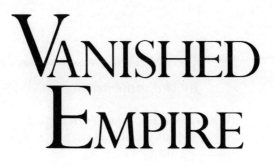

VANISHED EMPIRE

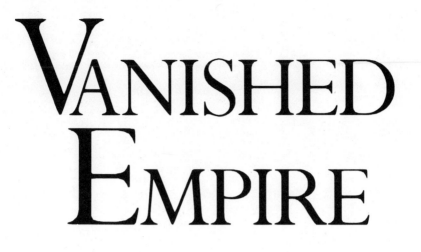

VANISHED EMPIRE

Vienna · Budapest · Prague
The Three Capital Cities
of the Habsburg Empire
as Seen Today

STEPHEN BROOK

William Morrow and Company, Inc.
New York

Copyright © 1988 by Stephen Brook

All rights reserved. No part of this book may be reproduced or utilized in any form
or by any means, electronic or mechanical, including photocopying, recording or
by any information storage and retrieval system, without permission in writing
from the Publisher. Inquiries should be addressed to Permissions Department,
William Morrow and Company, Inc., 105 Madison Avenue, New York, N.Y. 10016.

Recognizing the importance of preserving what has been written, it is the policy
of William Morrow and Company, Inc., and its imprints and affiliates to have
the books it publishes printed on acid-free paper, and we exert our best efforts
to that end.

Library of Congress Cataloging-in-Publication Data

Brook, Stephen.
Vanished empire : Vienna, Budapest, Prague : three capital cities
of the Habsburg Empire as seen today / Stephen Brook.
p.   cm.
ISBN 0-688-09212-8
1. Vienna (Austria)—Description. 2. Budapest (Hungary)—
Description. 3. Prague (Czechoslovakia)—Description. 4. Brook,
Stephen—Journeys—Central Europe. I. Title.
DB855.B74   1990
943.6'13—dc20   89-27254
                                                                                                              CIP

Printed in the United States of America

First U.S. Edition

1   2   3   4   5   6   7   8   9   10

CONTENTS

ACKNOWLEDGMENTS

I wish to thank Austrian Airlines, who flew me to Vienna and back, and Malév, who flew me to Budapest and back. While in Vienna, my friends David and Jean Bolton once again provided me with much hospitality as well as a place of refuge from work. Terry Sandell of the British Council was extremely helpful and put me in contact with a great variety of people. The Viennese tourist board gave me a pass that allowed me free entry to and consequently the luxury of drifting in and out of museums as I pleased. Georg Eisler did me the great service not merely of suggesting how I should spend my days in Vienna, but of simply telling me what I ought to be doing; and he was invariably right. Richard Bassett and Paul Sinclair gave me the benefit of their considerable knowledge of Central Europe.

In Budapest, the Hilton Hotel accommodated me in style for a number of days. Keith Dobson, formerly of the British Council in that city, was immensely helpful, as were Jane Walker and Brian McLean.

Dr Roger Scruton, despite our contretemps, put me in touch with a number of Prague residents, as did Neal Ascherson and Richard Escritt. And I am grateful to innumerable residents of all three cities, some of whom appear in the following pages and some of whom do not, for their warmth and hospitality.

FOREWORD

Close to the centre of Vienna, beneath the bland seventeenth-century Kapuzinerkirche, are coiled the cool interconnecting chambers of the imperial burial vault. Here for hundreds of years the bodies of the Habsburg royal family have been entombed. They are almost all here, the obscure archdukes of the seventeenth century, Maria Theresa in a sarcophagus large enough to accommodate her sixteen children too, the abstemious Joseph II in his suitably plain box, Franz Josef flanked by his assassinated wife Elisabeth and his son Rudolf, Maximilian of Mexico, and even a handful of archdukes and archduchesses who breathed their last in recent decades have been tucked away in the niches.

The bodies, however, are incomplete. To find the hearts of the Habsburgs you must walk a hundred yards to the Augustiner-kirche, which adjoins the imperial palace. Here, in a small room off the Loretto Chapel, shelves carry the urns that contain the hearts of fifty-four Habsburgs. And in the catacombs of Vienna's cathedral, the Stephansdom, you will find the imperial entrails, which have been tucked into urns that resemble hat boxes.

These bizarre burial practices are supposedly derived from the Spanish court ritual to which all the Habsburgs were addicted, even long after this royal house had ceased to exercise direct control over the affairs of Spain. The custom may be bizarre, but it is also fitting. For the bodies of the Habsburgs were in death dispersed as arbitrarily as their domains. The Habsburg Empire was never, at the apogee of its control and power, more than a collection of estates, assembled almost at random, occasionally by conquest, more often by marriage, and handed down from ruler to ruler almost as though it were a personal inheritance, an heirloom, less a coherent national unit than an embodiment of personal dynamic power. The Habsburg Empire was never conceived in nationalist terms, and its sole *raison d'être* was the legitimacy it was accorded by the other great powers of Europe. When, during and immediately after the First World War, those powers withdrew their recognition of that legitimacy, the Habsburg Empire didn't so much fall apart as vanish in a puff of smoke. It had proved enduring yet insubstantial. When its bluff was called, it had nothing to fall back on, no reserves of national sentiment. The allegiances that sustained it, usually in the form of loyalty to the Emperor, were simply transferred elsewhere.

The three cities visited in this book were the primary cities of the Habsburg Empire. Vienna, of course, was the Kaiserstadt, the Imperial City, but it was not always so. A few hundred years ago Vienna was simply one choice of residence for the imperial family. Prague and Wiener Neustadt also had spells of duty as court headquarters. Only after the Turks were halted at the very gates of Vienna in the late seventeenth century did the city begin to draw in the cosmopolitan collection of court officials and administrators and aristocratic hangers-on whose successors dominated the city until the Habsburgs' final departure. By the nineteenth century both Prague and Budapest grew not only in size but in confidence. Prague was not only a Habsburg city but a Bohemian one, while Budapest was not only the principal rival to Vienna but a magnet for Magyar aspirations. Since the Habsburgs were also kings of Bohemia and kings of Hungary – with different crowns for each region – the distinctive identity of each territory was left perilously intact, even while the Austrian Habsburgs imposed German language and culture on their domains. As the nineteenth century drew to a close, both Bohemians and to a greater degree Magyars wrested more and more control over their internal affairs from the imperial bureaucracy in Vienna. The interests of all three cities were incompatible, and the Habsburgs were forced over the decades to make various concessions to Czechs and Hungarians on the condition that the sovereignty of the Monarchy itself was not challenged. This was adhered to long after the Habsburg Empire, as a political entity, had ceased to make sense. Or as the narrator of Robert Musil's masterly novel about the collapse of the Habsburg Monarchy, *The Man Without Qualities*, put it: 'This is what happened to the Austrian and Hungarian Austro-Hungarian Dual Monarchy: it perished of its own unutterability.'

The Habsburgs have been gone for seventy years – though the widow of the last Emperor, the Empress Zita, is still alive – and they have been little missed, despite the occasional languishing

2

noises made by sentimental royalists. With the collapse of the Empire, and the later upheavals that convulsed central Europe, the three cities have been diminished in various ways. Prague and Budapest are no longer the glittering cultural centres they once were. The Habsburgs, while autocratic, were inept in their absolutism and cultural pluralism ran riot in all their principal cities. The present rulers of Budapest and Prague are more restrictive in applying their orthodoxies, and Prague in particular is about as culturally receptive as the bottom of the sea. Vienna itself, both in the 1920s and late 1940s, endured hardships probably not encountered in any other city of Western Europe, and even now, despite the return of prosperity, Vienna has a population smaller than that which it boasted at the outbreak of the First World War. If Prague and Budapest are culturally and politically diminished, Vienna is one of the few cities of Europe that has been physically diminished, and its grandeur seemed, the longer I explored it, to be more and more implausible.

VIENNA

This sense of Austro-Hungarian nationhood was an entity so strangely formed that it seems almost futile to try to explain it to anyone who has not experienced it himself. It did not consist of an Austrian and a Hungarian part that, as one might imagine, combined to form a unity, but of a whole and a part, namely of a Hungarian and an Austro-Hungarian sense of nationhood; and the latter was at home in Austria, whereby the Austrian sense of nationhood actually became homeless. The Austrian himself was only to be found in Hungary, and there as an object of dislike; at home he called himself a citizen of the kingdoms and realms of the Austro-Hungarian Monarchy as represented in the Imperial Council, which means the same as an Austrian plus a Hungarian minus this Hungarian, and he did this not, as one might imagine, with enthusiasm, but for the sake of an idea that he detested, for he could not endure the Hungarians any more than they could endure him, which made the whole connection more involved than ever.

Robert Musil, *The Man Without Qualities*, chapter 42

1

Brown is Blue

There are two ways to observe Vienna: looking in or looking out. Both are essential to an understanding of the city. From the 1500-foot Kahlenberg or from the other hills that rise to the northwest of the city, there are expansive views down onto the surprisingly tight urban circle of Vienna. Although there is some urban sprawl to the east and south of the city, there are other edges of Vienna along which the boulevards and streets slide to a halt and give way to fields and vineyards. Most capital cities peter out on their edges, with straggling lines of identical houses poking into the countryside. Vienna, for much of its perimeter, simply stops. From the hills it is easy to appreciate the salient geo-historical point that Vienna is the most easterly outpost of Western Europe. It is a cliché that the East begins at the Mexikoplatz along the Danube Canal, and like most clichés there is more than a grain of truth to it. Go west from Vienna and you are in the Alpine mountains and valleys that lead towards Italy and Germany, those unreliable repositories of western civilization. Travel east and you will find yourself taking the first of many steps that lead for hundreds of miles across the Hungarian plains into the lesser known quantities of Transylvania, Russia, Turkey, and the Slav lands that contributed so powerfully to the downfall of the Habsburgs. A mere twenty-five miles away on the Marchfeld, the Austrian extension of the Hungarian plains, are the extensive remains of the large Roman town of Carnuntum. With its population of over 50,000 it easily overshadowed Vindobona, the Roman settlement on the site of present-day Vienna. Innumerable trade routes converged on this spot, and gave it an importance both economic and strategic.

Vienna peers both ways, east and west, absorbing the remote into the familiar. Its cultural receptivity has become institutionalized in recent decades, as the city bid successfully to house the headquarters of various United Nations agencies. English accountants share offices with Polish economists and American scientists and Soviet computer technicians. In the previous century the mixture was less organized, for Vienna acted as a magnet to the various peoples of the Empire, to Galician nobles, Magyar officers, sailors from Trieste, Jewish merchants from Czernowitz, and anarchists from Bosnia.

This large influx from all corners of the Empire squeezed itself into a remarkably small space, as can be appreciated by looking out of Vienna. In the heart of the city is the Stephansdom, and from the viewing platform of its principal tower you can slowly spin on your heel and enjoy a view of the city around you. To the east, from the flat lands on the far side of the Danube, rise the hefty skyscrapers of the United Nations buildings and the newer suburbs around it. This part of the city is unfashionable, for the Viennese have always preferred to huddle closer to the centre, nearer to the vine-clad hills to the west on which they take so many of their pleasures. Despite flurries of new building – supermarket complexes, a few luxury apartment blocks, the oil refinery – the city, visually, is stable. With the decline of population since the early years of this century, there has been little call for new apartment buildings, and much of Vienna still looks as it must have done eighty years ago. In the working-class suburbs the long grey boulevards, flanked by the bland, evenly windowed walls of apartment blocks, push out to the edges and encircle the city; in the hilly northern suburbs, decorous villas still nestle among gardens and vineyards. Closer to the centre, the city seems an agglomeration of churches and palaces, for the flats built by the bourgeoisie in the nineteenth century were in their scale and flamboyance modelled on the great town houses and palaces of the aristocracy that cluttered the Inner City from the day the Turks were defeated in 1683. The Inner City and the inner suburbs, all within easy walking distance of the cathedral, are packed with buildings imposing in their scale. Vienna is a grand city, its love of display compensating for its lack of quaintness. Its charm is not to be found in the centre of the city but in suburbs such as Hietzing, where in the early nineteenth century the aristocracy and wealthier bourgeoisie, anxious to be close to the Habsburgs' summer palace at Schönbrunn, built charming villas in the style subsequently known as Biedermeier. Their city houses, in contrast, were for the most part raised in a rambunctious baroque style. Pomp at the centre, bucolic romps on the semi-rural edges – the pattern remains quintessentially Viennese.

From the south tower of the Stephansdom the city seems to hug itself tightly. The Inner City is semicircled by the Ringstrasse, built in the second half of the last century on the site of the old fortifications. Here, under Franz Josef, were built all the representative institutions of the Kaiserstadt: the Parliament and municipal offices, two great museums, and those showpieces of Germanic culture, the Burgtheater and the Opera. Less than a mile out from the Ringstrasse is a second girdle known as such in German, the Gürtel, on which are hung the heavy charms of a few railway stations, cheap hotels, and grim brothels. Beyond the Gürtel are the working-class suburbs to the west and the verdant suburbs of the rich to the north. These two circles are broken by the Danube Canal. The Danube itself lies a couple of miles further east, and the waterway that flows along one side of the Inner City is in fact the Canal. Until fairly recently the Danube was prone to serious flooding, and its marshy banks were unsuitable for building and settlement. The waters have now been regulated and tamed, and the river banks are gradually being reclaimed. The city authorities have also had the daring to construct an artificial cigar-shaped island in the middle of the river, an intrusion entirely given over to recreational use. The River Danube divides and dominates Budapest as the Thames separates and defines London, but in Vienna the river makes little impression. It is a sideshow, and the city's association with the river is almost entirely due to the astute PR work of Johann Strauss the Younger, who with a lilting melody persuaded the world that brown was blue.

As the thin grey light of a damp dawn edged its way round the heavy curtains of my bedroom each morning, my ear would catch the unfamiliar sound of horses' hooves. My pension room overlooked the central square of the Inner City, Stephansplatz, and along the north side of the cathedral the *Fiaker* drivers would line up each morning, in readiness for the first tourists eager for a chilly carriage ride round the city. The *Fiaker*, now a tourist attraction, is a genuine remnant of the fabric of Viennese life in earlier centuries. The first *Fiaker* hit the streets almost 300 years ago, and they flourished until taxis and the city's excellent public transportation system made them obsolete. The days have long gone when the *Fiaker* drivers had their own ball in the carnival season, and now, clad in bowler hats and adorned with side whiskers, they have accommodated themselves to the state of being merely picturesque. To compensate for their loss of function, the drivers charge high prices for their services but give pleasure to the unhurried tourist, both by pointing out the numerous sights of the Inner City and by causing traffic jams down every lane.

I could not help exulting in the centrality of my pension. While I was heating some water for my coffee, I would draw open the curtains and gaze down onto the Stephansplatz and directly ahead onto the coloured and patterned roof tiles of the Gothic cathedral. Once invigorated by caffeine, I could set off in any number of directions out towards the perimeter of the Inner City and know that each would be rewarding. Most pleasurable of all was the recognition that Vienna is a perfectly designed city for doing nothing. It was not difficult for me to slip into a daily routine along the following lines. Rising at eight, I would listen to the news in English and French on Austrian radio while I shaved. I would then prepare and sip my coffee while thinking about what I was going to do for the rest of the day. By nine I would be ready to leave. Crossing the Stephansplatz, I could turn right into the Graben, a broad pedestrian precinct on the site of the moat that once protected Roman Vindobona. The third lane on the left was the Dorotheergasse, and a few doors down was the unprepossess-ing exterior of the Café Hawelka.

The Hawelka is one of those Viennese institutions that enjoy a popularity for which there is no rational explanation. From mid-afternoon until the early hours of the morning the Hawelka is jammed, with artists, idlers, groupies, and disputatious bands of students, all exuding noisy cheerfulness. The café's pretension lies in its obliviousness to pretension. The flimsy lace curtains over the windows have not been washed for decades, and the gloomy interior is lit by yellow globe lamps, the kind that diminish light rather than provide it. Old hat stands are parked by the tables like ossified waiters. But at nine in the morning the place is just about empty. The students and artists are still fast asleep, and I could settle behind a window table – not that it was possible to see out of the begrimed windows – and punctuate my perusal of the *Herald Tribune* or *The Times* or the miserable rags that pass for news-papers in Vienna with sips of excellent black coffee.

Refreshed and informed, I might stroll through the gardens of palaces such as the imposing Belvedere or the Augarten on the other side of the Danube Canal. In the autumn large black crows fly in from Russia and caw loudly from their perches. They provided appropriate furnishing for the Augarten park, which contains two gigantic Flakturms, the indestructible defensive towers resembling gargantuan windowless Norman keeps and built by the Germans as a variety of huge overground bunker. They are literally indestructible, for any charge of dynamite sufficient to demolish the Flakturms would reduce most of the surrounding residential districts to rubble too. The bleak snarling of the Siberian crows, especially here, could be oppressive after a while, but it was always easy to take refuge in a baroque church or a museum, since Vienna has an abundance of both.

There can be few cities of Vienna's size that have so many galleries and museums worth visiting. After a Cranach or a Breughel at the fabulous Kunsthistorisches Museum, or a canter down the vast halls of the military museum, or a dip into the inexhaustible Albertina with its marvellous Old Master drawings, or a stroll through the well chosen modern art collections housed in a spare Liechtenstein palace, it would be time for lunch. The Inner City is dotted with wine cellars, some of which have been there for hundreds of years. Most are dependencies of one or another of the great Benedictine or Augustinian monasteries of Austria, and there is no such thing as an Austrian monastery that does not cultivate extensive vineyards. At the Augustinerkeller, tucked beneath the Albertina, the world's greatest collection of graphic art, or at the Esterhazykeller, where the wine still comes from one of the Austrian estates still in the hands of this immensely grand Hungarian family, I could order a *viertel* (quarter litre) of fresh white wine, a local Riesling or Weissburgunder or Gumpolds-kirchener, and a plate of blood sausage and potato salad or half a roast chicken.

After this modest meal I would return to the very centre of town and the street known as Wollzeile. Here I would try to resist the temptation of a pastry at Heiner, one of the best Konditoreien in Vienna, and pass on to the largest foreign-language newspaper shop in town. By now the morning editions of the British dailies would have arrived, and I could at least cast my eye along the headlines. I might glance too at the more outré Austrian journals, such as *Extrablatt*, which in one issue featured a story entitled 'Fuck Me' that failed to live up to its promise. If I was feeling weary, I could return in two minutes to my pension, where the feather bed would have been puffed high and the radiators, which I turned off at night, would be silently maintaining the room at a slow oven temperature. I could take a nap or visit another museum. In many weeks of sightseeing, I never ran out of museums.

11

If I felt like an outing which would make minimal demands on my energy level, I could hop onto any of the three buses that stopped outside the door of the pension, and alight along the Ring. Here I would take the first outward-bound tram that came along, and glide out to the suburbs, making the most of my weekly travel pass (available in Vienna for the price of a few pastries) by taking journeys at random through all parts of the city. By four, the increasingly crepuscular light and the weight of tradition would impel me to rest in a café. Wherever you are in Vienna, or all of Austria for that matter, there is always a café within fifty yards where you can be sure of a cool welcome but a hot cup of coffee and a slice of strudel or a bowl of soup.

One of my favourites in the later afternoon was the cavernous Prückel in Dr Karl Lueger Platz. Like the Hawelka, it is determinedly shabby, with its dusty pink ceiling, frayed beige wallpaper, and hideous chandeliers. Small square formica tables rest on cheap linoleum, and there is a choice of seating between ghastly old green chairs and the more comfortable banquettes that look as if the dog had died on them. In the Prückel's utter lack of pretension, its inability to cope with notions of taste or decoration, lies its frayed charm. The coffeehouse is popular with the lame and the elderly who on most afternoons invade the brighter back room and play bridge beneath a cloud of cigar smoke. I'd settle in the front room with *The Times*. Well, not always, for once a garrulous Viennese couple had commandeered the two English newspapers taken by the Prückel and placed them on the banquette beside them. 'Are the papers free?' I inquired politely. No, they told me. I moved off. Fifteen minutes later the couple were still chattering, and the papers remained untouched. I returned and repeated my request. With heavy sighs, the fur-stoled lady groaned: *'Nimm's, nimm's'* – take it, take it – as though I were being insufferably impatient and the papers were her personal property rather than the Prückel's. Their selfishness and rudeness was more extreme than is customary in Vienna, but any notion that the Viennese are hospitable and welcoming is erroneous. Whether it is innate beastliness or a xenophobic attitude to foreigners in their city, I don't know, though long-time British residents in Vienna complained bitterly to me that in fifteen years they had hardly ever been invited to a Viennese home.

Having read the newspapers, when I could get my hands on them, I would devote half an hour to the German illustrated weeklies, especially the one that featured photographs of newly married couples boating, walking hand in hand, running through fields, and, invariably, lying stark naked in bed as they gaze adoringly at each other.

To cool my sense of disgust – anyone who has sat on a Mediterranean beach while lobstery German holidaymakers are taking off all their clothes while yelling at the tops of their voices will have shared it – I would make my way to another monastic institution, the Göttweigerkeller. Here at the counter I could join a few dozen other devotees of new wine, and down a *viertel* of Sturm. The celebrated Viennese *Heurigen* traditionally serve new wine, but by this they mean the wine of the most recent vintage. Sturm is wine so new that it is still fermenting. The colour of watered milk, Sturm has a light prickle on the tongue caused by the activities of yeasts that have not completed their task. It is only available for a few weeks after the harvest, and I made the most of its limited engagement at the wine cellars of Vienna.

After this refreshment it would be time for culture, and I would stroll down to the Opera to see how the queue was coming along. After a couple of visits I was able to gauge quite accurately the point at which I would need to start queueing for a cheap standing place at the back of the stalls. For a really wretched performance I could safely turn up twenty minutes before the curtain went up and be assured of a good perch, but for any production that was half-way decent it was advisable to be at the Opera by five or five-thirty. Tickets were sold an hour before the start of the performance, which gave me just enough time to call on friends whose flat was conveniently located two short blocks from the Staatsoper. Burdened by a trio of small children, they could be counted on to be at home, and, such was their innate sense of hospitality, to offer me a Pilsener or a mug of Veltliner wine until it was time for me to hurry back to the opera house.

The administrators of the Staatsoper, who know that their clients must cram many and varied pleasures into the short span of every single day, do not, unlike their British counterparts, waste our time with long tedious intervals. The Viennese love their operas, but they like to get them over with as soon as possible. By ten I would be back out on the street. It was only at this point that difficulties might arise in my daily routine. It is easy to find a bar or *Lokal* open until two in the morning, but few serve food after nine in the evening. I dine late by preference, and it took me a week or two to find restaurants in the Inner City where I could obtain *Bauernschmaus* (a dish specially designed for gluttons consisting of the entire repertoire of central European cuisine piled onto a single plate) or *Paprikaschnitzel* and dumplings at ten-thirty at night. And by midnight I would be snug in my bed once more, weary after my arduous day, but confident that a good night's sleep would recharge my batteries and that at dawn the familiar grey tongue of light would trim the side of the curtains, heavy as old copes, just as the first *Fiaker* clopped into the square below.

2

Dynasty

European royalty has never taken much interest in the artistic world. Were I a monarch or a mere prince, I would scatter commissions to composers, pleading for another voluntary with which to herald my *levée*, and no royal wedding or state funeral would be complete without half a dozen cantatas or rock oratorios. Erotic statues would be dotted about the lawns of my residences, and eager young painters would be put to work on the bare-walled sistines of my castles. Of course the occasional royal lunatic, such as Ludwig II of Bavaria, came close to the ideal, but his exception proves the rule. The Windsors have always preferred the clattering of hooves to coloratura, and are also devoted to the Habsburg obsession with shooting anything on four legs or with wings. Royal families do have other things to do, to be sure. The Windsors have a constitutional role, a function that would have been incomprehensible to a Habsburg. A Habsburg ruler, such as Franz Josef, had to spend most of his time running his Empire, hiring and firing ministers, receiving dignitaries in audience, and threatening or evading wars and occasionally having them fought out. Not much time left at the end of such days for the niceties of the arts.

I visited a handful of Habsburg residences: the vast Hofburg in Vienna, Schönbrunn, the summer palace built by Maria Theresa in what are now western suburbs of the city, Franz Josef's summer residence at the spa of Bad Ischl, and his wife Elisabeth's Villa Hermes in the former private hunting grounds of the Habsburgs on the outskirts of Vienna. The conception of the principal palaces was grand enough – building big is never difficult if you have unlimited access to architects, cash and time – but their interiors are numbing in their dullness. The Habsburgs had no taste, except by accident. It is not that they had bad taste; they

15

simply had no conception even tangentially linked to the notion of taste.

A palace is, or ought to be, a statement, a declaration of purpose and principle. Buckingham Palace assails us with its lazy dullness, its presumptuous sprawl, its empty forecourts, its bland symmetry. It is orderly and unadventurous, grand but not flashy, a perfect architectural expression of the squires within. The White House in Washington is more subtle, its modesty a reminder to onlooker and occupant alike that the lease is not indefinite; its classicism reflects the neat tripartite Constitution. But the Hofburg makes no coherent statement. It scatters its message over facades and courtyards too numerous to count. The power of the Habsburgs was sustained by the very vastness of their territories, which were regarded as a private estate that happened to stretch across half of Europe, and their prestige derived from the almost hereditary assumption of the title of Holy Roman Emperor. (It was only in 1806 that a Habsburg, Franz II, adopted the title of Emperor of Austria and gave up the other imperial title, since it seemed likely to be declared defunct within a few years as Napoleon tightened his grip on Europe. In the process the Holy Roman Emperor Franz II transformed himself into Franz I of Austria.)

Since Vienna was merely one of a number of possible residences for the Habsburg rulers, the original Hofburg was little more than a local fortress. The earliest part of the structure, the Schweizerhof, dates from the fourteenth century, though there are few visible vestiges of the Gothic era. The bulk of the Schweizerhof, solid and dour, is vaguely Renaissance in style and dates from the mid-sixteenth century. From then on, various wings and blocks were added to the Schweizerhof: the Amalienburg and the Reichskanz-leitrakt, among others. With the single exception of the eighteenth-century Reichskanzleitrakt, which zips the length of a courtyard with undeniable panache and grandeur, these buildings are monumental and dull. Conventional too, a minimalist expression of the most conventional styles of the time, poker-faced and bureaucratic rather than exuberantly palatial. The Reichskanzlei-trakt owes the comparative vigour and liveliness of its facade to a rare collaboration between the two greatest baroque architects of Vienna, Fischer von Erlach and Hildebrandt, who between them raised about half of the aristocratic palaces of the city.

Fischer von Erlach's major contribution to the Hofburg is the Winter Riding School. It was Emperor Maximilian II who founded the Spanish Riding School in 1572, though the winter school itself dates from the first third of the eighteenth century and was completed by Fischer's son Joseph Emanuel. The vast chamber is almost as showy as the aristocratic Lipizzaner horses that caper within. Rows of columns march round the edge of the building and support a shallow gallery; spectators, whether at the Hofburg balls of the last century or the riding displays of today, are crammed along the gallery rails, and peer down onto the sawdust below. The morning training sessions are open to the public, and long before tickets go on sale the queue snakes from the entrance on the Josefplatz to the Michaelerplatz on the other side of the stables. Queueing in the November rain to watch a bunch of horses being putting through their paces was not for me a prime attraction of Vienna, so I pulled strings and to my pleasant surprise found myself ushered not into the spectators gallery high above the arena, but into the splendid box at ground level at the far end of the hall.

My eyes wandered upwards and I fell into a trance. The plaster ceiling is partly coffered and ornamented with rosettes and scallops and cartouches and other fancy footwork in plaster, which I found considerably more enthralling than the fancy footwork of the horses. It reminded me of the ravishing Senate House in Cambridge, a hall usually viewed only once in an undergraduate's career, during final examinations. The temptation to admire the plaster ceiling in preference to scribbling a few words on counterfactual conditionals was great indeed. Here at the Winter Riding School, there was no contest. The ceiling won. The immediate visual impact of riders and horses is splendid enough: the handsome white and dishwater horses mounted by riders clad in eighteenth-century uniforms and tricorns are beautiful to see, but not at length. To be sure, the horses do tricks. After doing a few sedate laps, their riders whisper the secret words, or tap them out with their crops, and the horses promptly do their hot-coals prancing number, or trot sideways. Others mark time, raising their hooves high in the air, like a nervous woman waggling freshly varnished nails to encourage them to dry. I like to see animals doing what their creator intended them to do – eating other animals or cantering across the range or being led into the abattoir – but clever tricks leave me cold. When I was ten, Michael Ingram would entertain my entire class at school by burping the alphabet, and my cat Phylloxera can perform phenomenal sideways leaps when spooked, but I would not recommend others to come and admire these activities at considerable expense.

17

More to my taste is another corner of the Hofburg, also completed from his father's plans by Joseph Emanuel Fischer von
Erlach. This is the National Library. It was built, of course, as
the Hofbibliothek, the court library, to house a collection that
had already been in existence for a couple of hundred years. The
Habsburgs may not have been notable readers, but they were
assiduous collectors, amassing precious objects by the container
load over the centuries. To house their library, Fischer von Erlach
trounced the competition by designing the largest baroque
library in Europe. The principal hall, the Prunksaal, is simply
vast, measuring 250 feet in length. Two long wings broken
by white marble columns reach out from either side of the oval-
shaped principal hall, which in turn is arcaded, galleried and
frescoed with a *trompe l'oeil* depicting spectators gazing down
from a balustrade. Empty spaces between columns are filled
either with display cases – they have to put the books somewhere
– or with scholarly accessories such as globes and life-size inspi-
rational statues. The gem of the collection is the 15,000-volume
library of Prince Eugen of Savoy, who won lasting glory by
masterminding the defeat of the Turks in 1683 and winning
subsequent victories over Turks and French. Thereby he greatly
enhanced the prestige of the House of Habsburg, and he was well
rewarded for his pains. That waspish observer Lady Mary Wort-
ley Montagu wrote disparagingly of Prince Eugen's 'finnikin and
foppish taste' in leather-bound books. Judging by the stunning
display of illuminated manuscripts and early printed books from
his library that I saw in the Prunksaal, Lady Mary could hardly
have been wider of the mark.

Fischer von Erlach had also devised plans for a wing that
would link the Winter Riding School to the Reichskanzleitrakt of
the Hofburg. In the 1880s Franz Josef ordered the theatre which
then occupied this space to be torn down; he resurrected Joseph
Emanuel's plans and a new range, the Michaelertrakt, was built.
It is dominated by the enormous gateway called the Michaelertor, an overblown structure, heavy with statuary and fawning
inscriptions to the Emperor. The lofty green copper cupola shel-
ters a huge oval passage, large enough to accommodate a full
complement of archduchesses in their carriages; from here
visitors gain access to some of the state rooms. The Michealertor
is a monument to political as well as cultural reaction.
Architecturally, it looks backwards; its scale is needlessly large,
its idiom bombastic.

But the Michaelertor looks positively reticent next to the Neue Burg. The large square between the baroque portions of the palace and the former fortifications, now the Ring, is known as the Heldenplatz (the Heroes' square), and here Franz Josef resolved to construct new ranges of buildings. Only one, the Neue Burg, a neo-classical monstrosity large enough to house no fewer than four museums, was actually built. Completed in 1913, it now seems, and must then have seemed, a symbol of imperial and autocratic power erected decades after such power had ceased to reflect political realities. By 1913 the Empire was on the brink of collapse, torn not so much by disputes with other powers as by dissension among and between the various national groups who rattled around within its borders. Only the potent figurehead of the aged Emperor remained as a unifying force within the Empire, and on his death, only three years after the Neue Burg was completed, the dissolution of the Habsburg Empire became inescapably linked to the fortunes of its ally Germany in the First World War. And we all know the end of that story. The Neue Burg blasts out the theme of dynastic might, but the sound is a hollow one. Franz Josef and his court were still occupying the 2600 rooms of the Hofburg – not to mention the additional 1500 rooms down the road at Schönbrunn – as though he were the Sun King himself at the height of his power, and the populace paid him a deceptive respect. He had come to the throne long before most of his subjects had even been born, he had been dogged by personal tragedy, and he was immensely dutiful and hard-working. He had been unpopular in his youth, but royalty acquires a patina with age: Queen Victoria, lampooned earlier in her reign and severely criticized for the profundity of her widowhood, reaped the same reward as she doggedly waddled towards the end of the nineteenth century. While the British Empire was at least on a sound territorial, commercial, and military footing, the same could not be said for the Habsburg Empire, and two years after Franz Josef's death Austria, without the formality of a revolution, proclaimed itself a socialist republic.

The interior of the Neue Burg, which is gently curved along its pillared facade, is more pleasing than the exterior, and its shallow marble staircases and immense plastered galleries are admirably suited to the displays of armour and of Greek art from Ephesus. Each emperor in turn seems to have collected suits of armour the way that Imelda Marcos collected shoes. The workmanship is stunning, as are the inlays of ivory and filigree on the handles of rifles and swords. An age of chivalry and its ugly cousin, war, gave the pretext for the most dazzling artisanship, whether in the form of ceremonial saddles from the late Middle Ages or wonderfully detailed engraved weapons, such as jewelled maces, captured from Syrians and Turks. A less romantic portrait of men at war is given at the Heeresgeschichtliches Museum, the military museum, housed in a stupendously hideous neo-Byzantine monstrosity out near the Gürtel. Here no vulgarity was spared. Its large gloomy halls are filled not only with weaponry but with maps and battle paintings and memorabilia of Prince Eugen, Radetzky, and other Austrian generals. I was astonished to find here a bust of the great Marxist historian E.H. Carr, until closer inspection revealed that the carved inscription read EH: CARL – Erzherzog (Archduke) Karl, another celebrated general. Like most Austrian military leaders, Karl was in the habit of losing battles, such as the Battle of Wagram against Napoleon.

At the far end of this oppressive museum, almost entirely deserted except for a handful of understandably bored attendants, is the car in which Archduke Franz Ferdinand and his wife Sophie rode to their deaths at Sarajevo. Here too is his death mask, and portraits and photos of this bullish, unsympathetic man as he strutted around the Empire he expected to inherit. The Habsburgs defended their realm with military force, as did all the other proprietors of Europe, but the Austrians were clearly lacking in military gifts. They had probably the finest uniforms of any army, especially the Hungarian divisions with their moustachioed hussars, but at fighting battles they were conspicuously unsuccessful. Many of the battles and wars were relatively minor, and seem to have been undertaken more for their ritual satisfaction than in pursuit of defined strategic goals. With each loss, the Austrians signed a peace treaty that often treated them more generously than their wretched military performance warranted, yet in the course of the nineteenth century, the Habsburgs gradually lost portion after portion of their inheritance. In 1914 they found themselves locked into a war that was no joke, and this time the peace treaty, that of Versailles, stripped the Habsburgs bare. Here in the Heeresgeschichtliches Museum the visitor can chronicle at leisure the slow attrition of the Habsburg Empire.

A less mournful note is struck in the rooms of the Hofburg that house the Habsburgs' collection of trinkets. In the Schatzkammer are dozens of reliquaries, thirteenth-century ceremonial swords and crosses, and a crown for each month of the year. The Habsburgs collected kingdoms and principalities as they married their way through European history, and with each new kingdom – Bohemia or Hungary – they acquired another crown. Each is heavy not only with gems but with symbolic portent. If a newly enthroned Habsburg wanted a fair chance of getting on with the disputatious Magyars, he would have to undergo a separate coronation in Budapest. Soon after the young Emperor Karl succeeded to the throne in 1916, he and his wife Zita made an appointment for a December coronation in Hungary, and how the crowds cheered. They must have cheered so loudly that he was deluded into believing the Hungarians would continue to offer him their loyalty after he lost his throne in 1918. He made two attempts to return to Hungary, the second in 1921, and both failed dismally. A year later he died in Madeira. The last Habsburg on the throne of Austria-Hungary lived for only four years after the collapse of his Empire.

Maria Theresa, if we are to believe the evidence of the Schatzkammer, breakfasted off golden plates, while Kaiser Franz Stephan had a toiletry set also made of solid gold – doubtless a gift from his wife, puzzled to know what to give a Holy Roman Emperor for Christmas. In another set of rooms, the Silberkammer, are displayed vast quantities of tableware, of gold and silver and finest porcelain. Cabinet after cabinet is stuffed with gold or silver trays, candelabra, cutlery, serving bowls, cruets. My own household could have dined off that lot for a year without ever having to wash up. It was a numbing display, divorced as it was from function, from table and chair and waiter. Which emotions should the Silberkammer summon up? Is the viewer supposed to feel stupefied, lost in awesome admiration, or angry? Or none of the above? The Austrians themselves seem to have little sentimental connection with the house that ruled over them for nearly seven centuries. Franz Josef may have been respected, even loved, but once his Empire had crumbled, the Austrians looked forward rather than backward, and were stubborn enough to refuse Empress Zita admission into Austria for sixty-four years after her husband lost his throne, on the grounds that he had never agreed to abdicate, thus putting the House of Habsburg in the unacceptable position of pretenders to the throne. At the age of ninety she was invited back by Chancellor Bruno Kreisky, and bygones were at long last conceded to be bygones.

*

Between the Heldenplatz and the Ring stands the ceremonial gateway known as the Burgtor, a hefty but uninspired neoclassical structure dating from 1824 that is now Austria's principal war memorial. Visitors mostly pass by without a further glance, but one November morning a crowd gathered around the steps leading into the memorial. A marching band was strutting, and a military ceremony, presumably to commemorate those who had died in Austria's many wars, was taking place in the stiff presence of military and civic dignitaries. A few old ladies, many clad in dark green *Loden* coats, dabbed hankies against their eyes. A chaplain gave a comforting sermon, on the lines of 'Judge not that ye be not judged', which he quoted. In the eyes of God, he observed, which flag you fought under is less important than whether you are a good Christian, and so on and so forth. The man was only doing his job, comforting the bereaved, seeking to justify brutal deaths on the battlefield, but the task was a problematic one, since the only war most ageing Austrians can remember is the Second World War, in which Austria had not fought on the side of the angels. His argument may have given comfort to the old ladies, but seemed deeply flawed, since if the flag you have fought under is of so little importance, then why should one be prepared to surrender one's life beneath it?

Military virtues were highly prized under the Habsburgs, even though military prowess was in scarce supply. As the narrator of Robert Musil's *The Man Without Qualities* puts it: 'Although, of course, the Austrians had been victorious in all the wars in their history, after most of these wars they had had to surrender something.' Franz Josef habitually made his public appearance in uniform, and slept, even at his summer home at Bad Ischl, on a hard iron soldier's bed. Unless one shared the Emperor's passion for hunting chamois, I doubt that a day spent in the imperial presence would have been much of a lark. Certainly, the imperial apartments along the first floor of the Reichskanzleitrakt are of a remarkable dreariness. The rooms seem largely identical: some have a tapestry or two slung down a wall, others are decorated with routine gilding or plasterwork. One room is filled with large bland paintings that record the great popularity of Emperor Franz I, the most reactionary monarch of his day. Franz Josef's bedroom is slightly less spartan than its counterpart at Bad Ischl, and Elisabeth's (separate) bedroom is decidedly more cheerful. Should the Hofburg administration ever be strapped for cash, they might consider renting a suite of the rooms to an

Indian restaurateur, for the maroon silk wallpapers and uphol-
stery would be admirably suited to a Moti Mahal. The food
would no doubt be an improvement on standard fare at the
Hofburg in Franz Josef's day. Those invited to dine with the
Emperor often took the precaution of booking a table at a nearby
restaurant for later that same evening. Court ritual prescribed
that no one could continue to eat after the Emperor had risen
from his seat. Since the service was somewhat slow, and the
Emperor's fork-to-mouth action exceedingly swift, it was not
unusual for some guests to leave the table before they had been
served a single dish.

No wonder the Empress Elisabeth kept her distance from the
court. She may have been dotty but she at least had a vital
personality, as the gymnasium adjoining her bedroom confirms.
Elisabeth was a fitness freak who probably dreamt of Nautilus
machines decades before they were invented. Obsessively she
feared the fading of her remarkable beauty, and exercised com-
pulsively to keep her figure as trim as it had been when she was a
young girl. Bored with and irritated by court ritual and official
routine, she turned her affections to horses – she was said to be
the best horsewoman in Europe of her day – and dogs, whose
portraits line the walls here, as they do at her other residences.
Elisabeth was less inclined to the spartan life than her husband,
and in the neighbouring room she had a bathroom installed, the
first such facility in the Hofburg. While she was adjusting the
bath taps with her toes, Franz Josef would lower his stocky body
into the round tub full of steaming water that his valets brought
to his room each morning. Oh, they knew how to live at the
Hofburg!

I doubt that there was much levity at Schönbrunn either.
Paintings depicting the wedding of Maria Theresa show two
banquets in progress, a tantalizing occasion, since only the
members of the royal family were given anything to eat. Her huge
palace at Schönbrunn is one of those structures that looks better
from afar. The gardens are lovely, and the Gloriette, ranged along
the crest of a slope at the far end of the park, is splendidly
dramatic. But the interior is almost as stifling as that of the
Hofburg. Franz Josef's rooms are, of course, the dullest. Painted a
dull cream and ornamented with spindly gilt rococo patterns,
they can only have been home to a man utterly oblivious to his
surroundings. Even more depressing, and oppressive, is the joint
bedroom of Franz Josef and Elisabeth, dominated by a huge ugly

bed flanked with religious paintings by Guido Reni and Dolci. However, there is little evidence that the royal pair spent a great deal of time romping beneath its sheets. Maria Theresa's bed, on the other hand, is a very grand four-poster with hangings of maroon velvet and gold thread. She also put the bed to excellent use, and bore eighteen children.

To be sure, there are some grander state rooms: a Hall of Mirrors – a routine example of the genre – in which the young Mozart played for Maria Theresa, and a Grand Gallery, above the main portal of the palace, and decorated in a grandiose style. The Chinese rooms are attractive, and so is the Millionen room with its rosewood panelling and fine inlays of Indian miniatures. Here and there the heart strings are plucked rather than tugged. There's the bed – an iron cot, of course – in which Franz Josef died, and the stuffed bird that belonged to the offspring of Franz I's daughter Marie Louise and, of all people, Napoleon Bonaparte. The lad died young, from consumption in 1832, and his favourite bird chirped no more shortly thereafter.

One chilly morning I was admitted to the Hofburg cellars, the Hofkeller. They sink into the earth for three storeys, but it was the top level that interested me, for here are deposited plaster casts of the statues that adorn the Hofburg and other imperial institutions, such as the museums along the Ring. Given Franz Josef's grandiloquent taste in architecture, no building was erected during his reign without a platoon of life-size statues gazing out from balustrade and niche. Here they all are, empresses and archdukes, generals and statesmen, mythological heroes and Greek gods, strewn about on the cold floors of the Hofburg cellar, their white plaster greyed with dust. Some are labelled, others not, and most are chipped or damaged. Why the authorities have bothered to keep these plaster casts I do not know, but the large figures, loitering along the underground passageways, constitute an almost complete Habsburg pantheon. Some portions of the cellars are the scene of a fatal but bloodless massacre, with heads and busts scattered at random along the floor. The statues, most of them, are still *in situ*, high above the Neue Burg or the Natural History Museum, and it's probable that they are observed and noted as infrequently as the huge collection of casts consigned to the subterranean darkness. The pomp and pretensions of the Habsburgs have worn less well than those of most other dynasties, as though they had been discredited long before they were deposed. The monuments still stand, but even in retrospect the Habsburg emperors and heroes seem, like the plaster casts in the Hofburg cellars, to have had the stuffing knocked out of them decades before they vanished from the scene.

3

Going by the Book

Had he been peering down from a cloud as fluffy as his billowing side whiskers, Franz Josef would have been appalled at the speed with which Vienna was transformed after the eviction of the Habsburgs. The old Emperor would have heard about socialism, and shuddered, but could not have dreamt that within weeks of the removal of Emperor Karl, Austria and Vienna would have opted for a socialist regime, even though there had been radical politicians in Vienna during the Monarchy, notably the notorious Dr Karl Lueger, who devised a peculiarly Viennese blend of municipal efficiency, populism, and vigorous antisemitism. He was a dashing figure, known to the citizenry as '*der schöne Karl*'. The son of a college porter, young Karl became a lawyer active in Liberal politics. He began his political career on the left. When the ruling liberals of the day refused to extend the franchise, it was easy for Lueger and his allies to step in as the champion of '*der kleine Mann*' against the Liberal establishment. Before long he had welded together a number of populist movements into a Christian-Social Party. He deftly exploited petit bourgeois resentment of the commercial competition that arose as Jewish tradesmen and artisans poured into Vienna; and Jewish bankers and financiers were always a handy scapegoat.

Lueger was elected mayor in 1895, but Franz Josef, who distrusted Lueger's alliance with the burgeoning lower middle classes of the city and was also out of sympathy with his antisemitic utterances, refused to ratify his election. But the populace disregarded the Emperor's disapproval and Lueger was repeatedly reelected. In 1897 Franz Josef had no choice but to give in, and Lueger remained mayor until his death in 1910. Lueger was not as rabid in his views as may be imagined on first acquaintance with his career. His antisemitism and, for that matter, devotion to the Catholic hierarchy were not so much deeply felt principles as useful devices for enlisting the broadest possible political support. Cynical he may have been, but he was also a remarkably successful politician, a great public speaker, a man of panache and vigour who never lost contact with the ordinary people who repeatedly elected him and, unlike many politicians who are all charisma and no achievement, he did a great deal for his native city. Lueger electrified not just the hearts of the swooning proletariat, but the street lights and trams of the city. He built markets and abattoirs and schools, preserved and expanded the parks and riverside beaches, and provided banks and pension funds and insurance agencies. His policies, as opposed to his rhetoric, scarcely differed from those the socialists promised to implement. Lueger's antisemitism, while a shamelessly opportunistic exploitation of the fears of his constituents, was at least tempered by his own awareness of what he was up to. In a celebrated saying, he declared: *'Wer a Jud is, bestimm i'* ('I'll be the one to decide who's a Jew'), and he never hesitated to associate with Jews when it suited him to do so. Despite the scurrilous side of his populism, *'der schöne Karl'* has not been forgotten by the city, even though it has now been governed by socialists for over sixty years. One of the Inner City squares is named after him.

When the socialists came to power in the city after the First World War, the groundwork for their urban planning had already been laid under Lueger. What the mayor had neglected to tackle, during his lengthy reign, was the deplorable state of housing in the city. Towards the end of the last century immigrants poured into Vienna from all parts of the Empire, and overcrowding reached horrific proportions, with many of the homeless in the city renting shares in beds in order to have a place to sleep. The working-class districts were crowded with sweatshops that employed the new immigrants, be they Czech tailors or Russian pedlars or Ruthenian peasants, at minimal wages. Tenements frequently lacked gas lighting and running water within the building. Disease, especially tuberculosis, was rampant.

So improved housing conditions became the highest priority of the socialist regime. In the course of the 1920s the municipality built a huge number of apartment complexes, so advanced and humane in conception and execution that they can still plausibly be offered as models of their kind. With astonishing energy, the socialists constructed no fewer than 64,000 flats in the space of ten years. Unlike the notorious tower blocks and other council dwellings erected in Britain and the United States in the 1960s, almost all the municipal blocks built by the city of Vienna are still standing and still inhabited. In the northern suburb of Heiligenstadt stands the most famous housing project of all, the Karl Marx Hof, which has a facade a kilometre in length. No one would claim that the Hof is lovely to behold. It is essentially an articulated block of buff stucco, with dirty-pink balconies enlivening the rhythm of the facade, as well as the lives of the tenants. Large semicircular openings like railway arches give access to the courtyards, which are laid out with lawns and playgrounds and wading pools. The remarkable feature of this block and the dozens like it is not simply that they provided cheap housing to many thousands of Viennese (and still do), but that they were equipped with useful amenities. Many of the larger blocks had their own kindergartens, as well as numerous shops on the ground floor. Children could play in safety on the enclosed lawns. The architectural design promoted a sense of community, for the flats looked both outwards onto the city and inwards onto the courtyards and across to the flats and balconies opposite.

The Karl Marx Hof has 1325 flats, each with two or three rooms. Although the most celebrated of the 1920s housing blocks, it is not the most successful from an architectural point of view. The Engels Hof, for instance, is taller and more spacious, and lacks the element of grimness that mars the Karl Marx Hof. (The tradition of naming these housing blocks after heroes of the left has not been neglected. In another part of the city, workers are housed in the Salvador Allende Hof.) The accommodation provided must have seemed, in the 1920s, positively luxurious after the noisome, unsanitary tenements the tenants had come from. Nowadays the basic layout of these flats disappoints modern expectations. Even today most of them lack baths, though lavatories have been installed. In some cases a pair of two-room flats have been knocked together to provide more generous accommodation. A quarter of the population of Vienna still lives in council housing, without, it seems, generating the social problems and disorders increasingly associated with subsidized housing projects in Britain and the United States.

After the Second World War, when the city spent a decade under the thumb of four-power occupation, there were few resources available for imaginative housing projects, and most postwar housing is drab and blank in design. In more recent years, as Vienna has become more affluent, the city fathers have begun to sponsor housing projects of greater originality. The most celebrated such exercise of recent years is the Hundertwasser Haus. Friedensreichs Hundertwasser, a popular and prolific artist who works from an eyrielike studio high above the roofs of the Inner City, was let loose on a plot of land in an inner suburb. Here he reproduced in architectural terms the naive fancifulness and bright colours that characterize his paintings. Like a fantasy castle in a children's book, the building astonishes by its implausibility, its wilful eccentricity. Scarcely any two windows are the same size or even on the same level. Bands of sometimes garish colour swoop up and down across the facades. Minarets peep up from unexpected corners, and undulating paving, made from a seemingly random dispersal of brick and stone and cobble, adds to the fantastical air. So confident is the Hundertwasser Haus in its playful anti-modernism that it even affects to be falling down, and a pillar – irregularly shaped, like all the pillars supporting the arcades around the building – strains at an angle of forty-five degrees. For all its fey cuteness, the Hundertwasser Haus shows that even so vast a bureaucracy as the Vienna city council can use imagination as well as accountancy in the running of the city.

The fifty flats in the Hundertwasser Haus are eagerly sought after, despite substantial down payments beyond the reach of all but the upper strata of those eligible for council housing. Although built and managed by the municipal authorities, the block seems more like a prestige apartment house that happens to have the city for a landlord. The interior design is less idiosyncratic than that of the exterior, and there is inevitably a greater degree of standardization within the flats. The exterior design is little more than the gaily designed wrapping around more predictable contents. I resist its quirky charms precisely because it is so childlike and eccentric; architecturally, the Hundertwasser Haus is a dead end, one of a kind. Nonetheless it is hard to avoid small stirrings of joy on walking past it. It is daft, a colourful guffaw, insufferably impish, but it has the undeniable merit of being utterly unlike any other building in Europe.

Although there is an official waiting list of five years for most municipal housing, there is a short-cut available to all. It is known as the *Parteibuch*, the party book. Join any Austrian political party, and you will receive a small booklet as confirmation of membership. Flash it in the right places and it can prove of enormous help in cutting corners and jumping queues. Because

Vienna has a socialist council, the best Parteibuch to wave here is that of the SPÖ, the socialists. On the other hand, an SPÖ book wouldn't do you much good in Salzburg, where you'd be lost without the book of the ÖVP, the Conservatives. Daily life in Austria is politicized to a remarkable degree. Opposition politicians rail, quite rightly, against the tyranny of the Parteibuch, but neglect to add that if they were in power they would operate the identical system to their own advantage. The system weakens the ideological distinctions between the parties, and one of the factors that gave rise to the widest yawns during the 1986 elections was the broad agreement on policies between the major parties. Party allegiance is a matter of self-interest as much as political conviction, though many ambitious people take the sensible precaution of joining more than one party, so as to be sure of having the right Parteibuch for every occasion. An itinerant cameraman I heard of belongs to three parties, so that he can be sure of obtaining work with minimal delay in any part of the country.

The system has honourable roots, even though it is widely perceived these days as a blight. Since the Second World War, Austria has been ruled largely by coalition governments. Politicians recalled the factionalism that tore the country apart in the 1930s, even before Nazism became a powerful influence within Austria. In 1934, for instance, the Karl Marx Hof became a battleground, as fascist militia were ordered to wipe out their left-wing counterparts, who had their power base within the great housing complexes. These battles marked the end of Red Vienna, and the beginning of the nationalist dictatorship under Dollfuss. It is also interesting to reflect that, with the important exception of the Spanish Republicans, the Viennese socialists and communists were the only working-class factions in Europe to put up armed resistance to the forces of fascism. (Alternatively, these events can be seen as a triumphant expression of the forces of law and order putting down communist insurrection.)

The battles left a bitter taste in the mouths of those who remembered their ferocity, and the leaders of postwar Austria resolved that polarization should have no part in modern Austria. Hence their disposition towards consensus and coalition. Coalition governments, however, have to operate on a basis of fairness, rewarding supporters of all the parties of which it is formed. Thus the Parteibuch came into being, to ensure that appointments were made on an equitable basis. If it was accepted that the headmaster of a certain school should be a SPÖ member, then it was equally accepted that his successor should belong to the same party. The same would apply to an ÖVP teacher or headmaster. In other words, jobs throughout the nation, as well as throughout the city, were dispensed according to political allegiance, and the system still operates. Even the banking system is divided up on a party basis.

The system can by its very nature lead to injustices. It's widely reported in Vienna that many municipal flats are empty, despite a shortage of housing, because housing managers are unwilling to admit tenants with the wrong Parteibuch. Whether jobs-for-the-boys is equivalent to corruption is debatable, but though the system developed for understandable reasons, it cannot be a basis for good decision-making and good administration. It arose not only as a consequence of coalition government but as a continuation of ancient practice in the imperial bureaucracy. During the Habsburg era, government procedures were so cumbersome that frequently the only way to get a decision made promptly was to know someone who would do you that favour. A whole network of personal contacts, and not only at senior levels of administration, developed over the years. Called *Protektion*, it was widely accepted as the only practical method of ensuring that the bureaucracy would work in your favour.

Protektion still flourishes. Karl, a secondary school teacher, told me that when his father entered an old people's home recently, he was informed that it would take three years before a telephone could be installed. The old man was justified in fearing he would be dead before the telephone engineer arrived. Karl, who is a passive SPÖ supporter, mentioned this matter to a fellow teacher, whom he knew to be an SPÖ activist. The activist recalled that one of his political colleagues was a senior post office official, and whispered a word in his ear. Three days later the old gentleman had his telephone installed. Stories such as this, and everyone has a few to tell, confirm that if you want something in Vienna – a job, a flat, planning permission – instead of applying for it in the usual way, it's better to broadcast your need to all your friends. It won't be long before one of them comes up with the comforting formula: '*Ich kenne da jemand . . .*' (I know somebody who works there . . .) The magic words usually work like a charm.

If you ask Viennese whether local politics is corrupt, they look at you with some surprise, and answer no. Outside observers answer yes. They are both looking at the same phenomenon through different eyes. Overt corruption, such as graft and embezzlement, is probably no more widespread than in any other large municipality. There are stories of municipal projects that end up costing twice as much as was anticipated, and it would not be straining the bounds of credibility to suppose that from time to time sums of money end up in people's pockets. For the most part, the corruption, if that is what it is, lies in the exchange of favours. The official who ensured that Karl's father jumped the queue for a phone knows, and Karl knows it too, that he is now at liberty to call on Karl next time he needs a favour. And so it goes on. In Britain we have the old boy network, and in Vienna they have *Protektion* in its modern guises.

This cosiness extends to the economy as a whole, though not all the practices are shady. Prices of basic foods – basic black bread, milk, butter and so forth – are subject to controls that keep them artificially low. Traders are also protected by import restrictions that enable them to sell off their old potatoes for some time after new potatoes ought to be available in the spring. This makes for good housekeeping but lousy potatoes. Although Austrians, whose economy has prospered in the past by the simple expedient of clinging to the coattails of the German economy, earn good money, there are plenty of ways, quite apart from the black economy, of supplementing one's income.

It is common for certain workers to be paid for a notional thirteenth or fourteenth month, usually in time for summer holidays or Christmas. This was instituted as a wheeze to get round wage freezes in days when the economy was more strictly controlled than it is now. Such bonuses are either tax free or taxed at a lower rate than official salaries. A system of bank confidentiality akin to Swiss practice means that many transactions on the very edges of legality can be made without fear of detection. When you buy a house in Austria, the vendor declares, with the consent of the purchaser, that the price is lower than in fact it is. This decreases the vendor's liability to capital gains tax and also benefits the purchaser, whose income alone may not justify the acquisition of an expensive property. Then a second contract using the real, high price is drawn up by the lawyers and signed; the purchaser hands over his bank pass book to make up the difference between the two prices, and then the contract is destroyed. Or so I am told.

4

Death is for Keeps

Once a year, on 1 November, half a dozen tram lines are diverted from their usual routes – not to transport the Viennese to the Prater stadium for a football match, but to allow citizens in their thousands, mostly elderly, to make a pilgrimage to the Central Cemetery on All Saints' Day. At the same time, car-owning younger folk and their families drive to the southeastern edge of the city in droves, creating enormous traffic jams all around the cemetery, which a regiment of whistle-piping police officers waves into temporary car parks. On both sides of the avenue which links the main entrances to the cemetery are a dozen or more stonemasons' yards, one of which was offering a timely half-price sale. It is a prudent Viennese indeed who ensures his or her own tombstone is bought at a bargain price.

For the Viennese, death is no laughing matter. It must be anticipated, coddled, honoured, and memorialized. Outside all the gates leading into the vast cemetery – another of Karl Lueger's legacies – stands sell flowers, wreaths, and memorial candles. And there's a *Wurstelstand*, since even mourners can be attacked by a swift hunger on a cold morning. Few of the thousands who walk into cemeteries all over Austria on All Saints' Day go empty-handed. Behind me on the tram sat two men, both dressed in *Trachten*, the traditional Austrian garb of green *Loden* and kneesocks. They did not look prosperous, and the younger man was clearly retarded, but they and the womenfolk seated across from them were almost obscured by the wreaths and bouquets on their laps. By the end of the day hardly a grave in Austria would be free from a scattering of autumnal wreaths.

The main alley of the Central Cemetery is of ceremonial grandeur, broad and long, passing, almost incidentally it seems, clusters of mausoleums and family plots. There were the usual rather limited flights of fancy, constrained by custom to a repertory of ringleted angels, truncated obelisks, closing doors, and perplexed cherubs. I was much taken by a marble mountain, into which was set a wooden door improbably guarded by two gnomes carrying shields and lanterns. Either the grave of a mine owner or a troll. I came across the brown marble classical temple that houses the bones of the Thonet family: the Thonets designed simple but strikingly elegant furniture that is still in production. Lettering on tombstones is very important, as no self-respecting Viennese is buried without his title. In the decidedly picturesque cemetery in suburban Hietzing, I came across a tomb inscribed with the name Jagdschriftsteller Hegendorf (Hunting Journalist Hegendorf!). Not that this was an official title, more a descriptive one, but it has been worn down by the Hietzing air longer than Herr Hegendorf was worn down by chasing hunters through the Wienerwald. Some gravestones are signed – a pretty touch, as though the deceased had been begged by the stonemason to scrawl his signature one last time. The grave of Robert Stolz, composer of sickly operettas, bears on the stone a personally handwritten and signed message to onlookers.

The Viennese have established the admirable principle that even if you haven't been buried in the Central Cemetery, there may be a case for deciding that you ought to have been. If you are eminent enough to merit such an honour, the authorities will erect an *Ehrengrab*, an honorary gravestone. Neither Schubert nor Mozart was in fact buried here, but their remains, when recoverable – which in the case of Mozart they were not – have been reinterred. Just as Westminster Abbey has its poets' corner, so the Central Cemetery has a clutch of corners to bring together the graves of Vienna's great musicians, actors, even politicians. Ex-presidents of Austria are deposited around a kind of drained wading pool in front of the huge domed cemetery church.

All Saints' Day was the perfect occasion on which to tour the honorary graves, as one could assess the relative popularity of the deceased simply by counting the amount of foliage and the number of candles scattered across their final resting place by grieving admirers. I was there during the late morning, and the final count may have altered as the day drew to a close, but scoring out of ten, I would estimate the following results: Mozart and Beethoven were neck and neck with seven each, with Schubert close behind with six. Johann Strauss (Parts One and Two) lagged with four, but were well ahead of Brahms, with merely two. Suppé was scoring a pitiful one, as he deserved. Poor Hans Pfitzner, the composer of a very slow opera called *Palestrina*, had been tucked away among the politicians, so he had an excuse for being overlooked, which he had been, entirely. Politicians, on the other hand, do very well, as various political clubs and associations scatter their wreaths like funereal confetti. I was surprised by the poor showing over the fresh grave of Helmut Qualtinger, a brilliant comic actor and satirist, who had died just a few weeks earlier. He attracted a few memorial candles, but the writer Franz Werfel scored zero. Even more popular than Beethoven was a former major in the Luftwaffe who had died in action in 1944: his grave was strewn with flowers and an Iron Cross, and enough candles to light the Hall of Mirrors at Schönbrunn. The Viennese like to honour their own.

The domed cemetery church, dedicated to the memory of Dr Karl Lueger, is a cunning blend of brutalism and Art Nouveau (known in Vienna, and henceforth in this book, as *Jugendstil*) designed by Max Hegele. It was packed, and one Mass took off only minutes after the previous one touched down. The interior, adorned with mosaics and an altar modelled on that of the Steinhof church built a few years earlier by the great Otto Wagner, was less aggressive. The crowds inside the church and along the avenues and alleys around it were in telling contrast to the Jewish section of the cemetery, which was deserted. This is unsurprising.

Across the road from the entrance gates to the Central Cemetery is the grand approach to the principal crematorium. The Viennese, however, greatly prefer interment to the fire, even though the Second Vatican Council relaxed the rules that previously discouraged cremation. I obtained this nugget by visiting the Undertakers' Museum, which is only unintentionally ghoulish. The museum occupies some rooms on the first floor of what appears to be a kind of undertakers' cooperative. Hearses were being hosed down in the courtyard as I made my way up the stairs. To the guide, disposing of corpses was a business as much as a rite. Since burials are still conducted with pomp and ceremony in Vienna, undertaking must be a rewarding business. It was certainly as mercenary in the last century as in this. You get what you pay for: the rows of candles by the bier, the quality of the coffin, the number of pall bearers – you could have what you wanted, as long as you paid up. Emperor Joseph II, with his customary busybody style of reforming zeal, tried to persuade his subjects in the late eighteenth century that lavish burials were not only costly but wasteful. To assist his people to economize, he ordered them to be buried in cheap coffins with a hinged bottom. After your shrouded remains had been tipped into the grave, the coffin could then be hosed down and prepared for a fresh (or not so fresh) occupant. Not surprisingly, this recyclable model was unpopular with the clients, and after a few years Joseph had to rescind his order, petulantly observing as he did so that from now on his subjects could bury themselves as they damn well pleased.

Another ingenious innovation dates from the 1820s. Some thoughtful character invented a bell-pull that could be placed by the rigid hand of the deceased within the coffin. Should the corpse awake, he need not perish for a second and more permanent time, panicked by the total darkness six feet under; by giving a hearty tug at the rope he could summon the servants to disinter him. The device couldn't have been a huge success, as it fell into disuse before long. Nineteenth century undertakers provided all kinds of pleasant services. Since the art of the portrait photographer was less widely available than it is today, it was common for corpses to be photographed after the cosmetic scrub and polish had been completed. The photographed features would then be tinted to simulate sleep rather than death, and in this way the mourning relatives could carry away a likeness of their beloved. This practice was discontinued in the 1890s, whether on the grounds of taste or necessity I do not know. The poor of the city couldn't always afford the brass knick-knacks, bearing valedictory mottoes such as *Ruhe Sanft* or *Auf Wiedersehn*, that decorated a coffin and gravestone. Obliging undertakers would provide papier-maché replicas – less durable than brass, to be sure, but they still made the appropriate impression on the day.

On the afternoon of my visit to the Undertakers' Museum, I found myself in the company of a couple from Düsseldorf. I was content to listen to the informative commentary of the guide, but the young woman was full of questions. Her special subject, so to speak, was embalming and mummification. This was a red-letter day for the guide, clearly a retired member of the burying brotherhood, and all kinds of recipes and handy tips came pouring forth. While he compared the length of time required for a corpse to mummify indoors and outdoors, I studied some of the documents on display. There were invitations to the funerals of great musicians, and the undertaker's receipt for the corpse of Franz Schubert. Also in the glass case was a suicide letter written in 1962. With true Viennese respect for form and ceremony, the

36

suicide-to-be outlined at length his funeral requirements. Suicide is a Viennese tradition; countless numbers of gifted thinkers and artists took their own lives. The writer Adalbert Stifter, the playwright Ferdinand Raimund, the Ringstrasse architect Van der Null, the theorizer Otto Weininger, the poet Georg Trakl, and the children of Arthur Schnitzler and Hugo von Hoffmannsthal were among their number. Vienna, like all gay cities, awash with music and *Gemütlichkeit*, still has an extremely high suicide rate. Jumping under trains is wildly popular. *Ruhe sanft!*

The Central Cemetery brought order to a previously chaotic system of interment. Beneath the streets of the Inner City ossuaries are as common as drains, and some can still be visited and contemplated. In the catacombs under the cathedral can be seen not only the hat boxes containing the guts of the Habsburgs but the niches allocated to the cardinals of Vienna since 1630. In less august corners of the catacombs, about thirty chambers were piled high with coffins. The average capacity of each burial chamber was about 500 coffins, and when full the chamber was bricked up. The plague was a regular visitor to the city, and the Graben and the Piaristenplatz have as their focal point the contorted baroque columns, thick with iconographical allusion, erected to commemorate the visitations and to thank the deity for sparing the survivors. The victims, as in other conurbations, had to be disposed of without too much ceremony, and during the final plague of 1713 the 2000 dead were flung into a mass grave. The ragged flesh has long since fallen from those twisted bones, and through a grille in the wall the visitor can ponder at leisure a billowing sea of bone and skull, knuckle and joint. Space was always a problem down in the catacombs, and from time to time it was thought advisable to empty some of the coffins down there so as to provide room for new arrivals. During these operations the stench was so appalling that Masses could not be held in the cathedral. Joseph II, among his other prudent reforms, closed the catacombs in 1783.

In the same year the crypt of the Michaelerkirche was closed. Four thousand bodies were buried here, though only 250 of them managed to stay in their coffins. The young lady from Düsseldorf would have been entranced, for in this crypt the constant temperature and atmospheric conditions are such that the bodies have been mummified. Even their clothing has remained largely intact. Stumbling about in this gloomy crypt was not unlike attempting a nocturnal visit to the cellars of a Transylvanian castle. Many of the lids of the coffins have been flung open to reveal their occupants. The preservation of the corpses, who were placed here in the mid-eighteenth century, has been a hit-and-miss affair. Often the lips have decayed, so that the cadaver greets its visitors with an open-mouthed toothy grimace that distinctly lacks charm. One 300-year-old body is much like the next, but it is the clothing that makes these macabre survivals – if that is the *mot juste* – so fascinating. Whenever I watch a historical drama or film or look at an Old Master, I can't help wondering whether people really dressed like that – all those ruffs and two-toned hose and Carpaccio codpieces and stocks and gaiters – but here was the confirmation. They did indeed. Here was a cross section of the Viennese middle classes, dressed with panache and elegance, but unfortunately dead. One woman, lying in her box, had evidently died pregnant, and this two-in-one boxing-in was especially poignant. The poet and librettist Metastasio is also buried down here, together with an assortment of nobility and clergy, but his corpse, sealed in its coffin, remained safe from the vulgar gaze.

The Viennese may be ghoulish but they are in other respects depressingly free of eccentricity. Pressure to conform is strong. Any weird behaviour is immediately blamed on the *Föhn*, a balmy wind that blows up from the Sahara, giving unseasonably warm weather that, the Viennese claim, can induce migraine, instil a mood of dopiness, or push the suicidal into action. The *Föhn* whizzed into town when I was there and the only effect it had on me was delight in being able to walk coatless in November. The Viennese have a kind of court jester, who, being *extrem* (a favourite Viennese word and not approving), is allowed to embody any tiny twinges of eccentricity felt but suppressed by the *bürgerlich*. He is Waluliso, the stage name, as it were, of a bald and beaming man of about sixty who wears a toga and holds in his hands a staff and an apple and other impedimenta associated with Peace. The words *WAHR HEIT* are painted onto his sandals. A laurel wreath would give him some resemblance to a character in *Carry On Caesar*, were such a film to exist. His name is an amalgam of *Wasser, Luft, Licht, Sonne* (water, air, light, sun), which Wickerl Weinberger – his real name – thinks are Good Things. Completely dotty, Waluliso radiates such benignity and his discourse is so amiably vacuous that parents leave their entranced children in his company for a minute or two while they buy pastries and postcards, some of which portray Waluliso himself. He has the rare gift of ubiquity. Whenever I emerged from the Stephansdom, or from the Hofkapelle after hearing the Vienna Boys' Choir pipe their way through an eighteenth century Mass, or from the underground passages near the opera house, he was always there, beaming, nodding, an apple held high.

5

Noch a' Flascherl

Although many of the charming villages that once surrounded
Vienna have now been engulfed within the city, many retain
their intimate character. Grinzing is the dorf most tourists are
taken to see. *Heurigen* line the sloping streets, and delightful
they are too, each with a maze of cosy rooms in which you can
drink the local wine (often made and stored in the cellars below
the house) and sample home-cooked dishes from the buffet, and
a garden in which hundreds of Viennese tipple their way through
long summer evenings. The Grinzing Heurigen have become
thriving businesses, and one I visited could accommodate a
thousand people at a time; its rusticity was as calculated as the
netting and straw flasks on the walls of an Italian restaurant in
England. These large Heurigen contain restaurants within their
walls, thus legally depriving them of the right to be called
Heurigen, though nobody seems to care. These inns have thrived
in a dozen or more villages just outside the city since at least the
eighteenth century, though the vineyards themselves are far
older. Originally, a Heurige was little more than the front
parlour and cottage garden of a wine grower where one could sit
and smoke and drink the new wine while his wife prepared a cold
plate of meats and cheeses. Imperial decrees enabled small producers to *Auszuschenken*, to display their wares on certain days.
Some small Heurigen – though not in Grinzing – retain this
family atmosphere. In villages such as Gumpoldskirchen and the
Burgenland wine towns, the Heurigen are known as *Buschen-
schenken*, alluding to the old decrees; in many such establishments, wine-making is the principal activity, with serving food
and drink a useful way of supplementing the income and estab-
lishing a reputation for the wine. Most Heurigen and Buschen-
schenken are only permitted to open for a certain number of days

each year, presumably so as to give every grower in the village an equal crack of the whip.

Because of its undeniable prettiness, Grinzing has been selected as the archetypal Heurigen village. Many tour groups, having slogged round the palaces all day long, end up here in the early evening, and Germans and Scandinavians in particular have a reputation for drinking themselves into a stupor. The wine is not that potent, but it is easy to put away too much, since the basic measure, the *viertel*, is equivalent to a third of a bottle. I spent many evenings in less picturesque villages, where the wine was more distinguished and the clientele overwhelmingly local. I found the best wine in Stammersdorf, where at one Heurige the Riesling was sensationally good, dry but racy and vigorous. The Viennese rarely go out to restaurants late at night, and except in quarters of the city frequented by tourists or students, it is hard to order a meal after nine in the evening. But eating at Heurigen is popular. You can wander up to the buffet and order sausages or cold meats or some roast chicken and salad. Conviviality, the famous Viennese *Gemütlichkeit*, is the goal of an evening out at a Heurige. Couples will meet other couples, and by the end of the evening a dozen or more friends will be crowded round a single table.

I saw little drunkenness at the Heurigen. Most drinkers instal a bottle of Romerquelle, the local mineral water, on the table and dilute the wine into a DIY spritzer. Most Viennese wine is white – Welschriesling or Weissburgunder – and though red wine is perversely popular, it rarely matches the quality of the white. A chatty and portly patron of a Heurige at Jedlersdorf told me that certain wines are given local names to characterize them. Some were of so indelicate a nature that he had to whisper in my ear. Those I understood included *Hemdzieher* (shirt-tugger), a wine so sour it sucks your shirt up your arsehole, *Hemdspreizer*, a wine that will make your stomach spread, and *Rabiatperle*, a wine that simply makes you go ape-shit. Few of the wines I tasted had these alarming properties. The folklore of the Heurigen includes the belief that the wines of Vienna rarely lead to aggressive or extreme behaviour, and instead induce a mood of gentle melancholy or intimate conversation. One astute Viennese lady speculated that psychotherapy never really caught on in the city of its birth because the Heurigen function as confessionals. Life stories are blurted out to strangers; profound anxieties are shared and mitigated. This, however, was not my experience. In the company I kept, football scores were of greater concern than baring one's soul.

Much of my eating and drinking was done in the company of Robert and Marianne, the caretakers of an expensive apartment building on the Hohe Warte, a villa-lined street that leads from Vienna to the former village of Heiligenstadt. Much of the village is filled by the Karl Marx Hof, but old Heiligenstadt is a charming place with numerous Heurigen on both sides of its narrow lanes, and a remarkable collection of houses where Beethoven lived and wrote a bar or two. Robert and Marianne lived for football. The walls of their flat were plastered with posters and pennants, signed photographs, souvenir programmes. Here and there Bruce Springsteen got a look in, his strained and sweating features in striking contrast to the bland smiles of posing soccer stars. A childless couple in their thirties, Robert and Marianne prided themselves on their capacity for gargantuan consumption. When I phoned Marianne one lunchtime, she confessed, 'Heute sind wir tod' (We're dead today), explaining that once again they had caroused until six in the morning and were now paying the price. Every three months they would disappear to Rome for a week and dream of the day when they could live forever in that sunny city, earning their living by setting up a *Würstelstand* outside the Juventus football stadium. It never seemed to occur to them that the Italians shared their passion for football but not for *Knackwurst* and *Semmeln* (rolls).

We had two principal venues: a *Lokal* in the Billrothstrasse or, on special occasions, a Hungarian restaurant in the 20th Bezirk (district). There, most evenings of the week, Marianne and Robert would meet a dozen of their friends for drink and talk. The group was varied: a plump doctor with soft pudgy features called Hans, a handsome heating engineer, a blank-featured young woman called Lotte who spoke only, and then rarely, to her nameless boyfriend, and two other women who spoke only to each other. Perhaps two-thirds of the total contingent would be present on any one night. They were united by two passions: football and gluttony. Every time their beloved Austria played, the entire group would descend on the stadium, where Robert and some of the other men worked as stewards, allowing them to see the match for nothing. Marianne operated a kind of ticket agency, and every week, around a table in the Billrothstrasse *Lokal*, she would distribute the latest batch of tickets. Introduced to the gang by Marianne and Robert, I was made welcome in the best possible way: greeted with handshakes and smiles, and then for the most part ignored. My sponsors and Hans were good company, and proved helpful and informative when I asked them about anything that was puzzling me. In general, however, I was treated as though invisible. I was there on sufferance, welcome to sit and drink with them, but it was clearly understood that I was not part of the Austrian football fraternity, and thus could never be more than an occasional guest – which suited me fine, since the only contribution I could make to the dominant topic of conversation was my celebrated impersonation of a drunken Scottish football fan in Leicester Square.

More serious revelry took place at the Hungarian restaurant owned by the Haller family in the 20th Bezirk. The 20th, a triangular-shaped district between the Danube Canal and river, is essentially a working-class area, though class consciousness is not a prominent feature of Austrian life. Robert's group may have been predominantly working class in its social composition, but the middle class was represented too. None of them, to judge by the amount they ate and drank every night, was short of money. Unencumbered by children and living, most of them, in subsidized housing, they were able to spend substantial sums on the habitual gratification of their pleasures. Even being on the dole didn't seem to cramp the style of two of the group, and everybody participated in the occasional evenings of unrestrained gluttony. One morning Marianne phoned me up with advance notification of a *Kerzelfest* at Haller's the following Saturday. The food would be good and the dining areas entirely candle-lit, and there would be music and dancing. I said I'd be there.

Half the principal dining room had been reserved for Robert's group, and above the table Frau Haller had taped some football posters in honour of her loyal customers. Another table was occupied by a birthday party, and all chatter ceased whenever a bouquet or a cake was brought in, while the disc jockey installed in the far corner flicked through his records and tapes in search of an appropriate song. I soon found myself enraptured by Frau Haller. She was about fifty, determinedly pudgy, as though a chin or two brought on by excessive consumption of dumplings and pancakes were a badge of honour. Her eyes gleamed, and her mouth was half-open with permanent merriment whenever she flounced through the room with another tray heaped with plates from which schnitzels poked over the sides just as beer bellies loom over belts. She swung her hips provocatively, and there was plenty of hip to swing. Yet this splendid woman, dressed to kill in black and gold, was in no way vulgar; she was stately and utterly sure of her own powers, drawn as they were from the appetites and thirsts she catered for.

We began the evening with an hour's drinking. We were purists – wine and beer folk – and disdained such popular concoctions as *Baucherl* (Weinbrandt and Coke) or Bonanza (Coke and red wine). Then we ate, copiously. Weighted with stuffed cabbage or schnitzel, we were slow to respond to the DJ's urgings to dance. One or two couples would dash in from the adjoining room, bop vigorously, then rush back to their beers. We preferred to do a little singing to get us in a more Dionysian mood. The songs were mostly boisterous traditional songs, thick with sentimentality. Some, like 'O Susanna, wie ist das Leben schön' ('Susanna, how lovely life is!') had a philosophical content, however watery, that found the singers raising their voices high with emotion. As soon as it was over, everybody switched gears either into another song or back into conversation. The *Vogeltanz* (bird dance) brought the house down on each occasion it went onto the turntable. This mindless ditty requires the performers – and listeners are trans-formed into performers in the convivial back room at Haller's – to attempt birdcall imitations, to flap their wings, jiggle their rumps, and so forth. This disgusting display epitomized to me the very worst of Germanic culture, showy, coarse and loud. But when I described the song to a Canadian acquaintance, long resident in Austria, she told me that the previous summer, when she had gone to Toronto to attend her brother's wedding, an almost exact equivalent of the *Vogeltanz*, anglicized, had been one of the star turns at the reception.

When Frau Haller felt the mood was flagging, she would sashay into the back room with a tray of small glasses filled with a clear spirit: Hungarian Csereszne, distilled from cherries. These were on the house. When the chef appeared, hot from the kitchen range, he was warmly greeted as the hero of the evening, and indeed the food had been delicious. A second round of Csereszne prompted more songs – including something about getting on my tractor – and we were now ready to take to the dance floor. Golden Oldies proved popular – 'Let's Twist Again' and 'Tutti Frutti' in particular – and the styles of dancing derived from gyrations popularized in the 1960s. The birthday party at the next table had expanded, and I was struck by the presence of a Louise Brooks look-alike, an unsmiling woman with tufted earrings, sharp pert

features, and an oddly attentive look, combining rooted concentration with boredom. She danced, unenthusiastically but
efficiently, with another woman. I'd noticed in Russian restaurants that the act of dancing was more important than whom you
danced with, and the same seemed to apply here.

We were now up to our necks in *Gemütlichkeit*. Robert's voice,
heavy with dialect, boomed out across the length of the table as he
told a story that had everybody collapsing with mirth. Sweat ran
down the cheeks of the men, as their bodies moved into high gear to
cope with the heat of the room and the alcohol in the blood. Still,
there were some people who were having difficulties measuring up
to all this jollity. Plump Lotte – oh, they were all plump, every
single one of our group – well, plump Lotte was beaming in a morose
way, but remained silent, while on the other side of me Anna
giggled a good deal and joined in all the songs, but never responded
to my attempts at conversation with more than a monosyllable. By
midnight, Robert and Hans and most of the other men had wearied
of joke-telling and clumped off to the front room, where the bar was
located. Here they could abandon the pretence of drinking only
beer and wine, and transfer to schnapps for the rest of the night. The
men's lavatory was awash, and one lad – nothing to do with our
group, I hasten to add – was inert on the floor while unnameable
liquids seeped into his clothes. While the men grew drunk – '*Noch 'a
flascherl!*' I could hear them call, as they emptied yet another
bottle of beer – the women acquired an increasingly glazed look.

By now I was bored. Having rejected the Austrian wine I'd
ordered as not good enough, I prevailed upon Frau Haller to bring
some of their special Hungarian white wine, which proved
delicious but very strong, and I wanted no more to drink. I didn't
feel like dancing, and the women on either side of me were doggedly
ignoring me. The men at the bar were deeply engrossed in their own
impenetrable conversations, so I paid up and left. The last tram had
long since switched off the current, and I walked back towards the
bridge across the Danube Canal. Nobody tried to mug me or offer me
drugs. Heroin addicts, I was told, tend to deal from the safety of
cemeteries, accessible only to those determined enough to climb
the walls. Soft drugs are also peddled at the Beiseln near the
Naschmarkt, but the Viennese prefer to drink rather than snort or
puff in search of their kicks.

Although it was late at night and the 20th is not the most
salubrious of districts, I felt entirely safe. Street crime in Vienna is
uncommon. I crossed the bridge and found myself in the small area

of the Inner City known as the Bermuda Dreieck – the Bermuda Triangle – so called because people go to the bars of the district and three days later can't recall where they've been for the past seventy-two hours. Until a few years ago the few streets that form the triangle were deserted at night; then a dozen bars and restaurants sprung up, catering to the trendies, students, artists, and yuppies to be found in any prosperous city. Late on a Saturday night – it was about one in the morning – some of the bars were so crowded that the revellers, many fashionably though informally dressed, had spilled out into the street. I fought my way into two of the bars, abandoned hope of getting a drink within fifteen minutes, and fought my way out again. Some of the bars offer live music, but there is little dancing – these are not discos – since the Viennese prefer, admirably, to talk to each other. Many of the bars stay open until four, and it is not uncommon for some energetic young people to return home at five or six, take a quick shower, then head straight for the office. In a fashionable restaurant, the Salzamt – too chic to identify itself on the facade – not a table was to be had. I didn't feel inclined to linger. Even though I was more likely to find good company in a Dreieck bar than in a Hungarian restaurant in the 20th Bezirk, I felt here the isolation of the stranger, whereas in Frau Haller's dining room I had felt, if not at home, then at least welcome.

Close to the chic bars of the Bermuda Triangle stands the principal surviving synagogue of Vienna. The exterior, along the steep Seittenstettegasse, is self-effacing, and on returning to the street by daylight I only realized that I must be passing the synagogue when I noticed that three Cobra guards, armed with sub-machine guns, were patrolling the street. Armed guards are not usually present in such force, but this was the Jewish festival of Simchas Torah and the synagogue was crowded. When I asked a young man standing by the door whether I could visit the interior, he said not at present, though I would be welcome to come back another time. I walked slowly back up the street and paused in the small square at the top. From here I could see the empty kosher restaurant, Noah's Ark, the fashionable Salzamt, and the ancient church of St Ruprecht, alleged to have been founded in 740 and still supported on walls that date from the eleventh century. Here I paused and began to make some notes.

A minute later a ginger-haired man of about twenty-five was by my side. Politely but firmly, he asked me what was I doing. Taking notes, I replied. About what? I said I was a journalist and could be found taking notes throughout Vienna on a half-hourly basis. He peered over my shoulder. It so happened that earlier in the day I had been talking about the general election campaign then under way and had noted down the name of Jörg Haider, the leader of the right-wing Freedom Party, which enjoys the support of some ex-Nazis. Not surprisingly, this engaged the curiosity of my new companion even further. I explained further. When he began to throw more questions at me, I threw a few back, asking him who he was. 'Security,' he replied simply. While we sized each other up, we were both being watched by two policemen seated in a car parked in a corner of the square.

I decided to take the security man into my confidence, not that I had much to confide, and mentioned that I was keen to visit the synagogue. He said the morning service should be coming to a close now and he would see what he could do. We walked back down the Seittenstettegasse and approached the guard who had rejected my earlier application. The security man told the guard that it should be all right to let me in. The man on the door nodded, and thanking the red-head for his help, I began to walk into the passage that leads to the main hall of the synagogue. A firm hand gripped my shoulder and I found myself being gently pushed into a corner. Here the guard frisked me, while another young man, who had suddenly materialized, kept watch on us both. Slowly, very slowly, the guard ran his hands down my body, poking into crevices, behind my ears, behind my collar. I was made to empty my pockets and take off my shoes, which were minutely examined. So too were my spectacles, and my jacket was turned inside out.

After five minutes of this, I was allowed to proceed, and there was no further attempt to watch me or hinder me. I kept my notebook out of sight, however. The synagogue itself certainly made the difficulty of getting in to see it worthwhile. Built by Joseph Kornhäusel in 1826, it is a most beautiful hall, circular in design with two levels of galleries supported and divided by tall white columns with gilt capitals. The domed ceiling is painted pale blue and dotted with dancing stars. Although the service was still in progress, it was as noisy as a railway station. The women were seated in the upper galleries where they could exchange hat recipes and shoe cocktails, while the men sat downstairs telling each other jokes. Between the two factions of worshippers ran their children, wild with excitement. God was being taken care of nearer the Ark, where a rabbi and cantor were chanting away busily, assisted by a few members of the congregation who had taken time off from gossip.

Smartly dressed bourgeois men in dark suits dominated the congregation; their wives wore expensive dresses and elaborate hats, their children scampered about in freshly laundered clothes and looked as though they were on their way to a birthday party. Another group of worshippers was far more shabby, the men badly dressed and ill-shaven, the women blowsy and loud. The first group consisted of Viennese Jews; the second of East European Jews who had come to rest in Vienna. Before the war there had been 200,000 Jews in Vienna, where they comprised one-tenth of the population, and, as is well known, had long been prominent in the city's cultural as well as financial life. A significant proportion of Vienna's musicians, writers, doctors, editors, and academics were Jewish or of Jewish descent. Now their population is reduced to about 7000. That, at any rate, is the number of Jews registered with the Kultusgemeinde, the Jewish religious authorities, and there are probably another few thousand who claim no religious affiliation. But of that 7000 there are probably no more than 200 families who can trace their ancestry back to Vienna or Budapest (where the proportion of Jews had been even higher) in the last century. The majority of Jews now living in Vienna are, as one prominent Viennese Jew put it to me, 'flotsam', concentration camp survivors from Eastern Europe, Romanian refugees, or Jews who had left the Soviet Union more recently. Many among this group did not consider themselves permanent residents of the city. Many of them, or many of their children, had moved on to Israel or other countries, though a number of Soviet Jews, who had had uncomfortable experiences in the Promised Land, had later returned to Vienna.

That huge prewar Jewish population had been reduced to shreds and tatters. The Austrians had made a less than glorious contribution to that decimation. One of the telling features of *Last Waltz in Vienna*, George Clare's book recounting his formative years in Vienna, is the fact that when he and his family fled from Austria in 1938 after the Anschluss, they took refuge in Berlin, where they encountered far less antisemitism than in their native Vienna. Until recently the presence, or absence, of Jews in Austria had not been a matter for much comment. The revelations about Kurt Waldheim's past changed all this. Austria once again took note of its scattering of Jews. Most Viennese Jews did not welcome this acknowledgment of their presence wholeheartedly. The suspicion that American Jewry had attempted to interfere in an Austrian election by hurling accusations at a respected candidate had revived allegations that antisemitism has always been latent in Austria – just as it has always been latent in other European countries such as France and Poland. At the same time more honourable sections of the community were doing their best to make amends for the suffering previous generations had inflicted on Austrian Jewry, and this was almost equally unwelcome to the Jews of Vienna.

'What most of us would like best,' remarked a Jewish journalist to me, 'is for the world to leave us alone. When the World Jewish Congress attacked Waldheim, not only did they win considerable sympathy for Waldheim from voters who wouldn't normally support the conservative party, but the very name of the organization brought up echoes of the World Jewish Conspiracy, and that was the last thing we needed.

'Austrian Jews know it's still not advisable to live in a small Tyrolean village and not go to church. That's asking for suspicion, if not hostility. But then hardly a single Austrian Jew would want to do such a thing anyway. Rural antisemitism, especially in the west of the country, is religiously based, because we Jews nailed the Lord to the Cross. It has nothing to do with the activities of contemporary Jews. A farmer in the Vorarlberg or Tyrol has a far greater chance of being killed in a car crash than of ever meeting a Jew.

'What irritates us is that politicians and media people now feel obliged to stroke a Jew every day, just to be sure we know that they love us. We can't do much to stop that, but we can object to those leaders of the Jewish community who pander to that kind of stroking. As we say in Vienna, "Wenn ein Jud blöd ist, ist er wirklich blöd".' ('When a Jew's stupid, he's really stupid.')

There was certainly a lot of stroking going on while I was in town. A TV documentary dealt, rather blandly, with the position of the city's remaining Jews. Claude Lanzmann's *Shoah*, his compelling ten-hour documentary on the Holocaust, was shown in four parts on Austrian television, and was followed a few days later by a lengthy televised discussion of the film and the issues it raised. Then there was a televised ballet based on the Anne Frank story, and a few days later a vigil took place in Stephansplatz to commemorate Kristallnacht, when Hitler's triumphant arrival in Vienna in 1938 triggered a wave of antisemitic violence. When I spent an evening with a musician and his friends, there was an almost competitive insistence on revealing, with pride of course, the proportion of Jewish blood that flowed through our veins.

To even the most idle observer, the contribution of Jews to Austrian culture and learning has hardly been obscured. Mahler, Schoenberg, Freud, Husserl, Wittgenstein, Schnitzler, Joseph Roth, Stefan Zweig, Karl Kraus, Hoffmannsthal – all were Jews or of Jewish descent. To these illustrious names can be added those of newspaper editors and academics and doctors whose reputation was more localized, but who were nonetheless influential in their day. Yet it would seem, judging by Austria's new-found interest in its handful of Jews, that the country has only belatedly recognized the contribution they made to the national culture. Certainly Austrian schools never took great pains to stress that contribution. The furore over Waldheim has restored the issue to prominence. Whether ordinary Austrians are much interested in the Jewish population is doubtful, but the media seem to be acting as the conscience of the nation. It's tempting to speculate whether a substantial special exhibition devoted to 'Judaism in Vienna' would have been mounted in November 1987 had the Austrian Establishment not perceived the need for some rapid refurbishment of its image. By a curious exercise of split memory, it is as though the Austrians are showing some willingness to come to terms with their largely discreditable past as far as the Jews were concerned, so long as such admissions steer well away from such personal issues as whether, to cite what must be a common example, their grandparents were Nazis or Nazi sympathizers. The progressive municipal government has installed in the former Town Hall, the Alte Rathaus, a moving permanent exhibition devoted to the activities of the Austrian Resistance. 65,000 Austrian Jews were put to death by the Nazis in camps such as Mauthausen. The Viennese were not slow to kick a Jew into the gutter when offered the opportunity, but there were also brave Austrians, communists as well as clergy and ordinary men and women of good will and great courage, who resisted the Nazi regime, often at the cost of their own lives.

By the time the war ended, not only was Viennese Jewry virtually extinct, but almost every other independent-minded soul, of whatever religious or racial origin, had either fled or been murdered. From this destruction of the nation's cultural and intellectual life, Austria has yet to recover. Even today, many distinguished Viennese-born writers, such as Erich Fried, continue to live abroad, even though they take a keen interest in contemporary Austria. Among those Jews who have returned to their native city there simmers a distinct disquiet at the resurgence of interest in them from their fellow citizens. Those who returned did so in large part because they wished to make their contribution to the Austria of the future. The last thing they want is to be recognized only in relation to the terrible past they were fortunate enough to have survived.

6

Kultur

The world's great opera houses generally make concessions to those who cannot afford high seat prices or who wish to attend a performance on the spur of the moment. Usually, after a fairly lengthy queueing period in conditions of marked discomfort, the worst seats in the house are sold off on the day of performance. In Vienna, in happy contrast, the Staatsoper administration seems to welcome the impoverished as warmly as the well-heeled. 550 standing places – supplying a quarter of the audience – are sold at wonderfully cheap prices an hour before the curtain rises, and except on certain star-studded occasions, the queueing takes place indoors, not on the chilly streets.

I turned up early one day to queue for *Simon Boccanegra*, which offered a splendid cast conducted by Claudio Abbado, just arrived in Vienna as the new musical director of the Staatsoper. First I had to wriggle my way through a niceness demonstration taking place in a corner of the plaza on which the opera house, like a dozing hippopotamus, sprawls. The protesters, overwhelmingly female, wore round their necks placards bearing legends on the following lines (my translation): 'Eat Eggs from Free Hens', 'My Fur's Fake', 'Don't Coop Up Calves'. I smiled a lot to speed my passage through the small crowd, and found my way to the rear of the queue. Here was that delightful international gathering, reminiscent of the higher orders of youth hostelry, always to be found on the pavements outside major opera houses. In front of me a Viennese girl was swopping stories about Great Performances with German youths from Stuttgart and Wiesbaden. Behind me two Viennese ladies squatted on stools and chatted as they crocheted. An Italian girl stood reading *Repubblica* for an hour. Small knots of American girls punctuated the queue. On other occasions I met a Swedish sociologist and a Polish doctor who asked me to translate

the German instructions for the digital watch he had just bought
for his son.

At four the queue moved indoors, and by six the first tickets
were being sold. I always opted for the standing places at the back
of the stalls. Because of their central location, the view of the
stage is perfect. These places were priced at 20 Schillings (about
the same price as a loaf of good bread or a cup of coffee at the
Hawelka), and standing places up in the balcony and gallery were
even cheaper at 15 Schillings. There is yet another queue for
students and other people entitled to special concessions, and
unsold seats are made available to them for 50 Schillings. Once
inside the auditorium, you can reserve your spot by tying a scarf
around the rail provided for leaning against. You are then free to
wander about until the performance begins.

The interior of the Staatsoper, which was severely damaged in
the last war and not reopened until 1955, is surprisingly plain.
There is no plush, and even the stalls seats are plain and wood-
backed. Plain golden fluting around the proscenium arch and
lightly gilt panels in front of each box around the many circles
give the interior a quietly elegant tone. The effect is cosy and
slightly dim, for the walls are painted a dull cream and the carpets
are a dusty red. A small Habsburg eagle looks down on the
standing places behind the stalls as one of the few reminders of
imperial glory, though Franz Josef is memorialized in an inscription on the facade facing the Ringstrasse. Ostentatious display is
reserved for the halls and staircases, which are littered with
statuary and daubed with frescoes.

At Covent Garden the plebs are still kept separated from the
more expensive parts of the house, just as in London theatres the
gallery is only reached by stairs mounted from another entrance.
Not so in Vienna, where the 500 or so holders of standing tickets
may mingle freely with the rich Viennese and the Japanese
businessmen in the boxes. Dinner jackets are far more common
here than in most opera houses, and the women dress with
somewhat funereal splendour. Close your eyes in the main
lounges and you can hear the swishing of taffeta and silk and smell
the glaze of hair lacquer. Fur stoles round the shoulders of
countless old ladies, and sequined purple jackets are worn with
matching shoes. Although the latest Italian fashions are widely
available in the shops along the Kärntnerstrasse, they are not
much in evidence at the opera, where wardrobes tend to be dowdy
rather than chic. Far too many outfits looked as if they had been

bought at vast expense in 1958 and would not be thrown away until the Angel of Death came for the owner. One young lady even wore a *Dirndl* over a lace blouse. Since everyone knows everyone else in Vienna (even I, on a relatively short visit, would meet an acquaintance by chance in the street once or twice a day), there was much cheek-pecking and broad smiles of recognition. Despite the formality of the audience, the orchestra, the wonderful Vienna Philharmonic, is dressed in dark suits.

The decor is typical of the plush vulgarity of the Ringstrasse style, its constituents borrowed from the multi-volumed catalogue of architectural and decorative motifs that had accumulated over the years as a kind of stylistic reference work. The detail is deplorable, but the overall effect admirable. Best of all, there is ample room for strolling about, especially in the upstairs salons. Smokers were directed to a special hall so as to keep the air pure in the remaining salons. Downstairs the parterre lounges, painted a dim cream, resembled the public rooms of dowdy hotels. There was a constant whiff of the boudoir, as ladies emerged from boxes and toilets; I sniffed powders and creams and sweet jellies. The Staatsoper is not only beautifully spacious, but admirably organized. The queueing is orderly, and any attempt to jump the queue or bend the rules is fiercely stamped on by the brown-jacketed attendants – jokey, obliging, vigilant – who patrol the lines. Banks of cloakrooms line one entire side of the ground-floor lobbies, and I never had to wait more than thirty seconds for my coat. Once I saw a plain double door opening silently to reveal a lady in a bath chair being wheeled down a ramp.

I was delighted to be seeing *Simon Boccanegra* again. I had first seem this same production at the Paris Opéra in the late 1970s. My seat was about as far from the stage as the white cliffs of Dover are from Calais, and I could see no more than a few mannikins in cloaks stumbling about in the gloom below. I fell asleep, indeed. Not this time. Not only was the singing very fine, but it was wondrous to hear the glorious sound produced by the orchestra. Like all opera house orchestras, the VPO can turn in a lousy performance when, as not infrequently happens at the Staatsoper, the conductor is a hack, but under Abbado they gave of their best. The audience was extremely attentive. Since 500 of them had been queueing for up to six hours to hear the performance, it was safe to say that the vast majority were nuts about opera and had no intention of missing a note. Even the fatcats were well behaved. On my visits to the Staatsoper, I was always struck by the fact that the audience actually listened and watched – in preference to reading the programme, sleeping, or munching Maltesers. They dispensed the sweets of applause with discriminating hands. When they bravo'd a curtain call, it was to honour a fine performance; when they merely pitpatted their fingers, it was to signal a polite lack of enthusiasm. At the Metropolitan Opera in New York, the often vulgar audience applauds widely any vulgarity on stage (Kings of High C's, and other such nonsense); but here in Vienna dramatic intelligence as well as vocal acrobatics were required and, if forthcoming, rewarded.

Nonetheless, I did walk out of the Staatsoper more than I have ever walked out of any other opera house or theatre. True, when you've only paid 20 Schillings for a ticket, you feel less guilty about vanishing than if your life savings have been exchanged for a seat in the stalls. But there were some astonishingly weak performances. When the horns of the VPO fluffed it during the overture of *Der Freischütz*, it was a bad omen, and indeed there was worse to come, from the stage as well as the pit. I left after the forest scene, while backstage, I later gathered, the set designer was raising Cain, alleging that this revival had travestied his intentions. Nor did I last the course the following night at Henze's ballet *Orpheus*. The *corps de ballet* wore paper bags on their heads, and began the ballet by squirming on the ground and counting to ten. The set resembled a loading bay at a major post office, and the sole visual suspense was provided by a metal-roller door. What we wondered, for lack of anything else to do, was behind it? Not much, was the answer. There was a *coup de théâtre* when the entire set sank beneath the stage, but on the whole it was an evening of barely relieved drabness and tedium. Through what must have been some travel agent's error, a Japanese business delegation of about thirty men still wearing their ID lapel badges found themselves in the standing places. About two-thirds of the way through the ballet (to torment the audience further there was no interval) there was a hurried conference among the Japanese. Following the body language, I gathered that the gist of the discussion, and certainly its unanimous and binding decision, was 'Let's get out of here'. Shrinking into my shoes, I did my best to act Japanese and slunk out behind my discriminating friends from the Orient.

The problem at the Staatsoper is the repertory system. At Covent Garden or the Met, perhaps four or five productions will run concurrently. The Staatsoper, on the other hand, may mount thirty or more productions per year, though some revivals may receive no more than a couple of performances. Inevitably, with pressures on rehearsal time, standards are bound to vary hugely. When the prestige of the house is at stake, no trouble or expense is spared. The opening production of Abbado's reign, which had only just begun when I went to Vienna, was *Un Ballo in Maschera* starring Luciano Pavarotti. It was first rate, and even Pavarotti sang with some grace and conviction. So too was *Simon Boccanegra* and a British production of *Maria Stuarda* with the glorious Agnes Baltsa and Mara Zampieri. But a production of *Die Entführung aus dem Serail* was – let's be kind – merely proficient. Perhaps it had been rehearsed, but if so it didn't show, and the conducting was dreadful.

The prestige of the Staatsoper is matched by that of the Burgtheater, which has been a leading exponent of classic German theatre since the eighteenth century, and the Musikverein, the home of the Vienna Philharmonic. It is no accident that the Staatsoper and Burgtheater were given magnificent sites along the Ringstrasse. They were always perceived as central cultural institutions, among the glories of the city. High culture has never been peripheral in Vienna, and in the nineteenth century was integral to bourgeois as well as aristocratic life. The levels of subsidy to theatre and opera from municipal as well as federal governments are extremely high. It is widely recognized that they have enhanced, and continue to enhance, the international reputation of the city, and it is prudent to invest substantially in those institutions so as to ensure that they can maintain their high standards and continue to draw free-spending foreign visitors to the city. This strikes most Viennese as mere common-sense, though when a similar attitude is expressed in Britain, it is dismissed as elitist and simple-minded. There are dissenting voices. A distinguished Viennese painter did mutter to me that he personally wouldn't lose any sleep if the Staatsoper closed down: it eats up three-quarters of the arts budget and thus deprives other worthy recipients of public largesse.

One night at the opera I was surprised when a young German standing behind me identified by name the double bass players, who were visible from the standing places. A VPO instrumentalist has a status inconceivable in any other Western city. Standards of teaching at Vienna's conservatories as well as of performance are extremely high. It is often noted that London sustains four or five full symphony orchestras, but Vienna too supports four orchestras, and this in a city a quarter of the size of London. Music, far more than theatre, is part of the fabric of Viennese life. Although the Viennese daily press is among the worst in Europe – it may never sink to the savage and mesmerizing banality and vulgarity of the British tabloids, but there is no newspaper that even approaches in quality a 'serious' British or German newspaper – even in the most crass Viennese tabloids you will find a *Kultur* page, with lengthy and thoughtful reviews of current productions and performances. Most Viennese do seem to take pride in the cultural distinction of their city, even if they never avail themselves of it. School trips from the suburbs and surrounding countryside to theatre and opera are encouraged, and a large proportion of children take music lessons at school. There is no shortage of free music to be enjoyed in Vienna. The best place to spend a cold Sunday morning, apart from the Café Landtmann, is the lovely Gothic Augustinerkirche near the Hofburg, where exuberant Mozart and Schubert Masses are sung complete with full orchestral accompaniment.

High culture, indeed, is followed as avidly by the Viennese as though it were a sport. Few directors of the Staatsoper complete their terms of office, so turbulent are the politics of culture. The press enjoys stirring up speculation, and it is said that the principal reason why Lorin Maazel abandoned the directorship of the Staatsoper is that he was sick and tired of the relentless hostility to his regime shown by the press. The Burgtheater also has a new director, the German Claus Peymann, and he had scarcely had time to unpack his suitcases before he too came under severe critical scrutiny. I went to see two of his current pro-ductions, Brecht's *Die Mutter* and Lessing's classic *Nathan der Weise*. I hope Peymann stays the course, for the Lessing produc-tion in particular was outstanding, fairly radical in style and projection, yet lucid and gripping. (Burgtheater programmes are filled not with ads for perfume but with the entire text of the play being performed. *Nathan der Weise* is extremely long, and many cuts had been made, all of which were indicated in the text. Thus it was possible for me to follow the entire play as I watched, and gave me more time to puzzle out passages that I had not fully understood when spoken.)

The Burgtheater, like the Staatsoper, stands on the Ring, facing out towards the hills, as though greeting the city around it. The two wings that stretch out into the plaza around the building both contain immense ceremonial staircases, decorated with excellent frescoes, including some early work by Gustav Klimt. This grandeur seems misplaced. Built in an age when men wore uniforms and swords, and medals rattled on their chests, and when women's dresses trailed breathily up the carpeted stairs, the pomp of these staircase entrances now seems overblown. The theatre is as spacious and well organized as the Staatsoper, though slightly less formal. Here too there are cheap standing places for the indigent, and the audience was astonishingly attentive, even through a marathon production such as the Lessing. Yet the audience did not seem especially responsive. Even I, with my imperfect understanding of the play, would occasionally venture a chuckle, but would rarely be joined in my modest participation by the rest of the audience. The atmosphere was altogether too respectful, too dutiful, as though classic theatre were a monument to be admired in silence, rather than a specimen of living drama to be entered into. It also seemed incongruous that a crude if stirring piece such as Brecht's *Die Mutter* should be played before an audience so relentlessly bourgeois. How could they relish a play in such opposition to their carefully nurtured values? Again, it was as though the play were like a statue on a pedestal, admirable but still, with no power to reach down and touch them.

Claus Peymann has been welcomed by the more discerning Viennese, but he has ample time to incur hostility. His staging of a new piece, 'March 13, 1938', that probes the Anschluss, may harmonize with the spirit of national reappraisal but it will also earn him enemies among the conservative Establishment. Moreover, any new director must make changes if he is to leave his mark on the institution, and that includes firing actors and staff associated with the preceding regime. Once blood begins to flow, intrigues will flourish and it will be interesting to see how, or indeed whether, the admirable Herr Peymann survives. And the same goes for Dr Drese and Claudio Abbado at the Staatsoper.

If the major cultural institutions are well supported by the city, so too are less fashionable manifestations of cultural vitality. The Scottish avant-garde composer Stephen Ferguson told me that the city supports five modern composers sufficiently well to allow them to live from their work. Should you receive a commission for a new work, the Arts Ministry will ensure that you receive a sufficient income to enable you to compose it. Ferguson was the first to admit that avant-garde music from Austria has not made much of a dent internationally, but pointed out that some Austrian jazz musicians do have a high reputation abroad. Jazz musicians have outlets through clubs, but for modern composers the radio is their principal medium, and audience reaction is often adverse. In Vienna, cultural life and the higher reaches of social life are closely connected, so if you do receive a commission for a new work to mark a civic occasion, you have at least a fighting chance to make or consolidate a reputation.

Local forms of music-making with broader appeal such as Schrammelmusik are still popular, especially in Heurigen, though my own acquaintance with this jaunty idiom was fleeting. But I was urged to go and see a recent example of Austrian movie-making, *Müllers Büro*. It turned out to be an agreeable parody of Chandler-style gangster movies, mixed in with burlesque elements. Directed at a fairly juvenile audience, it also contained some moderately explicit sex scenes that were handled with humour and sophistication. On the evening I went to see it, the scene which the audience – average age sixteen – loved most was when Müller wakes his sleeping sidekick by farting in his face. When the same incident was duplicated ten minutes later, the audience was even more ecstatic. If only Claus Peymann could draw on the central European addiction to lavatory humour, his future might be secure.

7

Third Palace on the Right

That Vienna would be grand I fully expected. That it would also be beautiful came as a greater surprise. I suspect it also came as a surprise to most Viennese. Only in recent years has there been a concerted effort to restore and spruce up the numerous baroque palaces strewn about the city. Strictly speaking, the French word *palais* should be used in preference to 'palace', since in Vienna *palais* denoted an urban residence, a town mansion, rather than a building on a truly palatial scale. Some, such as the Palais Liechtenstein next to the Burgtheater, are built on a massive and almost regal scale, but they are the exception rather than the rule. Although it is possible to pick out the individual stylistic contributions of the major Viennese architects, notably the two Fischers von Erlach and Hildebrandt, the design of the Viennese *palais* took on fairly standardized forms, and many are superficially indistinguishable.

Since the streets of the old city were and still are quite narrow, facades were relatively unimportant features. Some mansions, such as that at 3 Bäckerstrasse, are enlivened by the simple device of varying the forms of the hood and pediments over the windows; the effect is plain and dignified, yet rhythmical. But most facades are marked by their regularity. Each floor is lit by large windows that scarcely ever vary in height from storey to storey. The major ornamental effort was reserved for the main gateway or portal, which was almost invariably flanked by straining Herculean figures groaning under the weight of the lintel they were supporting. An outstanding example of this conceit is found in the Bohemian Court Chancellery designed by J.B. Fischer von Erlach. This comes complete with the standard statuary and also has elaborate pediments broken by emblazoned shields, and crowning the entire structure, a top pediment filled with martial emblems and crowned, literally, with a golden crown.

The palais gate gives access to a large courtyard, the *Hof*, and the entrance to the main rooms of the palace usually leads off from the covered passageway that connects street and Hof. More modest houses also have a Hof, and external walkways give the residents along each floor direct access to the courtyard, in which stands a fountain or pump from which they once drew their fresh water supply. One of the loveliest courtyards in Vienna is also to be found in Bäckerstrasse, at Number 7, which has retained its original stables.

Gothic Vienna has all but vanished. During the redecoration of a house on Tuchlauben, a busy shopping street that runs from the Graben to the Michaelerplatz, fifteenth-century frescoes were uncovered. Despite their crudity they are of interest because they depict secular subjects, including buildings. Only one solitary Gothic tower remains in the Inner City, but there are a few remaining examples of the Italian Renaissance style, notably the lovely portal to the Salvatorkapelle. But these are rare survivals, as are the Roman excavations beneath some of the principal open spaces in the Inner City. Above ground, Vienna is a baroque city, and took on its present-day appearance after the defeat of the Turks in 1683. As Vienna recovered its stability, the aristocracy became increasingly drawn to the Habsburg court. Great noblemen built their mansions around the Hofburg, and continued to do so until the late nineteenth century. Not all the streets of the Inner City are filled with patrician houses; many are lined with substantial early eighteenth-century dwellings of the bourgeoisie. Kurrentgasse, for instance, is packed with lovely tall houses, thoroughly urban in their shoulder-to-shoulder congestion, yet stylishly decorated with cartouches and panels in the vertical spaces between the windows.

The courtyards provided private space and access to water and horses, but public spaces were rare in the Inner City. There were a few major market squares, and, until the demolition of the city fortifications in the 1850s, the glacis, the open ground between the city walls and the suburbs, was used for recreational purposes. Parks such as the Burggarten attached to the Hofburg, and the immense riverside Prater, once a Habsburg game reserve, were not opened to the public until relatively recently, the Prater in 1766 and the Burggarten during the last century. Apart from the Habsburgs and a few very rich aristocrats, the principal landowners within the Inner City were the ecclesiastical foundations that drew their wealth from estates in the provinces. Many of these ecclesiastical headquarters are still intact, and behind their immense ranges of buildings are spacious courtyards, such as the Heiligenkreutzhof and the Schottenhof attached to the Schotten-kirche, which despite its name was an early medieval Irish foundation that ran a prestigious school that is still functioning. Both these courtyards are accessible through a number of gateways, and this too is typical of Vienna. On almost every street of the Inner City you will find a *Durchgang* or two, passageways, usually covered, that serve as lanes weaving through blocks of building, thus providing pedestrians with a link between two parallel streets. Their use can not only save a good deal of time in making one's way across the Inner City, but they can also protect one from inclement weather.

Vienna in its original guise was designed for the passage of Roman chariots. It remains a city for walkers, agile at manoeuvr-ing through the lanes and alleys. The municipal authorities, sadly, do not see it this way, and although through traffic is banned from the Inner City and many of the principal shopping streets are pedestrian precincts, the motor car is still a coarse and persistent intruder along streets where it does not belong. The Viennese are very good at obeying rules – they don't jay-walk or evade their tram fares – but motorists consider themselves exempt from such constraints. Not only are drivers reckless and incon-siderate, but they will park anywhere that a space is available, even if this blocks a pavement. The situation is only marginally better than in Rome, where in order to walk along a pavement without stepping into a very busy street I was once obliged to clamber over a Fiat that was obstructing my path.

The diversity of building styles within the Inner City led to the fashioning of odd corners that acquired their idiosyncratic charm accidentally, by juxtapositions and incongruities that arose over the centuries. In the cobbled Schulhof, for instance, the small square is dominated by one side of the Gothic chancel of the Church Am Hof. Facing the chancel are tall baroque houses, one of which contains a charming clock museum, while between the buttresses of the church a number of lean-to boutiques have been erected, some of them, in tune with the museum across the way, devoted to the sale and repair of antique clocks. A more coherent statement is made in other little squares such as the lovely eighteenth-century Piaristenplatz in the 8th Bezirk, and the

Minoritenplatz. Here too there is a fourteenth-century church, and close by is one of the wings of the vast and plodding Palais Liechtenstein. Adjoining it is the charming Palais Dietrichstein, with its tall windows and discreet elegant rhythms, and the Palais Starhemberg, painted pale green and olive, an imposing and dignified structure though its lack of variations from bay to bay thickens it with some of the monotony that afflicts the Palais Liechtenstein. (A family of unimpeachable lineage, the Starhembergs produced a twentieth-century prince who led the right-wing militia that eventually crushed the workers' resistance movement in 1934 and helped lay the groundwork for Hitler's *Anschluss* in 1938. The palace is no longer the property of the Starhembergs.) Here we are not far from the Hofburg, and these streets contain the greatest concentration of palaces, for proximity to the source of power was always desirable for ambitious families. The Herrengasse, which flanks one side of the Hofburg from the Schottenkirche to the Michaelerplatz, is so called because the Herren, the nobility, erected many of their mansions along its length.

Perhaps the most resplendent of the patrician palaces is not to be found in this corner of the Old City but along the Himmelpfortgasse. Here Prince Eugen of Savoy, the hero of 1683, commissioned Fischer von Erlach to build him a town house. Three massive portals punch through the facade, and the central one leads into a lofty arcade adorned on either side with large plaster panels depicting military emblems in low relief. On the far side of the Hof is a dummy wall, sketched in against the back wall of a neighbouring building; this dummy wall is lightly moulded and ornamented to ensure that the Hof is visually coherent and stylistically even. Before entering the Hof one can turn right into the main entrance, where a magnificent staircase, supported by four larger-than-life statues of Herculean body-builders, leads to the main apartments on the first floor. The landing is dotted with statuary, as well as fine rococo plasterwork and doorways surmounted by gilt crowns and swords. Almost cowed by so much grandeur, one can sample here the confidence and self-assertiveness that returned to Vienna after the Turks had finally been repulsed. Prince Eugen, of course, also built himself a pair of summer palaces, the glorious Belvedere no more than a mile from this spot. That was no modest undertaking either.

Of course it must not be supposed that the majority of the nobility actually occupied their palaces. The standard procedure was to commission the palais, occupy the mezzanine, and rent out the principal remaining floors to bourgeois families. Often the very top floor, divided into the smallest possible units, was rented out to artisans or other workers. These rents enabled the noble family that had commissioned the house to pay off the debts incurred during its construction. This pattern of habitation persisted until modern times. Nowadays, of course, few of the palaces remain in private hands, though the Liechtensteins, to cite one famous princely family, do still own a couple of palaces in Vienna (not to mention a little principality wedged into Switzerland). But most palaces are now used as government offices or museums. Outward grandeur often concealed inward squalor, except on the mezzanine. Viennese flats tend to be small and are notoriously lacking in modern conveniences. Despite external appearances, housing conditions in Vienna are among the worst of any western European city. Because the population has diminished since the early years of this century, there has been little need for the municipality to provide new housing stock. New blocks built to replace those bombed during the Second World War have tended to follow the adequate but somewhat primitive standards set by the Karl Marx Hof and other blocks built in the 1920s. Vienna is still a city of rented properties, and with housing costs heavily subsidized by the municipality, there is little incentive to buy flats when you can rent cheaply.

The flat of a friend of mine was typical. He had three spacious rooms in the 8th Bezirk, not far from the University, in an apartment complex dating from the late nineteenth century. The rooms are lofty and bright, but there is no bathroom and a shower has been installed in the kitchen. The lavatory, which he shares with other tenants on his floor, is out in the corridor. So common is this arrangement that it is known in Vienna as *Klo im Gang*. Because of this undesirable feature, the flat is officially classified as substandard and the monthly rent is derisory, roughly equivalent to a modest meal for two in a reasonably good restaurant in London or New York. Although such flats are extremely common, they are still not easy to get hold of. As always in Vienna, personal contacts are essential, not to mention good political connections.

There are two kinds of lease: *Hauptmiete* and *Untermiete*. Hauptmiete is the more desirable. With Hauptmiete, you pay rent on a contractual basis that effectively gives you tenure for life. Some Hauptmiete, however, come laden with restrictions that forbid subletting or even the sharing of a flat with friends or lovers. To obtain a Hauptmiete the would-be tenant must usually pay an

Ablöse to the landlord. This is a lump sum theoretically paid to compensate the owner for improvement costs. Although it is illegal to demand Ablöse without offering improvements, that seems to be the norm rather than the exception, and most tenants are so anxious to find somewhere to live that they will pay up without question. With an Untermiete you pay no Ablöse, but you also have fewer rights. People are prepared to pay high *Eintritsgeld* (entry money) to secure a flat with Hauptmiete – plus the usually exorbitant fees to estate agents – because of the security of tenure such a lease offers. Rents are index-linked and rise at the same level as inflation. Leases can even be inherited, and some choice flats have remained in the same family for generations.

With little demand for new building except in a few outer districts of the city, social change is as gradual as architectural. It is not only the facade of Vienna that has changed little over the past century. There has been little social mobility, and working-class districts such as Favoriten still have the same kind of population, though this is not to say that Favoriten or Leopold-stadt are slums. Far from it. Because population patterns have remained stable, gentrification is virtually unknown in Vienna. Any renovation or upgrading schemes are undertaken by the municipality, not the private landlords. Vienna is a city of flat renters, not of house owners, and it is common for a Viennese family to rent a flat on a Hauptmiete lease and buy a country cottage an hour's drive from the city.

The city has been responsible for some enchanting and skilful restoration projects. One of the loveliest is in the 7th Bezirk, where a few streets – the Spittelberggasse, the Gutenberggasse – crowded with modest baroque and Biedermeier houses have been sensitively restored. Even more significant than such individual schemes has been a change in the administration of property and rents. Rent increases, other than those in line with inflation, are only permitted if a proportion of that revenue is used for renovation. Before this measure was introduced, landlords, often with justification, could plead poverty by way of excuse for the neglect of their often magnificent properties. The city took action because far too many apartment houses and former palaces were either decaying or being left empty. The measures providing an incentive to landlords to renovate their buildings have not only improved the living conditions of the Viennese but saved the Inner City from urban decay. As property owners scrub and clean and mend, facades that for decades had been charcoal-coloured with grime are being revealed anew in almost pristine beauty, their gently pitted stone gleaming in the crisp air, their Herculean lintel-bearers squinting in the sunlight, and the firmly outlined pediments and sills casting lively shadows along the length of the building. Next on the agenda will have to be the inventive Jugendstil exteriors found all over the city. Some in the Inner City, such as Oskar Laske's extravagant mosaic angels in décolleté cocktail dresses soaring over the Engel Apotheke, are well cared for, but many suburban examples are beginning to suffer from neglect. But in the meantime one can at least be thankful that the true beauty of the baroque heritage of Vienna is at last emerging from the shade, and those who live in the city as well as we who come to visit it are the beneficiaries.

8

May the Best Man Win

Let us now praise famous men! There have been few enough in Austrian political life during the postwar years. Chancellor Bruno Kreisky certainly made his voice heard far beyond the borders of Austria, and Kurt Waldheim is probably much better known now than he was as secretary general of the United Nations. Despite the rancour and a heightening of mutual misunderstanding between Austria and the rest of the world, the Waldheim controversy had one beneficial consequence: it forced many Austrians to face up to a few home truths. The issue of whether or not Kurt Waldheim was responsible, directly or indirectly, for deportations of Jews and for the deaths of partisans, must be pondered in the context of the Austrians' self-image, and indeed of the image they were encouraged to hold of themselves, over the last forty years.

After the Second World War ended, when Austria had to endure a four-power occupation by its former enemies for ten more years, it was concluded that Austria had been not a collaborator in Nazi aggression and Nazi crimes, but a victim, a defeated nation. This degree of absolution did not prevent the Austrians, and the Viennese in particular, from suffering extreme hardships during the lengthy occupation. Nevertheless, while the German people have been obliged to contemplate the notion of collective guilt, the Austrians have been spared any such rigorous self-examination. Austrian education has always played down the fact that a large number of Austrians welcomed Hitler and his *Anschluss*. The idea that staunch little Austria was brutally invaded by the Nazi hordes in 1938 is a fiction, for the ground had been prepared ever since 1934 for closer ties with Germany. German nationalism had been a powerful force in Austrian politics for a hundred years, as the expression of the supreme sense of nationality within an empire of fragmented nationalities. German nationalism always had the edge because German culture was so widely accepted in Austria-Hungary as the pinnacle of artistic achievement and aspiration. Nor was it only the supporters of the right-wing regimes of Dollfuss and Schuschnigg that flourished from 1934 to 1938 who welcomed Hitler. Some socialists who had been persecuted by the fascist militias and the right-wing dictatorships were also receptive to Hitler's occupation.

The great self-deception proved remarkably successful. Austrian Nazis who survived the war – and there were hundreds of thousands of them – have lived out their lives in relative tranquillity. Occasionally antisemitism and the more unsavoury aspects of German nationalism have reared their heads, but in general the government of Austria has been in the hands of moderate men. Until very recently, the vicious extremism and race hatred of the National Fronts of Britain and France have been absent from Austrian political life. Since, as even Austria's former enemies agreed, the country had been a victim rather than a perpetrator of Nazism, there was no need for too vigorous a self-inquiry. Yes, perhaps a husband or father had done unpleasant things in the war, but then war is unpleasant and such things happen – and anyway, everyone has agreed it wasn't our fault. It was hardly necessary to inquire too closely into the wartime activities of Austria's fighting forces.

Then, all of a sudden, the rules were changed. Some Austrians, and many Americans, notably Jews, were making outrageous allegations about Dr Kurt Waldheim, who was running for the presidency of Austria. It was as though there had been a momentous breach of international etiquette. Questions which, it had been tacitly promised, would never be raised were raised once again, and in the most brutal and direct manner. If Kurt Waldheim were guilty, then so too were hundreds of thousands of other Austrian men and women, and that possibility was supposed to have been banished from the national consciousness. Nor should one underestimate the olympian status enjoyed by Waldheim. He was not, it is clear, greatly liked. Indeed, a less lovable individual in Western political life it would be hard to encounter. But he was a local boy who had made good. First Bruno Kreisky had put Austria back on the map, and then Waldheim had done the same as secretary general of the United Nations. That, by all accounts, he was a mediocre secretary general and a vain and greedy man did not trouble the Austrians. He may be a shit but he's our shit. Then out of the blue, at the peak of his career, when he was on the verge of being elected to the presidency of his native Austria (a largely honorary role, since political power is held by the chancellor, not the president), his reputation was being besmirched.

Ironically, Waldheim's political opponent Kreisky, a socialist, may have inadvertently set the ball rolling. Kreisky was Jewish, but that did not deter him from taking an anti-Israeli line on occasions and from making political contact at the highest level with some far from moderate Arab leaders. Such tactics alarmed the ultra-sensitive watchdogs of American Jewry and may have led some of its more crass leaders to adopt an anti-Austrian line that inevitably made Waldheim a target, for he had pursued policies at the UN that would have struck the more paranoid elements among American Jewry as blatantly pro-Arab. When the World Jewish Congress, so unfortunately named, began to impugn Waldheim's reputation, even some of Waldheim's political opponents took umbrage. 'It's beyond doubt,' a left-wing Viennese said to me, 'that the World Jewish Congress won Waldheim the election. I sometimes think its leaders must have been paid agents of Waldheim's.'

But Waldheim's political opponents in Austria, the SPÖ, also miscalculated and contributed to his victory. Their chosen candidate for the presidency was Dr Kurt Steyrer, who, it would not be unfair to say, was little more than a dutiful party hack. The retiring president, Dr Kirchschläger, although a socialist, had enjoyed wide popularity and support, and not only from the SPÖ voters. Steyrer was clearly not in the same league. No one can be entirely sure why the SPÖ put Steyrer up against Waldheim, but it seems probable that the party leaders, acknowledging Waldheim's prestige, didn't want to waste a first-rate candidate in a battle they felt they were likely to lose. There was also a suspicion that certain SPÖ officials were not unhappy when the allegations were made and believed, incorrectly, that they would gain the political advantage. Consequently, it was alleged and widely believed by many Austrians, some officials passed information to the World Jewish Congress and the press with the intention of besmirching Waldheim further.

'I don't know anybody who liked Waldheim,' a Viennese teacher told me. 'It's worse than that. Nobody I know, and I admit most of my friends are SPÖ supporters, could stand him. But once the American press began to attack him, we all felt outraged. Not only was there blatant misreporting in the press, but it was a clear interference in the political campaigns of our country. What really enraged us was the implication that anyone who voted for Waldheim had to be a Nazi or Nazi sympathizer. When in the spring of 1986 Bundespräsident Kirchschläger ruled that the documents containing the evidence for the allegations against Waldheim wouldn't support any formal charges that could be brought against him, that ruling was decisive. Remember that Kirchschläger had been the Austrian ambassador to Czechoslovakia when the Russians invaded in 1968. Waldheim had ordered the embassy to take in no more fugitives from the Russians, and Kirchschläger disobeyed. So there is no love lost between the two men, and no reason for Kirchschläger to slant his ruling in Waldheim's favour. I suppose the general feeling here was that if Waldheim had been considered good enough and decent enough to be secretary general of the United Nations for all those years, then he was good enough to be our Bundespräsident.'

'And did you vote for him yourself?'

'Yes.'

'Are you sorry?'

He shrugged. 'In a way he's the president we deserve. Waldheim represents much that is worst about Austria, and in that sense that makes him fit to be our president.'

The prestigious position at the United Nations that had won Waldheim the respect of his people had been curiously maintained. The superpowers, who must almost certainly have been aware of the rumours about Waldheim's past and may have had independent documentary evidence to support some of them, seemed perfectly happy to have Kurt running the show. And it did seem odd that his principal aides in the Secretariat were often Yugoslavs, since the activities that tarred his reputation had mostly taken place in what is now Yugoslavia. It is tempting to infer that some powerful member nations of the UN found it quite useful, given what they knew and what the world didn't know about Dr Waldheim, to have him as secretary general. As a no doubt cynical friend of mine put it: 'It seems increasingly obvious that the only people in the world who had nothing on Waldheim were the Austrians.'

The atmosphere had been distinctly unpleasant in the spring of 1986. Political campaigns are largely paid for out of the public purse, and posters bearing the features of the two main candidates had been slung around every lamppost and disfigured every hoarding in Austria. Waldheim posed as the statesman in some of these posters, dignified and benign, while in others he stood beaming next to his dirndled wife against a background of glorious Austrian mountainscape. It was the smile that was most insufferable, those foxlike features distorted into a sunny bonhomie that seemed, like Richard Nixon's grin, unrelated to what one had gathered was his true personality. Poor Dr Steyrer couldn't adopt this role of Father of the People, for it was well known, though nothing appeared in print thanks to the timorousness of the Austrian press, that he was in the midst of marital difficulties. He also campaigned as though he were running for chancellor rather than for the ceremonial post of president. He said he would do things that no president has the power to do. Meanwhile, Waldheim squirmed irritably but his denials and qualifications became increasingly feeble. His campaign managers during the first round of the presidential elections, devised the slogan, 'FAIRNESS FÜR WALDHEIM', and literally overnight it seemed that every single Waldheim poster – and there must have been tens of thousands beaming over Austria by then – was stickered with those three words in bright letters. It was an effective stroke, and clearly one to which my friend the teacher and his socialist friends responded. Waldheim may have been loathsome in their eyes, but outside interference was even less tolerable. 'FAIRNESS' ruled.

Waldheim, of course, never explicitly denied all the allegations. What excited concern was the implications of his activities. Oh, I may have signed a few documents here and there, but that doesn't make me a war criminal. Or: I was only following orders, like all good soldiers everywhere, and I simply didn't know anything about the full horror of what was going on. What was incontrovertible, however, was that Kurt Waldheim, a former secretary general of the United Nations, had lied about his past. Anybody who is in the slightest doubt about this need only consult the opening chapters of his autobiography in which he writes about how he spent the war. It bears only slight resemblance to the facts that Waldheim himself has reluctantly acknowledged in response to the allegations against him. Moreover, Waldheim, the wartime recipient of the silver medal of the crown of King Zvonimir with oak leaves from the pro-Nazi Croatian leader in Yugoslavia, consistently denied that he had ever been in Yugoslavia until he was rumbled in 1986.

It is hypocritical to feel too appalled by Waldheim's wartime record; it is no better and no worse than that of many other German and European political leaders who have yet managed to enjoy the confidence of nations during the postwar period. But I am appalled by the lies and deceit, and were I an Austrian that alone would make it impossible for me to vote for such a man. It also seems incredible that such duplicity counted for so little in the minds of the Austrian voters. The reason for this, as I have suggested earlier, is that Waldheim's guilt is the same guilt that would entrap tens of thousands of other Austrians. If it had been, after all, unacceptable, even wicked, for Waldheim to have skated over his contribution to the Nazi war machine, then the same taint would besmirch countless of his contemporaries. Many of those contemporaries may now be dead, but their widows and children lived on. The substitution, at this late stage in their rehabilitation, of truth for convenient fiction was more than many Austrians could bear.

Even after Waldheim struggled through the second round of the elections and won the presidency, there were many Austrians who still preferred to ignore the facts. Frau Mayr, a highly intelligent teacher, told me, long after the elections were over, that Waldheim had not tried to conceal his past, 'but perhaps it would have been better had he done so and made no concessions to his critics'. That so intelligent a woman could in all seriousness both deny the truth and recommend that her president deliberately perpetuate a lie is an indication of the lengths to which many older Austrians will go rather than acknowledge their past.

Even more disturbing than the arguably self-serving assertions of Frau Mayr were those of her daughter, now in her mid-twenties and a doctoral student at Vienna University. 'Most Austrians,' she insisted, no doubt on evidence provided by her mother, 'didn't know what was going on during the war – so how should Waldheim have known?' I decided not to point out that even Waldheim himself has admitted that his knowledge of the wartime deportations in the Balkans was considerable. 'How could the Austrians hold his past against him, when so many others of his generation had had similar histories, and when so many people had lost relatives in the war? Also we respect Dr Waldheim. He was a brave secretary general, who even put his life at risk in the Middle East. All these attacks against Waldheim really angered us. I have a friend who happens to be Jewish, and during the election campaign last spring he actually went on television and said that he no longer wanted to live in Austria. I tell you, I felt betrayed by him.'

She felt this sense of betrayal because, it seemed to her, his primary allegiance was not to Austria. He was not, unlike her, prepared to support his country and his co-citizens come what may.

To this young woman, her friend's anguish about what he perceived as the refusal to acknowledge the truth about Austria's past was less forgivable than Waldheim's deceit and his failure, even now, to come clean about his past. Who, I wonder, would find it impossible to forgive the activities of a young lieutenant forty-five years ago, given that a refusal to play his part would have called for a physical and moral courage that is granted only to a few? Equally, one must ask, who can forgive the man who even to this day is incapable of volunteering the truth, and can only acknowledge it when incontrovertible documentary evidence is thrust under the noses of the world? In his way, the wretched Dr Waldheim is paying some sort of price. He may be Bundespräsident of Austria, but few of the world's leaders show any inclination to be associated with him in any way.

Matters came to a head in February 1988, when the international historians' commission, an impartial body appointed by the Austrians themselves, presented their report on Waldheim's war years. The report was far more condemnatory than most observers had predicted. The seven historians rejected utterly Dr Waldheim's denials that he had been quite unaware of the deportation of Greek Jews who subsequently perished in concentration camps. The historians also showed how Waldheim's military units provided logistical support while civilians were being deported and even massacred. They stated: 'He repeatedly cooperated in illegal operations, thereby facilitating their execution.' He was, they added, 'far more than just a lowly bureaucrat'. Although the commission did not conclude that Dr Waldheim was guilty of actual war crimes, they did not absolve him of all moral responsibility. The failure of the commission to discover newsreel footage showing a cackling Waldheim enjoying a spot of Balkan butchery would have come as a relief to such prominent Austrians as Michael Graff, who declared that he would regard Waldheim as guilty only if it could be proved that he 'had strangled six Jews with his own hands'. This sensitive remark was made by none other than the secretary general of the ÖVP. His boss, the pedestrian foreign minister Dr Alois Mock, merely tut-tutted, though other figures in public life ensured that Mr Graff stepped down from his politically powerful position.

Nevertheless, the public response to the revelations about the president's inglorious past and decades of incessant lying was remarkably muted. The commission may have failed to find blood on Waldheim's elegant hands, but its conclusions are nonetheless damning and shaming. But not, it seems, in many Austrian eyes. Dr Mock rubbed his hands and said everything was fine since the commission had not established that Waldheim was guilty of war crimes. Dr Mock also threatened to bring down the coalition government of which he is the leading Conservative member if that government withdrew its support for the beleaguered president. More pressure was piled on the Austrian chancellor, the Socialist Franz Vranitzky, by Waldheim himself, who apparently threatened to use his presidential powers to dissolve the government if it accepted the commission's report – despite the fact that it had been the government that had commissioned the report in the first place. Vranitzky was undoubtedly swayed by clear indications that the greater the evidence against Waldheim, the more fervent the Austrian people grew in their support of their president. So Vranitzky dithered, Mock crowed, Bruno Kreisky and Simon Wiesenthal for the first time publicly denounced the president, the Austrian people were divided even more sharply than before – and Waldheim sat tight.

9

Desperately Seeking Lotte

It was only when the leaders of other nations began to distance themselves from Waldheim to the point of refusing to meet him that many Austrians, at last aware that the people's choice was an embarrassment to the nation, began to feel slightly uneasy.

'They'll try not to let the Waldheim affair trouble them for long,' said a foreign resident of Vienna. 'The Viennese would so much rather the whole matter would go away so that they could get on with more important matters such as eating *Sachertorte* and going to concerts.'

This somewhat flippant assessment is not without a measure of truth. Churning away within the ample frames of the Viennese is a strange mixture of hedonism and dourness. Conventional, rigid, absurdly conscious of appearance and status, the Viennese will at the same time devote much of their time as well as their incomes to gratifying the call of their stomachs and the yearning of their souls. They will eat five times a day, effortlessly. The coffeehouses and *Konditoreien* are full at most times of the day with elderly ladies tucking into a sandwich, two eggs in a glass, an ice cream, or a geological model of a cake stratified with creams and molten chocolate. The Austrians even have a word, *Jause*, to label that inter-meal snack. The ubiquity of coffeehouses means that even the faintest twinges of hunger can be instantly assuaged. If your local café is more than fifty yards away, you can always substitute your butcher. For – and this is a practice inconceivable in Britain – many butchers' shops have installed in one corner a small rotisserie, a counter and a few stools. Here, at any time of the day, a customer can walk in, order some *wurst* and a *semmel* (roll) or a piece of roast chicken and accompany it with a glass of wine or beer. No ceremony and you are not expected to linger over your pitstop, but such light and wholesome foods are infinitely preferable to the offerings of standardized fast food outlets.

Standard Viennese cookery may be of limited range but it does call for the most diligent shopping. *Wurst*, for example, is a family as extended and diverse as the descendants of the Mayflower pilgrims. Even a Würstelstand out on the street will offer five or six varieties of sausage. In a good butcher or delicatessen there will be dozens to choose from. Breads are equally varied, though nearly always heavy and substantial and pocked with whole grains. Most palatable cheeses are imported, though the Austrians do make a number of passable imitations of Emmentaler and Esrom, and some less acceptable copies of Brie and Camembert.

Although shops and supermarkets are well stocked and comprehensive in their range, a large number of Viennese still find it worthwhile to get up early on a Saturday morning and go down to the Naschmarkt. A ten-minute walk away from the Inner City is the long street known as the Wienzeile. It is actually divided into the Linke and Rechte Wienzeile, for the two sides of the avenue are divided by the lengthy expanses of the outdoor market, including rows of shops and boutiques. The market becomes progressively less smart and more chaotic as one walks down its lanes from the city end. Any apparent disorder is, however, intentional, an exuberant spillage of produce, for the market is strictly controlled. At the city end are small shops specializing in fish, cheese, or breads, followed by the fruit and vegetable merchants. Some of the proprietors and vendors are Viennese and their stalls have been in the same family for generations. Standing over a pile of dark gleaming cucumbers, her porky knuckles on her hips, a red-faced matriarch insisted to all and sundry that she was offering *'Beste Gurken die's gibt!'* and who would want to argue with her?

Her counterpart can be found the world over: the barrow women along the Portobello Road, fag in mouth, snarled profanity at the ready, or the harridans of the herring stands in Rotterdam. But in recent years these guardians of the gherkin and tyrants of the tomato have had to share their patch of the Naschmarkt with traders from other lands. The *Gastarbeiter* from Turkey and Yugoslavia – who do all the jobs the Viennese are loath to do themselves and are rewarded with contempt and fear – these guest workers are, most of them, here to stay, and so are their stalls. With their weather-beaten faces and stocky figures and accented German, I often found it hard to tell whether I was buying my

satsumas from Turks or Yugoslavs. Lacking the Viennese imperi-
ousness, they bounced with nervous energy and eagerness to sell.
At the back of their stalls or boutiques would be a clutch of friends
and relatives, often thin older men in cheap suits and white shirts
open at the neck, and their stout wives in shapeless dresses that
may have passed an earlier existence hanging from curtain rods in
rooming houses.

Beyond the fruit and veg are the flower stands, which managed
to put on a brave display even in November. At this point the
fixed structures, the cabins and shops, petered out and the
expanses of the open market are filled with trestle tables. Behind
them stand the battered cars and vans which in the hours before
dawn had carried into the heart of Vienna the produce now laid
out before our appreciative eyes. There were home-made
sausages, black puddings the size of an elephant's windpipe and
boiling rings muscular enough to pass through the nose of a bull.
There were flans and tarts, not always a success, for they had
grown weary during the journey from a Burgenland oven to a
trestle table at the Naschmarkt. Some offerings were more feeble,
such as a handful of leeks or cabbages, freshly tugged from the
ground but less handsome and appealing than the scrubbed and
organized heaps and piles at the upper end of the market. I would
make a beeline for the tables closest to the Linke Wienzeile, where
the winegrowers would line up their bottles. Every two weeks the
same families would arrive, and occupy the same positions. Here,
for considerably less than the price of mediocre supermarket wine,
I could find large bottles of zippy young Grüner Veltliner or fresh
Welschriesling brought directly from vineyards in Krems or
Langenlois. Some shoppers and traders would be refreshing
themselves at a Würstelstand, or in one of the *Beiseln* – the most
modest form of Viennese eating house – that line the Wienzeile,
but many others would gulp down a *viertel* of Sturm, red or white,
that could be bought by the glass at most winegrowers' stands. On
alternating Saturday mornings, the cider makers would set up
their stalls where the winegrowers had been the previous week,
and their litre bottles would be filled with the delicate, lightly
alcoholic pale cider in which they specialized.

Continuing down the market past the subway station I would
come to the flea market. Laden with half a dozen large bottles of
Herr Riedlmayer's Veltliner, I could not be persuaded to linger
over the detritus so pitifully offered for sale in the wan hope that
somebody somewhere out there might actually want to buy a

jockey's cap, an armless doll with cat-chewed vinyl hair, sheet music of forgotten popular songs, ceramic bunnies, large canvases of suffering Christs in lurid colours, carriage lanterns, a stringless zither, military medals from one or another of the wars that Austria has lost, old copies of *Playboy*, foxtails, and, least appetizing of all, the contents of cardboard suitcases from which the tattiest of old clothes spilled onto the cobbles.

This bric-a-brac – the grubby magazines, the discarded toys, the underwear and shoes rummaged from a dead relative's cupboards – is peddled beneath the shadow of one of Vienna's loveliest buildings. Along the Linke Wienzeile are two large apartment houses designed by Otto Wagner, who will surely prove to be the most enduring of Vienna's many turn-of-the-century architects. He brought Jugendstil to the greatest level of refinement and sophistication, and his love of surface decoration never distracted him from an underlying respect for function. Wagner, like Gustav Klimt, is rightly seen as an innovator and pioneer, but it is sometimes forgotten that both men began their careers within the rigid historicist confines of the Ringstrasse style. The building of the Ringstrasse proved a bonanza for architects and interior decorators, but the men who won the commissions were more or less compelled to reflect the prevailing bourgeois taste for bombast and showiness. Artistically, however, it was a dead end, a repetition of tired formulae or at best a cautious series of variations on narrowly defined themes.

Towards the end of the nineteenth century a group of artists and architects broke away from the orthodoxies of the academies and appropriately named their secessionist group the Secession. They did not have a bad time of it, these breakaway artists, for these were no *refusés* and it was not long before they were offered the patronage of both city and state. The city donated to the Secession a plot of land midway between the Wienzeile and the Karlsplatz, a plaza dominated by one of the masterpieces of European baroque, Fischer von Erlach's Karlskirche. On this site the architect Josef Olbrich built in 1898 the remarkable gallery still known as the Secession. A greater contrast to the historicist flourishes of the Academy and the Ringstrasse could scarcely be imagined. From a distance it seems to be a windowless white block topped by a curious bronze openwork ball of an intertwined laurel leaf design. The Viennese, who are addicted to nicknames – the cathedral tower is called the Steffl, the underground passage beneath the Opernring the Jonasgrotte, and there are countless others – soon dubbed the cupola of the Secession the gilded cabbage, and it remains a thoroughly appropriate name.

As one moves closer towards the Secession the remarkable wealth of detail on the building becomes more apparent. On either side of the main steps charming blue and gold mosaic owls rest on the backs of turtles; lizards slither down either side of the door, and owls in low relief hoot from side walls. Because of the lack of windows, the interior, which is far larger than the boxy exterior suggests, is effectively lit by skylights, and the capacious basement contains Klimt's celebrated Beethoven frieze, a seminal work that had worn less well than I had expected. Its symbolism seems overwrought, its exoticism effete. If detractors of Freud can point out with some justification that his theories were rooted in the social and sexual anxieties of the Viennese bourgeoisie at the turn of the century, it is even more fitting to locate Klimt's distorted nudes, his dream imagery and snaky textures, in that same moment of repression and awakening.

Otto Wagner, though not the designer of the Secession, was the obvious influence on Olbrich's design. Wagner, an architect of long experience, changed his ways late in his career. His eminence made it possible for him to undertake major commissions with which he could test his radical ideas and thus exert an influence over younger architects who lacked the opportunities that came Wagner's way. As artistic adviser to the Vienna Transport Commission throughout most of the 1890s, he had overall responsibility for designing the new underground system, and the system of dams and bridges required to control the waters of the Danube. His most massive contributions to these ambitious schemes of city planning are not easily visible, but the subway stations he built in the Karlsplatz are accessible to all. The charming Art Nouveau tendrils marking the entrances to many Paris Métro stations have become part of the image of that city. Wagner's far more substantial designs are surely of greater importance, if less well known. Two white cubes flank a taller semicircular-roofed structure that contains the main hall of the station. At first sight, the slightly gawky assertive little stations seem out of harmony with the baroque majesty of the Karlskirche, as if Wagner had deliberately designed them in querulous and brittle contrast. He was, surely, right to avoid any attempt to compete with the grandeur of Fischer von Erlach's design, but I do find echoes of the great church in Wagner's structures. With their cast-iron railings and complex gold mosaic inlays, their cornices and balustrades, they are as decorative and ornamental as the overtly fanciful baroque. The colour scheme too – green, white and gold – and the copper roof and the contours of the facade strike me as allusions, discreet and cautious, to the mighty backdrop of the Karlskirche, like an admiring footnote, or an echo that while distorted still repeats the same sounds.

Wagner's apartment buildings along the Wienzeile were built the year after Olbrich's Secession gallery. Until the 1890s the Naschmarkt had been held on the Karlsplatz, but as part of the river control system for which Wagner was partly responsible the River Wien was covered over and the space gained by so doing became the new Naschmarkt, which it still is. One of these apartment buildings is faced with majolica, while its next-door neighbour is ornamented with lovely inlays depicting golden palms, designed by Kolo Moser. Wagner was always innovative in his interior design, giving great thought to the layout of his buildings and the way they were to be used. In one of his greatest buildings, the Post Office Savings Bank (which, incidentally, was intended as a populist rebuke to what was perceived as the Jewish domination of capital through control of the major banking houses), function and ornament are exquisitely matched. The exterior bears the Wagner hallmark of projecting eaves and ornamental studding over sheets of white marble, but it is the main banking hall that is most remarkable. Now that we have grown used to the Centre Pompidou in Paris and other structures built on similar principles, we are no longer fazed by exposed pipes and lifts and other elements that used to be concealed behind walls and beneath floors. In the skylit Post Office banking hall Wagner left the heating ducts exposed, and the columns supporting the roof were lightly clad in aluminium. The hall may not be pretty, but it is clear, functional, airy, and grand. It also looks as though it had been built yesterday and, unlike Olbrich's more mannered Secession, has not dated in the least.

The sight of Wagner's apartment buildings looking stylishly down on the bustle of the Naschmarkt was invigorating but not invigorating enough. By walking for a few minutes from the Linke Wienzeile to the Gumpendorferstrasse, I would find on one of its corners the recently renovated Café Sperl. On Saturday mornings it was uncrowded and, depositing my cargo of bottles next to the banquette, I would call for my 'kleiner Schwarzer' coffee and spend an hour reading the newspapers and the titillating German magazines. The Sperl, unlike some of the Inner City coffeehouses, is spacious. With its dark wood panelling and comfortable banquettes, it is deliciously relaxing. About once an hour, plates of hot strudel are brought in, the odoriferous steam still rising from the light golden pastry. Any post-prandial urge for undemanding exercise can be satisfied in the adjoining billiard room.

Saturday, of course, was not only the day for stocking up at the Naschmarkt and wolfing strudel at the Sperl. I was also summoned to join Robert and Marianne at the football stadium in the Prater. The first time I went Marianne suggested I should meet her in front of – where else? – the Würstelstand outside the stadium. 'Lotte will be there too,' she added. I turned up in good time. I wasn't sure at first whether I was at the right Würstelstand, but when I spotted Lotte's hefty form bundled up within an unsightly woollen coat, I knew all was well.

I walked up to her. '*Bist du nicht Lotte?*' I said with a smile of recognition.

The young woman who had sat next to me for hours on end just the week before looked straight into my eyes and said: '*Nein.*'

I blushed, for it was obvious that the crowd standing about the sausage stand was assuming I had just made an unsuccessful attempt to pick up the blowsy blonde. Now I don't mind attempting a pick-up that fails, but the thought that a few dozen hearty Viennese actually believed I yearned for the favours of this living *Knödel* was crushing. I moved away. Some moments later, to my relief, I spotted Marianne, snugly encased in black leather, speeding in my direction. She had in tow a second Brit, the eight-year-old son of a diplomat, who was wearing a purple and white scarf, the colours of the Austria team. I later rebuked him for his disloyalty to the Crown. The mitigating factor was that he attended not one of the international schools favoured by the diplomatic and foreign community but the local state school, and had adopted the accent and mores of his classmates. The three of us then collected the woman who had snubbed me. She greeted Marianne but ignored me. Surely I could not have been mistaken! This was indeed Lotte, whose king-post thighs had brushed mine when we sat squeezed down one side of the table at Haller's. '*Bist du nicht Lotte?*' I ventured again, shaking my head in incredulity.

'*Nein,*' she repeated, sticking to her guns. '*Ich bin Anna.*'

The following morning I was talking to the British diplomat who had long cast a dispassionate eye on the Viennese. I told him of my embarrassing encounter with the wench. 'It was the right

81

girl, but I'd got the wrong name, the name of one of her friends. That may have been a lapse on my part, but since she didn't even recognize me at all, I'd have thought it was forgivable.'

'That,' said my guru, 'is typical of Viennese literal-mindedness. So many of them seem to lack imagination, and clearly the deduction that you had recognized her face but muddled her name was beyond her.'

The match was a great disappointment. There was no bottle throwing, no chanted obscenities, no racial taunts, no invasions of the pitch, no attempts to set alight the scarves of the fans from opposing teams. Indeed, such fans even sat side by side, though most of the noisier elements were herded into the cheaper stands high up behind the goals of the respective teams, Austria and Rapid. Beer and tea laced with rum were openly on sale and openly consumed, but the inebriation led to no knifings, no brawling, no puking. No wonder the Austrians are a third-rate nation. The most exciting thing that happened was when Marianne rebuked the Yugoslav (I think) sandwich seller for trying to overcharge her. Nor was my enjoyment increased by the dank chill weather, which nearly converted an incipient cold I was nursing into double pneumonia the following day. Nor did my ears appreciate the incredibly loud advertisements that came blasting across the sound system before the match and during the interval. My health was further affected by the cigarette smoke all around me. Marianne's group, without exception, smoked heavily, and there was no escape. I hacked and rasped and spluttered, but none of my companions seemed to suspect there was any connection between their poisoning of the atmosphere and my discomfort. Tobacco is a state monopoly in Austria, so there is little incentive for the government to persuade the citizens to give up smoking. Consequently almost everybody in Vienna smokes. I dare say even midwives have a cigarette between their lips as they tug at the forceps.

And the football? It too was uninspired, though enlivened by some disgraceful fouling from both sides. Even Marianne could barely suppress a yawn. When it was over Walter was instructed to give me a lift to Haller's. He did so, in total silence, and even when we were weaving through the car park to find his BMW, he made not the slightest attempt to see whether I was able to keep up in the dark, for the grounds were crowded with fans hurrying through the rain to where they supposed their vehicles had been parked. Once we were seated at the long table at Haller's, and we were the first to arrive, he did converse, quite amiably too, though as soon as reinforcements arrived he reverted to the more agreeable state of ignoring me completely.

Although my companions had munched one or two cold Knackwurst during the match, everybody was already hungry. Few could resist ordering Martinigansl. St Martin of Tours is the patron saint of the Burgenland, where he was born, and the date of his birth, 11 November, is traditionally celebrated by eating goose. Hence the name. Naturally the Viennese, whose thought processes are lubricated by their digestive juices, have extended this form of celebration by about two weeks, and right through November you can order roast goose in almost every restaurant in Vienna and Lower Austria. Haller's was no exception, though Hans had doubts about the propriety of consuming a quarter goose (the standard portion in Vienna) at six in the evening.

'*Gans um sechs?*' he wondered aloud. '*Wos moche' wir um zehn?*' (What will we do by ten?)

'*Noch a' gansl,*' said Robert without hesitation.

I didn't linger until ten to see whether the gang would actually launch into a second round of goose, though I was, as before, transfixed by Frau Haller, who every few minutes swung luxuriously through the room like a cross between Sophie Tucker and Clytemnestra. At nine I made my excuses, and took a streetcar back to the Ring, then walked to the 8th Bezirk and made my way to the Tunnel, a *Lokal* crowded with students. The Glaswegian composer Stephen Ferguson was holding court, surrounded by Erich, a painter; Molly, a Canadian sculptress, who spoke such authentically intonated Austrian that I was convinced she was a native until she informed me she had been married to an Austrian; a classically beautiful woman, complete with hauteur and apparently a neighbour of Stephen's, who disdained to speak to anyone other than Erich; and Dave, another Glaswegian who had busked his way around Europe for a decade. The group was deep in its cups. Another friend of Stephen's, a doctor, had just succeeded in getting a job at a leading hospital, and the celebrations had begun earlier in the afternoon. The object of all this festivity had long since stumbled home, but his friends continued to celebrate despite his absence.

Molly was loud in debate over the virtues and contradictions of feminism; Erich was doing his best to keep a level head while the beautiful woman who had no name spoke softly about her life and gazed into his face; Stephen was in his beatific mode, saying little but dispensing good will with his liquid eyes and broad smile; and Dave was telling me about his ten years on the road with a guitar and a sleeping bag. A benevolent scheme of Stephen's to bring Molly and Dave into a brief but blissful union met with no success. Whether Erich and the nameless beauty developed their relationship further that night I didn't discover till the next day (they did not, and Erich returned chaste and chastened to his wife at two in the morning), for I had to head off to my next appointment at the Blue Box, a fashionable bar on the quiet Richtergasse.

The painter Georg Eisler, aware of my *nostalgie de la boue*, had insisted that I go to the Blue Box to get a clearer idea of trendy night life, far from the boisterous *Gemütlichkeit* of Haller's and the Arab-packed strip joints of the Inner City. It had not been easy to arrange, but the painter had persuaded an acquaintance of his to take me with him on a bar crawl. We met at the Blue Box at 11.30. I expected to find a heavy at the door, a smoke-filled lobby where I would have to surrender my weapons to a bleached blonde cloakroom attendant, and then a dark atmospheric interior in which the hunched figures of conspiratorial adulterers and actors and politicians would be outlined against white marble tables. But no, the Blue Box was a slightly dingy, vaguely punk, and completely orderly bar, with plate glass windows. The music was loud, the beer excellent, and there were at least eight other people sitting around talking calmly. I had turned up the stone but there was no slime beneath.

The Blue Box is not very far from the Gürtel, where the whores hang out. Prostitution used to be a major Viennese industry. Nowadays, like shop prices and opening hours and pensions, it is controlled. Red faery lights flash and beckon garishly from the brothels which line the Gürtel, while out on the pavements the whores, usually bleached and blonde, sharp-featured and tiny-eyed, clip up and down in murderous high heels and skin-tight leotards. They look ferocious rather than inviting, and ten minutes in their bony grip did not seem a good way to part with 650 Schillings. The classier whores cruise the Graben and Kohlmarkt in the Inner City, but I never noticed any.

As I walked back to the pension it began to rain, and by the time I was crossing the Stephansplatz it was pouring. A few moments later I was standing by my window looking out across the deserted square onto the cathedral roofs. The immense south tower, the Steffl, was floodlit, and the spotlights caught the sheets of falling rain, which, tugged by a fierce wind, bent and buckled like a swishing curtain of water that was almost out of control. Such high drama is rare in Vienna, which, except for a handful of tower blocks on the outskirts and the vertical slabs of the United Nations complex, is not a city of tall buildings. Its beauties, apart from the broad facades and great vistas of Schönbrunn and the Belvedere, are small in scale. Even the Hofburg only consists of a series of wings attached to no body, and courtyards; only the bombastic Neue Burg – which in its very excess is atypical, an organ fortissimo during a clavichord concert – is on a monumental scale. The great bulk of the cathedral is the major exception, and the proud thrust of the south tower is an easily comprehensible symbol of the aspirations of the city. To see it whitened behind a band of needlelike rain showers was to realize the enduring romantic appeal of Vienna. If the Habsburgs had failed, until the final decades of their rule, to make the Kaiserstadt the beating heart of their empire, the Viennese themselves had never been in doubt about the building that would symbolize their city. When the roof caved in during a bombing raid shortly before the end of the war, the Viennese wept openly in the streets, and they were mourning more than the crippling of an ancient church.

10

Zlotys for Sale

The East, they say in Vienna, begins at the Mexikoplatz. All around this large bleak square facing the Danube and along the straight streets that flow into it are indistinguishable shops selling all manner of merchandise: jeans, watches, bolts of cloth, soft porn playing cards, rugs, cheap clothing, stereo and radio equipment. The general quality is poor, and so too are the badly dressed men and women peering into the windows. Crudely written signs give the game away, for they announce that the shops will accept foreign currencies, not just dollars and Deutschmark, but notes from Czechoslovakia, Romania and Hungary too. The Mexikoplatz is where traders from Eastern Europe and beyond earn their living. Many of the family names over the door are Georgian, though the clientele is more likely to be Czech or Bulgarian than Russian. The shoddy goods in the windows and on the shelves, which few Viennese or other west Europeans would have felt anxious to purchase, were clearly coveted by Hungarians and Romanians, who found the merchandise more enticing, both in terms of quality and price, than the stuff they could buy back home.

The Mexikoplatz is an uninviting spot, windy and raw, and many traders have moved shop to the steep lanes running off the busy Mariahilferstrasse. Walking down the Königsklostergasse early one evening, I was almost dragged into a Hungarian shop, identifiable by the national colours painted over the windows and from the rush of vowels and soft s's I heard all around me. It must have been assumed by the man on the door that only a Hungarian with forints to burn would be strolling down the street at that time, and that I had to be a citizen of Eger or Pécs on the lookout for a quartz watch. Down in these basement shops the Hungarians were lined up two deep at the counter and trade was brisk. The customers are not members of official delegations with an hour to spare, but coach loads of Hungarians who are driven into Vienna every day. While the coaches remain parked near the museums along the Ring, the passengers walk the few hundred yards to the Mariahilferstrasse, where they dive into the shops and spend the next couple of hours stocking up on food processors and cassette recorders before stumbling, barely visible behind their parcels, back to the coach. The goods are certainly cheaper than in most Viennese department stores, but few or no guarantees are offered. Since these customers, for whom foreign travel is an infrequent privilege, are unlikely to make the long journey back to Vienna just to exchange a faulty electric shaver, they are not greatly bothered by this lack of consumer protection.

The trade goes both ways. The geese I had eaten the previous week probably came from across the border, since many Viennese drive into Hungary over the weekend in order to stock up with butter, cheese, sausages, and poultry, all of which are far cheaper. Austrians travelling to Hungary are not required to have visas, so such journeys in search of provisions can be undertaken on the spur of the moment. Such is the warmth of feeling between the two nations that the former imperial tag *K. und K.* (imperial and royal) was said by wags to stand for Kreisky and Kádár, the leaders of the two countries.

Because of this constant trafficking, at governmental as well as personal level, with Eastern Europe and the Soviet Union, Vienna is now a far more international city than most people suppose. The United Nations has brought to the city a large semi-permanent population of diplomats, officials, and their families, though it is a source of slight grievance that this international community tends to keep to itself, renting houses and flats in the smartest districts and sending their children to the same schools. A British businessman married to an Austrian told me that they knew a number of families attached to the UN who had been in Vienna for twenty years but are still unable to speak German, and thus never mix socially with the Viennese.

This well-heeled international community can spend their sizable incomes in the smart Italian shops along the Kärntner-strasse and the luxurious hotels and restaurants of the Inner City and the Ring. Muslims can pray at the mosque near the Danube Canal before dining at Sacher's or the Bristol; they conclude their evenings not at a Lokal but at one of the nightclubs on the Opernring, one of which offers its clientele a Sauna Séparé. In the narrow lane behind the Stephansdom are two English-language bookshops and my favourite newsagents with papers and magazines from all over the world. The Japanese too are highly visible, especially among the students at the music conservatory. I was astonished one evening, when flicking on the television, to see and hear a diminutive Japanese woman singing – very well – a sentimental number by Robert Stolz. She had just won an important singing prize, which she blushingly told the interviewer was 'Grosse Grück'. In the 4th Bezirk, along the Faulmangasse, I found a Japanese delicatessen and emporium. And one Sunday morning, walking down the Kärntnerstrasse, I saw coming towards me five Buddhist monks in saffron robes, muttering monotone chants and beating drums the shape of badminton rackets. (I suspect they are the lads from Rent-a-Monk, who do weekly tours of duty in all the major cities of Europe.)

But it is the contact between the two halves of Europe that gives a certain piquancy and interest to an internationalism that in most other cities is predictable and standardized. Austria still has an open-door policy towards refugees, some of whom choose to stay on in Vienna. Many come from Eastern Europe, and though they tend to be economic rather than political refugees, they are not turned away. They usually spend some time at the refugee camp at Traiskirchen, just south of Vienna, until the paperwork has been completed and their new status established. Poles often linger in Vienna, but Czechs, who tend to speak English rather than German as their second or third language, prefer to move on, if possible, to North America. Czech refugees also seem to be concerned about the possibility of being dragged back across the border and like to put some distance between themselves and the frontier.

Austria's neutrality has also facilitated contacts with Eastern Europe at official levels. Many of the international agencies located in and around Vienna are staffed by Russians as well as Americans and British. An accountant at one of these agencies told me he found himself thrown into much confusion when the Polish government, retaliating against some penny-pinching from the US government, began to pay its dues in zlotys. Since zlotys were being devalued at a faster rate than he could process the payments, I would, he suggested, be doing him and his agency a great favour if I would take a few million zlotys off their hands at a favourable rate of exchange. But a second look in the windows of the Mexikoplatz bazaars, the only place in town where I could make use of zlotys, made it clear that this would be an unwise move, and probably to this day container loads of worthless zlotys are being buried on the outskirts of Vienna.

At the turn of the century, newly arrived migrants from distant corners of the Habsburg Empire would crowd into the outer suburbs. Now, a few generations on, the strong local character of these districts has diminished. An artist who had grown up in the 2nd Bezirk, Leopoldstadt, took me along the streets where he had spent his boyhood. Before the war Leopoldstadt had been thronged with Jews. Now only a few live there still, mostly recent arrivals from Georgia who have settled around the Mexikoplatz on the edge of the Bezirk. He showed me the spacious apartment block where he had lived and where his parents, ardent communists, had hidden comrades on the run. The semi-basement shops he had passed on his way to school were still there, but the names over the doors had changed. The stationer from whom he had bought his school supplies had worked for the Resistance during the war and been shot by the Gestapo. Of the Czech cobblers on the corner there was no trace. Streets which he remembered as filled with bustle and noise were placid now, and the district, no longer a comfortable middle-class Jewish enclave, had become tatty and slightly unsavoury. Even though younger families were moving back into Leopoldstadt because of its closeness to the Inner City, it is still a cold and unappealing corner of Vienna, despite the breadth of its streets and the grandeur of some of its apartment houses.

In the 5th Bezirk, another of the inner suburbs, a local family discerned little change in the social fabric despite the arrival of many Gastarbeiter and their families. The 5th was still a district of entrenched families and small workshops. Sitting in a small park off the Arbeitergasse one Sunday morning, I found myself sur- rounded by small children jabbering in a language I could not recognize. The daughters of the family I visited told me that between half and two-thirds of the children in their classes are not Austrian. Nor are all the foreign children the offspring of Gastarbeiter; there are Indians and Filipinos, as well as other nationalities. One of the daughters, a pensive and opinionated eight-year-old of rollicking good humour, said there was no great friction between the children of different communities, though she regretted, rather grandly, that Turkish boys tended to be cocky and unwilling to learn.

Lunching with this family, I was surprised by the modesty of their flat. It was warm and comfortable but it was also cramped. Yet the family seemed very pleased with this accommodation and prided themselves on having an indoor toilet, unlike some of their neighbours. For the Viennese, housing is not a high priority, so long as they have a roof over their head, security of tenure, and a moderate degree of comfort. With two incomes, the family might have been able to afford a more spacious flat, but, in common with many other Viennese, this is not what they choose to spend their money on. Food and drink attract a sizable proportion of their incomes, rents are usually low, and any money left over tends to be spent on holidays by the Italian coast, clothes, jewellery, a summer cottage, and a fur coat, not a luxury in Vienna when the wind comes howling across the Hungarian plains. With so many flats being hereditary, there is little incentive to move, and a greater inclination to fix up a place in the country. Rural properties in eastern Austria are quite primitive; a succession of invasions since medieval times persuaded the farmers of Lower Austria and the Burgenland that there was little point in building on a grand scale, since any structure was likely to be pillaged and burnt down every thirty years or so.

Viennese prosperity is measured outside the flats of the inhabitants. The dumb streets of Favoriten, one of the largest working-class suburbs in the southerly 10th Bezirk beyond the Gürtel, revealed little: behind the blank walls stuccoed in every conceivable shade of grey were, without doubt, the usual small apartments, warm and crowded. And on almost every corner there was a Gaststube with a Gösser Bier sign over the door. But turn the corner onto the long pedestrian precinct that cuts through the Favoriten, and the picture is entirely different. The shops, it is true, are not as stylish, nor as expensive, as the international boutiques of the Graben and Kärntnerstrasse, but they are well-stocked and lack entirely the dinginess of, say, many comparable suburbs of east London. The paved area was enlivened by a delightful and quirky building by the Austrian architect Domenig. A bank, its curved facade is lined with steel plates like an armadillo's back or the scales of an exceptionally large fish. The conceit is continued indoors, and even the little coffee bar on the ground floor has fittings to match by the same architect.

However, the pride and joy of the Favoriten is to be found a few blocks further down the precinct. Restored to its former glory only in the autumn of 1986, the Amalienbad is yet another example of the progressive munificence of Red Vienna. Built in 1926, these public baths have a magnificent tiled and columned Art Deco interior. There are two pools here, and facilities for sauna and massage. Public baths are often clammy, and prickly with the smell of chlorine, but the Amalienbad is positively sumptuous, a monument to public health now restored to its original function.

Not all the suburbs are as grey and monotonous as the streets of Favoriten and Ottakring. There are the villages of Heiligenstadt and Grinzing, and the suburb of Hietzing has a character of its own. Adjoining the grounds of Schönbrunn, the suburb flourished throughout the last century, as nobles and courtiers built their villas as close as possible to the royal estate. Here, a few miles from the baroque ostentation of the Inner City, one can enjoy Viennese domestic architecture at its most varied and charming. Along Lainzerstrasse, for instance, were built a number of substantial Jugendstil houses, but quite a few charming Biedermeier houses, pastel-coloured and elegantly proportioned, have been left dotted among them. On Maxingstrasse is the villa where the actress Katherina Schratt lived. Empress Elisabeth, inhibited from giving Franz Josef the attentions and consolations to which he was entitled as her husband, introduced him to this star of the Burgtheater. The relationship lasted for about twenty years, and Frau Schratt became his confidante and, possibly, mistress, installed by the Emperor in this conveniently located villa close to the gates of Schönbrunn.

The Gloriettegasse in Hietzing is a showcase of Jugendstil villas, including the extraordinary elongated piece of neoclassical pastiche that Josef Hoffman built for the financier Otto Primavesi. If in its way the Haus Primavesi is as debased in its idiom as any of the pomposities of the Ringstrasse, at least its debasement takes a memorable form. Given the unique quality of Viennese Jugendstil, it is sad to see that many of these large suburban mansions are poorly maintained. One on the Gloriettegasse was shedding and crumbling behind its glorious ironwork gates.

The most striking of these suburban villas were built, as one might expect, by Otto Wagner, in the 14th Bezirk close to the Vienna Woods. His Fuchs Villa is an extraordinary building, highly coloured, and, like the Haus Primavesi, not without elements of pastiche. For behind the classical portico is a coffered ceiling that could have been modelled by Wedgwood for an Adam country house; coloured urns are stashed into elaborate niches, while on either side of the main block there are pillared pavillions. The flat Japanese-style roof, with painted panels beneath the eaves, is one of Wagner's hallmarks, though the rest of the villa is designed in a far more eclectic spirit, since Wagner could hardly be imprisoned within a style he had not yet fully invented. This early villa of Wagner's is indeed a form of historicism, though so individual in style and imagination that it forms a class of its own. Close by is the Villa Werben, also by Wagner, with striking ultramarine decoration on the doors and between the windows. Here the studding and geometrical ornamentation familiar from his Post Office Savings Bank are given more flamboyant and decorative form.

The grandeur, the official imperial quality of the city, are on show in the Inner City and the Ringstrasse. But here in the suburbs, in the shadow of the woods and hills and winegrowing villages so beloved of the Viennese, domestic rather than official lives, from the Emperor's to the artisan's, were eked out in a more hedonistic manner and at a more leisurely pace.

11

Bow and Scrape

Even before Franz Josef found solace in the villa of Katherina Schratt, his wife, the Empress Elisabeth, had flown the coop. Brought up in the Bavarian countryside and addicted to horse-riding, she found the round of duties expected of an empress and the stifling court ritual at the Hofburg tedious beyond endurance. In modern-day Britain we still expect our increasingly tinselly royal family to behave in dutiful ways, launching ships, patron-izing charities, promoting exports, smiling a lot, watching military parades in hot countries, wearing expensive clothes. Even greater pressures of this kind bore down on a Habsburg empress, but Elisabeth simply wouldn't play. She had much to contend with, quite apart from mesmerizing boredom. Her mother-in-law was a fright, a politically powerful woman – Franz Josef was barely out of breeches when he came to the throne – whose sphere of influence encompassed the nursery as well as the nation. Elisabeth was seen less and less at her husband's side on his tours and official appearances, and went abroad for months at a time. A sudden passion for all things Hungarian, including its fearsome language, could just about excuse her absence in Hungary, but no such imperial thread linked her with Madeira, where she also liked to linger.

Franz Josef built her a villa close to the city where she could indulge her rustic hobbies. The Hermes Villa is placed in the middle of Habsburg hunting grounds that are now a game re-serve, the Lainzer Tiergarten. Buses run to the very gates of the park; from there it's just under a mile on foot to the lumpy villa itself. The Tiergarten is still a ravishing amenity for a city to have on its doorstep. Visitors step from suburban Vienna into a park so immense it resembles the open countryside. Only a few hundred yards away from the path, wooded hills rise towards the Wienerwald. Deer observe your progress as you approach the villa.

It is not hard to see why Elisabeth, especially after her assassination in 1898, became the object of a cult. She was quite spectacularly beautiful. In her youth she was exceptionally pretty, with straight eyebrows giving breadth and seriousness to delicate pointed features, marred only by a slightly bloblike nose. In her thirties, by then a veteran of imperial life, she was, if anything, even more ravishing. Her character emerges but faintly from the endless displays of lithographs showing her walking arm-in-arm with Franz Josef – a dapper, red-cheeked lad in those days – or rocking in her arms the infant Crown Prince Rudolf. No signs here of the tantrums that undermined her marriage, of the monumental if understandable selfishness that never ceased to wound her adoring if dull husband, or the growing signs of looniness that crept into her daily behaviour. All that's portrayed at the Hermes Villa and elsewhere is an ethereally lovely woman, perfect of figure and tiny of waist, fragile as porcelain.

Her bedroom, in which Franz Josef must have been an infrequent guest, is decorated with frescoes based on *A Midsummer Night's Dream*, her favourite play. Elisabeth may have sat on a throne in theory, but she sat on a saddle with much more regularity and pleasure, and one or two of her favourites are on display, together with the usual photographs of nags and hounds. Despite or perhaps because of her physical perfection, Elisabeth faced middle age with dread, and photographs of the ageing empress are all but nonexistent. The only one on display at the villa shows a woman still of striking appearance, though her figure had filled out slightly. Despite the fact that they seldom saw her, her assassination in Geneva at the age of sixty-one came as a shock to her people, especially since the killer was a demented Italian anarchist with no specific purpose in mind. The chilling memorabilia are still to be seen: the dagger with which she was stabbed, the torn black dress she was wearing on the fatal day, lithographs of her grieving husband. After her death the cult really got going: Fritz Kreisler composed a musical about her, and her apotheosis is depicted in a 1902 carving by Robert Weigl entitled *Elisabeth in Wolken* (Elisabeth among the clouds). Franz Josef was a great one for erecting memorials to commemorate traumatic experiences, whether joyful or tragic. He had built the striking neo-Gothic Votivkirche close to the Ringstrasse to thank the Lord for delivering him from a failed assassination attempt.

94

With the murder of his wife, it was time for another memorial, and the competition designs are on display at the Hermes Villa.

The Villa is at least maintained as a museum, but the hunting lodge at Eckartshau is a more sombre memorial to the decay of the Habsburgs. After the Emperor Karl found himself without an empire in 1918, he and Empress Zita and their children spent six months here before leaving Austria for good in March 1919. Eckartshau lies to the east of the city. The lodge is surrounded by a small melancholy park, and in autumn walnut trees drop their soft crunchy nuts onto the paths. The interior cannot be visited, and it's unlikely that there would be much to see. At least the lodge itself is quite imposing, which is more than can be said for the hunting lodge at Mayerling, where Crown Prince Rudolf met his end in 1889. The story is well known though the details and motives still remain unclear. It seems probable that the thirty-year-old Rudolf staged a double suicide with the young Baroness Marie Vetsera, with whom he was either having an affair or intending to. For decades now it has been suggested that a contributing factor to the prince's despair was his inability to make any political impact in the face of the unwavering opposition of his hidebound father. Rudolf was no fool, and engaged in lively political discussion with leading journalists of the time. But he had no way of implementing his ideas, no way of carving for himself a useful role in the affairs of the Empire.

What remains of the lodge in the woods near the great abbey of Heiligenkreutz is an unpretentious two-storey house painted yellow and cream. The bedroom where the bodies were found was torn down and replaced by a small neo-Gothic chapel erected by Franz Josef, ever partial to such memorials. Inside the chapel there is nothing to see, other than the usual ecclesiastical furnishings. Rudolf's tomb is in the Kapuzinergruft, alongside his father. Adjoining the chapel is an absurd reconstruction of a typically furnished room of the time – and 1889 was no *annus mirabilis* in the history of interior design – as though the guardians of this little shrine believed that visitors to this unrewarding spot had to be placated with some attempt at an historical display, however pointless. There are also a few portraits of the wretched Rudolf and lithographs of his grieving father.

Neither the lodge at Eckartshau nor the one at Mayerling tells us much about the Habsburgs, but the Kaiservilla at Bad Ischl is more revealing. Bad Ischl is still a spa town, attracting devotees of mudpacks and foul-tasting mineral waters to its modern baths and pools. During the last century it was a fashionable summer resort for the aristocracy, and an obvious choice for the Emperor's small summer palace. It isn't that small, but compared to Schönbrunn or the Hofburg it was a doll's house. Elisabeth, although she preferred the outdoors, had some minimal taste or at least consciousness of her surroundings. Franz Josef clearly had none whatsoever. His idea of interior decoration was to hang horns and antlers on the walls, with an occasional stuffed bird to provide a contrast. Somebody has earned a small medal for hagiography by counting the trophies, and there are over 1200 within the Kaiservilla, each one inscribed with the date of the hunt. The last is dated 23 August 1913, and was bagged by the Emperor at the age of eighty-three. In between hunting expeditions he occupied himself by signing papers and declaring war on Serbia. A glass case contains his boots and his hanky, his guns and his walking stick, and his *lederhosen*. Not only did the Emperor wear Tyrolean costume while clumping through the mountains in search of animals to obliterate, but he also, if the evidence at Bad Ischl is to be believed, wore a sporran too. Elisabeth has her fair share of memorabilia: her death mask, her prayer book and opera glasses, and, most eloquent of all, her riding crop. The only approach to a work of art in the Kaiservilla is a marble statue of Shadow, Elisabeth's favourite dog, depicted with its paw raised.

The Kaiservilla is a hard-edged house. There are few gracious touches, and no warmth. That is a common fate for houses that are no longer inhabited, but the Kaiservilla is not empty. It remains in the Habsburg family, and the current occupant is the Archduke Markus. I was summoned in for an audience with the proprietor, who received me in a kind of breakfast room where he was chatting to his steward. We didn't have a great deal to say to each other. The Archduke had caused a mild stir when he had taken a commoner, apparently a *Mädl* from a nearby village, as his bride, but I had no wish to embarrass my host by expressing my objections to this match *devant les domestiques*. The Archduke wore his spectacles at a tilt, but in other respects this authentic relic of the House of Habsburg made as little impression on me as I evidently made on him.

Although the central European aristocracy has lost whatever clout it once had, it's still hard to travel through some parts of Germany and Austria without tripping over dozens of counts and barons. I don't habitually move in such circles, but any reader of Patrick Leigh Fermor's admirable books about this part of Europe cannot help observing that in his day commoners constituted a minority. The use of titles is forbidden in the republic of Austria, but no one takes the slightest notice. Austrians, indeed, are so obsessed by rank that it would be absurd for them to object to aristocratic titles while clinging so fiercely to bureaucratic ones.

The correct use of rank and title is an arcane but essential skill in Austria. During the heyday of the Habsburgs, political power was kept firmly in the hands of the aristocracy. The rising bourgeoisie, while permitted to play the field in the guise of journalists or lawyers, was excluded from ministerial power, and its only access to influence, other than the pen, was through the imperial bureaucracy. With the founding of the Dual Monarchy in 1867, bureaucracies multiplied, as some matters came under *Kaiserlich* (imperial) jurisdiction, others under *Königlich* (kingly or royal) control, and yet others, such as the army, under *Kaiserlich und Königlich* command. To this day certain shops in Vienna display antiquated signs bearing the prefix 'K.K.' or 'K. und K.' before the name of the service they had been honoured to provide to the court. The novelist Robert Musil, naming his barely disguised fictional version of Austria-Hungary in *The Man Without Qualities*, called it Kakania. The allusion is a punning one, for it embraces not only the imperial formula but a German word for shit.

In the infinitely complex world of the bureaucracy, your place was rigidly defined by your rank. Titles not only earned you deference from your inferiors in the civil service, and a bow and a scrape from your concierge and tailor, but provided a culturally and ethnically diverse society with a sense of structure. Obsequiousness is still a central feature of Viennese life. A doctor would not introduce himself by using his full title, but he would be miffed were he not addressed by it. Even rebels against the system are limited in their protest: persons with academic and professional qualifications are obliged to parade them on their stationery. A long-time British resident thought little of my historical and sociological explanation for the Austrian addiction to rank. 'It's all a game,' he insisted. 'Viennese are simply eager to gather enough letters after their name so that they can get a piece of the action. Once you're important enough, or sound important enough, then you're more likely to get your cut.' Another British friend of mine, an academic, has taken this analysis to heart. Though he does not enjoy professorial status in England, he promotes himself on visits to Austria, and the results, he assures me, are most efficacious.

There have always been plenty of titles to choose from. On a memorial tablet in the Votivkirche, I found the following attached to a list of a mere twelve names: Sekt.-Chef Dr; Oberschulrat; Red.-Rat; Landesrat, Generalsekr.; Komm.-Rat; and the very grand Min. Rat Prof. Moreover, titles, like the pox, can be transmitted from man to woman. The wife of a Herr Doktor is to be addressed as Frau Doktor, though a woman with a Ph.D. of her own will not be addressed by her doctoral title. A university professor will be hailed as Herr Professor, but so will a schoolteacher. When in doubt, it is always safe to promote the person you are speaking to. A professor at Vienna University told me he and his brother were travelling in a taxi. The driver called him Herr Ingenieur and his brother Herr Doktor. On leaving the taxi, the newly demoted professor asked the driver why he had honoured his brother with a doctorate. 'Because he is wearing glasses,' he replied. There is one undeniable advantage to the mania for titles: it comes in handy when you can't remember somebody's name.

Hierarchical niceties can work both ways. Your local baker will fawn over you – 'Sofort, Frau Professor!' – but you must address her correctly too. It took me a few weeks to get the hang of this. Sometimes, on entering a shop, I would be the object of an attentive inquiry; on other occasions I would be ignored entirely. In search of a friend staying at the Imperial Hotel, I approached the front desk where a porter was consulting the register. He scribbled and fussed and scratched – and paid no attention whatever to me. I had, I later gathered, failed to observe an elementary rule of Viennese etiquette. The instant you walk into a shop or café or other place where some kind of service is expected, you must sing out: 'Grüss Gott!' At this point you become a Person and will be accorded the basic courtesies. Failure to produce the formula at the strategic moment will identify you as a Non-Person who can be ignored with impunity. There seems little middle ground in Vienna between rudeness and servility, though I must pay tribute to the salesperson at my local cheese counter who actually apologized for keeping me waiting while she wrapped my sliver of Emmental into an elegant package.

Of course rank and title no longer entail wealth and privilege. While I was in Vienna, much fuss was made of a crone who was photographed scrubbing the front steps of her little Palais. This attracted attention because the woman in question was a Countess Esterhazy and she no longer had an army of servants to do the scrubbing for her. Few aristocrats enjoy the wealth they used to, and none wields political power. Endlessly intermarried and interconnected, they have stitched themselves into a closed circle and tend to know each other and help each other out. Their base is in the countryside, where some large estates have survived. Once powerful families such as the Harrachs and the Schwarzenbergs are still around. The Harrachs own a few castles east of Vienna, and the Schwarzenbergs have profitably converted their magnificent palace near the Belvedere into a luxury hotel, which must compensate for the loss of their principal estates in Bohemia. On the other hand, families such as the Czernins and thousands of Hungarian nobles lost all their property, while others, such as Dr Paul Esterhazy, present head of a family that once owned ninety-nine estates, now live in Switzerland, within walking distance of the bank.

Unwilling or unable to enter politics, Austrian aristocrats can enter the army or the diplomatic service or the professions. Lacking wealth, property, and influence, their titles and the good society and entertainment they can offer one another are all that is left to most of them. As for mere commoners, deprived in a republic of any possibility of ennoblement, the authorities have placated them with a substitute, a kind of social methadone. Instead of having the usual multi-digited licence plate on your car, you may, in exchange for a handsome sum, purchase a two- or three-figure number plate, which will indicate to pedestrians as you run them over that you are, title or no, a person of consequence.

12

Mollycoddled

Historians of music and of the city of Vienna have not been idle in their search for every single house or room where an eminent composer may have sat down and scribbled a few bars. Writers seem to have been equally peripatetic, and by my reckoning the dramatist Grillparzer holds the record for the highest number of moves in a single lifetime. Not that Beethoven is far behind, for he is associated with about thirty addresses in the city and suburbs. A number of these places have been turned into museums, but I found them curiously unrevealing. Schubert's birthplace on Nussdorferstrasse, a modest house with balconies overlooking a central courtyard, is typical. The rooms on view are not furnished, and merely house portraits, photographs of places associated with the composer, two pianos, and facsimiles of scores. Only one exhibit made the heart leap: Schubert's spectacles. There are so many portraits of the composer wearing those fragile wire-rimmed glasses that it came as a shock to lay eyes on the object itself, reminding one that he may have seen poorly but he understood everything.

Mozart's house on the Domgasse, where he wrote *Figaro* and the Haydn quartets, is touted as giving an exemplary idea of the furnishing and layout of a Viennese flat in the late eighteenth century, but to me it was dumb. Ugly spotlights suspended from metal frames along the ceilings effectively wrecked any atmospheric authenticity, while the exhibits were of scant interest. Artists, however great, who led impoverished embattled lives leave behind few memorabilia: they leave their work, and perhaps we should be satisfied with that alone, rather than seek to erect shrines. Exactly the same is true of one of the principal Beethoven houses, on the Mölkerbastei, the former bastion overlooking the Ringstrasse and the University.

Weary of these desolate memorials to men who left little behind other than inexhaustibly satisfying music, I went in search of contemporary culture. Molly, the Canadian sculptress who had been immersed in Vienna's art world for a few years, agreed to lead me through the galleries. We met, of course, in a coffeehouse to plan our itinerary. The Café Central has recently been renovated, and a superb job the restorers have made of it. Tucked into a lofty corner of the Palais Ferstel, it consists of a marble-pillared room that's spacious enough for confidential conversations, while compact enough for profitable eavesdropping. Enormous windows look out onto the Herrengasse, and I loved sitting in the Central at dusk watching passing pedestrians looking more and more cold as the temperature dropped. Earlier in the century the Central was one of the most famous of Viennese coffeehouses. Trotsky was among the many regular clients. Just inside the door is a life-sized and most realistic model of a balding figure in a black leather jacket seated at a small marble-topped table. This is the monument to another distinguished and persistent client of the Central, the writer Peter Altenberg.

After a milky *mélange* coffee, I set off with Molly for the galleries. The art business has been doing very nicely in Austria in recent years. The Allied occupation until 1955 delayed the baby boom that hit the rest of Europe immediately after the war. But now there is a glut of men and women in their thirties, eager to form movements and establish their reputations. The most widespread movement is the Austrian branch of the *Junge Wilde*, the James Deans of the painterly world. Their style is *extrem*, as the Viennese say, and is characterized by violent colours thickly applied. We began our pilgrimage at the Galerie Nächst St Stephan. The sign – in English – by the door was not encouraging: 'DON'T TOUCH THE WORK OF ART – OFFENDER WILL BE AVENGED.' Since any would-be visitor must climb several flights of stairs and negotiate heavy doors and brave granite-faced women at the reception desk, the chances of any sticky-fingered children or adults rushing into the gallery for a quick smear seemed remote. The word 'avenged' suggested the sign might have been intended as humorous, and I consulted my guide on this point. She doubted it, as did I, and we concluded that the sign was just a bit of good old-fashioned intimidation to induce in visitors a suitably reverential frame of mind. This gallery is a high-class operation, under an influential director, Rosemarie Schwarzwalder. Unfortunately the work on display was mightily dull:

large canvases representing, if that's the word, abstract shapes, and immense expanses of uniformly coloured surfaces.

I yawned loudly and Molly nodded sympathetically. 'The work here is large because the artists have nothing to say. And they're hoping to sell it straight off to a museum or corporation.'

'Just like the stuff you see in SoHo. Unless you have a ten-thousand-square-foot loft or a family skyscraper you can't even contemplate buying it.'

'Exactly.'

'*Nun. Weiter.*'

We moved on to a small gallery called the Cajetan Grill. It was a strange place, more a high-class jumble sale than a gallery. Strewn among the nineteenth century landscapes and the modern mobiles were Maori artefacts. I asked the girl at the desk for more information. Her accent, as she politely told me she couldn't give me any, was familiar. She was English, a Sloane Ranger on loan.

'Is there some kind of policy pursued by the owner, or is everything just random?' I asked.

'I really couldn't tell you. I did try myself to ask the owner more about the various items on display but he wasn't very forthcoming. In fact he told me that if anyone asked me about the paintings and other stuff in the gallery I was to tell them to get lost. And if they persisted with their inquiries I was to tell them to get fucked.'

'I think,' I observed to Molly, 'that this is our cue to leave.'

'No, you're very welcome to look round,' said the Sloane. 'I just can't tell you anything. Take a look at this before you leave.' And she directed me towards something that looked like a large fried egg with a transparent yolk. By pressing a switch on the side, painted sheets, presumably on pulley devices, would rotate, providing combinations of layers of painting within the yolk. Highly intriguing, perfect for minutes of innocent fun in the nursery, but also hideously ugly. The Sloane agreed.

Back on the streets, Molly had a spell of getting lost while I trotted behind. On Schönlaternegasse we passed the Artothek, a splendid institution from which the public can borrow prints and drawings much as they borrow books from a library. Eventually she found the Pakesch gallery. Peter Pakesch had begun life as a painter himself before setting up as a dealer specializing in the work of his classmates at art school. Pakesch is the great sponsor of the Junge Wilde, and may even have been said to have invented them. Nobody was about, so Molly walked into the stock room and began pulling out canvases.

'This is a Danner. And here's a Brandl.' She plucked from the racks small canvases assaulted with thick clotted blobs of highly coloured oils.

'How can you tell them apart?'

'It's not easy. In fact the only way is by the colour they're keen on this year. Brandl's got a thing about red this year, while Danner's into green. See? Pakesch tells them what to paint, they do what they're told, and then he sells their work for vast sums. It's simple.'

At this point a receptionist, another Viennese, an indigenous Schloane, approached. Could she be of service? she snarled. Molly, who knows no fear, said she was showing her writer friend the work of certain artists represented by Pakesch. Whereupon the Schloane grilled me: what, she wanted to know, was I proposing to write about these artists' work? That, logic compelled me to reply, was impossible to say until I had seen it. She was not cooperative, and so we left in a simulated state of high dudgeon.

On the Seilerstrasse, the first floor of an old-fashioned apartment block has been acquired by Ursula Krinzinger, who made her name with a gallery in Innsbruck, and had now come to Vienna to muscle in on the art scene here. There was little to see in the gallery, since a new show was being hung in the immense rooms, so we moved on to the friendly Galerie Wurthle, where we were actually welcomed by the staff. The only work I liked was by Eduard Angeli, a most elegant painter whose canvases reminded me of Milton Avery's – and were thus entirely atypical of most trail-blazing Austrian art.

It was now getting dark, so we walked across the Ringstrasse, which was beginning to fill with rush-hour traffic, and made our way towards the Karlsplatz. Shortly before reaching the square we stopped at the Café Museum, another coffeehouse that had enjoyed a glorious past. Its interior had been remodelled by the radical Viennese architect Adolf Loos in the early years of the century, but since then it has been messed around so much that Loos's contributions have been obscured. Loos is a much revered figure, for he was the greatest enemy of the ornamental style. On his drawing board, lintels and pediments had no place; surfaces were flat and symmetrical, and rigour ruled his pen. I can quite see that Loos, like a dose of salts, was necessary at a certain time, but I am not an admirer of his work. In 1910 he scandalized Viennese society by erecting opposite the Michaelertor of the Hofburg one of his rather blank-featured apartment houses. Its lack of mouldings and its even fenestration deeply affronted the Habsburgs, and it is said that Franz Josef refused to use the Michaelerplatz entrance to his palace after 1910, which shows his strength of character and stupidity. The building is clean and quite stylish, and unlike so much turn-of-the-century architecture in Vienna has not dated. On the other hand I was never able to warm to it, and I don't share the regret that the Michaelerplatz structure is the only major work of Loos's to be seen in Vienna itself.

The present-day Café Museum is a somewhat dingy place, with dirty cream walls and an excessive proportion of chain-smokers. It is popular with young people, and Molly, who moved in arty circles, clearly felt at home there. I, however, preferred the bourgeois comforts of, say, the Café Landtmann next to the Burgtheater, where the waiters and cloakroom attendants treat you like shit, but the coffee is excellent and a formidable range of newspapers is always available. It also did not take me long to discover that the luxurious coffeehouses are no more expensive than the trendy smoke-filled ones where the *Herald Tribune* is often two days old.

After a beer at the Café Museum, Molly returned to her studio to continue work on a full-length nude model of her ex-husband –not a pretty sight – and I went back to my pension. It was a Tuesday night, one of two evenings each week when the higher toned of the two Austrian television channels presents *Club 2*. There was not a great deal to rivet the attention on Austrian television, and the news was presented with more seriousness and better coverage on radio, but *Club 2* was an exception. The format is simple enough: half a dozen people with a shared interest in a particular topic sit slumped in chairs and sofas and debate. The atmosphere is that of a Senior Common Room, and cigarette smoke curls slowly upwards towards the shades of the standard lamps behind the armchairs. Feelings sometimes run high, but decorum is always maintained under discreet but efficient chairmanship. Topics under discussion included, on the occasions that I watched the programme, the existence of the soul, should women fight in wars, feminism and psychoanalysis, Lanzmann's *Shoah*, and liberation theology. The starter's pistol was sounded at about 10.15 and the discussion continued, uninterrupted by advertisements, until well after midnight. There were deeply boring moments – grave jowly bishops intoning orthodoxies were guaranteed to induce me to turn down the sound for a while – but it struck me as admirable that such a programme could flourish at all.

The following Saturday I was back at Ursula Krinzinger's gallery. She was breaking all traditions by launching a new show on a Saturday morning. Molly had tipped me off, and clinched my determination to go by saying that there was usually a good spread at Krinzinger's. She was wrong about the spread – there was nothing at all to eat or drink – but there was certainly a good crowd of people; a few hundred must have come traipsing through the palatial rooms. The overdressed Dallas look was popular among the women; the men, on the whole, were elegantly suited, but there were a handful who affected the pseudo-unworldly Bertolt Brecht look, with cloth caps perched over crewcuts, and baggy trousers. The work on display was hot from New York, and was being exhibited under the umbrella title of New Strategies: New York City One. These new strategies consisted of backward-looking work, such as David Bowes' crudely executed reinterpretations of Greek and other legends. The show was hogged by two gentlemen called McGough and McDermott. Wearing wing collars and with their hair stiffly greased, they pose as nineteenth-century artists of the Hudson River Valley School. I was not much taken by the work of this camp comedy duo, though less meretricious work from more quiet-spoken artists did appeal to me quite strongly.

In another historic first, the crowd of visitors was invited to return at eight that evening for a lecture and a discussion at which a number of the artists would be present. It seemed unlikely that many people would come here on a Saturday evening for a second dose of New Strategies and no drink, but I was wrong. There must have been 150 people crammed into the largest salon, where a slide show and a commentary were in progress, together with an overflow crowd in the other rooms. The commentary was delivered by one of those uniquely blasé and conceited Americans who pronounce their fatuous judgments in so elevated a drawl that any counterview could be dismissed with a sneer as impossibly gauche. This was, I confess, like a red rag to a bull. A *viertel* or two had passed my lips earlier that evening, and I was in no mood for nonsense. I had also been in Vienna for a few weeks now, and felt a sense of responsibility to the citizenry; I could not allow them to be bamboozled by this drivel.

'What these artists have in common,' intoned the voice, 'is a sense of loss, of looking back. David Bowes in particular – next slide, please – has a sense of the past that's apocalyptic.'

'Maybe,' I heard a voice, mine, murmuring, 'but he's still a lousy painter.' I froze, waiting for the heavy hand on my shoulder and the firm tug towards the exit. Nothing happened.

The voice continued, and turned to the work of McDermott and McGough, who contributed to the commentary. 'Our latest work,' twittered the more fey of the pair, 'is dated 1928.' An earnest Viennese voice translated this for the audience, who remained solemn-faced throughout. The artist continued: 'The reason for this is that we're hoping our paintings will be bought by antique dealers and end up in flea markets.'

'At flea market prices?' I interjected, but there was no response. I was quite shocked by my own behaviour, being usually of more timid disposition. However, a heckler unnoticed has no choice but to escalate his actions. When McDermott (or McGough) simpered: 'Our motto is: We've looked into the future – and we're not going,' I yelled 'Why?' No response. I regret to say that when the lecturer rabbited on about the uniqueness of their 'oovre', my own counter-commentary was reduced to cries of 'Rubbish!' and 'Piffle!' and a final despairing 'How can you all listen to this crap?' I stumbled out, and found Erich the painter in one of the other rooms. I directed a diatribe at him, and he nodded sympathetic-ally, presumably in an attempt to shut me up. It worked, and I walked briskly back to the pension, lamenting that a cultural hunger, attested to by the crowds of earnest listeners at the gallery, should be appeased with such stale crumbs.

The Viennese, of course, have a bad reputation for artistic receptivity. It has become a cliché to observe that the composers and artists so revered nowadays by the Austrians and the world were scandalously neglected in their own city. The struggles of Mozart and Beethoven, the failure of Mahler, while director of the Staatsoper, to obtain performances of his indigestible symphonies, and the hostility that greeted Klimt, Schoenberg, and many others have been amply documented. The tradition continues: the *Hetz*, or chase, is how the Viennese refer to the popular and journalistic pursuit of their cultural icons, which these days tend to be theatre directors and conductors rather than creative artists, who are thin on the ground in modern Vienna. On the other hand, the Viennese must be mindful of their reputation – shared with other cities such as Paris – for brawling during first performances of works later acclaimed as masterpieces. Perhaps this, in addition to the good manners which I myself neglected to display, accounts for the docility of the crowd at Krinzinger's. Loath to be thought philistine when exposed to the cutting edge of American art (which a term such as New Strategies must have led them to believe the works on offer must represent), they swallowed with rapt gratitude a shovelful of the reactionary and second-rate.

13

The Clash of the Midgets

Travelling around Austria in the spring of 1986 I soon tired of the thousands of political posters both of the unappetizing Dr Wald- heim and his Socialist opponent. In November that same year I, in common with the entire population of Austria, had to endure the same thing all over again, though at least this time around the Waldheim smirk was absent from the hoardings. A general election had been called shortly before I arrived in Vienna, and the campaign lumbered on throughout my stay. The Socialists, the SPÖ, had been in coalition with a third party, the FPÖ (Freedom, or Liberal, Party), a bizarre assortment of anti-clerical liberals and German nationalists and the far right. Its previous leader, Norbert Steger, had been, by FPÖ standards, a moderate, but at the 1986 party conference he had been ousted by a youthful and charismatic politician called Jörg Haider, who, as everybody remarked, looked exactly like the skiing instructor of every girl's dreams. Dr Haider was also more extreme in his political views than his predecessor, and the SPÖ declared that they were not prepared to maintain the coalition with Haider taking Steger's place in the government. And so an election was called.

The main candidates were Chancellor Franz Vranitzky; Alois Mock, the ÖVP leader; and Jörg Haider. Since the FPÖ rarely mops up more than 5 per cent of the vote in general elections, the principal contest was between the SPÖ and ÖVP. Or to be more exact, between Dr Vranitzky and Dr Mock, since the entire campaign focused on personalities, such as they were, rather than policies. This was predictable, not because the Austrians are instinctively entranced by American-style election campaigns, but because there was little to choose in terms of policies between the principal parties. Since 1945 moderation has been the name of the game in Austrian political life. The armed battles of the 1930s, and seven harsh years under the Nazis, have not disposed the Austrians to endorse extreme policies and politicians.

Socialist and Conservative leaders alike have mostly been men of centrist views. The aggressive confrontations that mark the politics of other European countries are rare in Austria, and powerful and well-organized Chambers of Commerce and Labour, empowered to negotiate between industry and unions on a nationwide basis, have taken the sting out of industrial relations, which have been the bane of other democracies.

Nor are the parties especially ideological. Which party you support has less to do with programmes and policies than with family affiliations. Most people join the party they were born into. If you dislike its policies, you may abstain but you are unlikely to vote for the opposition, though this did happen during the atypical Waldheim campaign and it seems probable that such unshakable party loyalty will grow ever less firm. The SPÖ is supported by working people and a sizable segment of the population who have always believed in interventionist policies that will supposedly confer social and other benefits on less affluent citizens. The ÖVP attracts Catholics of firm belief, and those people convinced of the virtues of private enterprise. Nonetheless Thatcherism and Reaganism, or any doctrinaire belief in the merits of the unfettered marketplace and a firm antipathy to any system of comprehensive social welfare, have little support in Austria.

Nor is the socialism of the SPÖ ideologically intense. It is characteristic that Chancellor Vranitzky ran a bank before he ran a political party and then the nation. Few in Austria are prepared to snip through the elaborate social security net woven since the 1920s. Austrian politics is a politics of consensus. Such political debate as was taking place in 1986 pondered the role of the nationalized industries. The ÖVP favoured a degree of privatization, but this did not provoke yelps of indignation from the SPÖ, since the Socialists too had proposed selling off chunks here and there on the grounds that certain sectors of those industries were undercapitalized. Nationalization is not an especially contentious issue in Austria. In 1955 most industries were nationalized because there was no choice. Some sectors of the economy had been drained by the Russians during their ten-year occupation of eastern Austria, and there were few industrialists with sufficient resources to take over and run the nation's industries. The nationalized industries had long been used by the SPÖ to control

109

the labour market, but with harsher economic times in the late 1970s the Socialists too realized that they could not continue with this kind of featherbedding. Overmanning had become a luxury that Austria could not afford, and the two parties differed only in the extent to which they would pursue reform. Furthermore, pertinent questions were being asked about whether Austria could continue to afford its extremely generous social welfare payments. With the exception of the few decades when an adult is employed, the Austrian state cares for its people from cradle to grave. Even though no one proposed to dismantle the system, even SPÖ leaders were admitting, *sotto voce*, that some reforms were necessary.

Thus in 1986 there were few burning issues to engage the passions of the politicians, let alone the voters. Such accord may be admirable, but it makes for stupendously dull election campaigns. The small groups that espoused more extreme views had virtually no chance of entering Parliament, since under Austria's proportional representation system any party must earn a majority in at least one constituency before their votes have any bearing on the handouts of parliamentary seats. It is for this reason that the Communist Party has not held a seat in Parliament since 1959. It was thought that the Greens might do well in 1986, until a major split seriously diminished their chances of making any significant electoral impact.

Although Vranitzky presented himself throughout the campaign as a party manager of impeccable competence rather than as a rabble-rousing ideologue, it was as custodians of the economy and of the nation that the SPÖ were most vulnerable to attack. They had been a dominant force in Austrian politics for many years, and had grown sluggish. Bruno Kreisky – that rarity among Austrian politicians, a man of true dynamism – had done much to put Austria on the map throughout the 1970s, though not always to the satisfaction of the electorate. Nevertheless, it had been thanks to Kreisky's daring foreign policies and skilful brokership that it was no longer possible for the rest of the world to confuse Austria with Australia. He had successfully exploited Austria's neutrality to present the nation as an honest broker in dealing with other countries. But Kreisky was now in retirement, and his successors had been a dull lot. Then too the overall image of the SPÖ was scarcely virginal. There was little evidence of corruption at ministerial levels, but there were uncomfortably close ties between financial institutions such as banks and building societies and the treasuries of both political parties. It was widely accepted that many politicians kept a mistress on the payroll, drove a large car they hadn't paid for, enjoyed a generous housing allowance and other privileges denied to their fellow citizens. Since such abuses of power were as much a feature of local politics as of national politics, there was no reason to castigate the Socialists more than the Conservatives; but since the Socialists were running the country, it was easier to point the finger at them by accusing the SPÖ of feathering their own nests while mismanaging the nation's affairs.

Apart from lolling in limousines and luxury, Austrian politicians were just as likely to enchant the populace with sexual peccadilloes as British politicians are traditionally required to do. However, so reticent is the Austrian press – part of its badness is its excessive discretion – that you will search the newspapers in vain for information on the lustful adventures of elected officials. Some years ago a prominent broadcaster and the mayor of Vienna took the afternoon off and inspected the facilities at one of the city's many brothels. Unfortunately the broadcaster overexerted himself and expired in the arms of his moll. The mayor, to his credit, immediately told the police what had happened. Within hours the story spread through the city, since numerous whores, cops, doctors, and municipal officials couldn't help knowing what had occurred, and there was no way to seal their mouths. Yet not a word appeared in the press – which prefers to devote its tabloid pages to titillation, parochialism, and the occasional antisemitic slur – and Gossip had to take on the role of informing the nation.

It may be clear that Austrians do not have a particularly elevated notion of how figures in public life should behave. Since the electorate has low expectations, politicians can survive scandals that would ruin the careers of their counterparts in other democracies. It is also recognized that politics in the form of parliamentary debate and the enactment of legislation is a relatively minor aspect of political life. Power broking is equally important, and certain industrial leaders and union bosses wield tremendous influence behind the scenes, often making deals that may benefit the nation but that also may bear little relation to the views and expectations of the people they supposedly represent. That so many of Austria's industries are state-owned contributes to this concentration of power. The deals that were struck probably increased the vulnerability of the government when certain sectors of the economy were perceived as mismanaged.

Dr Mock, accordingly, went on the offensive, jabbing away persistently at the staleness of the SPÖ government. Dr Vranitzky affected to be above the fray, and serenely floated through the campaign as though he couldn't descend to Mock's nitpicking level of debate, since he was too busy running the country. He treated the somewhat petulant Mock as though he were an excitable schoolboy – a strategy hard to resist – but Vranitzky's pose as elder statesman was somewhat presumptuous, given that he had only been chancellor for a few months. Although the campaign was projected as a clash of personalities, the strategy was less than successful since nobody could discern much 'personality' in either candidate.

Dr Mock's television ads were particularly vacuous. One ad opened with children running joyfully through fields, followed by shots of the candidate talking to assorted citizens and pausing to listen attentively to a small child. Images of Tyrolean costume alternated with images of computer terminals. In a gripping portrayal of life on the farm, a farmer was shown leaping off his tractor to be greeted by an exceptionally well-groomed woman and two impeccable children. What on earth any of this had to do with ÖVP policy remained a mystery. So too did a particularly repulsive poster, showing two little children about to kiss; the slogan read 'Höchste Zeit fur bessere Zeiten' (High time we had better times), which gives you some idea of the level of debate in 1986. Mock's campaign literature was more revealing, since it consisted mostly of snapshots of the candidate shaking hands with assorted conservative leaders from all over the world. In his capacity as secretary of an association of conservative politicians, Mock has had occasion to pump every sympathetic hand in the universe. The campaign managers had clearly decided it was important to project their candidate as a man of international status. This wheeze had helped Waldheim earlier in the year, when he seemed to have convinced most Austrians that he had ruled the world, and the ÖVP scriptwriters clearly hoped it would work the same magic for Mock.

Another brochure showed Dr Mock through his wife's eyes, on the grounds that Frau Mock knows him as no other person can. He is, you will be amazed to learn, a good and gifted and kindly man, though of his sexual prowess she writes not a word. To illustrate her essay, the reader is regaled with photographs of Mock wearing *Trachten*, Mock dancing with Frau Mock wearing *Trachten*, Mock with four little girls on his knees, Mock playing the piano, meeting the workers, chopping wood, yelling into the ear of Jacques Chirac. The soporific quality of his campaign was exemplified by one of his slogans: '*Mit Mock.*'

Not that the Vranitzky campaign was any less glib. The chancellor, in his brochures, was portrayed as a family man and man of affairs, and many of his posters depicted him wearing a three-piece suit, perfect garb for a banker but an unfamiliar costume for the leader of a socialist party. If Mock protested too much, Vranitzky protested too little. One of his campaign slogans droned: '*Vor uns liegt das neue Österreich. Gehen wir den Weg gemeinsam.*' ('Before us lies the new Austria. Let us tread that path together.') This pompous reworking of the words Vote For Me was countered by the thrilling formulation of the ÖVP: '*Mock. Der Mann der's besser macht.*' ('Mock. He'll do a better job.') Blandness followed blandness, as during the final days of the campaign the Vranitzky people came up with a new appeal: 'If you want Vranitzky to be chancellor, then you have to vote for him.' Well, yes, that is a thought.

I noted with some relief that certain sections of the electorate were as fed up with this pap as I was. One of the Green factions boldly took the bull by the horns on one of their campaign posters, which beneath a portrait of Dr Waldheim printed the words: '*Um es klar zu machen er ist nicht unser Präsident.*' ('To make it clear that he's not our president.') I could sympathize with the sentiment, but it was a curiously inept slogan, with its suggestion that the Greens refused to accept the democratic choice of the Austrian people. A new political group began to hand out its own campaign literature in the streets of Vienna, and this fringe party gloried under the name of '*Mir Reicht's*' ('I've Had Enough').

It was the candidacy of Jörg Haider that spiced up the campaign. As FPÖ leader, he was in charge of a motley crew. Liberalism in Austria has always had slightly different connotations from liberalism elsewhere in Europe. In the nineteenth century the Liberals favoured constitutional controls over the Habsburg monarchy, greater entrepreneurial freedom, and close cultural, even political, links with Germany. German nationalism was always a powerful force within the Habsburg Empire, if only because of the primacy of the German language within it. Even after the fall of the Habsburgs, German nationalism remained strong. Austrian socialists felt strong links with the Social Democrats in Germany, and many favoured a union between the two countries. By the 1930s, of course, German nationalism took on more sinister associations.

Why German-speaking Austrians should feel so drawn to Germany, when German-speaking Swiss feel no such tug, is something of a mystery, but such nationalism is by no means extinct in Austria. The Liberal tradition, anti-clerical and sentimentally linked with Germany, is moribund but not dead, and for some years has played footsie with more strident German nationalists who espouse distinctly right-wing views. When the Second World War ended, over half a million Austrian Nazis, plus their families, remained alive and well. The Socialists were particularly anxious to prevent former Nazis from joining the conservative ÖVP, where their combined forces might easily swamp the SPÖ electorally. So the right wingers were encouraged to form their own political groups which, given the preponderance of the two large parties, would be reduced to perpetual insignificance. The right-wing groups have undergone many transformations over the years, and their current party is the FPÖ.

I found it very difficult to establish what it was that the FPÖ stood for. It would appear to be a party of dissent and sentiment rather than programme, a luxury permitted to parties that can never muster enough support to exercise power. It was primarily in local politics that the FPÖ made its presence felt. Its power base lay in Carinthia, where Haider had been party leader before his election to its national leadership. Many Austrian provinces incorporate small minorities. In the Burgenland there are parcels of Croats and Hungarians, and in Carinthia live pockets of Slovenes. There is no reason to doubt that the overwhelming majority of Carinthian Slovenes are loyal Austrians, but they are anxious to preserve their language and culture. Moreover, under the terms of the 1955 State Treaty which is the constitutional foundation of modern Austria, they are entitled to translate placenames into their own language and to have their language taught in schools in communities with large Slovene populations. These simple demands are met with fury by the German nationalists in Carinthia, under the guidance of local FPÖ bosses. Under Haider's leadership, the FPÖ has become ever more implacable in its opposition to Slovene demands, raising the spectre of Slovene links with Yugoslavia across the border. The neo-Nazi elements in the FPÖ are fiercely anti-Slav as well as antisemitic, for bigotry has an unappeasable appetite. The fact that Slav and Jewish populations form tiny minorities within

Austria doesn't seem to modify the strength of extremist feeling against them.

Haider has also been fortunate enough to inherit huge estates in Carinthia, making him one of the richest men in the province. Nothing wrong with that, except that the estate was originally acquired by his benefactor in a curious way. When, after the *Anschluss*, it became clear that Jews would be well advised to get out of Austria as fast as they could, it was common practice for Jewish landlords and landowners to be met with the following suggestion: 'Since the SS is about to confiscate all your property, why don't you sell it to me now before it's too late. Of course I can only take it off your hands at a low price, but that's going to be a lot more than the SS will give you.' By such means large chunks of property fell into the hands of scavengers. I put it to a Viennese socialist that Haider, who wasn't even born when the war ended, could hardly be blamed for the unscrupulous behaviour of the previous generation.

'Of course not,' said my friend, 'but it is surely unseemly for the leader of a political party to be enriched as a result of the exploitation of other people's desperation.'

'So what do you want him to do?'

'I'm not sure, but I think the least he could do is turn part of the estate into a holiday camp for retired National Socialists.'

Haider has also made various comments that could be construed as vaguely sympathetic to extreme right-wing, even neo-Nazi, views. Not that anyone was prepared to accuse him of being a neo-Nazi himself. He is seen by some as an opportunist, a shrewd manipulator who, more than Mock or Vranitzky, has his finger on the pulse of the people, especially in the provinces. Others see him as a puppet, the mouthpiece for strands of political and racial feeling in Austria that are unsavoury and even evil. Haider is skilled at making statements and speeches that, while overtly innocuous, carry echoes that bring joy to the hearts of neo-Nazis. Haider has the good sense to dissociate himself from some of his supporters who, in moments of ecstasy, shout 'Heil Hitler!' during FPÖ meetings, but it is significant that his election was so rapturously received by the nastier elements on the Austrian political scene.

Frau Mayr, who was proud to be a German nationalist, could scarcely restrain her glee when I spoke to her of Haider. 'Some people are antagonistic to Haider because he is very handsome and very rich.' I dare say, but there had to be more to it than that, and I decided to attend his major campaign rally in Vienna. I had already been to hear Mock address a rather modest crowd in the Stephansplatz. This had been a deeply boring occasion, with the candidate speaking in a monotone, emphatic enough but unvarying in its emphasis. He had attacked the record of the SPÖ but said little about the ÖVP's policies. 'We can't go on like this . . . new hope . . . ensure a better future for our children . . . stop the rise in unemployment . . . work for a better Austria . . .' and so forth.

Haider, interviewed in English on Austrian radio, declared that his party's policy was to reform the political system which had been structured by the two main parties. Nothing to object to there. When asked whether he was on the liberal or the far-right wing of his party, he replied cryptically that his position depended on the standpoint of the person observing him. The interviewer boldly asked whether there were many ex-Nazis in the FPÖ, to which Haider replied that the question was stupid, because you can find ex-Nazis in all Austrian political parties. The interviewer did not, alas, pursue this evasion.

The FPÖ held its largest Vienna rally in a shabby hotel on the Gürtel. When I arrived, I found a line of police politely directing latecomers to an overflow meeting around the corner, since the hall where the rally was being held was already full. Since the police were few and the latecomers many, I was able to slip through the line, murmuring 'Presse, Presse.' The hotel ballroom was filled with tables and chairs; waitresses balancing large trays on the palm of the hand like lily pads swooped between the tables bearing refreshments to the faithful, some of whom had been there for over two hours. A band played cheerful tunes such as 'Teddy the Toad' to keep us in good humour while we were waiting. The crowd was mostly middle-aged and working class, though there was a fair sprinkling of snappily dressed younger people. I had noticed, when spotting FPÖ leafletters at underground stations, that the right had recruited the highest proportion of pretty young girls. A beaming party official wandered through the hall handing out yellow roses to all the women. Flower power comes to the right two decades late.

My gaze, roving around the hall like lazy radar, rested on a familiar figure making his burly way back to his table. It was Robert, bringing a couple of beers to Marianne. I wandered over to say hello. Robert was surprised to see me there, so I muttered something about journalistic duty, but he wasn't nearly as surprised as I was to see them. I had assumed throughout our acquaintance that they would be SPÖ supporters. That my drinking and soccer companions should be active fans of the FPÖ gave me pause. Robert was slightly defensive as we spoke. Haider, he told me, was an excellent speaker and I would enjoy the evening. A wooden spoon, one of many strewn across the tables, was resting alongside Marianne's yellow rose, and I asked why. It's our campaign symbol, explained Robert; it's a spoon because we're going to stir things up.

There was no more room at their table, so I made my way back towards the front of the hall. A speaker was mounting the platform to explain the delay: at this very moment Jörg Haider was addressing an overflow audience a thousand strong in the streets outside. There was powerful applause when he ascribed the revival of the FPÖ's fortunes to their new leader. Other FPÖ candidates rose to their feet and spoke to us, but Haider's predecessor, Dr Steger, was both absent from the rally and from the speeches of his erstwhile colleagues. Haider's takeover of the FPÖ was complete. One of the Viennese candidates, Frau Partik-Pablé, spoke belligerently, distinguishing those who were genuinely unemployed from those who didn't want to work.

Some moments later a huge cheer rose from around the entrance as Jörg Haider struggled through the welcoming crowd and made his way to the platform. I couldn't help thinking, despite the vigour of his manner and speech, that to the breezy youthful Haider it must all be a game, that he was playing at running a party, pushing his charm and rhetoric and seeing how far it would carry him. He spoke well, poking fun, which was not hard to do, at the other parties, and observing that the abuse of the Parteibuch was shared by both of them. For decades now the Austrian Socialists have been known as the Reds, and the Conservatives as the Blacks, and Haider showed real sensitivity when he made a joke drawing a connection between the Blacks and apartheid. It seemed peculiarly Austrian that politicians should make comments implying some affinity, however tenuous, with racist or antisemitic views, while at the same time their cheering auditors take enormous offence because some of us beyond the borders of Austria happen to be listening.

Haider attacked the Greens on the grounds that they had not invented the notion of a better quality of life, and he spoke at length about the television debate between Mock and Vranitzky. This two-hour exercise in boring the nation had indeed been dire. Dr Mock had yapped in his excitable voice and stabbed the air with his finger, while the chancellor had seemed barely able to rouse himself to respond to the issues raised. The beneficiary of this lacklustre debate must, it seemed to me at the time, have been the FPÖ rather than the two gentlemen conducting it, and certainly Haider turned the occasion to his own advantage with panache. Again and again Haider referred to '*der kleine Mann*' whom he claimed to represent. The bland term has unfortunate overtones. Indeed, the entire controversy over Haider has to do with echoes and overtones, for he is too skilled to present his opponents with ammunition in the form of overtly extremist rhetoric. Previous champions of '*der kleine Mann*' had included Dr Karl Lueger and Herr Adolf Hitler, and Haider was clearly well aware that such allusions would not be lost on certain sections of his audience. When, a few days later, I asked Robert about his support for the FPÖ, he was at pains to tell me that Haider was no fascist (I hadn't said he was) but did speak for '*der kleine Mann*'.

On behalf of the little man, Haider attacked tax privileges that are paid for with the taxes of workers, the proliferation of bureaucrats, and excessive controls over shop hours and other aspects of daily living. He attacked waste in government. The politics of paranoia got a brief look in when Haider declaimed: 'The more we're defamed, the stronger we become.' He won a loud cheer when he said that the FPÖ was the only party prepared to accept responsibility (whatever that meant) for those former Austrians in the South Tyrol and Sudetenland. Here, at long last, was a firm declaration of German nationalist feeling. It could be made safely, since the South Tyroleans are now Italians, even though their language and culture remain largely Austrian. It is not difficult to take on burdens and responsibility for those you will never represent. Haider's declaration was thus sentimental rather than practical, but it won him some of the loudest applause of the evening.

It is one of the legacies of Dr Waldheim's weaseling evasions that it has become possible for such views, with their unsavoury subtext, to be advocated openly once more. And it is Jörg Haider's gift that he knows how to exploit currents of feeling that ought by now to be defunct. There are Austrians, and indeed Viennese, who even now perceive themselves as surrounded by hostile Slavs who threaten their Germanic superiority. The spokesman for those who feel this way is *Der Herr Karl*, the creation of Carl Merz and Helmut Qualtinger, the comic actor who first portrayed their invention on stage in 1961. Herr Karl is a typical backward-looking Viennese worker, reminiscing in thickest dialect about the old days. He is a victim of nostalgia, and the savage twist to his longing for the past is that by any rational standards the times he yearns for were far worse than the present. Karl wants a quiet life, so he can get on with the important business of drinking. He'll fit in, whether with Hitler before the war or the Russians after the war. As he shuffles about the basement of the grocery where he's supposed to be working, he reminisces and prides himself on muddling through. He talks about the bad times of high unemployment, but now he has a job he does absolutely nothing, while an apprentice boy, 'der junger Mensch', piles up the cartons around him. Playing the innocent, Herr Karl implicates himself more and more by demonstrating the kind of passivity in which evil can flourish. It was no coincidence that the Akademietheater revived Der Herr Karl during the election campaign, but the chilling comic monologue did not play to full houses.

There was another week or so to go before polling day. The political atmosphere – excitement would be too strong a word – prompted every pressure group in the city to mount a demonstration in Stephansplatz. That the European Security Conference meeting in Vienna overlapped with the election campaign was a further boon to political activists. There were demonstrations in favour of Soviet Jewry, in favour of the Sandinistas in Nicaragua, and against Biotechnology, whatever that may be. A small but noisy group with banners hoarsely demanded that the Soviet Union withdraw from Latvia, Estonia, and Lithuania: 'Was wollen wir? FREIHEIT! Wenn Wollen Wir's? YETZT!' ('What do we want? Freedom! When do we want it? Now!') A few days later music students protested in the streets that 2500 of them had only twenty practice rooms, and the following day 3000 unemployed doctors in white coats marched into the Stephansplatz chanting: 'Wir wollen arbeiten – aber sie lassen uns nicht'. ('We want to work, but they won't let us.')

And the election results? The two major parties both lost support, and the Greens, although split, attracted a large enough number of votes to give them nine seats in Parliament. Some socialist friends of mine in Vienna had dismissed my interest in Haider on the grounds that the FPÖ was electorally insignificant. 'They'll be lucky to get 5 per cent of the vote,' I was told. In the event the FPÖ won 9·7 per cent and increased its number of parliamentary seats by 50 per cent. In Vienna itself the FPÖ only increased its vote by 1·3 per cent, while the Greens picked up 6 per cent more. Certain foreign observers predictably rushed to the conclusion that the neo-Nazis were on the march once again in Austria, but it was obvious that Haider's success was largely due to the resentment felt by many voters at the complacency and indeed cynicism of the major parties. It had been perfectly obvious from the start of the campaign that no party would win a clear majority and that the outcome would be a coalition. Since the SPÖ had called the election in order to dissolve the coalition with Haider's new-look FPÖ, and since some prominent ÖVP leaders (though not Dr Mock) had categorically ruled out a coalition between themselves and the FPÖ, there was only one possible outcome: a 'Grosse Koalition' between the two major parties. This meant many more years of stability, caution, compromise, lack of reform, jobs for the boys, and the Parteibuch. Although this outcome was accepted as inevitable, many voters wanted to register a protest and this, rather than ideology, accounts for the success of the smaller parties.

It is tempting, in the light of Austria's past and the campaign waged by the loathsome Dr Waldheim, to assume the worst about the country. The truth is that Austria is a small neutral country on the fringes of Western Europe. Despite the best efforts of Bruno Kreisky and the internationalist Dr Mock, its people are almost myopically inward-looking. Although those old enough to re-member the postwar occupation remain wary about Soviet intentions in central Europe, younger Austrians feel more secure. It is arguable that Kreisky augmented the Austrians' sense of their own security by bringing various United Nations agencies to Vienna, thus diminishing the chances of any future foreign occupation. Austrians remain absurdly prickly about what they perceive as outside interference, but perhaps their history of precarious and short-lived democratic institutions offers some justification for their oversensitivity, just as Jews from other countries are justified in feeling concern when so many Austrians seem oblivious to the truth about Austria's role in the Third Reich. When Ronald Reagan, with the simple-mindedness of the simple-minded, divided the world into good and evil empires, the statement rattled many Austrians. Reagan's dogma implied that neutrality was a failure to choose between right and wrong, and such stark views, coming after American disapproval of what they perceived as Kreisky's excessively pro-Arab stand, merely strengthened Austrians' determination to go their own sweet way, regardless of what other nations thought. And this they have done, and in the process opportunist politicians such as Kurt Waldheim and Jörg Haider have flourished and festered.

14

National Slumber

The orderly blocks of the Psychiatric Hospital of the City of Vienna line the wooded slopes of a hill in the western suburb of Hütteldorf in the 14th Bezirk. Near the summit of the hill, overlooking city as well as hospital, stands an enormous domed church, the Kirche am Steinhof, one of Otto Wagner's greatest buildings. Erected between 1904 and 1907, the church is a triumphal expression of all Wagner's principal ideas, its details repeating and elaborating motifs found in many of his other buildings. As in the Post Office Savings Bank, the portal rests on pillars of a screw design, though the columns here are more elaborate and are topped with wreaths. The marble cladding that sheathes almost the entire church is decorated with copper nailheads, and the outer dome and the four immense angels over the facade are also of copper that was originally gilded. The basic design is geometric; windows are either square or round, angles are sharp. The Steinhof is, like the churches of Hawksmoor, ugly yet magnificent.

The vast interior is a single space. Slit-shaped skylights alive with stained glass are set into the roof, and the large transept windows also contain superb glass mosaics by Kolo Moser. Like the outside, the interior is mostly marble-clad, with gilt square-dotted nailhead ornament and fluting that quicken the texture of what might otherwise be an oppressively pure and rigid design. Wagner employed a battery of other Jugendstil artists to assist with the ornamentation; the most notable included the sculptors Othmar Schimkowitz and Richard Luksch and the painter Kolo Moser, though Moser lost some of his commissions after .his conversion to Protestantism. One of the commissions he was unable to execute was for the ornamentation behind the altar, which now consists of mixed-media mosaics of indifferent quality. Some of the side windows overlooking the altar contain thin panels of alabaster, an idea used to even more stunning effect decades later in the Beinecke Library at Yale, which is softly illuminated through thin marble panels rather than glass.

Walking back through the grounds of the hospital, I wondered why it had been considered necessary to design such a capacious building. I learnt that at the time the church was being erected, the hospital housed about 4000 patients, though about a third of them, in those days before routine sedation, were never allowed out. I tried to imagine the bands of worshippers, many of them severely disturbed, tramping up through the woods to Wagner's immense church. Wagner had kept them in mind too, and the functionalism demanded by the needs of patients became allied to his imaginative genius in remarkable ways. The church was oriented from north to south rather than from west to east so as to admit as much light as possible. The floors were laid with sloping white and black patterned tiles that could be easily cleaned, for some patients were liable to fits of vomiting or incontinence. Pews were designed so that patients in need of prompt medical attention could be moved without delay and with minimum distress to other patients, and rooms on either side of the altar were fitted with beds, toilets, and medical facilities. Aware that a holy water stoup could spread infection, Wagner designed a fountain instead, so that patients could dip their fingers into continuously running water.

This marvellously coherent church is increasingly a museum piece, for only about fifty patients and doctors attend the services held there, and even tourists are admitted to the church on guided tours only about once a week. For half the year, the Steinhof is too cold for services to be held. Within the church one can see the grilles through which central heating was to have been pumped, but money ran out before the system could be completed. The Steinhof is magnificent but melancholy, a mausoleum entombing its own idealism and aspirations. Built for a closed society, it cannot be adapted as that society changes. Yet to this day the vast church, lavish and loving, ministers exclusively to a city of the mad.

Vienna has always attracted such institutions. Joseph II founded an immense hospital complex in 1784, part of which still survives. The medical museum at the Josephinum gives one a striking idea of the sophistication of the anatomical arts two centuries ago. Two of the rooms are filled with photographs, busts and medals commemorating eminent men, together with photographs of boils and lesions, definitive studies of suicide by hanging (1895: illustrated with engravings of the sitting and kneeling methods), and cabinet after cabinet filled with gleaming surgical instruments, an orchestra of hack and gouge, saw and slice. The remaining two rooms contain anatomical wax models executed in Tuscany in the 1770s and brought to Vienna by order of the Emperor. Individual organs are lovingly modelled, with their veins and vessels and ventricles presented in section. On a kind of bier, a life-size waxwork of a woman has been sliced open from chin to vagina, revealing beneath her robe of skin a tumble of spaghetti around lungs and kidneys and heart, along with bulbous sacs, torn tubes, glittering surfaces and dark recesses. Her knee is slightly raised, and her hand thrown back, as though taken by surprise. There is, though it seems ghoulish, even necrophiliac to suggest it, a sexual allure in the pose, for her eyes and lips are half open, and real hair seems to have been used, both on her head and around the pubic area. (It may be a coincidence, but in Vienna's Museum of Modern Art you will find a sculpture by John de Andrea called *Woman on Bed* modelled in an equally naturalistic pose, with a comparable languor and identical tufts of pubic hair.) In the adjoining room lies the male counterpart of this ripped-open woman, and this figure, posed as though lying on his side in the park reading a book, is simply flayed from ear to toe.

Those whose diseases and infirmities the skills of the Viennese doctors could not touch ended up in the cemeteries of the city, and, from the late nineteenth century to the present day, in the vast Central Cemetery, the city of the dead that offers an eternal extension of the sense of community, of the *Gemeinde*, to those who no longer breathe. These institutional refuges, the great hospitals and cemeteries and the ubiquitous rites of the Catholic Church, offered their security in the course of a life; that Vienna has so many gives the city a strange integration. Just as the Habsburg emperors sought to unify their people, however diverse their ethnic origin, under a single dynastic claim, and just as the successor to the Monarchy, the Austrian state, cares for its citizens from cradle to grave, so too the city can direct you to the appropriate refuge in times of crisis, responding to every need. If psychoanalysis blossomed in Vienna rather than any other city in the world, it was not only because neurosis and repression flourished within the complexities of its society, so socially rigid and so intellectually fertile, but because the people were accustomed to the notions of care and cure. The favourite resorts of the vacationing classes were spas such as Bad Ischl and, closer to Vienna, Baden, which even today is a mere hour's tram ride from the heart of the city. Both these spas were patronized by the imperial house. At Baden one can still visit the former eighteenth-century bathhouse, which has now been converted into an art gallery, with paintings hung individually in what were once the changing rooms.

Freud, of course, offered an approach rather more sophisticated than the application of mud packs and dips into thermal springs,, which may have been very agreeable but did little to treat hysteria and schizophrenia. Given that Freud made such an astonishing impression on our century, irreversibly altering our notions of human motivation and sexuality, his tangible presence in the city where he lived and worked for sixty years is modest indeed. Half a century lapsed between his final departure from Vienna and the Austrians' decision to honour Freud by placing his features on the new 50-Schilling note. In 1891 the young doctor moved into a flat on the mezzanine of 19 Berggasse, and there he remained until he left Vienna for good in 1938. With fourteen rooms it sounds large and spacious, but none of them is especially large, and the impression is of a maze of interconnecting spaces. Freud's consulting rooms have been converted into a small museum, mostly consisting of an exhaustive display of photographs and documents. Of course Freud took most of his possessions to London, where they now furnish a second Freud Museum, but many items, including the ancient figurines and books and some furnishings, have been loaned by the Hampstead custodians to their opposite numbers in Vienna.

Visitors are expected to be attentive and thorough. Over 400 items are listed, and each visitor is handed a catalogue in a language of choice, and briefly instructed on the order in which the items are to be viewed. It would be an act of *lèse majesté* to fail to spend more than an hour in the museum, even though it consists of only three small rooms. I left, as I was surely intended to do, with my respect and awe for Freud's achievement enhanced. The museum can do little to increase our understanding or assessment of his work, but it does round out our grasp of Freud the man: the family man, the aspiring doctor, the jealous guardian of his disciples, the breadth of his cultural interest. Even the father of psychoanalysis had, we learn, to pay his respects to his Emperor. In 1902 Freud was finally awarded the professorship that had been denied him for far too long. A few months later – and this was seven years after *Studies on Hysteria* and two years after the *Interpretation of Dreams* were published – the great doctor was obliged to go down to the Hofburg to thank Franz Josef for the great honour that had been conferred upon him years after it was due. Freud wryly commented in a letter: 'Congratulations and bouquets keep pouring in, as if the role of sexuality had been suddenly recognized by His Majesty, the interpretation of dreams confirmed by the Council of Ministers, and the necessity of the psychoanalytic therapy of hysteria carried by a two-thirds majority in Parliament.'

It has often been said that Freud developed his theories in Vienna because social conditions among its middle classes encouraged the repressions and neuroses and hysteria that his theories uncovered and his therapies attempted to treat. This may well be so, and even today there is an oppressive quality to the city than can suddenly come swooping down. On many an evening, walking back from the outer suburbs to the Stephansplatz, I would tramp through street after street of compact blank-facaded municipal apartment blocks before reaching the more elaborate blocks in authentic baroque or pastiche historicist styles. Dim yellow lights the colour of mottled parchment would press against the double windows of a few rooms, and there might be some activity around the entrance to a Lokal on the corner and in the distance a car door might slam. The streets would be empty and the home-loving citizens bundled up in their small hot flats watching a dubbed episode of *Dynasty*. I never felt threatened as I strolled late at night but there were times when I felt I had never walked down streets so grey and dim and buttoned-up. At such moments the warmth of the city, its *Gemütlichkeit*, the conviviality of the Heurigen and the cosiness of the coffeehouses, could seem utterly remote.

The sheer orderliness of Vienna could be oppressive too. Even the punks are immaculate, with not a safety pin or leather thong out of place; one lovely girl on the train, her hair dyed blue and elegantly pointed on either side of her ears and chin, wore a galleon-full of rings and necklaces and brooches, all set off stylishly against her black blouse. There is a clothes shop on the Mariahilferstrasse called Yuppie, but only in Vienna have I encountered Yuppie punks. One morning on a streetcar I sat near a snotty little boy and his parents. After another round of unappetizing snuffles, his mother handed him a handkerchief and

told him to blow his nose: '*Aber mach's ordentlich!*' ('Do it nicely!')
Jay-walking, a useful touchstone of attitudes towards authority, is
uncommon, and, worse, foreign residents of Vienna tell me they
have been rebuked in the streets by fearsome old ladies for such
transgressions as crossing the street against the lights, walking on
the grass where forbidden to do so, and allowing their children to
walk along with their coat buttons undone.

The Viennese have only a limited notion of casualness. They
dress not only for the opera and theatre, but also take immense care
over their appearance when going for a stroll or streetcar ride. On
the tram I would find myself sitting across from a pair of old ladies –
it sometimes seemed as though the old lady were a Viennese
invention – dressed as if in uniform. In cooler weather, each would
be wearing a fur or cloth coat (often beige) buttoned tightly to the
neck; any gap remaining between coat and flesh would be bunged
with a scarf tucked tightly behind the buttons. Footwear consisted
of boots, or fur-lined bootees during more clement weather. Heads
would be covered with a beret or Tyrolean hat with feather. With
legs slightly parted, the old ladies would fold their hands over their
handbags and sit impassively until they reached their stop. They
never closed their eyes, but were quietly watchful, and steadfastly
refused to communicate with other passengers. I grew to dislike the
sight of these grim tight-lipped women and their equally inexpres-
sive but more bewildered husbands.

Their immobility seemed like a physical reflection of a static
quality in Viennese life that must be stifling to more radical spirits.
The sheer comfort of Vienna – the flawless public transportation,
the network of affordable places to eat and drink, the safety, the
compactness – militate against change. The energies of the
Viennese are devoted to pleasure; the boundaries are rarely
stretched. A student at the university told me regretfully that
Austria had fallen asleep. Even Vienna University, in her experience, is a somnolent place, though unless you travel to study at
other intellectual centres in Europe or America, you don't even
realize it. One is never challenged in Austria, she felt; all is safe and
comfortable. Thus there was no reason for Austrians to develop any
flexibility or adaptability. Struggle is unnecessary. Austria is like a
deep armchair, so cushioned and enclosing that it scarcely seems
worth the effort to rise from it.

Culturally, Austria lives in the past. It is not only a question of
Verdi at the opera, Lessing at the theatre, and Schubert evenings at
the Musikverein, for cultural institutions in most cities tend to

draw from the glories of the past rather than respond to the stirrings of the avant-garde. Rather it is that the entire sense of the city, its self-perception, is wedded to the past. The ball season still thrives in the winter months, with almost every professional group in the city – doctors, lawyers, whatever – holding its own ball, in addition to the grand social events such as the Opera Ball and the Philharmonic Ball. Walking through the inner suburbs you will pass dancing schools every couple of hundred yards, for participation in the balls is not restricted to the wealthy, and knowing how to glide through a waltz or quickstep is almost a *sine qua non* for Viennese adolescents.

Every Thursday afternoon in the elegant café of the Imperial Hotel, brilliant with chandeliers, a small ladies' orchestra, dressed in long skirts and boaters, fiddles unsmilingly for the delight of a small audience as they tuck into pastries and cream. Of course such entertainments are laid on to meet the expectations of tourists, but by no means all of the patrons were visitors to the city, and there was a solid brigade of *Loden*-clad Viennese. And once a month at the lovely Café Dommayer at Hietzing, a similar band (perhaps even the same one), the Damensalonorchester (Wiener Walzmädchen), duplicates the entertainment at the Imperial.

If the Viennese seem more comfortable at reworking the past than at reshaping the present, it is no doubt partly the result of the insecurities of the past. After both wars there was severe devaluation, and many Austrians lost all their money as well as their property. Before the Second World War the Austrians even lost their nation, though it has to be said that this absorption into the Third Reich was warmly welcomed in many circles. Older people in particular have strong memories of the years of occupation, when many of them suffered extreme deprivation; prostitution as well as poverty was rampant. The animals in the Lainzer Tiergarten were slaughtered to provide food. Photographs taken during those years by Ernst Haas record with shocking vividness the suffering many Viennese endured long after the war ended. With such memories and the fears that spring from them, caution and stability have become the supreme values. They are not to be sniffed at: coalition governments, political neutrality, excellent industrial relations, and a docile press have brought the country to an enviable degree of prosperity and a sophisticated level of social security.

And if there is a price to be paid, if the Viennese, for all their *Gemütlichkeit*, are smug and self-regarding, thickly and fearfully bourgeois, content to repeat the cultural certainties – Strauss waltzes on New Year's Day, the ball season, dressing up for the opera, pastries from Demel's – and uneasy about any radical or progressive movements, well, it is hard for outsiders to condemn the Austrian desire to play safe. The shrunken nation, shorn of a role in the world and under Kurt Waldheim shorn even of respect for its much proclaimed civilized values, is also unable to compete against its own opulent artistic and cultural heritage. Far better to settle for the languid and the comfortable, the tried and tested. Vienna once drove out the likes of Mahler and Freud; now it seems indifferent to the probability that the city will never again generate the intellectual vigour needed to produce men and women of that stature. In Joseph Roth's novel *Die Kapuzinergruft* (*The Emperors Tomb*), set in 1913, one of the characters remarks with a prophetic force that still seems appropriate: 'Austria's essence is not to be central, but peripheral.'

BUDAPEST

For the Hungarians were first and last only Hungarians, and counted only incidentally, among people who did not understand their language, as also Austro-Hungarians. The Austrians, on the other hand, were primarily nothing at all, and in the view of those in power were supposed to feel themselves equally Austro-Hungarians and Austrian-Hungarians – for there was not even a proper word for it. And there was no such thing as Austria either. The two parts, Hungary and Austria, matched each other like a red-white-and-green jacket and black-and-yellow trousers. The jacket was an article in its own right; but the trousers were the remains of a no longer existent black-and-yellow suit, the jacket of which had been unpicked in the year 1867. The Austrian trousers since then were officially known as 'The kingdoms and lands represented in the Council of the Imperial Realm', which naturally meant nothing at all, being a name made up of names.

Robert Musil, *The Man Without Qualities*, chapter 98

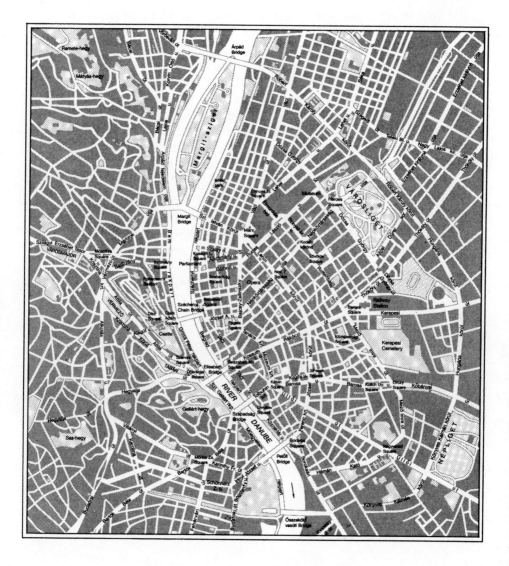

15

Made in Britain

First impressions matter. And my first exposure to Budapest could scarcely have been more promising. I took the airport bus into the centre of Pest, the commercial side of the twinned cities, and then took a taxi to the Hilton, where I was staying for a few nights until I had found longer-term private accommodation. The taxi sped towards Buda across the Chain Bridge, and then zigzagged up the side of the very steep Castle Hill. Dusk had fallen rapidly. There was snow on the ground, and as we reached the plateau of the hill, where a few old streets spread like antlers along the ridge, the dim yellow streetlights shone pallidly down onto the white mounds which, heaped along the sides of the road, both cushioned and feebly reflected the soft light. It was cold and the streets were deserted. The taxi pulled up outside the hotel, which is in the heart of the old district, and my luggage, shadowed by myself, was whisked into the warm cavern of the lobby and thence to a room overlooking the glinting Danube a couple of hundred feet below.

After I'd unpacked, I took a walk along those same yellow-lit streets to see whether my initial impression had been correct. It had indeed. I had unknowingly deposited myself in one of the few corners of Budapest that one can without hesitation call charming. Castle Hill is a conservation area, and since the last war many of the old houses – and most of them are at least two hundred years old – were thoroughly restored and in some cases virtually rebuilt. The result is spectacular, and entirely convincing. Whole streets, such as Úri utca, which runs like a gently bent bow across the ridge of the hill, are lined with splendid patrician houses, mostly baroque: entered through powerful stone gateways, they are more modest cousins of the monumental Hercules-flanked portals of Viennese palaces. Pediments, that prominent calling card of the neoclassical style, are finely carved, and some of the grander houses are dented with niches within which statues of nameless saints or ancestors pose flamboyantly. Many windows are guarded with ironwork grilles, elaborately turned and curved so as to give them a gracefulness that masks their defensive function. Many of the houses are more ancient than their facades, and the next day, on strolling into the now open gateways, I would often see, along either side of a passage leading through a house into the courtyard behind, a row of Gothic arches or sedilia. The next day would also reveal the gentle pastel colouring of the houses, a posy of lime, mustard, salmon, olive, and ochre. The diplomatic community has understandably snapped up some of the houses, while those on a more imposing scale, such as the Erdödy Palace, have been converted into museums. Even by day the streets were peaceful, for Castle Hill is out of bounds to traffic, apart from buses, taxis, and the cars of local residents.

At night lamps glow outside the entrances to the handful of restaurants and wine cellars on Castle Hill. These cater very much to the tourist trade – understandably so, given how pretty and romantic their interiors are – but are priced accordingly. In the less imposing little restaurant where I ate, I was the only customer, for in February the tourists tend to be Russians and East Europeans, and they are tucked away each evening in less ritzy parts of the city. Returning to my room, I stared out over the river and the city of Pest on the opposite bank. Directly below me were the mock-Romanesque turrets and platforms of the Fishermen's Bastion, a touch of nineteenth-century nonsense that has now become one of the symbols of the city. Its seven towers are supposed to allude to the seven tribes that originally founded the city of Buda, but I was struck instead by a resemblance – in a hideously debased form – to the terraces and towers of the great Mughal palaces around Agra. One of the turrets has now been converted into a discotheque and from my window I could see some heavily wrapped couples treading gingerly along the icy paths. By day organized groups of tourists climb up and around the Bastion, devising a dossier of photo opportunities.

My own first glimpse of the city by day was less romantic than by night, for a heavy mist crouched along the river and I could see no further than the first bend. The Danube itself was thick with ice floes, massive grey chips that surged downstream. The ice clotted the river, of course, but its rapid downstream flow gave visible evidence of the power of the water, its relentless churn through the city. Far more than in Vienna, the Danube defines the city, which it curves through as sinuously as a hand stroking a woman from neck to thigh. The Thames in London or the Seine in Paris also snake through their cities, but since those cities are essentially flat the river plays a small role in their self-presentation. The rivers are observed at their moment of passing and their fading into the distance, but from the Buda hills the Danube can be surveyed as it sweeps through the city, steady, implacable.

The charm and beauty of Castle Hill are an anomaly. The rest of Budapest resembles it not at all. The other Buda hills are either parkland or terraces of villas and brand-new apartment complexes of an almost Mediterranean elegance. Pest, however, is utterly flat, a Parisian city of squares and boulevards. There are baroque churches on both sides of the river, and charming relics of the Turkish occupation – mostly bathhouses – in Buda, but Pest in particular is a nineteenth-century city. Hefty apartment blocks and office buildings line the boulevards, a legacy from the days when the grain trade brought prosperity to the city. Although tremendous efforts have clearly been made to restore Castle Hill – and how splendid the photographs look on the tourist brochures, and what a false impression they give of Budapest – the rest of the city, especially its commercial centre, is coated with the grime of decades. In winter the thundering buses, with which the city is copiously supplied, and the putting, chugging Trabants and Wartburgs spew out filthy blue smoke. The pollution is thick and pungent, and I suspect that even were the boulevards of Pest to be scrubbed and renovated, exhaust fumes would undo the good work in a matter of years. There were times on Kossuth utca and Rákóczi út, the main drag that leads from the Elisabeth Bridge to the main Keleti railway station, when I was reminded of London in the 1950s, when fogs were still common and a pall of grime seemed to smear the whole city.

Despite the risk of asphyxiation I found it worthwhile to peer upwards from time to time at these palaces of commerce, for they celebrate an era that is long gone. After 1867, when the establishment of the Dual Monarchy gave the Hungarians a considerable degree of self-government, Budapest enjoyed a period of extraordinary commercial expansion. In just a couple of decades it became a prosperous sophisticated city – the Parisian example of Haussmann was not lost on city planners and architects in Budapest – exuding a brashness and vulgarity almost as exuberant as anything found along Broadway or in the Victorian City of London. Buildings that were essentially mundane in their structure and layout – offices and department stores – were topped with complex superstructures, motif piled upon motif, eclecticism rampant. It's easy to scoff at the vulgarity of it all, but at least these commercial boulevards display a vigour and energy that have not been recaptured in a more decorous but monolithic twentieth century.

There was nothing parochial about Budapest by the end of the last century. Despite Franz Josef's concessions to Magyar nationalism, German was spoken as much as Hungarian, and old photographs show shop signs either printed in both languages or, quite frequently, in German alone. Coffeehouses were just as pivotal to social life in Budapest as in Vienna. Insularity, whether commercial or cultural, did not go hand in hand with nationalist fervour. In Roosevelt tér (square), facing the Chain Bridge, is a monumental office block built in a very debased Jugendstil style, with lilies and peacocks ornamenting its grand iron gateway. What these motifs have to do with life assurance is lost on me, but a closer look at the inscriptions on either side of the entrance reveals that the block was built in 1906 by the Gresham Life Assurance Company of London. The Chain Bridge itself, and the tunnel beneath Castle Hill to which it leads, are also British imports, for they were constructed in the 1840s by the Scottish engineer Adam Clark. Indeed, the small plaza between river and tunnel is named Clark Adám tér (in Hungary the order of names is reversed) in his honour. The bridge was the first to link Buda and Pest and the joining of the cities stimulated municipal adminstration as well as commercial development.

Far more distinguished than the Gresham Building is the National Savings Bank along Münnich Ferenc utca, with its interior of tinted glass walls, its vaguely Jugendstil marble staircase and its imposing brass doors. And as lovely an example of Jugendstil as one can find in central Europe is tucked inside the flower shop along Budapest's most stylish shopping street, Váci utca. Budapesters are well aware that their city was once one of the most cosmopolitan and dynamic in Europe, and conscious attempts are being made to reclaim at least some of that glory. Western goods are widely available at the Váci utca shops and boutiques, and when the smartly designed Adidas shop opened there in February 1987, long queues formed outside and were topped up all day long. It is one of the attractive features of Budapest that long queues are practically unheard of, except when, as on this occasion, the latest flavour in consumer goods suddenly becomes available.

The eclecticism of Pest is seen at its best along boulevards such as Üllői út, where heavy nineteenth-century neoclassical buildings jostle against vaguely Art Deco apartment blocks surmounted with a golden eagle. As in Vienna, the blandest facade may conceal a lovely and tranquil courtyard, and so it is along Üllői út too. Dominating the boulevard is the neo-Byzantine monstrosity of the Applied Arts Museum, an eyesore redeemed by its spacious interior, which has two levels of whitewashed Moorish-style arcades and a glass roof reminiscent of one of Paxton's constructions. Along Népköztársaság útja, which, despite its unpronounceable name, is the city's principal boulevard, leading to the vast space of the museum-lined Heroes' Square, are historicist buildings more reminiscent of Vienna. Here stand the Opera and other theatres, slightly diminished versions of Viennese Ringstrasse architecture, while up near Heroes' Square, and thus about a mile from the commercial centre of Pest, are scores of stately villas set in small gardens. Unlike the balconied villas and chalets of Buda, which are unashamedly suburban in conception, those along Népköztársaság and adjoining streets such as Dósza György út are clearly town houses, imposing and impenetrable. Also close to the Heroes' Square is Hungary's own version of Disneyland. Set in a pleasant park, Vajdahunyad Castle is like a stone catalogue of different architectural styles – Transylvanian turrets, Romanesque chapel, baroque portico – all cobbled together to form an eminently silly but undoubtedly picturesque building. Its romance, however, is best appreciated from afar, for the real thing becomes increasingly crude and unconvincing as one approaches its walls. The principal wing contains a museum of agriculture and hunting, which is more absorbing than it sounds.

Despite decades of social levelling, I was surprised by how easy it was to read Budapest in terms of its demography. Journeying into the southern suburbs towards Csepel Island, it was perfectly obvious that I was in an overwhelmingly working-class district. On the other side of the river, walking along the steep streets of Gellért Hill past flamboyant nineteenth-century villas and small elegant apartment houses, it was correspondingly obvious from the architecture, as well as from the cars imported from West Germany parked outside, that I was among the professional classes. An apartment close to the city centre is as prized in Budapest as it is in Paris or London, and only foreigners and very prosperous Hungarians can afford to live in one of the exquisite medieval or baroque houses on Castle Hill. The nouveau riche of Budapest favour the curving streets of Roszadomb (Rose Hill) and the other Buda hills now dotted with villas and gleaming, glass-fronted apartment blocks. Some of those blocks are built against slopes so steep that, as in the Hollywood canyons, street access is to the top floor, while the rest of the house lies on floors below, propped against the hillside.

After a few days of luxury in the Hilton it was time for me to move into the city. The Hilton itself, though only ten years old, was a controversial building. Just a few yards from the historic Matthias Church, it occupied one of the prime sites on Castle Hill. Opposition had been strident when the plans were drawn up, but although the river-facing front has a bland monumentality quite out of keeping with the neo-Gothic spires of the Matthias Church and the fussy turrets of the Fishermen's Bastion directly in front of the hotel, the facade facing Hess András tér is a delight, incorporated as it is into the late seventeenth-century baroque façade of a former Jesuit college built by the Austrian architect Hildebrandt. Within the hotel precincts is an even more precious relic: the ruined nave and cloister of the thirteenth-century Dominican church. In summer, concerts ring out among the ruins, but now the flagstones were covered in snow.

I had no trouble finding private accommodation in a small block close to the exit from Adam Clark's tunnel. It was no different from countless other such apartment blocks in the city. The stucco was peeling away to reveal brickwork beneath, the stairways were barren and dirty and the window panes overlooking the courtyard were broken and jagged. Powdery mortar whitened the tiles of the entrance hall, and there was a smell of damp and decay around the rubbish bins. Yet this was no slum dwelling. The interiors of the flats I saw in this building and many others like it were snug and comfortable. Since flat-dwellers have no financial interest in the building they occupy, there is no reason for them to spend good money on carpeting the stairs and replacing broken windows, when that same sum is good for a new dishwasher or redecorated bedroom.

In the Antals' flat the windows were double-glazed to keep out the roar of the buses emerging from the tunnel below. My room was packed with furniture: a large bed and a day couch, two wardrobes and a desk, and it was reached through a living room. This was never used and formed a buffer zone between landlord and lodger. A symmetrically arranged suite of armchairs filled about an acre, and complexes of shelving carried row upon row of books. Glass sliding doors kept unused crystal dust-free. An enormous television impaled on a stand gawped like a mouth. The large floral carpets were vacuumed regularly as though in honour of guests that never came, and one morning Mr Antal took proud delivery of a new easy chair that nobody ever sat in. The Antals themselves lived in their kitchen, which adjoined their own bedroom. We had little contact, which suited us all, and whenever out paths did cross, we simply beamed at each other or exchanged a polite '*Guten Tag*'.

I soon began to explore my new neighbourhood, which differed considerably from the spick-and-span restorations of Castle Hill, even though from my lodgings on Alagút it was no more than a ten-minute climb up to the Matthias Church. Adjoining my building was the dingy Alagút Büfé. Like most cafés and small restaurants in Budapest, its windows were heavily curtained to ensure that the interior remained gloomy even on the sunniest of days. The display area between curtain and window was filled with a kind of gingham backdrop, dried flowers in vases, and bottles of domestic Vermouth on pedestals. None of this suggested that the Büfé was one of the city's more enticing establishments, an impression confirmed after I strode in one lunchtime. Apart from a few pickles on a counter, I saw little evidence of food being consumed, and far too much of beer being guzzled, and I walked right out again.

Next door stood a small but well-stocked florist. I have never seen a city with so many florists. Indeed, just fifty yards up the road and close to the bus stop flourished another flower shop, equally well stocked. And even on a winter's day it was delightful to pass the open-air flower market along Fehérvári út. Adjacent to the florist's was an equally well-stocked greengrocer's, but the tone dropped next door, where lingerie was sold; its window display reminded me of the truss shops, now I hope a thing of the past, that used to give the Charing Cross Road much of its aura of sleaze. On a nearby corner stood a video rental shop, which serves some of the 200,000 owners of video recorders. This remains an expensive form of entertainment, since daily rental fees for a cassette are ten times the price of a cinema ticket.

Just beyond the bus stop a large Eszpresso faced Krisztina tér. It was divided into two rooms, one containing apparatus for making somewhat diluted coffee and a glass cabinet filled with not very appetizing open sandwiches and pastries. The other room was a salon, where the clientele could linger over their refreshments at small tables covered with yellow cloths, the only cheerful note in the place. Its salmony marble floor was so dirty I at first took it for linoleum; the wallpaper, an unbecoming beige in colour, was imprinted with sketches of unrecognizable plants. The salon was partitioned by iron hatracks and by simple frames with square panels filled with geometric straw and with cacti in curved iron potholders. The ubiquitous long net curtains flopped onto the low sills, curdling the natural light so that the room relied for its brightness on two rows of bulbs cupped within white glass shades; all the fittings hung loose from the ceiling. Here, by eight-thirty most mornings, misty-eyed men and women of all ages were ordering their second beer since dawn, while they exhaled cigarette smoke through their noses and stared dolefully at the net curtains. It was not an inspiring start to the day, and just my bad luck that I happened to live very close to one of the few repellent Eszpressos in Budapest.

I liked my neighbourhood best late at night. Once, returning from a late-night film screening, I missed the last bus and had to walk back through the maze of streets between Alkotás utca and Attila út. Through the February mist, a mushroom of white and yellow light was falling from streetlamps over the sleeping cars, some of which were wrapped in tarpaulins to aid their hibernation. It had been a wet day and overflowing gutters had turned one cobbled street into an urban version of a trout stream, all gurgle and glitter. The few cars and taxis still on the road at that hour would splash past at an excessive speed, given the twists and ruts of the surface. The windows of the flats above the shops were fastened shut against the damp and the cold, but the double doors opening into the entrance passages of the apartment buildings were still open and illuminated with the pallid light of under-powered bulbs that plucked from the darkness the rounded forms of rubbish bins standing in a row. Here and there net curtains were parted to reveal a chandelier suspended from a high ceiling or a mighty wooden bookcase. These interiors were solid and warm; slightly fuggy, I imagined, and made piquant yet familiar by cooking smells and the aroma of old dogs. My intrusive gaze would drop from those lit windows to the wet street below, gleaming as though doused by a film crew. If there were such characters as the Third Man nowadays, they would not, I suspected, inhabit the glum but no longer sinister streets of Vienna, but would emerge from a doorway right here, before my eyes. But nothing stirred, and I wandered home to Alagút, to my own cosy interior, blustery with the noise of the gas fire, and as solemn and comforting as the dictionaries and encyclopedias that filled the bookcases.

16

A Whole Lada Trouble

What is one to make of a country where the word for bookshop is
könyvesbolt, and the word for fruit *gyümölcsük*? And where any
attempt to take a girl home must be preceded by seductively
whispering, '*Hazakisérhetem*'? Philologists observe that the Hungarian language is akin to Finnish, but fluent Finnish speakers
should not dash to Budapest in the expectation of understanding
or of being understood, for although the two languages share some
syntactical structures, my Hungarian friends assure me they can't
understand a word of Finnish. No, Hungarian is *sui generis*, a
language of bewildering difficulty, heavy with suffixes that,
because of an impenetrable principle known as vowel harmony,
are modified according to the vowel sounds of the root word to
which the suffix is appended.

I soon gave up. To be sure, I could order a cup of coffee, even two
or three, in Hungarian, and thank the waitress once she had
brought my order, but even the standard greetings began to slip
from the mind an hour after I'd emerged from my morning dip into
the phrasebook. Hardly surprising, when the word for goodbye is
Viszontlátásra. I found this deeply frustrating, not merely because I like to communicate with fellow human beings, but
because I am an inveterate eavesdropper. What's the use of a
private conversation that cannot be overheard? Why buy a
newspaper when it's so easy to read over someone else's shoulder?
In Budapest none of this was possible. Hungarians have a highly
developed sense of hilarity – a single peal of laughter can take ten
to fifteen seconds – and it was vexing to be surrounded by
merriment without having the vaguest notion of what was
prompting it. When I found myself in a coffee bar a yard away
from a gypsy couple being belligerently interrogated by plain-
clothes policemen, I would have given much to have been able to

understand what was happening. A short gypsy woman, probably no more than thirty-five but looking far older thanks to a complexion like burnt omelette and a lack of teeth, was stumbling about importuning customers, some of whom were reacting with extreme disgust. One man had to be restrained by a friend as he kept pushing away the ugly little woman. But I couldn't follow what was being said and had to content myself with enjoying the rich music of the language, its *dy*, its *ok* and *tek*, its *hey* and *hogy*, its *ush* and its *ersh*.

Since I had a few other languages at my disposal, I could negotiate my way around the city easily enough, and I spent many a damp afternoon riding bus and tram through centre and suburb. The city has a superb bus system, slow and express, but both reliable. Cheap too. My monthly city-wide travel pass cost me 170 forints, £2.50 or $4 at current rates of exchange. The people of Budapest do complain about the bus system, but then they complain about everything. 'Complaining,' the novelist György Konrád told me, 'is a way of life here. It's routine to criticize the way things are, though not to analyze why they are that way. Complaining is a strategy for survival, an expression of the gap between expectation and awareness.'

The bus drivers complained too, for a shortage of drivers meant that work shifts were being increased to up to twelve hours a day. So desperate were the authorities that they even advertised on television for new drivers. The transportation bosses were well aware that it was easy for disaffected bus drivers to hand in their cap and badge and make much more money driving a taxi. Given the difficulties under which the system laboured, I found it worked remarkably well, as did the somewhat skeletal subway network. The number 1 subway line, which runs the length of Népköztársaság, dates, I was repeatedly informed, from 1896 and is thus the oldest subway line in Europe. Its rickety wooden carriages retain a quaint charm, though their capacity for accommodating passengers is clearly inadequate in a city of two million. One of its stops was right beneath the Opera House, and after an evening at *La Bohème* it was delightful to step out of one period piece and into another.

Budapesters also like to complain about their phone system, which indeed operated haphazardly. Sometimes a friend calling me from half a mile away would sound as if he were speaking to me from within the eye of a Siberian blizzard. That the system functioned in a somewhat random manner I soon learnt to live with. At least it had no pretensions to being modern and efficient. Budapest has a limited exchange capacity and a lack of cables, and you can't expect perfection. There are entire suburbs where a telephone line is a rarity, though, as in every other aspect of Hungarian life, if you want something badly enough, you can get it. In such districts, a phone can be yours for 25,000 forints – equivalent to four months' pay. Telephonically, Budapest is probably better off than the rest of the country, as I was later to discover when visiting a series of wineries throughout Hungary. Unexpected snowstorms and unploughed roads meant that I fell many hours, and eventually an entire day, behind schedule. So I asked the winery near Badacson to inform its counterpart in Pécs that I would be very late indeed. My contact informed me that this would not be possible, since there was no direct phone link between the two parts of the country. The good news, however, is that the World Bank is coming to the rescue and a new digital system will, one of these days, be installed.

Many Budapesters were surprisingly appreciative of the television programmes they were offered, though inevitably the more serious programmes, including debates on economic issues and social policy, were usually shown late at night. There are no soap operas – the Ewings have not become weekly guests in Hungarian households yet – though the radio does feature the chronicle of the Szabó family. The series is thoroughly up-to-date, since one of the Szabó kids has recently died from glue-sniffing. A sizable chunk of time, between programmes rather than during them, is given over to advertisements. I occasionally sat through five minutes of local Perl and Din, trumpeting the merits of Malév (the national airline), the City Grill, make-up, Wrangler jeans, and an ad for the Crazy Cabaret to the distinctively Habsburg tune of the Radetzky March and illustrated with naked ladies.

No Hungarian, especially one who has travelled to other parts of Eastern Europe, could conceivably complain about the food. The shops are well stocked, and good quality meat and fish are readily available. A visit to the huge covered market at Dimitrov tér is a revelation to those who assume that all Eastern Europe is a land of unmoving queues and perpetual shortages. Since I was visiting the city in February, some of the fruits and vegetables were looking a little tired. I found bruised and shrivelled apples neatly boxed into trays, the elegance of presentation only highlighting the antiquity of the produce. Parsnips were long and spindly and woody, carrots as ungainly as dildoes, sprouts and pumpkins dry and crinkly. The most attractive stalls were those selling peppers. Masses of cherry-red and yellow paprika pods, strung into wreaths and other elaborations, were hanging from the beams and walls framing the stalls, while on trays below were scattered hundreds of shiny pale green sweet peppers. Beans and nuts and herbs were abundantly available, and in a far corner of the market a few stalls specialized in whole goose livers. Not cheap, of course, at 900 forints, but probably a tenth of the price you would have to pay in a Périgord town square. The market is spacious enough to accommodate bakeries, clothes shops, sausage and *lángos* stands, peasants behind trestle tables selling locally produced honeys and jams and orchids boxed in transparent plastic. I bought some *lángos*, a lump of pale dough that is slung into hot fat, where it writhes until golden and dimpled; in the mouth it is soft, juicy, and delicious, a kind of *extrem* doughnut that regrettably leaves a nasty oily taste in the mouth, no doubt an honest reflection of the nasty oil in which it attained its succulence.

The fish stands were splendid, if brutal. Carp, mostly, were crammed into large tanks and pools, hundreds of them, scale to scale and fin to fin, until liberated by the swift dip of a skilfully wielded net. Still gasping, the scooped-out fish are whisked into plastic bags, weighed, and handed to stout kerchiefed shoppers. It was not wise to stare for too long at the fish, for the tanks were right alongside one of the main avenues through the market, and every two minutes there would be a clatter of wheels and a snarl of foul language as porters would race through, pushing trolleys loaded with pig carcases or boxes of fruit. The porters seemed perfectly capable of treating your feet as part of the floor if necessary.

There were times, even in February, when it seemed as though all the main streets of Pest were a giant marketplace. In Moszkva tér, where half the trams of the city halt or at least chug through, gypsy women stood clutching small posies of flowers, proferring them to commuters. Near an exit to the subway station at Kossuth utca, a woman sold hot corn on the cob, as yellow as the daffodils peddled by gypsy women nearby. More surprisingly, along Váci utca, men and women in heavy peasant garb – kerchiefs and long flower-patterned dresses – held up embroideries and clothing in the feeble hope of persuading chic Budapest shoppers to buy them. Similar offerings were to be found in the underground concourses at major subway stations. These peddlers were not all gypsies, but often Poles and other migrants from Eastern Europe, who, denied more forints because of restrictive currency regulations, were selling decorative embroideries and other craftware at a loss in order to procure more local currency which would enable them to prolong their stay in bountiful Hungary. Such peddling is frowned upon by the authorities, and at the first glimpse of the law, the Poles would pack up their wares in a matter of seconds and be bounding up the steps into the concealing flurry of the open streets.

More unofficial trading takes place in markets far from the city centre. Early one Saturday morning I took a succession of buses and trams to Ecseri piac, a flea market on the edge of the city. The tram passed through grim industrial suburbs, where derelict and weed-ridden rail tracks lead only onto rubbish-strewn acres, and grubby brick warehouses are surrounded by broken glass. There followed a suburban district of small one-storey houses, tightly packed, painted in flat ochre and russet colours, some incomplete. I had no difficulty working out when to leave the tram, for almost all the passengers, most of whom were clutching well-stuffed bags, dismounted at the same stop and crossed a modest motorway to the market entrance. Just inside the gates traders had spread cloths and blankets over the lingering snow; the goods for sale included old, and empty, Scotch and Rioja bottles, unmatched shoes, bags of nails, broken toys. Chilled, I made for the buffet, where I slurped hot coffee while gypsy women knocked back apricot brandy at the counter in full view of the nude calendars. In the permanent halls of the market you can find transistor components, drill segments, tools of all kinds, furniture, chandeliers, carpets, furs, jeans, denim jackets, disco music cassettes, and spare parts from cars including tyres and an artistically arranged row of suspended exhausts. Out in the open air the tables were decked with secondhand clothes, soft porn magazines from Germany, ceramics, rusty knives. Most of the indoor traders looked as institutionalized as a loud-mouthed brass merchant on Portobello Road on a Saturday morning, but the outdoor peddlers tended to be gypsies, tightly bundled into heavy overcoats, their hair parted down the middle and smoothed beneath headscarves. At Ecseri, anything goes, and the police were conspicuous by their absence. I heard of, but never witnessed, Russian soldiers who come to Ecseri to sell the uniforms off their backs.

The flower sellers and the *lángos* and sausage stands kept the street life lively, but the Hungarians have other ways of entertaining those who enjoy a stroll through their city. I know of no other city where car crashes are so spectacular and so bloodless. Near my local bus stop, two cars, including a costly Mercedes, bounced off each other so skilfully that they left a gap between them large enough for the traffic, admittedly reduced to a single lane, to pass between them while the drivers hurled abuse at each other. Moreover, the impeccable siting of the accident allowed an entire bus queue to be diverted on a frosty morning. Near the overpass at Hegyalja I watched with awe as a tremendously gifted driver swerved screechingly to avoid another car. Instead he hit a traffic light, knocking it over, and caused an old lady in a mauve coat to jump for her life. The car that had caused the accident in the first place headed for the sunset, leaving the driver of the bashed-in Lada no alternative but to scream murderously at the old lady in the mauve coat. How we all laughed!

The Hungarians looked at me in astonishment when I remarked on the awfulness of their driving. On the contrary, they assured me, they were excellent drivers. Indeed they were, except when they hit another car. I must remark in their favour that their numerous accidents sprang more, it seemed, from high spirits and an irrepressible adventurousness than from excessive speed or drunkenness or other traditional methods of reducing a few thousand pounds' worth of metal to scrap. Viennese drivers in Budapest – of which there were many, since favourable exchange rates enable the Austrians to lord it over their less affluent neighbours – tended to be belligerent and inconsiderate, and many were the times when I emitted a stream of Hungarian viciousness as a BMW with Viennese plates shot the lights and missed my toes by the width of a *würstel*. 'Könyvesbolt! Gyümölcsük! Gyöngyös!'

Considering how difficult and costly it is to get one's hands on a car in Hungary, one would imagine that the coveted objects would be treated with more respect. A new Lada 1500 costs about 170,000 forints (more than two years' average salary) and you may have to wait five years for the privilege of owning this piece of junk, which is widely regarded as the best car you can buy in Hungary. I rented a new Lada for a week and by the end of it felt fully qualified as a tank driver. Moreover, the car shuddered to a halt on a snowy lane in western Hungary, and if I hadn't been giving a ride to a pair of Hungarians who were able to summon spanner-bearing colleagues, I would no doubt still be sitting there. A Lada also consumes more fuel than a Porsche. On ordering your car, you must make a down payment of 50 per cent, but the balance, payable on receiving the car, is calculated at 50 per cent of the delivery price, which after five years is bound to be higher than the purchase price. If you are unwilling to wait so long for delivery, it is possible to buy a car more promptly on the black market, but the price will be double the already exorbitant official price. It is not permitted to sell a car until it is three years old, and if you acquire a secondhand car on the black market you may then be stuck with the vendor's registration papers, which can cause problems if, as is extremely probable, you are ever involved in an accident. Budapest is full of foreign cars – Mercedes and Volkswagens are popular – acquired by the many Hungarians who work abroad for a year or two and import a foreign car despite the heavy duty payable on such transactions.

If Korea can produce snazzy and economical cars, there would seem to be no reason why the Soviet Union and the Eastern Bloc can't do likewise. Yet the design of the Lada has remained unaltered since 1964, when the licence was purchased from Fiat, and the unspeakable Trabant is based on a forty-year-old design. The fibre-glass Trabant is the cheapest car on the market at 85,000 forints but is probably even worse value than the Lada. Romanian Dacias are so badly made that some purchasers take the cars to a specialist mechanic: for 20,000 forints he will take the car apart and rebuild it in the correct order. Some years ago, I gathered, Honda offered to build a car plant in Hungary in exchange for Hungarian uranium. The government said no, both because the Russians wanted to keep their hands on Hungarian uranium, and, of course, because the other Eastern Bloc countries that manufacture cars wanted no competition from Honda. The Japanese thought they were doing the Hungarians a favour when they offered to sell the cars for less than the East European cars. They forgot that the last thing those manufacturers want is efficient competition. For decades now they have been exploiting what is in effect a network of monopolies to ensure that demand outstrips supply, thus ensuring that Lada et al. can sell at extortionate prices as many of the lousy cars as they can produce.

A friend in Budapest once drove to Scotland in his Trabant. As the horrible little car chugged into petrol stations, he would be greeted with looks of disbelief and remarks such as: 'Oh, did you build this yourself?'

17

Canucopia

From my room at the Hilton, with its panoramic view onto Pest, and then from my wonderfully convenient rented room on Alagút, I could rapidly build on my first favourable impression of the city. I was leading the life of a boulevardier, strolling through the streets and stopping frequently for coffee, pastry, or a glass of Tokay. With Benetton and Adidas factories humming away within Hungary itself, not to mention the many boutiques in Budapest, it was not surprising that many Budapesters were as well dressed as their counterparts in Western cities. Some young men favoured trousers identical to those worn by prosperous Germans of the same age, loose-fitting and charcoal-coloured and Pollocked with paler flecks. Some girls made touching attempts at a punk style: grubby clothes, patched jeans, and a denim jacket with stitched-on Union Jacks or CND patches and the names of favourite groups such as Iron Maiden crudely stencilled onto the back. Here and there a half-hearted safety pin would jut from knee or elbow. The rest of the women of Budapest, young or old, were more conservatively dressed and impeccably coiffed. Hairdressers are as ubiquitous as florists, and most salons are open from six in the morning until eight or nine in the evening, so as to give office workers the greatest possible opportunity to whip the thatch into shape in readiness for dinner or date, funeral or assignation. One morning I allowed a scrupulous and attentive scissor-bearer to trim my locks, which she did for 30 forints. I knew there would be hell to pay when I returned to London and had to confront my usual barber, Philip of Ormonde Yard. ('Sorry about deserting you, but the hair was getting too long. Budapest handiwork. Not very good, is it?' 'Since you ask my opinion, no, it isn't. It's bloody awful.')

But as I gradually got to know more Budapest residents, a

different picture wobbled into focus. Despite the apparent prosperity of the city, its plush suburban villas, its beautifully dressed young women, the Hungarian economy was reaching crisis point. Its foreign debt is the highest in the Eastern Bloc, and the programme of economic reform pursued by Kádár has increased expectations as well as the standard of living. Yet for some time Hungarians as a nation have been living beyond their means, as the government is well aware, and the bonanza cannot continue indefinitely. With growing trade deficits and inflation at 9.5 per cent by 1987, drastic action was inevitable. In March 1987 the export director of a small enterprise told me that huge increases in the price of basic commodities would come into effect by late spring; he was spot on, and rises of up to 30 per cent were announced in June.

There is a huge discrepancy between salaries earned and actual incomes. Hungarian salaries are low, on average 6000 forints per month, and most workers seem to have second and even third jobs. (On the other hand, 5 per cent of the employed earn ten times the average, so differentials are considerable – and being permitted to grow wider.) Moonlighting is a way of life, and it's estimated that three-quarters of all employed Hungarians have second jobs. The habit first took hold in the countryside, when labourers on collective and other state-owned farms would get up at 4 a.m. to tend the private plots where they grow, and sometimes sell, fruit and vegetables. Because in the 1950s Marxist ideology lifted skilled workers to the peak of the social pyramid, professional people, tainted with suspected bourgeois tendencies, were less well paid. The Marxist ideology is admitted to be more or less bankrupt in modern Hungary, but professional workers and technicians remain poorly paid. One woman told me her son-in-law plays in one of the country's top orchestras and earns 4400 per month. Engineers, teachers, and doctors also survive on low salaries, on which it is impossible to make ends meet. I heard about an opera chorus singer whose daily routine was not atypical: he rehearses each morning, does odd jobs in the afternoon, performs in the evening, and is a night watchman during the small hours. The official justification for low salaries used to be that social services and housing and education were all virtually free, but that too has changed. State-owned housing is almost impossible to obtain, and many families must spend a large proportion of their incomes on finding and keeping a roof over their heads.

The authorities acknowledge that most employees are obliged to take second jobs and frequently work on their secondary jobs during some of the hours when they are supposed to be working on the primary one. The consequence of this, inevitably, is that many primary jobs are inadequately done. Inefficiency and maladministration are rife within state enterprises, which still dominate the economy, but everybody's mind is on more lucrative forms of employment pursued elsewhere. An architect told me that he'd been employed on designing many buildings and projects over the years, yet not a single one had come to fruition.

Many Hungarians complain not so much about the long hours they find themselves working – without them they could not afford their villas and cars and leather blousons and Barbie dolls – but the stress the system places on their personal lives. The divorce rate is very high. 'I have a second job,' one woman told me, 'because although I can survive on one income, I cannot afford to go to the cinema or theatre or buy books on my salary alone. So I have another job, but I also have no more time to go to the theatre or read the books I buy.'

While I was in Budapest I attended the screenings of new Hungarian films at the film festival, and was surprised by how closely most films reflected the current preoccupations of the people. János Rósza's *Love, Mother* paints a satirical yet convincing portrait of an upwardly mobile Budapest family. They live in a villa in the Buda hills, of course, and although the house is unfinished – shortages of building materials, don't you know – the family has already moved in. It is filled with gadgetry – sophisticated alarm clocks and coffee makers and microwaves – which enables each member of the family to rise each morning at a different time. Consequently they never see each other. The children wish to consult their father about various matters, but he never has the time, is always rushing out of the door – but, we soon gather, he has time enough to cavort with his mistress. The principal means of communication between the members of the family is through notes left on the refrigerator door – hence the film's title. The ten-year-old son has been playing truant for three weeks, but no one has noticed.

The film takes a more serious turn when we learn that a grandmother is seriously ill. No one except the daughter has the time to visit her, and she dies. The daughter, desperately seeking to draw attention to the appalling state of her own family, attempts suicide. The father at last acknowledges that his family is on the verge of disintegration, and institutes a Family Day once a week, when, with painful awkwardness, they sit around on their unfinished terrace and try to talk to each other. As the film ends, it is quite clear that this solution is makeshift and that within days everyone will have reverted to their earlier patterns of behaviour. *Love, Mother* is a very funny film, but it is also a deft recognition of a very common state of affairs. By striving for a material success that is, after decades of austerity, at last within their grasp, Hungarians are in danger of neglecting the other values that make life precious.

Despite the industriousness of the people, the economy remains stagnant. The trade deficit in 1986 was $400 million, and Hungary's total foreign debt is over $14 billion. Hungarian economists now predict that by 1989 92 per cent of all export earnings will have to be squandered on servicing these debts. The expectations of the resourceful Hungarians have risen far faster than the ability of the economy to meet them. After the failed revolution of 1956, the regime felt that the best way to restore calm was by providing higher living standards. This it has achieved, but the result is that Hungary is living well beyond its means. Underinvestment in industry has been a problem, as it has in many other Eastern Bloc countries, and former export markets, such as Algeria and Nigeria, have just about collapsed. Some Hungarian economists look longingly at the EEC as they are convinced that Hungary suffers from its exclusion from the club. The club which Hungary is a member of, Eastern Europe's Comecon, is sometimes described as seven thin cows milking each other. Hungary's dependence on trade became strikingly evident after the Chernobyl disaster; for a month no foodstuffs could be exported and the consequences were worrying, though official figures claim that the loss to the economy was a mere $20 million. The official line from the Chamber of Commerce is that Hungary has potentially impressive exports in the form of energy, buses, medical instruments, fashion, and machine tools, even though there is room for improvement within manufacturing industry as a whole. Tourism too provides additional foreign earnings.

Other observers with no ties to the government take a less confident view. A leading dissident told me: 'The American government used to guarantee the loans Hungary took from US banks. It won't do so any longer, and we have to look to Japan and Italy for fresh loans. Drought and Chernobyl have damaged our exports. The state enterprises can probably weather the storm, but there are a lot of smallholders left in Hungary and they can't absorb the losses so easily. There's plenty of talk about new industries, but the problem is that our infrastructure is so outdated. Investing in sophisticated computer technology is a splendid idea, but unfortunately our phone system is so antiquated that the new technology can't operate efficiently by using it. What worries me is that all the signs indicate that Hungary is drifting towards Third World status.'

On a personal level, the jauntiness of most Hungarians conceals the difficulties encountered every time a major decision is to be made. Finding somewhere to live can be a nightmarish business. Although there is a great deal of state-owned housing, flats mostly, it seems virtually impossible to gain access to it, and the government would clearly prefer to hand over the business of housing its people to cooperatives and the free market. Moreover, the waiting lists for municipal housing are so long it can be five or ten years before anything becomes available, unless you are in a position to take advantage of the burgeoning black market in such flats. In the meantime a young couple must live with parents or in shared flats in a dingy part of the city. (This is offered as another explanation for the high divorce rates. Even after a couple divorce, they often cannot afford to go their own ways and must continue to live in the same flat for years, separated by flimsy partitions.) Since the going rate for a flat in fashionable Buda is 25,000–30,000 forints per square metre, though the same patch of living space may only cost half that in a suburb of Pest, the cost of purchasing is extremely high, since an average salary is only about 75,000 forints per year.

Consequently, would-be homeowners must take out hefty loans, and they will also require a cash down payment which may take a couple many years to save up. Loans, whether from the National Savings Bank or from an employer, are cheap enough, and often free of any interest. Nevertheless buying a reasonably sized flat for a million forints can commit a purchaser to repayments of about 6000 forints per month, equivalent to one person's salary. Of course those who were lucky enough to obtain loans fifteen or twenty years ago find themselves with much lower repayments. One professional couple I met complained to me that their rent had doubled over the past four years, but they have the good fortune to live in a spacious, high-ceilinged flat in a central part of Buda, and despite the increases in rent their monthly repayments are no more than 960 forints, which, in relation to their income, is peanuts.

Some Budapesters are more lucky. They may have inherited a flat – and rented municipally owned flats may be inherited as well as privately purchased property – or married someone who also inherited some property, which can be traded in for something quite grand, a villa in Buda, say, costing anything from four million forints upwards. Others take advantage of some of the wheezes the city council has devised to ease the problem. Many elderly people live alone, often in quite spacious flats, since the rest of their family is either dead or dispersed. The council introduced a scheme whereby young couples could move in with a solitary elderly person, subject to that person's contractual consent. The couple undertake to look after the aged one – shopping, cleaning, making sure it takes its medicine, and so forth – and after the death of the pensioner are rewarded with the flat. A couple who had acquired their flat in just this manner told me it had been a most unpleasant arrangement, since death was the hinge on which the whole arrangement swung. A frail seventy-year-old can often keep the undertaker at bay for a further twenty years – senile, perhaps, but alive – and the frustration of the couple can increase unbearably as they find themselves nearing their own pensionable ages while they're still spooning apple pap into a twitching old mouth. There are, apparently, few abuses of an eminently abusable system, since neighbours are instructed to report any evidence of mistreatment; if complaints prove justified, the contract can be annulled.

Many Hungarians feel that although they are told that their salaries remain low because of the splendid free provisions of the social security system, such assertions carry less and less conviction. Not only must they mortgage themselves up to the hilt for the next century in order to afford a flat, but even medical services must be paid for. The medical system is, of course, notionally free. If you are seriously ill or injured, you will be well taken care of, agreed most Hungarians I spoke to, but at the level of routine operations or the treatment of chronic diseases the system functions poorly. There is also a shortage of nurses and evidence of poor administration at many hospitals – complaints that are doubtless made of every hospital thoughout the world. Doctors and dentists are poorly paid and supplement their incomes by giving private treatments for which they of course receive additional payments. What is unusual about the Hungarian system of health care is the prevalence of tipping. A tip to a doctor who had decanted a baby into the world might once have been a spontaneous expression of gratitude on the part of beaming parents. Nowadays, however, it is customary to tip the doctor before the operation rather than after. The going rate for a delivery is between 2000 and 3000 forints. The practice is, of course, illegal, but that does not prevent it from being endemic, for there is a widespread feeling, probably not without some justification, that unless you make a special claim on a doctor's attention by greasing his or her palm, you may well be neglected at your time of greatest need.

An engineer with whom I was discussing the matter said: 'In my view it's against human nature to get something for nothing. Tipping is an oil that greases the machinery. Because all our social services are centralized, the people whom they are supposed to serve have no say or influence over how they are run. Without tips the system would be even more sluggish.' In this argument there did seem to be a fuzzing of the distinction between a tip and a bribe. Tips, or bribes, are also essential for making shortages, like tough stains, disappear. You may find yourself tiling the patio of your little house in Buda, when all of a sudden the building materials depot runs out of tiles. The rapid production of some forints in notes of a high denomination will almost certainly ensure that the manager will make that extra special effort to locate a further supply in the weeks ahead.

Already beset by grave problems, both in the economy of the nation and the economy of the family, there is much talk of how to deal with them. I had supposed that poor economic performance might jeopardize the programme of reform that, pursued over the last twenty years, has transformed Hungary into the least regimented and most relaxed of the Eastern Bloc countries. Hungarians shrug off Mikhail Gorbachev's talk of *perestroika* (restructuring) with justifiable smugness, since the reforms he has been urging on his own people have been commonplace in Hungary for the past two decades. Although more hard-line states such as Czechoslovakia and East Germany claim that their economy is doing splendidly without reform, there seem to be no politicians in Hungary who wish to turn the clock back to that extent. Arguments rage not about whether to continue the programme of economic reforms, but about the pace and exact nature and emphasis of those reforms. In 1986 a two-tier banking system was introduced, two foreign banks were allowed to open branches in Hungary, and companies in need of capital may issue bonds at attractive interest rates. In general, the regime has shifted the emphasis in controlling the economy from centralized *diktat* to a system of credits and profits related to the performance of different sectors. The new prime minister, Károly Grosz, allows such words as 'entrepreneur' to pass his lips. Income tax and value added tax were introduced in 1988 and other reforms will continue the decentralization of the economy and the tightening of monetary controls.

Although these moves towards a more market-oriented economy suggest that the Hungarians are adopting Thatcherite remedies for their economic woes, there are limits even to the Hungarians' wide-ranging thinking on these matters. In official circles, at any rate, there remains a concensus that the primary means of production will remain collectively owned. There is no way, at least not in the forseeable future, that the Ikarus bus factory will be privatized, even though it seems probable that restrictions on private enterprises in Hungary will be further eased. At present, no more than twelve people may be employed in, say, a privately owned restaurant or car repair workshop; that number could well be increased before long to fifty. (About 200,000 people work for private firms, mostly in the service or construction sectors.) Nor is it clear to what extent the regime can afford, politically, to acknowledge the existence of unemployment, even though it is increasingly reluctant to use the profits of successful enterprises to prop up the unsuccessful ones. Officially, there is no such thing as unemployment; but the new laws on bankruptcy will speed the closure of unprofitable enterprises. Should a company shut down, the affected workers will receive handouts from the government for up to six months, but this is regarded as a period of 'retraining' rather than dole. It has been calculated that if all unprofitable state enterprises were to be closed, 350,000 men and women would be out of work, a sizable proportion of the workforce in a country with a population of just over 10 million.

There is also an ideological objection to excessive (in the eyes of the regime) economic pluralism. If companies have greater freedom of action and manoeuvre, unfettered by meddling centralized control, if state subsidies (which swallowed one third of the 1986 budget) are increasingly withdrawn from unprofitable enterprises, then the logic of such reforms is that the people should be able to invest in this newly fledged market economy. At present you must be a practical participant in any venture in which you wish to invest. Government economists now contemplate intro-

156

ducing forms of stock ownership that will supplement the present system of corporate and municipal bond ownership. Once you have achieved economic pluralism, and Hungary is moving slowly but steadily in that direction, then the next demand, inevitably, will be for political pluralism – and that is another matter entirely.

18

Thermal Lunch

The Hungarians, discounting Budapest's earlier incarnation as a Roman city, believe that their capital was founded as a Magyar city in the year 896 by King Árpád. That date, or part of it, is kept bubbling in Magyar consciousness by the deliberate decision made in the last century to build both the dome over the Parliament Buildings and the one over the vast and pompous St Stephen's Basilica to a height of ninety-six metres. The House of Árpád established its court at Esztergom, north of Budapest, which remains important not only for its medieval ruins but as the primary archbishopric of Hungary. Gradually the court was transferred to the castle at Buda, and Pest too began to be settled more vigorously. King Matthias Corvinus, who died in 1490, brought a cultural sophistication to the city, just as the Bohemian king Charles IV had done to Prague a century earlier. Matthias' achievements were to crumble away thirty years later, as the Turks began their assault on the Hungarian lands, which in those times extended eastwards into Transylvania. The Budapesters had to suffer the indignity of an occupation which began in 1541 and continued until the end of the next century.

The Turks left their mark on the country. In Pécs two great mosques are still standing, and in Budapest their legacy takes the form of the tomb of Gul Baba and numerous bathhouses. The cliffs of Buda are studded with hot springs. The Király baths on Fő utca, with their cupolas surmounted with Turkish crescents, are the most picturesque and have been in continuous use since 1570, as have the men-only Rudas Baths near Gellért Hill. My acquaintances in Budapest were none of them aficionados of therapeutic bathhouses, and on hearing that I wished to visit one, recommended that I avoid the old Turkish establishments, where the hygiene was questionable, and sample instead the more modern baths at the Thermal Hotel. This new hotel stands on Margaret Island, a long flat reefer that lies in the centre of the Danube, its two ends touched by bridges linking it to Buda and Pest. The entire island is given over to pedestrians and their recreation, to sports facilities and restaurants and cafés – and to therapeutic springs. Few of these facilities were being used, since there was two inches of snow on the ground, though I did see some intrepid joggers plunging through the slush and mud.

I walked through the large and largely empty lobby of the hotel, through its coffee room, and into an area of tiles and women in white coats. I was handed a large thin cotton sheet and the key to a walk-in cubicle. After I'd changed into my swimming trunks, I stepped through the foot pools into a large hall. The walls were lined with lurid tiles the colour of Seville oranges and immense picture windows looking out onto the snowy woods around the hotel. There were two main pools – one lukewarm, the other hot – as well as subsidiary pools equipped with various torturers' surplus stock such as pulleys and neck clamps. Depending on the mineral properties of the water, different treatments are recommended at different establishments. Specialists in such matters are known, in Hungary at any rate, as balneologists, and trained personnel are available for consultation at all the principal thermal springs throughout the country. Hypochondriacal visitors to the Gellért Hotel, to which some of the most spectacular baths are attached, frequently undertake a two-week course of treatment. At the Thermal Hotel you will find not only a squad of balneologists but an X-ray laboratory and a dental department, much beloved by Austrians, who come to Budapest both to shop and to get their teeth fixed at rates far below those they would have to pay at home.

I lowered myself into each pool in turn, mindful of the notices declaring that it was unwise to remain in either for more than twenty minutes or so at a time. As I floated in the sumptuously warm water I gazed around me, at the amputees and obese men and women in the water and at the bodies laid out on mattresses by the poolside. One person lay beneath a yellow sheet, entirely concealed, and it was impossible to avoid the speculation that this might be a corpse, pickled by a surfeit of chlorides and sulphates, mud packs and underwater jet massages. The more I lingered, the more I hated the place. The baths were a repository of aches and pains and malaises. It hadn't sufficiently occurred to me that thermal bathing is only partially seen as recreational in Hungary, but is also taken very seriously as a form of therapy by the very ill. A sense of squeamishness grew on me, as I realized I was sharing the waters with, for the most part, the diseased, and when I emerged from the water I felt far from cleansed.

I enjoyed myself more at the Gellért baths, which were opened in 1918, though the management claims that the ten springs here have been tapped for two thousand years. These baths were constructed on the grandest scale, and the main hall, which gives access to the various pools and treatment areas, is large enough to double occasionally as a ballroom for the adjoining hotel. The men's baths are located at one end, the women's at the other, and between the two is a lovely pillared and balconied swimming pool for use by both sexes. As at most of the bathhouses, many different services are available: steam baths, mud packs, underwater massage, and a mysterious treatment called CO2 fog. A full round of treatment – dips in the thermal pools, lolling in the steam room, and a massage – takes about two hours, and after that pummelling the clients are required to rest for a while before emerging. I skipped the bathing and physical assault but did wander into the men's section, where I met the cook of the Gellért Hotel wrapped in a towel and sweating off a few pounds. Back in the main hall I joined the dozens of old folk, who, their health-giving exertions over for the day, were queueing up for a mid-morning snack at the buffet, which does a roaring trade. Those who do not have easy access to thermal springs can drink the waters rather than sit in them. Hunyadi János, for example, must be swigged before breakfast if the desired effect of a 'single drastic purgation' is to be achieved. In Jósef Nádor tér a shop is devoted exclusively to the sale of mineral water.

Of course it's not hard to see why such purgative treatments are in heavy demand throughout Hungary. Everybody eats so much, and in order to savour the Hungarian experience to the full, I joined in. I soon discovered Ruszwurm. This tiny café is easily overlooked, tucked away in a side street on Castle Hill. For me it was the best in town. Its pale green banquettes and delicate chairs, its furnishings and glass cabinets full of dolls and other such knick-knackery are a relic of Biedermeier tastes and its atmosphere one of Biedermeier intimacy. The coffee is as good and strong as any in Budapest and the pastries both delectable and inexpensive, even by Hungarian standards. Ruszwurm is marred by sour though efficient service – I resented not being recognized after drinking coffee there almost every day for a month – and occasional invasions by groups far too large to be accommodated in a room considerably smaller than most people's living room. One morning a dozen Russians wrapped in fake furs came charging in, and a few of them, forgetful of Mr Gorbachev's anti-alcoholism campaign, skipped the coffee and ordered Tokay instead.

The most famous coffeehouse in Budapest is Gerbeaud, a palatial suite of three salons filling one side of Vörösmarty tér. In the 1940s the name was changed from Gerbeaud to that of the square (named, I was informed, after a singularly dreary nineteenth-century poet), but the populace paid no attention whatsoever and so the name was officially changed back again. The coffeehouse is stately and comfortable, large enough so that one can nurse a cup of somewhat dilute espresso for an hour or more at one of the green marble tables. The pastries are excellent, though twice the price of Ruszwurm's, and on Sunday mornings the counters are thronged with elegant women buying a trayful of goodies to take home for lunch or tea parties. Buying a take-away pastry requires saintly patience, for you must queue first to select your sweetmeats, then again to pay for them, and then once more to wait for them to be wrapped and handed over – a sequence that rarely takes less than ten minutes.

Since Gerbeaud is in the heart of Pest, close to the international hotels, it is always packed with tourists. I preferred to loiter at some of the other coffeehouses under the same management, such as Különlegességi on Népköztársaság, and Művész on the same boulevard. Művész is just across the street from the opera house, which I found convenient, and I enjoyed the spaciousness of its tall back room with its gilt rococo ceiling and panelled walls. Különlegességi has a gaunt ground-floor room scarcely more attractive than a railway buffet, but up on the mezzanine is a much prettier if somewhat dingy cream and gold room. I used to come here for the delicious chestnut cakes – but only when I had a good half hour to spare, since the service is dilatory. Not all the cafés of Pest are on this grand Viennese scale. Some reminded me of the Soho coffee bars where I wasted many evenings as a teenager. One, along the boulevard called Bajcsy-Zsilinszky út, showed nonstop rock music videos on a screen above the counter, a seamless procession by Dire Straits, Elton John, and Queen, a group that had won the hearts of Budapest some months before at a vast concert heard by 200,000 people packed into a sports stadium.

There is, of course, one major difference between the coffee-houses of Vienna and those of Budapest. There are no newspapers available at the latter. Visitors who read no Hungarian can buy at kiosks the official paper *The Daily News*, published in both English and German; it provides a reasonable coverage of international news, as well as tedious commentaries on Hungarian political developments and the state visits of African chieftains and Mongolian trade delegations. There is no difficulty obtaining Western newspapers in Budapest at any of the international hotels, and I knew Hungarians who subscribed to the London *Observer* until they could no longer afford to do so.

After my mid-morning coffee and pastry I might visit a museum or take a stroll until lunchtime. Luncheon is a major meal, as it is throughout Europe, only in Hungary it is matched by a meal of comparable bulk at dinnertime. I avoided hotels, restaurants and tourist haunts, though I did make one foray into the famous Mátyás Pince in Pest, close to the Elisabeth Bridge. This cellar restaurant has two large rooms. In one of them you are in constant danger of being coated in honey by gypsy musicians, who play ancient Hungarian melodies such as 'If I Was a Rich Man', 'Never on Sunday' and 'Zorba's Song'. I opted for the musicless room, where I sat in a comfortable and secluded booth. I knew I was in a tourist joint when the waiter brought me salad instead of *sholet*, a most tasty bean smush that would accompany perfectly the roast duck I had ordered. He had assumed that, as a foreigner, I couldn't possibly mean *sholet* when I said *sholet* and must therefore mean *shalad*. Moreover the markup on wine was fourfold, which is excessive.

I had a better time at the more rustic Margitkert in Buda, where to the accompaniment of music performed by a band who gratifyingly failed to molest me as I ate, I ordered pork stuffed with goose liver. I turned up late in the evening, and although the restaurant was still full, mostly with the kind of cigar-puffing Austrians who wouldn't be seen dead in anything smaller than a Mercedes Million or its equivalent from the BMW stable, the waiters had little to do and one of them came over for a chat. I had noticed that the walls were decorated with the signed photographs of dignitaries, mostly politicians, who had eaten at Margitkert: Willi Brandt was shaking a hand, portly Helmut Kohl was beaming from jowl to jowl, and François Mitterrand was doing his best to look regal.

'No picture of Mrs Thatcher, I see,' I remarked to the waiter. 'She was in Budapest about a year ago. Didn't she eat here?'

'No,' he scowled, and added with what seemed complete

seriousness 'She only eats yogurt and tea, and we don't serve them.'

'Quite right. *Galuska* and goose liver would be wasted on that woman.'

'Hey, you heard this one? What's the difference between the United States and England?'

'Gosh, you've got me. What *is* the difference between the United States and England?'

'Well, America has Ronald Reagan, Bob Hope, and Johnny Cash.' Pause. 'England has Lady Thatcher, no Hope and no Cash.'

There was no repartee at the Kárpátia, a spacious restaurant in downtown Pest, divided like the Mátyás Pince into a gypsy music zone, and a room where it was possible to talk or read. As a state-run restaurant, the Kárpátia offered smooth efficient service but made no conspicuous effort to please. That didn't bother me, since I was content with the excellence of the food, the fair prices, and the privacy. Here the booths were tall and high, and the gaudily painted pseudo-Gothic vaults and the thrones on which we sat and the lofty wooden partitions between the booths gave the room a resemblance to a cluttered sacristy. There were the usual raised eyebrows when I ordered a whole bottle of wine with dinner, but the waiter couldn't know that this was my first sip of the day, while the majority of Budapesters had been knocking back the *palinka* and beer since dawn. The Kárpátia also dispensed with the irritating habit of putting the sign 'FOGLALT' (Reserved) on every table as a matter of course, so as to convince diners that the restaurant was the most fashionable spot in Budapest, when the truth was more likely to be that on a winter's night they were lucky to fill ten tables in the course of the evening.

I tried some of the small private restaurants in town. These offer food that is a far cry from the hearty but heavy cuisine of my other haunts. As the discreet Szindbád, a cellar restaurant hidden away off Bajcsy-Zsilinszky in a street where the city ambulances are parked overnight, I could eat by candlelight at large round tables decked with immaculate white linen. The kitchens produced dishes that were idiosyncratic, tasty, and occasionally disastrous. The pork fillet stuffed with chicken livers and served with barley and green noodles in a cream sauce left me reeling, but there were more delicate dishes such as a game soup spiked with lemon and tarragon and ingenious fruit flans. The Szindbád attracted an elegant clientele, both foreign and native. It was here that I overheard a young Hungarian woman, clad entirely in designer

163

denim, telling her escort how she'd answered an ad placed by a rich Buda man seeking marriage: 'If he has a Mercedes, I'll marry him. If a Lada, no.' She smiled sweetly, and with a firm nod of her forefinger flicked the ash from her cigarette.

For true European sophistication, at true West European prices, there was nowhere to match Legrádi's, a pretty cellar restaurant, its tables laid with fine linen and expensive glassware. The service was so attentive that the waiter opened a second bottle of wine before my guest and I had finished the first, thus enabling the manager to charge me for both, even though I hadn't been consulted about the second. The food was splendid, as indeed it should have been at prices that would give me pause even in a London restaurant: we sampled a selection of fine pâtés, leg of venison in a rich lemony sauce, and quails cooked with sprouts (better than it sounds). The gypsy violinist smarmed over and asked me whether I had a special request for the charming lady at my table. I resisted the temptation to say 'Silence', left the choice up to him, and then handed over a few dollars. When the meal was over and it was time to pay the bill, I protested at the various and ingenious ways in which it had been padded. For instance, when I 'order something the menu calls a Grand Marnier soufflé, I don't expect to pay a hefty extra sum for the liqueur. The manager shrugged shyly and I paid up.

I never again went to Legrádi's, but stuck to the cosy neighbourhood restaurants where the service might be less smooth and the cooking less clever, but at least no one cheated me. I dined repeatedly at the söröző (beer tavern) on Maros utca, which served cheap and generous portions of well cooked food, and washed them down with good Czech beer, while an accordionist tootled and wheezed in a far corner. Or I'd take the bus up the Fillér utca in a chic part of Buda and dine at Kikelet, which resembled a cabin in the woods. The food wasn't brilliant, but the cheerful check tablecloths, the relaxed service, and the indefatigable fingerwork of a very old man at his accordion added up to a pleasant evening. The old man, who'd apparently played here each night for decades, had the cockiness of someone who could never be fired; he enjoyed poking quiet fun at the diners, who, myself apart, were all Hungarians and able to respond wittily, it seemed, to his taunts.

But the best of these places was Kis Pipa in Pest, an extremely popular and unpretentious restaurant. There was no sultry lighting or fancy linen – just a large split-level room packed with as many tables as could conceivably be crammed into the space. About a hundred people could be accommodated at one sitting, and Kis Pipa was a great favourite with groups that could well have been office outings, ten or fifteen people of all ages, eating at speed and then prolonging the evening over dozens of beers and bottles of red wine. It was a marvellous place to pig out, as a four-course menu featuring game would cost a mere 130 forints (£2). The service was slow, but when you're enjoying yourself so thoroughly, who cares?

Indeed it was this capacity for enjoyment that I so relished about the Budapesters. The economy may be in a perilous state, everyone may have to work twelve hours a day to make ends meet, there are harsh restrictions on freedom of expression and movement, but for all that life is to be enjoyed, and anyone who has sat, as I did repeatedly, in Kis Pipa and listened to the roar of conversation and the shrieks and howls of uncontrollable laughter, can't help suspecting that the Hungarians know better than most how to squeeze every conceivable pleasure from their lives. This *joie de vivre* is not, as I was to sense later in Prague, a passive recognition that since the political life of the nation is so thwarted the citizens may as well console themselves with material satisfactions and rewards for their hard work; in Budapest it struck me as an inextinguishable attitude, an inability rather than a refusal to be cowed. Hungarians, immensely vain as they are, like to portray themselves as a people of volcanic energy and charm. Six weeks in the country persuaded me that the Hungarians are just that.

One frosty morning I tried to board a crowded bus. By the time I got my foot on the step the bus was full, so I retreated. A woman ahead of me, seeing me step back, shouted at me, as did one or two other people on the bus. Their gestures made it clear that they were urging me not to give up so easily. I hurled myself towards them, they obligingly squeezed up, and I slid into the bus just as the doors were closing. They beamed at me, glad I hadn't given up after all, and as we bumped across the Chain Bridge I found myself being simultaneously beamed at and squinted at by a man with a glass eye. The Viennese would have kept me off the bus, in Prague nobody would have cared one way or another, but in Budapest my half-heartedness was clearly interpreted as a failure of character that had to be corrected by the community.

19

Send in the Crowns

On some wintry days the mist and the exhaust fumes drove me out of the city centre. Trams took me down the Danube shore to the hilly southern suburb of Budafok, where it seemed as though modest village houses had been lifted over the fields and dumped along either side of the steep streets, complete with chicken runs, vegetable patches, and rows of vines. Many Budapesters also own allotments just outside the city, where they grow fruit and vegetables for their families and may also spend occasional weekends in small cabins.

One morning I took the fast HEV train south to the working-class suburb of Csepel. It seems odd to speak of working-class districts in a country where in theory class distinctions have been eradicated, but this is so patently not the case in Hungary that the tag remains descriptive. The HEV chugged past stockpiles of coal, logs, and new cars – so many of them, indeed, that I wondered why it was necessary to maintain a five-year waiting list for new cars. From the HEV I transferred to a bus that passed through valleys between high-rise blocks on either side. Beyond the deadening high-rises lies a huge district of mostly one-storey houses behind wooden or metal fences. The boxy houses are stuccoed and decorated with two or more bands of earthy colours, ochres and russets and buffs, a cheerless form of ornamentation. As in Budafok, vegetable gardens and vines are common. Some buildings had new storeys added, many incomplete. Because it is so difficult for young couples to find their own accommodation, many parents obligingly build extensions to their homes to make room for their immobilized offspring. The side streets giving access to the acres of little houses were unpaved, and since the blanketing snow was now beginning to thaw at long last, the lanes resembled finger lakes more than streets.

At the end of the line I took a short stroll before returning to the bus stop. Behind some railings rose mounds of cigarette butts. Since smoking is not permitted on the buses, and most Hungarians would faint dead away if they couldn't have a fresh cigarette in their mouths once every ten minutes, I often saw dozens of still lit cigarettes being tossed aside as passengers prepared to board the bus. The small heated missiles had burrowed their way into the snow piles, which, melting now, were gradually exposing to view their unappetizing contents. Back in the centre of Csepel I wandered into a large restaurant for lunch. There was hardly anybody there apart from a few men sipping beer. I asked for the menu, but instead received a three-course meal and a half litre of beer. While spooning my soup, I heard a crescendo of chatter from the entrance as dozens of children aged between eight and thirteen raced into the restaurant, flicked their satchels off their shoulders and arranged themselves at the tables. With grim efficiency the waiter brought the children their lunch, a meal identical to the one I was eating. They were charming kids, and gifted too, for they all spoke fluent Hungarian, and I tried not to envy them a meal better than anything I was ever served in school at their age. I still shudder to recall the formidable headmaster's wife at Hereward House School standing over me while I refused to eat the slab of fatty corned beef on my plate, or the lumpy custard that followed; when her threats grew too dire to bear, I would take some of that stuff into my mouth and retch. But here were nine-year-olds tucking into their pork in paprika sauce with *galuska* (small dumplings) as if they had every right to be properly fed.

Another day I travelled up to Óbuda, just north of Buda and the site of the Roman garrison town of Aquincum, which flourished until the fifth century. Part of the attraction of the site may well have been the presence of hot springs, which provided the drearily practical Romans with central heating. Much of the Roman town has been excavated, and one can visit the forum and two large amphitheatres. Unfortunately Óbuda has been wrecked by insensitive urban redevelopment, alternatively known as razing the place to the ground. Great slabs of ten-storey apartment blocks have been slapped down at various angles like karate chops rendered in concrete. Between some of them desolate green spaces are planted with saplings that seem reluctant to grow in so denatured an environment. Since Flórián tér in the centre of Óbuda is bisected by large roads bearing traffic north from the city and over the Árpád Bridge to Pest, the pedestrian is thrust down into a Nibelheim of underpasses and bridges. Some underpasses function as a depository for Roman and medieval remains dug up when the redevelopment was taking place.

With great difficulty I found my way to Fő tér, one of the few spots in Óbuda where the character of the old city can still be felt, albeit in a spruced-up form. The square itself is an oasis encircled by a concrete desert. Frail saplings are propped up by wigwam frames among the cobbles. The low baroque and neoclassical buildings around the square carry carriage lamps and have been converted into pricy restaurants. One of them is the famous Sipos. Only it isn't the famous Sipos at all, since the original Sipos had to be moved here from its original site during the rebuilding of Óbuda. Opposite the Mark II Sipos a carriageway leads to the Zichy Palace, a charming two-storey, pink and grey mansion with a fishscale-tiled roof. There are more vestiges of old Óbuda just south of the Árpád Bridge: a pretty eighteenth-century church, its facade punctured with niches populated with statuary. A couple of hundred yards away on Lajos utca is the two-toned grey synagogue, a neoclassical building beneath an immense portico, its pediment topped by the Tablets of the Law. The synagogue, which is far larger than the nearby church, is now used as television studios. Opposite, a row of low eighteenth-century buildings has been restored and converted into art galleries, a reminder of how Óbuda used to look before most of it was demolished. Judging from old photographs the lanes of Óbuda must have been fairly noisome places, frequented as much by animals as humans, malodorous in summer, muddy and damp in winter. On this particular corner one can compare the two approaches to urban dwelling side by side, for the ten-storey blocks begin their stomp across the landscape just a few yards from here.

Were one to continue north from Óbuda on the Esztergom road, one would pass Békásmegyer, an even larger development of high-rise buildings, designed to house 35,000 families. The most disheartening feature of such enterprises is the loss of any sense of locality. Modern Óbuda or Békásmegyer are scarcely distinguishable from similar developments not just in Eastern Europe but in London or Singapore. Such estates are a deplorable contribution to the architectural history of a city with so interesting and complex a past, which can be recaptured at the Aquincum museum and the Budapest History Museum inside the castle. Although the exterior of the present castle dates from the seventeenth to nineteenth centuries, the structure dates back to medieval times, and as one descends into the handsome vaulted chambers of the museum one has the sensation of burrowing too into the history of the city, for it is here that are deposited its medieval and Renaissance relics. Another wing of the palace, almost completely rebuilt inside in pale grey marble, now houses the National Library and a small exhibition hall, while other remodelled salons of the palace contain the National Gallery, and the former Throne Room is now a showcase for superb Gothic altarpieces.

Also absorbed within the vastnesses of the palace is the Museum of the Hungarian Labour Movement. None of my acquaintances in the city had ever been there, but I went twice, to the astonishment of the dozy old ladies who guarded these collections in which no one is interested. They kept following me at a discreet distance in case I had the urge to paint a moustache on Lenin's portrait. The first time I sauntered through this exhaustive display of documents, books, posters, reconstructed workshops, photographs, news sheets, machinery and tools, and memorabilia of leading communists, I encountered no one at all. The second time I ran into a guided tour of Russians, and followed them as they neared the room in which are documented the events of 1956, including the famous and still vivid photographs of secret policemen being summarily executed. I longed to understand the captions with which these events were explained to visitors, but here, as in all the other museums of Budapest, captions were in Magyar only, which is taking nationalism rather too far. The Russian group was driven rapidly though this room and out of the museum.

The other museums on Castle Hill, such as the Military Museum, proved more interesting than I expected, as did the Museum of Catering (in Hungary, as in France, cooks such as Gundel enjoy a status akin to national hero, which makes sense to me), and the Music Museum within the lovely Erdődy Palace. Here it took a while to get to the exhibits. First I crossed the splendid baroque courtyard of the palace to the entrance, where I bought a ticket. Next I handed in my overcoat at the cloakroom, and was striding into the first hall of the museum itself, when I was called back and informed that to protect the parquet flooring I would have to put on cloth overshoes, a comical item resembling cuddly moonboots. I had the consolation of knowing that the other visitors to the museum looked just as foolish as I did.

169

Dreary winter afternoons provided ideal occasions for lengthy visits to the Fine Arts Museum, with its splendid and eclectic collection, and the Applied Arts Museum, which had a special show that season devoted to Hungarian Art Deco, a somewhat ungainly branch of the style. But the museum to which all Hungarians, as well as visitors, make a beeline is the National Museum, a powerful neoclassical building in the centre of Pest. It houses a fine collection of medieval artefacts, as well as displays tracing the history of Hungary through its many phases of invasion, Mongol and Turkish, and of Habsburg domination. The prize exhibits, however, are the crown jewels, so heavily guarded that it is very difficult to study them in any detail. Of course Hungarians are awed less by their artistic merits than by the symbolic power of having once again within their national possession the Crown of St Stephen and the rest of the coronation regalia, which after the Second World War were kept at Fort Knox as booty and were only returned to Hungary as recently as 1978. The crown, said to have belonged to the great King Stephen, who came to the throne in the year 1000, resembles a soufflé, its soft buff leather rising puffily above a band of enamels and jewels and pearls. It is a relic symbolizing national pride and continuity far more ancient than anything the Austrians have to offer, and it's easy to understand the emotional power the regalia holds for Hungarians. The treasury room also contains the orb and sceptre, both later medieval work, and the fragile and extremely beautiful eleventh-century coronation robe.

Both the historical museum at the castle, and the exhibits at the National Museum, which trace Hungarian history up to 1849, are a salutary reminder that in the Middle Ages and Renaissance Hungary was very much part of the mainstream of European culture. Nowadays Hungary is shrunken to much the same size as Ireland, but in the fourteenth century, when it reached its greatest territorial size, it was many times larger and extended far to the east into what is now Romania. Nevertheless the Hungarian court looked westwards for its cultural inspiration, as the ruins of King Matthew's sumptuous summer palace at Visegrád, just north of Budapest on the Danube Bend, demonstrate. Matthew's wife was Italian, and that country's influence was powerful indeed in the late fifteenth century. A visit to the ravishing red marble chapel dating from the sixteenth century and now incorporated into the nineteenth-century cathedral at Esztergom confirms how richly sophisticated this influence became.

After the Turks invaded, Hungary left the mainstream and slid into a side channel, where it remained until the Turks were driven from Buda in 1686. The Hungarian lands had been dismembered under Turkish control: the western and northern regions fell into Habsburg hands. After liberation from the Turks, the entire country was swallowed by the Habsburgs and, despite armed uprisings in 1703 and 1848, it remained in their grip until the Dual Monarchy was established in 1867. Thereafter the numberless Hungarian nobility gave tacit support to the Austrians, so long as they themselves were left undisturbed to continue their oppression of the peasantry. Even though many aspects of administration remained in the hands of Austrian ministers in Vienna, Hungarians enjoyed a considerable degree of freedom, including the freedom to assert their nationalism in opposition to Habsburg rule. Austrian domination meant that certainly until 1844, when Magyar became the official language, German was the principal language of administration and commerce, and remained a powerful cultural force despite the rise of Magyar nationalism. The Magyars, after all, never constituted a majority among those who dwelt within the borders of Hungary; they were merely the largest minority. Inevitably, Hungarian intellectuals allied themselves with the cause of nationalism. Under the Austrians, it was the intellectuals who sought to define a Magyar national identity. Literature was put at the service of national goals, and it was entirely in character that the rebellion of 1848 was led by a poet, Sándor Petőfi – and equally in character that he died in the attempt. Hungarian literature has long concentrated on national themes, which may account for the failure of Hungarian writers such as the prolific novelists Mór Jókai and Zsigmond Móricz and the poet Endre Ady to make much impact on Western literary history. In 1956 too, Hungarian writers and intellectuals were in the forefront of those who opposed the Stalinist regime.

The external influences on Hungarian culture were not solely German and Austrian. Hungarian intellectuals also looked to Paris for inspiration, and the layout of nineteenth-century Pest is very much on the Parisian model. Even after the Communist takeover in the late 1940s, West European and American literature continued to have some impact. Hungarian access to Western literature tends to be fairly random, for much depends on who gets translated when. I.B. Singer's fiction was widely read in Hungary long before he won a Nobel Prize, and writers such as Joseph Heller, Eugene Ionesco, Samuel Beckett, and the

practitioners of the French *nouveau roman* caught on fast in Hungary. On the other hand, Hungarians have been spared the vogue for the novels of Hermann Hesse, whose writings inexplicably gripped the imagination of an entire generation of Western college students, simply because he wasn't translated into Hungarian until very recently.

Despite the constraints of living under an authoritarian regime, there is still some vitality left among Hungarian intellectuals. Western ideas filter through with little hindrance. There is no routine jamming of broadcasts from the West, and many western Hungarians receive Austrian television transmissions. The days are long over when different literary reviews were edited from neighbouring tables in the fashionable coffeehouses, but literary societies in Budapest still meet at restaurants or, more commonly, in the more private surroundings of somebody's flat. The number of intellectual reviews and journals published in Hungary remains high in relation to the size of the population, and intellectuals and writers retain considerable prestige in Hungary. Politicians' opinions aren't valued, as they sometimes are in democratic societies, for Hungarian politicians, however intelligent, are not free to express their own ideas. The same applies to journalists. Although required to work within the constraints established by the Ministry of Culture, writers and filmmakers have a degree of freedom of expression that can occasionally give rise to alarm in official circles.

There are, however, limits to the regime's tolerance, as the Great Row within the Writers' Association was demonstrating while I was in Budapest. The Writers' Association is less tightly controlled than its Soviet or Czech equivalents, but this official body took on a previously unheard-of significance in November 1986. Elections to official positions within the association used to take place by a curious method. A member was given a list of seventy-two candidates, which could be amended, but which usually resulted in the election of a slate friendly towards the regime. In 1981 the system was democratized, so that open sessions would toss into the ring up to 100 nominations, and from their number seventy-two would be elected to office. Under this method, many Party loyalists failed to secure election. The government took the punches with fair grace. In November 1986, however, members took advantage of the open session to voice their grievances, addressing senior officials and even members of the Central Committee of the Party by name. Members

protested in particular against the banning of three literary journals.

This insubordination exasperated the regime. The Ministry of Culture denounced the governing body of the Association as 'unrepresentative' and persuaded twenty-seven writers to quit and set up a new organization on the grounds that the newly elected officials were too confrontational in their attitude. Not all those who left were hard-liners; some were religious writers who hoped for a quieter life in a less argumentative association. Since there are 612 members of the Writers' Association, the defection of twenty-seven was hardly a wounding blow, and suggests the regime lured them out in a fit of pique. Many intellectuals interpreted the government's testy response to these elections as a sign of its essential weakness, a conclusion it is indeed difficult to avoid. Yet, despite its irascibility, the Hungarian government, while undeniably authoritarian, still tolerates a degree of freedom of expression that would be unthinkable in Czechoslovakia or Romania or East Germany.

20

Z'zi Meets Mimi

A fiction prevails in Budapest that it is difficult to obtain seats at the Opera. I never had the slightest problem, and spent many an evening comfortably seated in the stalls for approximately one-thirtieth of the price charged at Covent Garden. The Operaház, with its *porte cochère* and grand staircases, was reminiscent of its Viennese precursor, the Staatsoper, though of course on a smaller scale. There were three tiers of boxes, separated by sphinxlike creatures wearing helmets. The basic decorative motif set heavy gilding against a lime-green background, and this was supplemented by frescoing on an exhaustive scale. I passed the intervals in the large salon at the circle level, where I could refresh myself with fruit juice or Hungarian champagne or the lightly sweet Tokay wine called Szamorodni. The salon is flanked by wood-panelled corridors lined with banquettes, rather like a Victorian railway carriage.

The opera provides the Budapesters with an excuse to dress up, though for many the wardrobe must be severely depleted. The audience was overwhelmingly elderly. Venerable women, presumably widows hunting in pairs, tottered slowly on their heels along the corridors. Less well heeled, in every sense, than their grandchildren, they wore strange clothes probably kept in mothballs since the 1930s, or ill-fitting blouses cut by computers from rolls of Shimmerlene and Crumplex. Unable to find clothes entirely suitable to the occasion, they went to work on embellishing their bodies. Hair was freshly coiffed and curled, gently tinted or bleached; faces, well powdered and rouged, had taken on form and feature thanks to the liberal use of eyebrow pencil; a jangle of gold bracelets and the muted sheen of heavy gold rings distracted the eye from vanished waists and mudcake necks. The formal note was echoed by the orchestra, resplendent in white tie, and thus a cut above the mere black tie of the Covent Garden orchestra, not to mention the lounge suits of the VPO.

The opera house is blessed with an extraordinarily deep stage. During a production of Tchaikovsky's *Eugene Onegin* that was by far the best performance I saw in Budapest, Tatiana had at one point to sprint from backstage to front, where Onegin was waiting for her. Although this was no doubt intended as an expression of her ardour, it was also a physical necessity if she hoped to get to Onegin's side before the curtain fell. Not all the performances were up to this standard: *Rosenkavalier* was drab indeed, and the dutiful hamming from Baron Ochs elicited hardly a single twitter from the geriatric audience, some of whom probably went to school with the Marschallin.

Music critics mistakenly inform us that *Manon Lescaut* is one of Puccini's lesser operas. Since I hold a contrary view, I treated myself to a seat in a box. The curtain rose on a rooftop scene, smoke curling up lazily from a garret chimney. The set had a French feel to it, but seemed far removed from the courtyard of the inn where Act 1 of *Manon Lescaut* takes place. I soon realized that I was to be treated to a Puccini opera that I like a good deal less, *La Bohème* – or, in Hungarian, *Bohémélet*. During the interval I addressed the old ladies with whom I was sharing the box. One spoke rusty German. Why *Bohémélet*, when I had bought a ticket for a different opera?

'That is because the singer is ill.'

'What, all of them?'

'*Nein, nein.* The soprano is ill.'

'And for that they change the entire production? Why don't they find an understudy?'

At this point our German vocabulary failed us both, so I reconciled myself to sitting through this opera out of a masochistic desire to learn whether Rodolfo's singing could actually get any worse as the opera continued. It did. There was also something mesmerizing about hearing Puccini sung in Magyar, as are all operas performed at the Operaház. The language has an abundance of syllables, far more than Italian, and it was intriguing to follow the scramble as the singers crammed, say, '*uruggyel*' into the musical space reserved for '*si*.'

A week later I was back at the Operaház for *Così fan Tutte*. The usherette, with whom I was by now on smiling terms, sold me a programme. As I moved away I glanced at the cover and stopped short. Mozart, to the best of my knowledge, never grew a bushy moustache, nor did he wear stripy neckties. A closer look confirmed my worst fears: the gentleman whose photograph gazed from the cover was Giacomo Puccini, and the opera I was about to hear was *Bohémélet*. I remonstrated with the usherette, explaining to her that this was the second time this had happened to me in two weeks, and didn't the opera company have any other work in its repertoire? A singer was ill, she told me.

'So? Why can't you find another Fiordiligi or Ferrando? This has to be less troublesome that mounting an entirely different production! And why must it always be *Bohémélet*? I actually *wanted* to see *Così*! If I'd wanted to see *Bohémélet* yet again I could have bought a ticket for it.'

She beamed. 'Puccini! *Schön*!' And with a kind of pirouette she began to prance about crooning an unidentifiable snatch of song from, I must assume, *La Bohème*. Then she wrinkled her nose. '*Così*,' she growled disdainfully, and began to mince before my eyes – 'Ti-ti-ti-t-ti' – parodying, unknowingly, Don Basilio's capers in the final act of *Figaro*. In other words, I should be grateful for the change of programme. I decided to respond stoically and took my seat. The performance was gratifyingly bad. Győző Leblanc, the Singing Squirrel, was an abysmal Rodolfo. When Mimi returns to the garret in Act 1, the stage lights failed, and Rodolfo had to grope for her tiny hand in near darkness. The lights came back on after a minute, followed by two backstage thumps so loud that even the cellists in the pit reeled with alarm. I left at the end of the act.

Scanning the pages of the Budapest equivalent of *What's On* I spotted the name of Shakespeare recurring with extraordinary frequency. It is no exaggeration to say that in a week in Budapest it was possible to see more Shakespeare plays than in the same period in London. When I asked György Konrád why Shakespeare seemed to be an honorary Hungarian, he told me that Shakespeare was popular because of the German cultural influence: most of the plays had been translated and performed in German from the early nineteenth century onwards. Moreover, according to Konrád, the concreteness and density of Shakespeare's language translates well into Hungarian.

I chose *Ahogy Tetszik* at the Katona József Theatre. The delectable Dorottya Udvaros was a lively Rosalind, and Sándor Gáspár a vigorous Orlando given to bursts of Samurai yells, but the production as a whole was somewhat inept. The audience was packed with teenagers, which suggested that *As You Like It* was a set text that year. The following week at the same theatre I saw a compelling performance of Harold Pinter's *A Kind of Alaska* starring Juli Básti. Almost all the leading roles in the productions at the top theatres, such as the Katona Jószef, were taken by actors and actresses who were also Hungary's most popular film stars. There was no evidence of the division of talent between film and theatre common in Western Europe. In a small country, versatility is *de rigueur*.

I found no trace of Operaház stuffiness when I attended a packed Sunday morning concert at the Liszt Academy. This, together with the beautifully restored Vigadó Concert Hall (where Mahler's first symphony and innumerable works by Béla Bartók received their first performances), is the main concert hall of the city. Like all central European theatres and concert halls, it is laid out on a lavish scale. Before the concert begins, the audience dispose of their coats at the many cloakrooms on both floors and strengthen themselves with coffee and a sandwich at the equally numerous buffets. It was surprising to find how small and cosy is the hall itself. I sat in the balcony, which consists of five rows running down the side of the auditorium and facing another five rows opposite. The green and gold interior of the auditorium was so encrusted with ornamentation that only a general impression remains of gilt foliage panels, deities, friezes, bas reliefs, organ pipes, and a flurry of Egyptiana. A squad of buxom usherettes in blue housecoats more appropriate to a hospital than a concert hall marched concertgoers to their seats. The concert opened with a Zemlinsky symphony, followed by Orff's *Carmina Burana*.

Gazing down into the stalls, I soon spotted someone I knew: in the third row sat my friend Gábor, with his small son perched on his knee. I enjoyed the familial atmosphere of the concert, for there were countless toddlers getting an early infusion of classical music while bouncing on a parental knee. Opposite me, in the front row of the balcony, a tiny and bewilderingly pretty girl swayed her long head of hair in time to the music, and when that made her dizzy, thumped her little palms on the rail. A woman sitting close by mouthed the words of the entire piece, including all the solos. After the undemonstrative audiences of the Operaház, who always seemed stone deaf, it was a revelation to see the responsiveness of this audience, stimulated both by the informality generated by the presence of dozens of children and by the catchiness of Orff's music, which is riveting enough, though it does go on for an hour too long.

I couldn't leave Budapest without going to see Z'zi Labor, a hugely popular rock group. Such was the demand for their concerts that the management of the Erkel Theatre, a remarkably ugly though capacious hall near the Keleti railway station, had laid on an extra concert for which I managed to obtain a single ticket. Directly in front of me sat a young man with an Afro haircut. He had a strong throaty voice and did his best to get a chant going – 'Z'zi, z'zi, z'zi!' – by leaping up and down and thrusting his hands rhythmically into the air. He had some slight success, but also attracted the attention of the ushers who appealed for calm. He was, however, irrepressible, and as soon as their backs were turned he was on his feet again, chanting and yelling. Nor was he deterred when the lights went down, and throughout the concert I would see his arms shoot into the air, as though he were a puppet manipulated from above.

The curtain rose to reveal a dozen women in peasant costume – the colourful petticoated short skirts billowing out from gargantuan hips that I would later see in rural Hungary. They sang and danced stiffly, either parodying a folk song or, for all I knew, producing the real thing, and twirled their hips and their hot-air buttocks. Since some of the women were tall as well as broad, the effect, while crude, was unquestionably hilarious. Z'zi Labor themselves wore more restrained black and white clothing, but went in for a good deal of clowning around in nightshirts and hard hats. It soon emerged that their inventive cavortings and the trappings of their show rather than its mediocre musical content were the secret of their enormous success. To the noisy delight of the young man in front of me, still leaping and cheerleading, the band kept producing fresh surprises for us: a brass band, six dancers in grass skirts, the peasantry reappearing as a hip-swinging backing group.

Since the working day starts early in Hungary – many shops are open by six, and offices by seven – there is little late-night entertainment on offer. The cabarets and night clubs, I was reliably informed, were thoroughly awful. Since the idea of sitting alone nursing a bottle of sweetish Hungarian champagne while a line-up of lovelies showed me and a dozen visiting Bulgarians their knickers didn't appeal to me, I gave them a miss. Instead you must create your own entertainment along the streets of Budapest, which, fortunately, are fairly safe late at night.

There was always good value to be had at the Keleti railway station, for Budapest is one of the main stops along the route of the Orient Express. I'd been told that all manner of illicit goings-on, presumably including drug dealing, take place in the pedestrian zones beneath the station, but the only importuning I experienced was from unshaven men loitering near the currency exchange office. They would offer me forints, but since the official exchange rate was generous enough, I dismissed them with a wave of the hand. Casual observers may walk freely onto the platforms at Keleti, and an hour spent at night wandering up and down can be enthralling. During the hours before the eastward-bound Orient Express departs for Bucharest, the platform is crowded with passengers, usually whole families guarding trolleys laden with cheap suitcases, boxes, and shopping bags from which loaves and bottles of cola and beer peeked out. Whatever the nationalities of these laden travellers, they were definitely not Hungarians. The weather in Budapest at this time of year was chilly but scarcely cold, but these travellers were dressed for Siberian conditions, the men in belted leather coats and fur hats, the women in ankle-length sheepskin coats with fur collars. They were, I guessed, either Russians or Romanians, perhaps of Hungarian descent, who had come to Budapest to visit relatives and take advantage of the wide range of consumer goods available here, just as Hungarians travel to Vienna for much the same reasons.

One night I was strolling along the Jószef körút, part of the succession of boulevards that encircles inner Pest, when I saw coming towards me some men who were stumbling and unsteady on their feet. Drunk, I deduced, but a minute later I realized there could be another explanation. I found myself approaching Rákóczi tér and being approached by some singularly ugly women of indeterminate age. The square is nocturnal home to the whores of Budapest, and the men I had seen were either dazed with horror at the sight of the hags or, harder to imagine, were recoiling with disgust from their embrace. It is my custom, on encountering ladies of the night in different parts of the world, to inquire as to their *tarif* for the various acts they undertake to perform. Not this lot, though, and I passed on rapidly and in silence, both because the women were so unprepossessing that I feared catching some airborne ailment from proximity alone, and because they were guarded by pimps, who, weary of loitering in distant doorways while their charges failed to attract custom, had strolled into the square itself to chat and exchange criminal records. Some of the dazed clients may well have been Hungary's own brand of *Gastarbeiter*, from Cuba; these, I was told, can show distinct reluctance to board the flight home at Ferihegy Airport when their spell of duty is over.

There was more salubrious entertainment on Castle Hill. One night I donned a jacket and my only tie, an all-purpose number that matches any clothing, and made my debonair way through the Hilton car park to the night club located in the furthest corner of the Fishermen's Bastion. The dance floor is situated beneath one of the cupolas, and the surrounding alcoves are filled with comfortable armchairs and coffee tables. Many of the women were young and travelled in packs so as to present a defence against the leering and nudging of the parties of diplomats who crowded into the club. I'd seen German cars parked outside, and a car bearing diplomatic plates disgorging some Syrians. I'm a shy soul, unskilled at approaching pretty leggy girls in patterned black stockings, and lasted all of ten minutes at the disco. I left the Syrians and the Germans to their sport, and walked down the flights of steps that descend from the back of Castle Hill to the sleepy streets around my lodgings.

21

Testing the Limits

Since for me contemporary Hungarian literature was – forgive me for putting it this way – a closed book, I was glad to have an opportunity to attend the screenings of the Hungarian Film Week. Images being harder to censor than words, it is not surprising that film rather than literature has turned the coolest eye on contemporary Hungary. Since the film week was attended not only by thousands of Hungarians but by visitors from all over the world, including the film critic of *The Times*, it amazed me that Pressinform, the official agency that assists visiting journalists to obtain the information they require, seemed to know nothing about this major cultural event. With only hours to go before Film Week opened, I decided I had nothing to lose by indulging in a touch of screaming and yelling. I sought out my contact and put it to him straight.

'The festival begins this evening, and I want to be there. You tell me there are only limited facilites for foreign translation at the screenings, but every other foreigner in town has heard differently. Get on the phone to Hungarofilm and tell them I want a pass.'

'But I spoke to Hungarofilm this morning and they said that most showings were sold out.'

'If you have a pass, concepts such as "sold out" lose their meaning. I don't want tickets, I want a press pass.'

He made another phone call while I pretended to fume. Hungarians, who pride themselves on that good old volcanic energy, might respond if faced with an eruption themselves. Well, something worked, for he returned with good news: 'Go straight down to the Novotel. Behind the hotel is the congress centre. Ask for Vera. She will give you a pass.'

And Vera did. A lovely badge, which entitled me to attend any screening I wished and to a set of headphones which would provide simultaneous translations into English, French, German, and Russian. The festival was extremely well run and I was able to fulfil a long nurtured fantasy: nonstop movie-going from nine in the morning until midnight. The simultaneous translations varied in quality, and one woman was both irritatingly mechanical in her delivery and delightfully uncertain of English idiom. One day I had the pleasure of hearing her translate: 'Why don't you . . . kiss my ass?' Then she left her microphone on as she checked with her colleagues: 'Kiss my ass? Is that right? It is "arse"? Oh, kiss my ass. I see.' And she tried it out a few times to get the hang of it, while the English-speaking contingent in the auditorium chortled. But later in the day she delivered a rebuke to us all, by simply giving up for five minutes in the middle of one of the most eagerly awaited films, *Banana Skin Waltz*. Eventually she agreed to return to her duties, but interspersed her increasingly lackadaisical translations with sighs and yawns.

There were a good number of lightly satirical films shown that week. *Love, Mother* was one of the best, and Péter Bacsó's *Banana Skin Waltz* was much talked about before the screening. It was Bacsó who broke new ground in 1969 with *The Witness*, one of the first Hungarian films to allude to the events of the 1950s, though the film was not released until ten years after it was made. *Banana Skin Waltz* shows how a succession of accidents and coincidences can wreck a life. The hero, Dr Kondacs, is on his way to his wedding when he sees a young woman who, unhinged by the tedium of her office job, is parading naked through the street. He wraps his coat around her as she is being led away by the police. Arriving at the registry office, the groom, having surrendered his coat, is unable to produce his identity card. 'No identity card, no wedding,' says the registrar, and the ceremony is off. So is the engagement, for the bride finds the doctor's explanations unconvincing. The poor doctor stumbles from misadventure to misadventure, and the result is a lightweight comedy of no great merit, though it deftly alluded to a variety of current Hungarian preoccupations.

The reception after the non-wedding takes place in a Buda villa which, of course, is unfinished. The house belongs to the bride's father, a rich dentist, who shows off his new dental chair to the guests. When it spins out of control and seems in danger of self-destructing, the dentist murmurs: 'Oh, to think how much foreign currency we spent on that chair!' When an agricultural cooperative boss recovering from surgery leaves a demijohn of wine for Dr Kondacs, the surgeon is accused of corruption by a committee of colleagues who, incidentally, spend far more time practising Mozart quartets than in the operating theatre. Fun is also poked at the police, who are portrayed as amiable idiots, and at the privileges conferred by Party membership: a senior Party official in hospital with a game leg insists on 'no frills' treatment and is promptly surrounded by three nurses who cater to his every whim.

A number of films dealt grittily with problems encountered by families in the course of their, I hope, atypical daily lives. Pál Erdőss's *Tolerance* depicts an ill-educated couple, both of whom have spent time in prison for petty crimes, trying to get back their children from the foster parents to whom they were consigned. It's a sympathetic film, with no sugary message in the final reel, for no sooner is the family reunited than it disintegrates once again. Livia Gyarmathy's *Blind Endeavour* traces, quite separately, incidents in the lives of two groups of people plagued by misunderstandings and recriminations: a pair of middle-class lovers, and a factory foreman on a binge. Only in the final moments of the film do the two stories converge, and with tragic consequences. For me the interest of the film lay in its unblinking portrayal of misery and drunkenness, just as Pál Erdőss's film made no attempt to round off his story with a happy ending.

The documentary *Pretty Girls* chronicled the 1985 Miss Hungary contest, which was remarkable on two counts: this was the first such contest to have been held in Hungary since 1931, and the winner, Csilla Molnár, killed herself not long after her victory. The film exposed the crass commercialism that scavenged off the successful beauties. Girls no more than sixteen or seventeen years old were photographed in the nude without anything being said about subsequent exploitation of those images, which would later appear in soft-porn magazines under such cheap captions as 'If Lenin only knew . . .' Miss Molnár bore some resemblance to Lauren Bacall, and it was heartrending to imagine this seventeen-year-old girl killing herself a few months after being judged the loveliest girl in Hungary. She was not alone: Hungary's suicide rate is alarmingly high, especially among the young. Despite the temptation to mouth clichés about the volatility of the Hungarian character and the romantic cachet of a tragic death, I am lost for an explanation. Nevertheless four times as many Hungarians kill themselves as in the United States, and five times as many as in Britain.

But for me, and to judge from the crowds filling not only 2000 seats in the auditorium but standing at the back and seated cross-legged down the aisles, the most exciting films were those which tried to come to terms with the terrible years before 1956. These were the years of the worst Stalinist excesses, of show trials and executions, of denunciations and disappearances, of torture and indefinite prison terms. Above all these were the years of fear, when a chance word or a casual rebuke could result in a knock on the door from the secret police, whose powers seemed unlimited. In Hungary Mátyás Rákosi had been general secretary of the Party since the late 1940s, and it was his regime that was credited with the chilling slogan, 'Those who are not with us are against us.' Nor had this been an idle threat, for during the years of the terror some 150,000 people were arrested and imprisoned.

When in February 1956 Nikita Khrushchev at the Twentieth Party Congress in Moscow denounced the crimes of Stalin, this was taken as a relaxation of the regime, though Khrushchev surely didn't intend it as a signal for the repressed peoples of Eastern Europe to try to displace those leaders most closely associated with the Stalinist era. A matter of months after Stalin's death in 1953 Rákosi acknowledged under pressure that he had made 'errors' and was replaced as premier by Imre Nagy, whose reforms, though long overdue, antagonized many of the surviving old guard. The outcome of the ensuing power struggle was that Rákosi, who still held the post of general secretary, succeeded in having Nagy stripped of his party membership. Rákosi's triumph was short-lived, for Khrushchev's speech gave fresh ammunition to the reformists in Hungary. Dissent crystallized around the aptly named Petőfi Circle. Pressure from Moscow led to Rákosi's dismissal and his replacement by Ernő Gerő, another hard-liner, on 18 July 1956.

In retrospect it is not difficult to see why even in 1986, thirty years after the revolution, the Party had found the strife within the Writers' Association unsettling, for the chorus of demands that led to the 1956 revolution also had their origins within what was then known as the Writers' Union. On 17 September the official slate of candidates was rejected, an ominous sign. In the weeks that followed, student assemblies began to propagate demands that ranged from the trivial – the removal of Stalin's statue – to the momentous: the withdrawal of Soviet troops; multiparty elections; freedom of the press and the release of political prisoners; and the open trial of Rákosi's closest associates. On 23 October a demonstration in Budapest brought hundreds of thousands into the streets, many calling for the reinstatement of Imre Nagy. The state security police, the AVO, opened fire on the crowd, but the momentum was with the demonstrators. Many soldiers joined them and turned their arms over to the students. The statue of Stalin was torn down. Nagy returned to his former position of premier, and radical reforms were introduced, such as the restoration of a multiparty system. Soviet troops had been called in but were forced to withdraw, and the reformers tried to negotiate their further demands with the Russians; the most threatening of these was the withdrawal of Hungary from the Warsaw Pact. In the meantime the street fighting continued, and so did the hunt for secret policemen, many of whom were murdered on the streets.

On 1 November Nagy announced Hungary's withdrawal from the Warsaw Pact and appealed to the world to recognize Hungary's neutrality. It was too late. Soviet troops were crossing the border once again. It was the end of the road for Nagy, but not for his colleague János Kádár, who promptly switched sides and headed the new government, which stamped out any remaining signs of armed resistance and reimposed order on the country. 25,000 people were killed in the course of two weeks, and almost ten times that number fled the country. Imre Nagy and the other reformers in his government were arrested. Tried in secret, Nagy and three 'accomplices' were sentenced to death and executed, and the remaining defendants received lengthy prison sentences.

It is impossible not to be moved by the story. The 1956 revolution was a communal act of heroic defiance. In retrospect it seems doomed to failure. The expectation that the Soviet Union could have accepted a declaration of neutrality by a member of the Warsaw Pact seems preposterous, though survivors of the period assured me that many people, including Nagy himself, believed the Soviet Union could be persuaded to go along with the idea. After all, the terms of the Austrian State Treaty of the previous year had stipulated a status of armed neutrality for Austria and the withdrawal of Soviet troops. But then Austria was not in any sense a member of the Eastern Bloc. The radicalism of the students' demands in 1956, the support they received from hundreds of thousands of citizens, the clear willingness of the Hungarians to fight against overwhelming odds, and even the language of defiance and despair used by Nagy in his final broadcasts to the nation and the world – these, in their very passion, make the reforms of the Prague Spring in 1968 and the response to the grinding of Soviet tanks across the Czech borders seem mild. Yet the less combative Czechs too were to be crushed by Soviet and other Eastern Bloc troops, including, ironically, Hungarian soldiers.

The man who suppressed the revolution, János Kádár, still rules Hungary, and it is one of the paradoxes of recent central European history that this turncoat should have presided over the gradual transformation of his country into the most market-orientated and least repressive nation in the Eastern Bloc. Kádár knew well that simply crushing the revolution would not diminish the Hungarian loathing of the Soviet Union a single jot. So to distract people from their bitter disappointment at the failure of the revolution, he gave them material prosperity and, beginning in 1968, a programme of reform that continues to this day, now with the blessing of the Soviet Union. Under Kádár, too, there has been an extension – gradual, but nevertheless an extension – of the boundaries of cultural freedom. One of the consequences of this has been that certain topics, hitherto taboo, are now allowed to be discussed.

Here lay the fascination of the film week for all of us who attended. Films were to be shown, the synopses made clear, that would deal with the 1950s, and with the events of 1956. How far would they go? Would, indeed, one or two of the films be shown at all? There were doubts about Márta Mészáros's *Diary for My Loves*. Its precursor, her film *Diary for My Children*, was made in 1982 but apparently delayed by the Russians for two years on the grounds, somewhat implausible given Soviet disdain for the niceties of copyright law, that some historical clips used in the film were a breach of their copyright. Eventually Hungarian footage was substituted and the film was shown. *Diary for My Loves* was shown at the film festival, and it came, we were told, hot from the cutting room. Three films, however, were not shown. One had been made ten years ago, another two years ago, and the third was banned at the last minute. So despite the relative freedom of Hungarian cinema, there are still formidable constraints, and the decision as to whether a film will be screened is, of course, a political one.

One of the films that just scraped through was Gyula Maár's *Mills of Hell*. Set in the late 1940s and early 1950s, the film shows how the academic career of the protagonist, Flandera, is sabotaged by an anonymous letter of denunciation. Forced to work on

186

a construction site, he becomes friendly with a count who, though sympathetic to the communist cause, is considered suspect because of his background and is arrested on trumped-up charges. Meanwhile Flandera falls in love with the beautiful crippled daughter of the Stalinist prosecutor Altschuler – by now it should be clear that we are entangled in nets of melodrama – and jettisons his pregnant girlfriend. Altschuler has Flandera tortured to clarify his mind, but his daughter's will proves stronger than his own, and finally Altschuler consents to the marriage of the young pair. Flandera's subsequent infidelity leads his wife to suicide, where-upon Altschuler guns Flandera down in the street. Yes, it was a terrible film, in which all the characters were stereotypes, and where every scene pointed to a moral. The reaction of the audience interested me. The solemnly mouthed Stalinist certain-ties, such as 'An aristocrat has to be an enemy of the people' and 'Communists are special people', provoked howls of derisive laughter. The voice of Mátyás Rákosi on the radio was also received with sniggers. The contempt for the attitudes that prevailed in the 1950s is now universally shared. Bad though the film was, it did show AVD men administering torture to the obnoxious hero, and that scene no doubt provoked some heated discussion at the Ministry of Culture before permission was granted to screen the film.

Far more successful was Péter Gárdos's *Whooping Cough*. Set in Budapest in October 1956, it shows how an ordinary family responded to the rush of events during that momentous week. The charm of the film is that it resists that very momentousness by being set almost entirely inside the family's flat, a haven of admittedly anxious tranquillity while mortars thump in the streets outside. The warmth of this disputatious family – and the eight-year-old daughter is played with voracious energy by an enchanting little actress called Eszter Kárász – and their heavily furnished, dimly lit flat, are beautifully conveyed, and the prevailing comic tone only sharpens the sense of brutal reality when the family occasionally ventures into the battleground of the streets. A series of vignettes brings those days vividly to life: the relatives phone from America and the overexcited family has difficulty working out what it is prudent to tell them; and, short of fuel, the family tosses the collected works of Stalin into the stove.

The film with which the festival ended was *Diary for My Loves*. As in her previous film, Mészáros incorporates historical footage into this broadly autobiographical account of a young woman seeking in 1949 to become a film director. The film is long and somewhat diffuse, but avoids the triteness of *Mills of Hell* by alluding to the horrors of the 1950s rather than crudely depicting them. The conflict between the heroine, Juli, and her foster-mother, a grim colonel in the state security forces, and later with the authorities who disapprove of the candour of her films, make abundantly clear the kind of repressive society in which she is living. Nor does Mészáros gloss over the fact that millions of people, kept in the dark about Stalin's crimes, grieved bitterly when he died, shaken by the loss of the avuncular figure who, in the case of young people such as Juli, had presided, as it were, over their entire lives.

Since Mészáros is keen on using newsreel footage in her films, there was great curiosity as to which segments she would include in this film. We saw the unveiling of the statue of Stalin, and the funeral of László Rajk. Rajk had been Minister of the Interior until 1948, but Rákosi deemed it expedient to get him out of the way. In 1949 he was accused of every conceivable offence – from spying for the United States to conspiring with the hated Tito to overthrow Rákosi – and prevailed upon, with the help of well-applied torture, to confess 'for the sake of the Party'. The confession didn't save his skin, however, and he was executed, despite an assurance given to him that he would merely be exiled to the Soviet Union. It gives one a fair idea of the loathesomeness of the Rákosi regime that Rajk's wife Julia was compelled to witness the execution and that his son, also named László, was taken from Julia and reared under another name by a foster family. When, some years later, Rákosi was forced to admit his own 'errors', Rajk and three other 'co-conspirators' executed with him were formally rehabilitated. When eventually his remains were given a proper burial, the funeral procession attracted a crowd of 200,000. Behind the coffin walked his widow and his small son.

Since Rajk had been formally rehabilitated, this film clip had doubtless been seen on occasion since 1956. What was unprecedented was the incorporation of a newsreel showing Imre Nagy delivering a speech in Parliament. (*Whooping Cough* had shown the cooped-up family listening to Nagy's poignant final broadcast.) This was received with a gasp of astonishment and then a burst of applause, for, unlike László Rajk, Nagy has not been rehabilitated and it is unlikely that he ever will be.

After the screening I walked out into the lobbies with Keith Dobson, then the British Council representative in Hungary, and his wife, whom I had met by chance in the auditorium. He introduced me to another film director, who criticized *Diary for My Loves* because it failed to show the confrontation that occurred when released political prisoners met up with those, often in their own family circle, who had denounced them. I suspected some envy here, since this director had just made his own film about 1956 as experienced in the villages.

'When will it be shown?'

He laughed. 'Who knows? From what I've heard it's more likely to be banned than screened.'

We all approached a tall man of great handsomeness who was telling a small group around him of his own surprise at seeing Nagy on the screen. Keith, who seemed to know everybody in Budapest, said he wanted to introduce me to him.

'Who is he?'

'László Rajk – junior.'

22

Printers Don't Read

Quite apart from relishing the dramatic transformation of Rajk from a small boy on celluloid to the grown man standing before me, I was delighted to have run into him. For some weeks I had been trying to get in touch with Hungarian 'oppositionists', as they like to call themselves, but it had proved extremely difficult. The phone numbers I had brought from London were out of date, and even supposedly current numbers obtained in Budapest proved useless. In some cases I had the addresses of oppositionists who were not on the phone, and despite repeated visits I could never find them at home. Some of those I was able to contact, such as the writer János Kenedi, were 'too busy' to see me, which usually is a code for needing to keep a distance between oneself and Westerners at a particular moment. I had despaired of ever getting in touch with László Rajk, but here he was before me offering me not one but two phone numbers. I had also given up hope of ever finding Miklós Haraszti, who in 1973 wrote a controversial book called *A Worker in a Worker's State*. Earlier that evening, chatting to Keith Dobson in the auditorium, I had been complaining of my frustrations, when he glanced ahead of him and said, 'You're in luck. Haraszti's ex-wife is a few rows in front of us. She's bound to have his current number.' And she did, and a moment later so did I.

Some days later I climbed the stairs of a large apartment building not far from the Liszt Academy. I came to the end of a corridor where I expected to find Rajk's flat. The name on the door was not his, and there was no reply when I knocked. The tiny kitchen window of another flat looked out onto the corridor and an old woman was peering out at me. '*Rajk, kérem?*' I inquired, but she clearly had no idea what or whom I was talking about. '*Nem, nem,*' she replied, and I gave up. Just as I was setting off

down the many flights of stairs, I saw the tall figure of Rajk
bounding up the steps.

'I am sorry,' he said, in his almost perfect English. 'Had you
given up hope? I am a bit late.'

'No, but I couldn't find your flat.'

'Ah, you must go to the very end of the corridor,' he said, as we
approached the door on which I had knocked in vain. He turned
the handle and as we passed through I realized that this was not
the entrance to the flat but led to an extension of the corridor. At
the very end we came to another door. There was no name on it –
Rajk, I gathered, was peripatetic – but behind it there was a
cordial welcome from a young woman, who ushered us into an
enormous and meagrely furnished sitting room.

László Rajk is doubly blessed. He has a name that renders him
virtually untouchable: as a public relations exercise, it simply
would not do for the Hungarian authorities to arrest someone who
bears a name with such powerful and haunting associations.
Moreover Rajk has a commanding presence. Unusually tall for a
Hungarian, he is extremely handsome, with dark eyes and hair,
grave furrows running from the nostrils to the sides of his broad
mouth, and a winning smile. He speaks with measured calm and
authority. He has presence, he has charisma, and is not afraid to
exploit his untouchability in order to maintain some kind of
opposition to the Kádár regime – not that it was really possible to
speak of an organized opposition in Hungary.

'We're more of a loose association than a formal organization.
We have differing interests. Some of us are interested in human
rights issues, others are more concerned with environmental
issues or the problems of the gypsies or the poor or alcoholism.
Even if we wanted to combine in some way to put together a
united programme, it would be very difficult for us to do so, not
only because the regime would put obstacles in our way, but
because we lack information. It's so hard for us to argue about,
say, defence spending or our position within the Warsaw Pact
when none of the relevant information needed to make judgments
and form policies is available to us. On the other hand, we gain
strength from all knowing each other. Hungary is a small country,
and it's overcentralized, with Budapest at the hub, and everybody
knows everybody else.'

'Are there factions within the opposition?' I wanted to know.

'Not really. Any factions that may spring up are tactical and
tend to be short-lived. I'll give you an example. During the

protests about the dam that the Austrians are building along the Danube, the environmentalists thought their hand would be strengthened if they excluded from the protests oppositionists whose goals are primarily political. Of course, this was naive on their part. As soon as the police began to take an interest in their protests, and they soon did, the environmentalists woke up to the fact that no protest in Hungary can be apolitical.'

Nevertheless, I suggested, the regime was prepared to tolerate a measure of dissent. I had heard no reports of trials and long prison sentences for oppositionists, and compared to their Czech counterparts, Hungarian dissidents have an easy time of it.

'That's true. There is some harassment but it never reaches newsworthy levels. Your flat might be searched, or you can lose your exit visa, or you can lose your job. Right now the oppositionists are tolerated because the regime desperately needs loans from Western banks, so it has to retain its liberal image. There is even some contact between oppositionist groups and government officials. Not that you should have too rosy a picture of the situation here. In the field of publications, in particular, we remain very restricted.'

In Hungary, where samizdat flourishes, it is not simply a question of a few people surreptitiously cranking the roneo machine. There are many layers of samizdat. 'You can even speak of "State samizdat" in Hungary. There are publications with a restricted distribution, usually to Party secretaries and branches. They're usually translations from the Western press, but can also be books. I remember that Marcuse's books were published in this way. Then there are the semi-legal publications, usually research papers from the universities. The institutions publish these themselves and avoid the official routes. There are also private publications. This route is used, say, by poets whose work is not banned but also not supported by the state publishing houses. Even though the author has to pay for such publications out of his own pocket, he must still submit his work to the censors in the usual way. The other drawback, other than the expense, is that the author will have no access to bookshop distribution, though he's allowed to make his own deliveries.'

'And then there is the true underground samizdat.'

Rajk showed me a journal called *Beszélő* (*The Talker*), which appears irregularly at 100 forints per issue. It is a roneod publication of over a hundred pages, expounding what Rajk calls 'a realistic pluralism' that acknowledges the limitations prevailing within the Soviet sphere of influence, while still arguing for greater freedoms within the system. Some issues contain articles by Hungarian oppositionists, others carry translations of Western writers. Very little fiction is published in samizdat, which is mostly used as an outlet for articles by oppositionist sociologists, historians, and economists. On the title page are printed the names and telephone numbers of the editors, a practice first devised in Poland, the purpose being to focus the attention of the authorities on a front line of prominent people, usually intellectuals with an international reputation whom it would be foolish for the police to arrest. Nonetheless, to admit to being an editor of a journal such as *Beszélő* is a courageous act, for no one can be sure of remaining immune from prosecution. 'It's also a moral act,' Miklós Haraszti was to tell me later, 'to dare not to be faceless.'

Beszélő has a readership estimated at over ten times its print run, which varies from 1500 to 2000 copies. Although civil servants would be reluctant to admit it, samizdat journals are also read in government circles. 'The important function of samizdat,' said Rajk, 'is that it extends the boundaries of what may be discussed. It can bring new issues into public debate and encourage the approved writers to be more daring in the subjects they deal with. We're trying to break down some barriers. You'll have heard of the second economy in Hungary. Well, we like to think of samizdat as "second public opinion".' Or, as Haraszti put it, 'the government has no fresh ideas, and has little choice but to draw on the ideas of the radicals.'

Although the samizdat publishers have a fairly cosy understanding with the regime, their continuous prodding at the boundaries can be dangerous and forces the editors to continue to act in a clandestine manner. Acquiring stocks of paper and arranging for the printing can prove logistically tricky. Printing equipment has to be portable, and is moved from location to location so that there is no such thing as a printing office that can be closed down. The organizational model is that of a linked chain, and every effort is made to keep the various links in ignorance of who else is involved in the chain of production. The printers don't know who does the binding, and vice versa. Distribution is taken care of by individuals, using their personal contacts. One way to publish, for example, a translation of Orwell is to make no reference on the cover to the contents of the book. 'Fortunately,' says Rajk, 'printers don't read.'

Samizdat is also a vehicle for expressing indignation about the treatment of Hungarian minorities beyond the borders, especially the two million or so who now live in Romania. There is indignation that the regime does little to assist those people, even though János Kádár has stated that this is Europe's worst human rights problem. One of the editors of an officially approved journal – his views on the regime were so virulent as to be unprintable – was one of those who felt passionately about the matter. 'In the 1920s Hungary lost half of its population and two-thirds of its territory. Consequently almost everyone in present-day Hungary has relatives in what is now Czechoslovakia or Romania. The Romanians have a particularly terrible record of suppressing the Hungarian minority. They are rewriting history to deny the fact that Transylvania was once Hungarian. Records are being destroyed, people are being systematically misinformed, and populations are being dispersed and relocated. The Hungarian schools and university are being closed down, and it's almost impossible for newspapers and books to be imported from Hungary. The situation isn't quite as bad in Czechoslovakia. The Czechs are a more sophisticated people, so the oppression is more sophisticated. It takes place mostly at the educational level. Whatever they may say about respecting the rights of minority groups, their policy is assimilationist.'

'If the outrage you express is so strong within Hungary,' I wondered, 'how come the government doesn't adopt a more forceful attitude on the issue? Wouldn't that be a way of bolstering support for the regime?'

'I'm not sure of the answer,' said the editor. 'It certainly seems that our government doesn't care, and I suspect the reason is that they don't have Soviet support on the issue. Remember that the Russians don't have a clear conscience either when it comes to the treatment of minorities.' Nor, I was tempted to add, do the Hungarians, for the treatment by the Magyars of the many other nationalities living within Hungarian borders in the nineteenth century was very far from tolerant. Indeed, the hub of the problem may well be the Romanians' long memories of their own suppression at the hands of the Magyars during the Habsburg Monarchy.

I tapped more memories some days later when I rang a doorbell within a pleasant modern block on Rose Hill. The door was opened by a short, rather stocky man, well groomed, who invited me in to a comfortable living room, stacked with books and with access to a balcony overlooking the hills. I was calling on Miklós

Vásárhelyi, now seventy years old. He had been the official spokesman for the short-lived government headed in October 1956 by Imre Nagy. Brought to trial in June 1958 as one of Nagy's accomplices, he received a five-year sentence.

'Before the Second World War I was an old-time communist,' he told me, 'but I had to wait until Stalin's death in 1953 to press for the kind of communism I'd always believed in. Our opportunity came in 1956 and I joined Nagy's team.'

'Don't you feel, in retrospect, that the Nagy government was naive in expecting the Soviet Union to go along with its wishes?'

'Not really. We were optimistic in October 1956, we had no sense of impending doom. We felt the USSR would accept the changes we advocated as long as the fundamental tenets of socialism were not threatened. But we were wrong, and what's more the Russians cheated us.'

'And after the Russians invaded?'

'My whole family was deported and I was arrested. As you know, I was tried and imprisoned, and released four years later. After my release I worked as a clerk in a cooperative. Since 1972 I've been active in the fields of culture and literature and science.'

'Don't you regret the failure of 1956?'

'Of course. Had we succeeded, Hungary might have developed into a Western-style pluralist democracy or – who knows? – into something entirely new.'

Behind his immensely courteous, soft-spoken manner there clearly lurks a strong will, for in 1986, on the thirtieth anniversary of the revolution of which he, at ministerial level, was the sole survivor, Vásárhelyi helped to organize a conference in commemoration of October 1956. Its outcome was an international declaration, signed not only by Hungarians but by East Germans, Poles, Czechs, and even three Romanians, stating that what had occurred in 1956 was part of the democratic heritage of Eastern Europe. Naturally, this kind of talk didn't go down well with the Kádár regime, which responded angrily, attempted some half-hearted harassment of the participants in the conference, and then appeared to give up. But then a few months later, some days before I went to see Vásárhelyi, he received the news that, although his passport had not been withdrawn, he would not be given a visa enabling him to attend a scientific conference in Italy as a Hungarian representative. A price had been exacted after all for daring to raise his head over the parapet after a silence of thirty years.

195

I asked Vásárhelyi whether, in all these years, he had ever been tempted, like hundreds of thousands of his fellow countrymen, to leave Hungary for good. He shook his head.

'No. And the same goes for my family. This is my country. Why should I leave? The others – let *them* leave.'

23

Jolly Roger

Having at last succeeded in obtaining Miklós Haraszti's phone number, I used it. He suggested I might like to come to his flat the following Sunday when a philosopher whom I might know – I didn't catch the name – would be addressing a small group. This might be interesting for me.

At seven on Sunday evening I was admitted to Haraszti's attic flat, though there was no sign of my host. Instead I was astonished to see, holding forth quietly in an opposite corner of the room, none other than the Wicked Witch of the Right, Roger Scruton. So this was the philosopher I might have heard of. Indeed I had, and for years had been throwing his newspaper articles at the wall or into the fire. The New Right, I would gather during my visits to Budapest and Prague, was making a concerted effort to win the hearts and minds of East European dissenters, an effort I could scarcely disapprove of, since it presumably filled a gap, ideological and physical, that the West European democratic left was failing to plug. I kept my distance from Dr Scruton and went in search of my host. Miklós eventually emerged from some room or other and came to say hello. He was a slight figure, quite unassuming in manner, and with bags under his eyes plumped up, I assumed, by wakefulness.

Although the room was quite large, there weren't enough chairs to seat twenty of us, so Miklós threw a couple of mattresses onto the polished wood floor and I sprawled across one of them and waited for the guest speaker to begin. Dr Scruton announced that he proposed to focus his remarks on issues relating to the environment. He argued, plausibly, that such issues are naturally congenial to the right, since 'conservatism is the philosophy of the future, of conserving what exists'. He observed that air and water pollution are more grave problems in Eastern than in Western

197

Europe, and that this was not unrelated to the opposed political ideologies. In a system where all means of production are in public ownership, there is no course of action open to those who wish to combat pollution, whereas under capitalism private citizens may take legal action against those who damage the environment. Unfortunately, in his view, the environmental banner had been commandeered by the anti-capitalist left in Western Europe, represented by political groups such as the Greens in West Germany.

By now Dr Scruton had warmed up, and, though still slouching elegantly in his chair, had kicked off his shoes and delivered the rest of his remarks in his socks, which I found mildly endearing. He now embarked on a series of wide-ranging smears against the *New Statesman* journalist Duncan Campbell ('almost certainly a Soviet agent'), the Greenham Common women (ditto), and Neil Kinnock (of suspect allegiance, since he belonged to the Nicaragua Solidarity Campaign, which, Scruton revealed, was funded by the Communist Party). Moreover, the Labour Party, Britain's Loyal Opposition, was no longer loyal, since its attacks on policing constituted an attack on the rule of law (disloyal) and its policies condone the revelation of state secrets.

Smears completed, he moved on to political philosophy. The crux of his argument was that there can be no individual rights without the right to own property, and once the right to private property has been conceded, then the rule of law must be established in order to defend it. It is the sovereign power of a nation (the terms grow a bit hazy here) that validates the law, and that power must be defended against subversion. However, only the state itself can decide what constitutes state security. By now it was clear to me, if not to the speaker, that Dr Scruton was scoring a spectacular own goal. When he stopped speaking, the response was total silence. After a while Gáspar Miklós Tamás (a prominent oppositionist who, with László Rajk, had attempted to stand as an independent candidate in the 1985 elections), who had gleefully introduced Scruton as 'one of the most hated men in the world', solicited questions. There were none. Hungarians abhor silence, so perhaps the audience was in a state of shock. Here had come a celebrated missionary from the New Right, a man opposed to the very roots of his being to the Communist system which had oppressed his audience for decades, yet his peroration ringingly endorsed the power of the state. As Scruton eulogized 'state security', I couldn't help thinking that almost every Hungarian present had probably, within recent memory, experienced a few uncomfortable interviews with the state security police; their attitude towards the concept was not likely to be as commendatory as Dr Scruton's. After all, it was entirely possible that the gathering that evening might well have been monitored by the secret police.

I kept silent for a while, since I was a guest here and could, if I chose, take issue with Scruton any day of the week back in England. However, since the Hungarians were tongue-tied, I decided to speak. First I responded to the smears. As a regular contributor to the New Statesman I did not take kindly to what he had said, and as an erstwhile apparatchik in the British Labour Party, I equally resented accusations of disloyalty. Not wishing to restrict my remarks to the settling of scores, I also challenged one of his assertions on environmental matters. Scruton had stated that the Chernobyl disaster had provided the Greens and others in the West who thought like them with a pretext for attacking all nuclear power, whereas, in his view, the real argument should be against the public ownership of nuclear power.

'This,' I observed, 'is disingenuous since nuclear power is as tightly in the hands of the state in the West as it is in the East. You were implying, falsely, that nuclear power stations are privately owned in the West.'

'Perhaps they should be,' murmured Dr Scruton.

I didn't reply, hoping that a Hungarian might offer a few words at this stage. But no. Now it so happened that Scruton had not only smeared a respected journal in the presence of its wine correspondent, but he had also rubbished the West German Greens in the presence of one of the movement's most ardent supporters. A soft German voice rose from behind my chair, as a journalist from a Frankfurt biweekly recorded her stupefaction at Dr Scruton's distorted representation of the Greens' views and strategy. Indeed, Dr Scruton missed an opportunity to score a hat trick that evening, for unknown to either of us the newly posted New York Times correspondent was also present. Gáspar Miklós Tamás rushed to his friend's support at this stage, declaring that Hungarians had to choose sides, and that any action that undermined the West – by Duncan Campbell, the Greens, whoever – had to be deplored.

That struck me as fairly silly too, so I had another crack of the whip, especially since we were nearing the hub of my distaste for Scrutonism: the strong note of authoritarianism implicit in all his remarks. The state was as much at the controls of his ideal system as of any East European regime, and his defence of the rule of law at all costs and his insistence that only the state itself could determine what constituted a threat against its security, would surely be met with heavy nods of approval in the Kremlin or in the Party headquarters about a mile away from where we were sitting. Myself, I didn't particularly want to hear what Roger Scruton had to say about this, but I would be most interested to hear what our Hungarian friends thought of the argument. Silence for a while, and then a long speech from János Kis, most of which I could not fathom, though the following observation would probably have been echoed by everybody else in the room: 'When I hear you call a British journalist a Soviet agent, I feel uneasy, since I am sure that I and many others here tonight have been called CIA agents by those who do not agree with us.'

And Miklós Haraszti asked whether, given Scruton's attachment to the rule of law, it was permissible for East Europeans to oppose the state by acting in defiance of the law.

'Yes,' replied Scruton ingeniously, 'because in your country you have no legal system within which you can work.'

Dr Scruton had clearly been taken aback to find a cross-section of the Western press squatting on the floor as he spoke. This had truly been a matter of chance, since I had been invited along at the last minute and Elisabeth, the German journalist, had been brought along by a Hungarian friend on the spur of the moment. Miklós had provided us with snacks and wine, but the West European contingent was now confessing to a sharp appetite. Gáspar Miklós Tamás wanted to take the most hated man in the world to dinner, and Scruton, who had not taken long to find his shoes and approach me so as to learn the identity of his unexpected critic, asked whether I would like to join the group. I would. Since some of the other diners had already gone ahead to the restaurant, my willingness to join Scruton was particularly welcome since I was the only one left who knew how to get to the restaurant. We set off for Alföldi, a scruffy bistro, recommended by many but never enjoyed by me. The food was acceptable, the wine the most routine products from the state farms, and the service casual.

Our party consisted of Scruton, Elisabeth, Gáspar, Sándor Szilágyi (an editor of Beszélő), two women who spoke not a word, an extremely drunk and tiresome man who became increasingly belligerent as the evening continued, and myself.

200

Being in a public place did not seem to constrain the Hungarians in the slightest, and Gáspar bafflingly and noisily described himself to me as a 'Tory anarchist', a rare species in Hungary. He spoke admiringly of monetarism, and I had to bring him the sad news that even among the most fervent of Thatcherites, the word 'monetarism', not to mention the practice, had been consigned to history. We then turned to foreign policy, and he was most dismissive of my claim that Gorbachev, compared to his pre-decessors in the Kremlin, was to be welcomed.

'Would you rather have an idiot running the Soviet Union?' I asked him.

'Yes,' he replied.

'You are naive, you are stupid,' said the drunk, lunging across the stuffed pancakes in order to reinforce his point by poking me in the chest. 'You know nothing about the Russians. You are naive.'

Having had a go at a sentimental leftie such as myself, they then turned their attention to Elisabeth. Gáspar and Roger Scruton began to spin some theory showing that feminism was essentially a male conspiracy to befuddle women, or some such nonsense. I said that I couldn't help noticing that women did not seem to play much of a part in the oppositionist movement, though every dissident I had encountered had been waited on by a lovely young woman. Nor were the charming women at our very table prepared to open their mouths except for the purpose of shovelling food into them or plucking at cigarettes. Since the temperature of our discussion was rising pleasantly, we ordered more wine with which to fuel our debates. Scruton conceded, reluctantly, that it was just about conceivable that one could be a Labour Party member without betraying one's country, and we had a rare bout of unanimity in discussing the dreadfulness of a publishing house I had once worked for and he had once written for.

It was past midnight, and we were the last tipplers left at Alföldi. Lights dimmed and we took our cue. Roger – we were all on first name terms now – called for the bill. I admired him for at least trying to address the waitress in Hungarian, even though his attempt was as unsuccessful as mine was always to be in Budapest. Generously, he wanted to pick up the tab.

'I've got to get rid of this funny money before I fly off tomor-row,' he said, chucking about a week's average earnings onto the table.

I insisted on paying my share. 'It's ideologically unacceptable for me to let the *Salisbury Review* pay for my wine.'

'You're right,' said Roger. 'Socialists sponge quite enough off the rest of us as it is.'

Elisabeth also said she would contribute.

'Yes, yes,' said Roger, gaily, replacing a few day's wages in his pocket. 'Greens must pay too.'

I think the principled parties may have overdone it, and that Roger Scruton and the *Salisbury Review* probably made a profit on the evening, which no doubt would have been entirely consistent with their philosophy.

My only regret was that I had not had any opportunity to talk to Haraszti himself. But a few days later I joined him for a prolonged breakfast of salami, yogurt, and fresh bread, and we had a leisurely talk. Haraszti's first major confrontation with the authorities had been when in 1973 a Budapest publishing house decided that it would be imprudent to proceed with the publication of his book *A Worker in a Worker's State*. Denied official publication, Haraszti distributed typewritten copies, of which nine were pounced upon by the police. The author was arrested and his trial was conducted at the highest level of the judiciary. Haraszti had mistimed his book, for during 1974 there was a lull in the spate of reforms that had been under way since 1968 and a renewal of repressive measures. György Konrád had also found himself in custody for a week at around this time. Haraszti's trial was clearly intended to warn the intelligentsia not to stray too far from the straight and narrow, though, as is common in such trials, the legal charge was essentially a technicality. There was no discussion of the content of Haraszti's book, only of the improper methods by which it had been circulated. It soon became evident that the trial was turning into something of a damp squib, and Haraszti received a relatively mild punishment of eight months' suspended sentence.

This was the last trial of its kind in Hungary. Kádár was shrewd enough to realize that such attempts to gag the intelligentsia were counterproductive and simply generated martyrs. Repressive laws such as those prohibiting words or deeds that 'undermine socialism' are still on the statute books and are even used on occasion, though mostly for fairly trivial offences such as the drunken indiscretions of students and soldiers who rail too noisily against the Russians. Police powers of search and confiscation are also still used from time to time, but rarely in so draconian a fashion as to attract wide publicity, especially in the West. (I recall visiting a Western correspondent when he was telephoned by a dissident whose flat had just been searched; the dissident was clearly dismayed that the news item was unlikely to hit the front pages of the Western press.) In 1980, when samizdat publication took a leap into the modern age as duplicating machines replaced typewriters, there was further government action, and in 1983 more charges were brought against samizdat publishers and distributors, but these charges were dropped because even the authorities realized they generated more bad publicity than the matter was worth. Haraszti himself discerns in the abating of police actions against the underground press a gradual coming to terms with the existence of samizdat.

Haraszti detected a changing consensus in Hungary. Kádár maintained a degree of popularity, despite his inglorious role in October 1956, both by effecting economic reforms that brought material benefits to the people, and by his tacit agreement not to govern in a totalitarian way. Of course there is no such thing, despite electoral reforms, as political pluralism in Hungary, but there has been a broadening of the boundaries that allows Hungarians a greater freedom of expression than that permitted in most other Eastern Bloc countries. There may be searches and confiscations and other harassment of oppositionists, but in the last ten years there have been no actions comparable to the jailing of the Jazz Section officers in Czechoslovakia in 1987. Even the fiercest critics of the regime acknowledge that indefinite arrest and torture are no longer part of the Hungarian manual of government. Kádár let it be understood that he would seek discreet compromise in preference to overt confrontation, and only those who acted blatantly in opposition to the interests of the regime would be acted against. In the summer of 1987 the new prime minister, Károly Grosz, went so far as to admit that critics of the government were not necessarily 'enemies of the system'. It was, he went on, permissible to hold views that differ from the official line on a whole range of issues. What was not permissible was the organization of parties or pressure groups to advance such alternative views.

Even this modest degree of tolerance is remarkable in an Eastern Bloc country, especially since the remarks were made not by an incautious minor official but by the prime minister. It may not be sufficient, however, to forestall Haraszti's prediction that oppositionists will be less willing than before to express their views *sotto voce*. Those who oppose the regime on ideological and idealistic grounds are joined by groups who feel passionately about single issues, such as the Hungarian minorities or the exploitation of gypsies. Although the numbers of those willing to press their case forcefully enough to risk losing their jobs and exit visas are fairly small, Haraszti sees a distinct possibility that the various groups will gradually form some kind of coalition and thus establish themselves as a pressure group. A first step in this direction was taken in June 1985 when oppositionists of various views met both to make contact and to see where the possibilities lay for joining in common cause.

Given the difficulties I had experienced in contacting the oppositionists, I was surprised by the ease with which, once I was suitably equipped with addresses and telephone numbers, I had access to them. Although some, deprived of their jobs and dependent instead on translating work or other occasional commissions, undoubtedly found it hard to make ends meet, I did not sense that dissidents lived too far out on the margins of society. Many lived in comfortable flats, well equipped with stereo systems, short-wave radios, and, in a few cases, costly IBM typewriters. György Konrád, whose powerful novels are not available in his own country, lived in a state of disorder I found congenial – papers and articles all over the place, empty envelopes with colourful stamps from all over the world, translations of his works into languages almost as remote as Hungarian, thick well-worn armchairs. Friends dropped in and out, small children ran excitedly into the room, then swiftly backtracked, and innumerable cups of coffee and a valedictory dram of scotch were served while the novelist, burly, bespectacled, almost doleful in manner, spoke to me gravely of 'the economy of the soul'.

24

Moving the Rubicon

'Nowadays you can say what you want, but nothing happens.'

The speaker was a middle-aged woman, a doctor who practises in a Budapest suburb. Her cynical appraisal is a fairly typical reaction to the continuing political and economic reforms in Hungary, if only because it is so obviously double-edged. Everyone acknowledges that there have been many improvements in recent years. There are fewer restrictions on foreign travel than before; the standard of living is relatively high; there are more opportunities for private enterprise and, for the successful, high earnings; Western newspapers are available at a price; and reformed electoral procedures now require a choice of candidates in each constituency.

All this is accepted and welcomed, but if there seems little enthusiasm for the changes, it is no doubt because the nature of the system remains unchanged. There is still little access to the true sources of power. It is now obligatory for certain elections to offer the people two or more candidates, but the system ensures that they tend to be Tweedledum and Tweedledee; there is thus no opportunity to effect change, as László Rajk and Gáspar Miklós Tamás demonstrated when they attempted to stand as candidates in 1985 and were outmanoeuvred by the Party committees. Free discussions were allowed at caucus level, but it was clear that no one was going to be elected whom the Party couldn't stomach. Miklós Haraszti told me that the electoral reforms, which some time ago included instituting secret ballots, didn't add up to much in themselves, but were significant in that they prepared people psychologically for the possibility of real democratic reforms at the expense of the influence of the state.

The prolonged refusal to allow the populace to participate in the political process has led to a well-founded distrust of the process itself, reforms included. No one doubts the economic reforms begun in 1968 were politically motivated: Kádár wished to keep his volatile people calm and content by offering them greater access to material goods. To a large extent, the policy has worked. One British observer remarked to me: 'The Hungarians are basically not interested in politics. But take away their blue jeans and their rock music and all hell will break loose.'

Most Hungarians are convinced that the repression and terror of the 1950s could never be reinstituted, though some who lived through those days sound a note of caution. 'Anything can happen,' they'd murmur to me. Yet it seems unlikely, since there is no longer the ideological foundation for repression. The climate of fear has given way to one of accommodation. Even György Konrád, who in *The Loser* wrote so powerfully about the 1950s, sees no possibility of a recurrence of such terror: 'The Second World War bred an atmosphere of violence. The culture accepted violence as a way to solve problems. In those days we had a kind of civil war. But the collectivist ideological fervour that seemed to justify the extremism that locked up and tortured thousands of men and women has disappeared. Those who applied the torture were not so much evil men as victims of their times and circumstances.'

Konrád may be overcharitable in his eagerness to let bygones be bygones, but Miklós Vásárhelyi, who paid a heavy price for his participation in undoing the evil wrought by Rákosi and his henchmen, also believes those days are well and truly over. 'Of course there are no constitutional safeguards to prevent a return of repression, but it's unlikely to happen. It's possible that if our economic decline continues, some politicians may speak out against the greater freedoms granted us since 1968. Then too, if the economic problems become so grave that more and more people take issue with the regime, the government may invoke counter-measures to keep people in line. Declining living standards always pose a threat to stability. But everybody, even senior Party officials, agrees that the only way out of the mess is not a return to Stalinism but further reforms.'

Despite the total control exercised by the Party, the ruling body, unlike its Czech counterpart, is prepared to entrust important jobs to non-members. Only about 9 per cent of the population consists of Party members – admission, of course, being not a right but a privilege – and about a third of members of Parliament are non-members too. Before one jumps to the conclusion that political pluralism is now flourishing in Hungary, remember that Parliament has very little power, and that all major decisions are taken by two Party organs: the Central Committee and the Politburo. I was given an idea of how little respect the Party commands when, some weeks later, I was driving through the countryside with a group of employees of a state wine farm. As we passed some rows of straggly, unkempt vines, one of the men remarked, to the amusement not only of myself but of his colleagues: 'Look at those vines! What a lousy pruning job! It's obvious they're tended by somebody who doesn't know what he's doing. He must be a Party official.'

If the economic future seemed clear to most Hungarians – the reforms must and will continue – the political future was far less certain. János Kádár has now ruled Hungary for thirty-two years. It is widely accepted that he must bear considerable responsibility for the economic mess in which Hungary finds itself, both because of decisions he has taken and decisions he has delayed taking. Both his impetuousness and his procrastination expose him to criticism. He is old too, and must surely step down soon. Miklós Haraszti was fairly hopeful about the future, and said that the lower ranks of the Party were well stocked with members with quite radical ideas, though they may lack wide support among the Party bosses. He also thought it probable that once Kádár goes, there could be a considerable increase in cultural freedom. But according to a young executive I met, some of whose policy forecasts proved startlingly accurate after I left Hungary, 'Kádár's successor has already been chosen – in Moscow. Any new leader will take a more pro-Soviet line, as in Russian eyes Hungary is too out of step with the other countries of the Bloc.' She too, it was clear, had no great faith in Mikhail Gorbachev. My friend the magazine editor was more acerbic: 'We're in a period of great political uncertainty now. Kádár is clearly out of touch and the government is slow to make decisions. Meanwhile the country sinks deeper and deeper into debt. The government won't take the risks of forcing redundancies and of limiting imports. The trouble is that Kádár is dreadful, but his would-be successors are no better.'

Miklós Haraszti had no doubt in his mind about the reforms that were necessary: 'These will have to include the right of companies to grow or die, free flow of capital within companies, and, most urgently, less control of the media, free discussion of issues and no more censorship or self-censorship. That's what ought to be happening. The difficulty is that all reforms entail some sharing of the power that used to be monopolized by the Party. If the final outcome of the reforms is to remove the party from control of economic production – and the kind of decentralization we're talking about will amount to this – then the Party itself becomes an irrelevance. Whatever happens, the road ahead will be painful for the government. Everybody recognizes that there's no future in the notion of the centrally planned economy. Radical changes must come. But industry and the Party are one and the same – that's where the pain comes in. Those who oppose the reforms, the hard-liners, are mostly union leaders, who represent the working class, the industrial proletariat. They defend the "achievements of socialism", such as the absence of unemployment in Hungary, though we all know that this is an artificial state of affairs.

'The union leaders naturally want to defend the standard of living of those they represent. But the reforms will include phasing out the subsidies that uneconomic industries now receive from central government. That's going to mean price rises and austerity. Now the government knows that people are only going to accept such measures, which amount to a lower standard of living, if the pill is sugared in various ways. If factories are to close there must be unemployment benefits and resources for relocation. There must be greater autonomy for local councils and a public bargaining role regarding wages and conditions.'

A couple of months after I left Hungary the pain began. Many prices were increased by up to 30 per cent and in early 1988 a graduated income tax (beginning at 20 per cent and rising to a maximum of 60 per cent) as well as a value added tax of up to 25 per cent were introduced. Various other systems for levying taxes – hitherto there were twelve operating simultaneously in Hungary – will be phased out or rationalized. Salary increases will be granted to offset the taxes that would be due from lower salaried workers with a single source of income, but earnings will be increasingly tied to productivity. Whether the reform package as a whole will be as radical as Haraszti and other oppositionists would wish is unlikely, since the prime minister, Károly Grosz, despite his embracing of what he calls 'the principle of performance', has tended to defend the old centralist model of the economy. Other contenders for the leadership, such as János Berecz, also fear too rapid a pace of political reform. Soon after the tax measures were announced, a number of members of Parliament strongly opposed the package on the grounds that they would hit hardest those least able to pay. For once the government found the usually docile Parliament troublesome, and had to accept numerous amendments to the new law. Whatever the solutions proposed, there is greater unanimity on the ultimate goal: to improve Hungary's trade performance and diminish its immense foreign debt.

It seems unlikely that the strides towards a market economy will be reversed. In July 1987 you could read in the Budapest *Daily News* statements such as the following bit of awkward prose from the Central Committee: 'New, flexible, profitably operating small and medium-sized business must be encouraged. Household economies, cottage industries and private businessmen are part and parcel of the socialist economy.' This is nothing new in Hungary. Some years ago, for instance, it was acknowledged that there was a shortage of taxis in Budapest. The authorities could not afford to buy a new fleet of cars, so they devised the following system. Private individuals were allowed to apply for licences to use their own cars as taxis. The authorities profited from the annual licence fee of 18,000 forints (plus 2000 forints per month for National Insurance), while the drivers could earn up to 25,000 forints gross per month. There were indeed times during my stay in Budapest when, to listen to people telling me how wonderful free enterprise was, one might have been forgiven for assuming that capitalism was, like Rubik's cube, a Hungarian invention.

Whether or not one takes the cynical view that all Central Committee decisions are in fact taken in Moscow before they are endorsed in Budapest, there is no doubt that the attitude of the Soviet Union has been of crucial importance over the years. In the past the authoritarianism and sluggishness of successive Soviet regimes could be used as a justification for not proceeding more rapidly with reforms within Hungary. It could safely be pointed out that Leonid Brezhnev was no enthusiast for radical change, and no Hungarian needs to be reminded that Yuri Andropov was the Soviet ambassador to Hungary in October 1956. Hungarians in positions of authority employed, on appropriate occasions, a gesture of pointing their finger upwards. This signified: 'However, the Russians . . .' In other words, Soviet intransigence could always be used as an excuse for not permitting greater cultural freedoms or whatever. With Gorbachev making speeches every week about *glasnost*, Party leaders can no longer rely on Soviet disapproval as an excuse for not implementing reforms. Miklós Haraszti observed, somewhat loftily: 'Marxists speak of a general crisis of capitalism, but Gorbachev signals the general crisis of communism. The whole impetus in central Europe is away from communism.'

One does not need to be in Hungary for more than ten minutes before realizing that the Russians are deeply, implacably loathed. It is not only the memory of 1956 that keeps the hatred warm. The Russians have been loathed for over a century; it was the Tsar, after all, who assisted the Austrians to crush the 1848 revolution by sending in his troops. Plenty of Russian tourists, neatly rounded up in groups, come to Budapest, but they must be the only foreign tourists in the world who keep a fleet of their own buses in a foreign capital. Russian tourists do not gawp at the sights through the windows of an Ikarus with Hungarian plates, but through a red and cream Russian bus, its provenance obvious not only from the licence plates but from the Cyrillic script along its flank. No doubt the Russians, while they cash in their roubles for goods unavailable back home, tut-tut about the capitalist leanings of the Hungarians, but their hosts suspect that in private they are deeply envious.

Hungarians have an ineradicable sense of the Russians, despite their ritualistic insistence that their presence is provisional, as an occupying force. Haraszti put it this way: 'Communism in the Eastern Bloc is the same thing as Russian occupation. The Soviets must eventually realize that militarily and politically Eastern Europe is of no benefit to them. Some of us hope it may one day be possible for Hungary to transform itself into a neutralized buffer zone in central Europe.' Other Hungarians express their dislike of the Russian presence with a joke: 'We have a saying: "Long, longer, provisionally . . . "' Driving north across the hills from Budapest towards Esztergom I passed numerous Russian patrols and the hideous barracks in which they are incarcerated, for there is no fraternization with the local population. Russian NCOs are confined to barracks, probably as much for their own safety as to protect them from such Hungarian viruses as private enterprise, delicious food and drink, and contempt for Russians.

Hungarians are given a *gavage* of Russian language studies at school. Miklós Vásárhelyi remarked: 'Despite ten years of compulsory Russian in school and college, the Russian language and culture have made no impact at all on us. During the years of the Monarchy, the Hungarian middle classes all spoke German as a matter of course, but no one in Hungary speaks or reads Russian. There's a psychological resistance to the very idea. Our culture is a

European one, mainly Catholic, and there has never been any profound Slavonic influence here.' My friend the vineyard manager made the same point more succinctly: 'I learnt Russian for twelve years. We all had to. And what for? It's almost impossible for me to travel to Russia, and the only Russians in Hungary are the soldiers and they aren't let out of their barracks.'

When I asked him what he thought about the Russians, he was not lost for words: 'Is it true that the Americans are really afraid of the Russians? That amazes me. If you'd seen them at close quarters for forty years you couldn't possibly be frightened of them. Once you've had to work with their stupid Ladas and the lousy tractors, you soon realize what a hopeless bunch they are. It's very difficult for a simple man like me to understand the Russians. They're always blaming their predecessors. Khrushchev blamed Stalin, Brezhnev blamed Khrushchev, and now I hear that Gorbachev is blaming Brezhnev. "The other guys, *they* got it wrong." So it's hard for us Hungarians to know which is the true colour red. As for Gorbachev, well, perhaps he'll improve some things. He sounds a bit better than the others. But knowing the Russians, it'll take twenty years before anything changes over there. People will tell you that we all hate the Russians. Not really. We just feel sorry for the poor bastards.'

Totalitarianism fits the Hungarians as badly as an ill-cut suit. Although their direct experiences of democracy have been few and far between, Hungarians have always managed to gouge a measure of liberty from whichever regime or occupying force has been ruling over them. From the Habsburgs they forced a major concession in the form of the Dual Monarchy. Under Dualism, suffrage was extensive and a multiparty political system could and did flourish. Despite the rigidity of a class system dominated by half a million men and women with claims to nobility, the bourgeoisie both participated in and prospered from the political processes of the late nineteenth century. Between the world wars, when Admiral Horthy ran a regime akin to fascism, certain freedoms were permitted, and Horthy, for a variety of reasons, kept a distance between his regime and the Nazis, until in 1944 the Germans occupied Hungary. Finally, from 1945 there was a last fleeting experience of democracy until the gates of Stalinism slammed shut in 1948. In 1956 the Hungarians made a desperate and doomed attempt to break out of their straitjacket. What is more astonishing is that from the jaws of that terrible defeat, they yet managed to snatch a victory of sorts. They have wrested from their leaders a degree of personal freedom, both economic and cultural, unmatched in any other Eastern Bloc country with the sporadic exception of Poland. It is precisely for this reason that many Hungarians feel so bitterly about the freedoms they have not yet attained. It should be clear by now that the Hungarians are as sophisticated and shrewd a nation as any in Europe. Being fobbed off goes against their grain. Grateful for existing reforms, their response is nevertheless to demand more, and their leaders, for economic as well as political reasons, are likely to acquiesce.

I asked György Konrád what you cannot do in Hungary. 'You don't openly criticize Politburo members. You can't found a new political party or organize an unauthorized lecture series. You can't publish a book without permission of the state, nor can you produce a play. It has been ten years now since I had a book published here in Hungary.'

László Rajk added to the list: 'Taboo subjects? There are many. There is no public discussion of whether Soviet troops should be in Hungary, or the status of Hungarian minorities in other Eastern Bloc countries – except Romania, a country unpopular with everybody – or the growing problem of poverty in Hungary, or the serious pollution in some areas that the government acknowledges but won't do anything about because it would, they say, not be economically viable for them to do so. You don't talk about the gypsies, who form the country's largest pool of unskilled labour. There's much prejudice against them, and if the economy declines further they could be made a scapegoat by some people. Loathing gypsies is an up-to-date version of antisemitism, which has a long tradition in Hungary. The gypsies, who are about 4 per cent of the population, also have the highest birthrate, and that also worries people. You don't discuss 1956 and you don't discuss censorship. You don't draw attention to the fact that our government made a deal with the Vatican by which we permit some religious education in our schools, and in return the Vatican agrees not to support the hundred or more jailed Hungarian conscientious objectors who base their objections on religious grounds. And you don't discuss the dam.'

That the Hungarians would participate in the Gabčikovo-Nagymaros barrage dam project was confirmed in the Party newspaper in August 1985. The scheme has excited bitter resentment within Hungary. Construction is being financed and undertaken by the Austrians, who in return for their money and technology and labour force will receive 78 per cent of the energy that will be generated over the next twenty years. In addition, they, rather than the Hungarians and Czechs, will benefit most from the employment provided by the huge construction project. Hungarian objections are numerous: tampering with the water table around the Danube between Bratislava and Budapest could threaten the latter's water supply; a large area will be flooded, and many archaeological sites destroyed. The alterations to the landscape will sever roads linking a number of Czech villages, many with Hungarian-speaking inhabitants. There is even fear that a successful terrorist attack on the dam could lead to the flooding of Budapest. The Czechs will benefit from the scheme, say the Hungarians (though not the Czech dissidents), and Austria and the Soviet Union will benefit from a shipping route that will link Vienna to the Black Sea ports.

Opponents of the project point out that the decision was taken by Kádár in a fit of table-thumping pique and that feasibility studies were carried out only after the decision had been made. Even some ministers concede in private, I was told, that the dam is a terrible idea and that the go-ahead should never have been given. In 1984 a petition against the dam collected 10,000 signatures, but had, unlike some of the Austrian environmentalist protests, no effect. One oppositionist took furious and patriotic objection to the scheme: 'Hungary has become the perfect colony for Austria. The Monarchy is dead, of course, and Austria no longer has to feed and defend us, but we're still a colony. They come swarming over the border to buy our food, enjoy our spas, and get their teeth fixed. They already plunder us, but now they're taking our energy away from us too. Austria gets "clean" energy, and we get the environmental damage. In fact, Hungarians get nothing from the dam – except lies.'

Hungarians are still constrained in their freedom to travel, though to a lesser extent than their East European neighbours. A Hungarian is permitted to visit the West once every three years (or once every year if invited, as many are, by the innumerable relatives living abroad, without whom no Hungarian is complete), but is permitted to purchase only about $300 in foreign currency, which doesn't take you very far. On day trips to Vienna, Hungarians may buy only 700 schillings. When they cross the border again on their way home, most of them, clutching video equipment and Japanese stereo systems, have some explaining to do. Documents, invariably bogus, are produced to show that the hardware is a 'gift', and more often than not the shopper will get away with it, though the authorities are fully aware that the system is being abused constantly. Hungarians with forints to burn can also sign up on trips organized by Ibusz, the state travel bureau. But they are very expensive: four days half-board in London will cost 30,000 forints, which is close to £500 or a few months' average salary. Hungarians may travel freely to most other Eastern Bloc countries, but show little interest in doing so.

Despite the constraints under which they live, the restless Hungarians will keep pushing at the boundaries of the possible. The austerity measures announced in the spring of 1987 will hit them hard, the frustration at living within a system they openly despise is palpable, the restrictions on freedom of expression, both cultural and political, are, for all their relative moderation, nonetheless intolerable to anyone who has had a taste of more democratic systems. It is hard to feel depressed in Budapest. I left buoyed and encouraged because of the sheer irrepressibility of the Hungarians, who will not curl up in a corner and go to sleep while their leaders flounder, and who refuse to accommodate themselves, except as an interim measure, to the system in which they find themselves enmeshed almost as an accident of history. Their most fervent hope is that you cannot have economic reform without political reform; you cannot introduce economic pluralism, as the government is indeed doing, without eventually opening the doors to political pluralism.

'If,' it was suggested to me, 'the Rubicon is inconveniently located, you can count on the Hungarians to move it.'

PRAGUE

Finally there was nothing left of Kakania but oppressed minorities and a supreme circle of persons who were the actual oppressors and who regarded themselves as being outrageously hoaxed and pestered by the oppressed.

Robert Musil, *The Man Without Qualities*, chapter 107

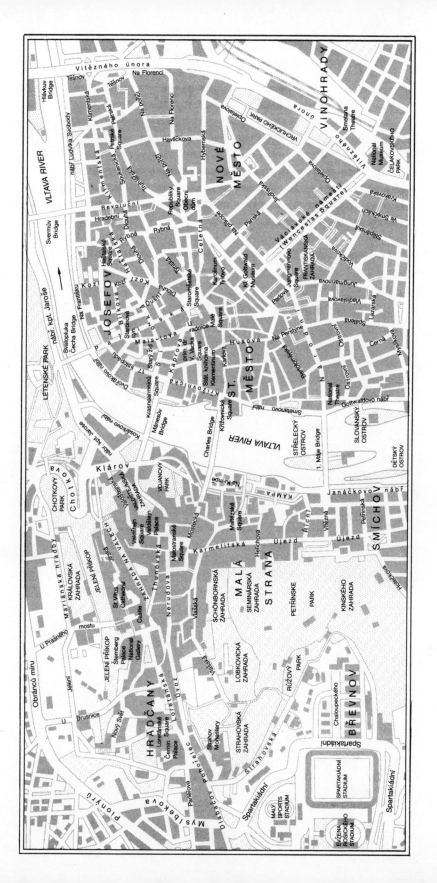

25

Go Away

While Vienna was still a provincial city, Prague was already the cultural and intellectual powerhouse of central Europe. The magnificence of medieval Prague owed nothing to the Habsburgs: it was the almost single-handed creation of the Bohemian king Charles IV, who came to the throne in 1346. This superbly accomplished monarch – he was fluent in five languages – rebuilt the castle, laid out new sections of the city, established a university that is still functioning, and rebuilt the fortifications. After Charles's death, the cohesion of Bohemia – and its other domains in present-day Poland and Germany – began to crumble, and revolts and wars dominated the region for decades. For a brief spell, Bohemia and Hungary were united under the rule of Matthew Corvinus, but the Turkish invasions of central Europe put an end to that. In 1526 the Habsburg prince, Ferdinand I, the brother of the great Charles V, was elected ruler of what is now Czechoslovakia and Hungary. The Habsburgs ruled Bohemia with a heavy hand. The largely Protestant nobility fought against them but were defeated at the Battle of White Mountain in 1620, after which many of their lands were confiscated. Maria Theresa centralized the administration of Bohemia in Austrian hands; and she and her successor Joseph II imposed the German language on Bohemia. Nevertheless Czech nationalism could not be eradicated entirely, and during the nineteenth century it proved as noisy, if not so effective, a force as Hungarian nationalism.

Prague is often described as a baroque city, and so it is in many respects. Entire streets and districts were rebuilt under Habsburg rule and parts of the city still seem saturated in supremely elegant seventeenth- and eighteenth-century houses and palaces. But describing Prague as baroque does an injustice to Charles IV, for he transformed too the physical appearance of the city. The towers and bridge and churches that he founded still remain, though some are inevitably obscured by the more domineering styles of later buildings now alongside them. There are still vestiges of the medieval Charles University to be seen, and many of the monasteries and fortifications that he established and built remain visible. The Charles Bridge itself, which dates from 1357, marries the essentially utilitarian solidity of Charles IV's construction plans with the more fanciful decorativeness of the many baroque statues on its balustrades, embellishing the bridge's progress across the Vltava River. Throughout Prague the medieval and the baroque blend and bow to each other, their differing styles rarely in conflict. Prague is a marvellously harmonious city, as harmonious as Venice, which juxtaposes along its canals and alleys a variety of architectural styles that never jar.

Yet the Czechs themselves seem somewhat reluctant to persuade tourists, at least from Britain and the United States, to come and take a look. Visitors' books in museums are filled with the names of Germans from both sides of the wall and, for some reason, Italians, but there is scarcely a British or American signature to be seen. The queues for the visas at the Czech embassies I have visited in Vienna and London may deter some. I left my passport at the London visa section for an hour or so, and on returning to collect it was informed that no visa would be forthcoming for at least two weeks. I had been warned by the Czech tourist office, Cedok, that the word 'Writer' in my passport would lead to delays in issuing a visa. Nonetheless I inquired: 'Why the delay?'

'It is necessary for us to consult with the Czech authorities.'

'I thought you were the Czech authorities.'

The official scowled at this pleasantry and muttered something about sending my passport to Prague. I should telephone in a fortnight, when it might be possible for me to collect my passport. The authorities completed their mysterious investigations on time and I reported just over two weeks later to collect my visa. I paid up the required £14 – quite a hefty fee for the privilege of spending hard currency in Czechoslovakia – and was then hit for a further £3.

'Oh yes? And what's that for?'

'Telex to Prague. Three pounds please.'

'It does seem to me,' I reflected aloud, 'that if you insist on telexing Prague to pursue your inquiries it should be at your expense rather than mine.'

The response was a shrug with which I would later become familiar. Its unspoken message was invariably: take it or leave it. I took it, paid up, and left with my visa in triplicate.

I was prepared for more trouble at Prague airport, but there was none. There were no inquiries, other than into how much currency I had changed, and no searches of luggage or person. Members of my family, on entering Czechoslovakia some years earlier, had been required to surrender their British newspapers, but my copy of *The Guardian* entered Prague intact and was later given away to news-hungry Czechs.

From the airport I took the bus into town, and from the terminal lugged my suitcase the few hundred yards to the Cedok offices. A taxi swam up alongside me, and a burly man sprang out to offer me not only transportation but money-changing at favourable rates. Even if I had been disposed to change money on the black market, I would not have done so on one of the main streets of Prague in full view of half a dozen policemen and four hundred informers. In any event, Czech currency regulations had already obliged me on entering the country to change vast sums into Czech crowns, and the last thing I needed was any more of them. I declined the offer, and staggered onwards.

I had enjoyed staying in private accommodation in Budapest, and intended to do the same in Prague. I chose to visit the city during the few weeks between Easter and the Prague Spring musical festival, and so I was hoping that the city would not be too crowded. Indeed, the plane on which I had arrived had been close to empty. So I was astonished, on reaching the Cedok office devoted to finding accommodation for tourists, to be told, with some relish, that there was no private accommodation available. It had not occurred to me that, even though Prague may attract few Britons or Americans, it is a favourite trough of the beer-swilling Germans, whose extensive border with Czechoslovakia is a mere two hours' drive from Prague. Perhaps Cedok could find me a room for tomorrow night? Nothing available! Well, how about the following week? I was, after all, proposing to spend a few weeks in the city.

With considerable impatience, the woman behind the counter responded: 'There are no private rooms available in Prague. Not today. Not tomorrow. Not for the next few weeks.' She could, however, offer me a room at the Hotel Flora, which was only a couple of miles from the city centre. When she told me the price of a single room, I realized that I would soon run out of money.

However, I had little choice, and booked in for two nights. On the street outside I was accosted by a sad-looking woman. I thought she was going to ask for money, but no, she was offering me a room. It seemed a long way out of town, and the price in dollars seemed higher than the going rate, but at least it might provide a safety net if all else failed. I took her card and thanked her.

The Flora proved acceptable, if spartan. Although Cedok had told me the room had its own bathroom, this proved not to be the case. It did have a bed, a small table, and a plastic-covered armchair. It also had a radio, familiar from Moscow hotel rooms, of the Amazing Nontunable model. It had no On/Off switch, only a volume control knob. I had been given no choice of accommodation, and there was no choice of radio station either. Fortunately I had brought with me a small transistor powerful enough to pick up the morning news in English from Radio Austria each day. The window looked onto the courtyard, which itself was overlooked on all sides by the other wings of the hotel. On most of the sills were perched German teenagers here on a group tour. They would call to each other from storey to storey, from room to room, appearing and disappearing like colourful figures in an Advent calendar.

After a wash, I headed back into town. Like a child using up a magic wish, I decided I had to start drawing on some of my contacts in order to find more affordable and more discreet accommodation. Going through my list at random, I settled on the number of a man who worked at a museum. I got through immediately, explained who I was, and asked him directly whether he knew of anyone with a room to rent. He thought not, and then he asked me to hold on for a moment while he checked with a colleague. He returned to the line a moment later and said he knew of a room on Wenceslas Square. This was rather like arriving ignorant and disorientated in London and being offered digs on Piccadilly. Moreover the price was lower than that demanded by Cedok for private accommodation.

The following day I was taken to meet the landlady and inspect the room. She opened the double doors into an enormous room that contained two huge beds in a creamy neo-rococo style. The sun was pouring in from the courtyard, where pale green leaves, newly unfurled, were flapping cheerfully in the strong spring light. I could scarcely believe my luck, and took the room immediately. I later moved into an equally spacious room across the hall; it faced onto the square and had its own sink. This space I shared with a toy dog, a spinning wheel, a guitar, two picnic hampers, a photograph of a chimpanzee smoking a cigarette, four coffee services, dozens of painted eggs, and two wigs, both the worse for wear. Among this memorabilia I stayed for the next three weeks, fussed over by my good-hearted landlady, who was convinced my health would suffer if I did not consume, at the beginning of each day, a tub of yogurt, a ham omelette, two rolls, and two or sometimes three slices of cheese or nut cake, usually all but invisible beneath an avalanche of whipped cream. Returning to my room in the late afternoon, it was hard to avoid an interception from the kind woman, her brow creased with worry, her lips a-tremble as she implored me to refresh myself: 'Ham an' eggs? Ham an' eggs? Tea? Tea?'

It was only after I had established myself in Mrs Plička's enormous apartment that I began to explore the city. Staying at the Flora had been irksome, even though it was no great distance from the city centre. The hotel itself provided restaurants and a coffee shop, but I avoided them because I couldn't stand the constant yawing and yelling of the German teenagers, who marched through the public rooms as though they were on a hiking holiday in Bavaria. Morning coffee was hard to find in the dull streets lined with stuccoed apartment buildings that flowed in all directions from the corner on which the hotel stood. There was a tavern close to the Metro station, but the owner took a strange delight in wilfully misunderstanding my order and giving me two mugs of beer when I had only wanted one. Still, I could sit out on the grubby terrace of the pub and watch the inhabitants of the neighbourhood slowly drink themselves into a state of good humour.

But from my room on Wenceslas Square all amenities were instantly available: restaurants and airline offices, the café of the Europa Hotel and the chic photographic gallery on Jungmannova Square, ice cream sellers and the sausage stands selling a *kolbasy* that seemed largely composed of pig tumours. It was, of course, Charles IV who laid out the half-mile-long Wenceslas Square – rectangle would be a more accurate term for it – though the horse market that originally occupied the space has mercifully disappeared. In recent years the square has been turned into a pedestrian precinct and the trams that once trundled up and down have been diverted elsewhere. Whenever the Czechs decide to scribble a footnote on the pages of European history, they usually do so here. The Republic was proclaimed here in 1918, Red Army tanks made a truimphal procession though the square in 1945, and after their return in 1968 the philosophy student Jan Palach incinerated himself in January 1969 not far from the statue of St Wenceslas which stands at the top of the square near the massive National Museum.

The museum is one of those palatial neo-Renaissance palaces of culture that could just as easily have been built in Vienna or Budapest. And it was by another nineteenth-century home of art, the National Theatre on Národní, that I met Helena, the friend of a Czech emigré I knew in London. She worked as a translator, and her English was good, if strangely artificial: her vowels whooped. Although she had trained as an English interpreter, she was obliged to spend most of her time translating for visiting Germans, a task she did not enjoy. The Germans were not her favourite people, she let me know, and the East Germans, in her view, were even more boorish than those from the West. We walked across the bridge by the National Theatre to Mála Strana, the Lesser Town, so called, I assume, because its narrow streets wind up and along the steep slopes that lead up to the castle.

Malá Strana is utterly delightful, a maze of baroque and rococo streets. The citizens of Prague never tire of telling visitors that much of the film *Amadeus* was shot in Malá Strana, which more closely resembles eighteenth-century Vienna than present-day Vienna resembles its former self. What particularly enchanted me about Malá Strana is the way gardens and greenery are tucked into unexpected corners. On Kampa Island, which is separated from the shore by a narrow inlet crossed by bridges – Prague's Venice – there is a park overlooked by palaces. Before the Second World War the island was privately owned by the occupants of a palace that, like so many of the loveliest and grandest buildings in Malá Strana, is now an embassy, in this case the Dutch embassy. Close to the shore is the formal Voyanovy Sady, with its weeping willows and, in the spring, budding magnolias and squadrons of scarlet tulips. Behind the splendid facade of the Valdštejn Palace, which fills one side of the square that bears its name, are more gardens, which are open only in the summer. On hot days strollers can tread the gravel paths between hedges and clumps of bronze statuary, and then shelter from the sun beneath the superb lofty Renaissance loggia that forms part of the garden front of the palace. Shelter can also be found in a corner of the gardens where immense chestnut trees shade the paths, while alongside this little grove peacocks spread their tails and shriek at the world from a large aviary.

I often used to come here in the late afternoon to read for an hour after a day of strenuous sightseeing. I rarely made it through the hour, however, thanks to the steady intrusion of *Gruppen*, bands of roving Germans who would spread themselves across the benches near Pieroni's loggia and then yell at each other. One would imagine that the Germans, having within living memory loutishly invaded this most delicate of central European cities, would have set about their second, more pacific invasion as tourists with more discretion and greater sensitivity. But no: for many Germans, as for many Americans, Europe is little more than a picturesque clump of scenery and backdrops over which they are free to stomp with heavy tread as though it were a ghost town. The loud guffawing *Gruppen* in the Valdštejn were quite oblivious to the fact that the gardens provide for the citizens of Prague and for tourists alike a refuge, a patch of calm and solitude in a crowded city.

So I soon forsook the Valdštejn gardens for the Vrtba gardens, which are almost impossible to find. They are reached through an unmarked passageway that tunnels through a house in Karmelitská. This early eighteenth-century garden, laid out on narrow terraces Tuscan-style, climbed the hillside beneath the castle, and from its upper levels there were wonderful views over the domes and spires of Malá Strana as well as across the river and up to the palaces around the castle itself. Few tourists here. Instead Czech office workers with briefcases and students with a textbook would quietly crunch along the gravel paths or sprawl on one of the benches, occasionally raising an eyebrow as somebody walked by. There are a few other such terraced gardens in Malá Strana, such as the Fürstenberg and the Kolowrat, but they were never open.

Helena took me up the steep lanes of Tržiště and Vlašská, past the great facades of palaces that are now embassies or government offices. From Úvoz, we descended into the large area of greenery that lies south of the castle. This series of interlinked parks is far less formal than the gardens closer to the river, and there is a wildness that is always pleasing when encountered in the heart of a city. Near the top of the hill is the Hunger Wall, part of the fortifications built by Charles IV in the 1360s. It's said that the wall was constructed so as to provide employment for the burgeoning population of Prague, a kind of medieval New Deal. After six centuries the fabric needs repair, and the towers and crenellations are now being restored. 'We can't help noticing,' observed Helena, 'that it's taking the authorities longer to restore the Hunger Wall than it took Charles IV to build it.'

We returned via Nerudova, where I begged Helena, who marched with a vigour inappropriate on such a warm day, to allow me to refresh myself at a pub. The pub, any pub, is a Czech institution, and there is no nannying in the form of licensing laws to prevent a constant slaking of one's thirst. The pubs on Nerudova, one of the loveliest lanes of all, were fairly trendy, packed with chain-smoking students and tourists whiling away a Sunday afternoon. And the beer, despite rumours that Czech lager is increasingly adulterated, was cool and delicious, though its monotony of flavour usually dissuaded me from downing a second mug. While I drank, Helena amused herself by teaching me the Czech word for ice cream.

'*Zmrzlina.*'

'*Zemerzerlina.*'

'No. Once more. *Zmrzlina.*'

'*Zrmzl* – '

'No. That's not right. Try again, more slowly. *Zmrzlina.*'

'It's hopeless. I find Czech more difficult to pronounce than Hungarian, which doesn't exactly trip off the tongue.'

'Oh yes,' replied Helena happily, 'Czech is a very difficult language. Even for Czechs.'

Helena was pleasantly indiscreet. I had expected Czechs to be more buttoned-up than the happy-go-lucky Hungarians, and in general they were, but Helena spoke with open scorn about the Communists. Nor did she have a good word to say for the social and economic organization of the country. I had come to Prague a fortnight after Mikhail Gorbachev (dismissed by Helena as 'just another Russian Communist leader'), and was thus able to receive at first hand a batch of newly minted political jokes. Helena provided a typical example, prompted by some horticultural remarks I was making. 'Do you know why spring is so late this year? It's because President Husák promised Gorbachev that things would improve here by the spring.'

26

Greeting the Glorious May Days

During the last days of April, thousands of schoolchildren and squads of handymen are employed in fastening bright red banners across the face of every official building in Czechoslovakia. On either side of almost every window sill in the land, small tubular sheaths fixed permanently to the walls are filled with wooden sticks to which are attached the flags of Czechoslovakia and the Soviet Union. Sometimes a plain red flag is substituted for the hammer and sickle. Even though I do not underestimate the ideological brotherhood and solidarity between Czechoslovakia and its eager liberator from the East, it did seem peculiar to see throughout the land the flag of another country waving in tandem with the Czech colours. Moreover, every shop window in Prague was filled with comparably patriotic displays, usually a poster of a dove (symbolizing peace, doncha know) or a Russian tank, the two concepts being, it appears, inseparable to the official mind. Even a modest butcher's in Karlštejn had devised an elaborate backdrop of such posters, in front of which stood the usual pile of tins of Luncheon Meat. One resourceful shopkeeper had persuaded a trail of ivy to adorn his poster, though the greenery had to be guided here and there with a few pins. And a pub had found some festive faery lights (no doubt surplus stock from an East German *Tannenbaum* store) with which to illuminate a dove.

The reason for this burst of patriotic fervour was the imminence of May Days. No, not May Day, but May Days, for the Czechs cram no fewer than three holidays into the space of nine days. There is May Day itself, when parades march joyfully through the streets and squares of every city and town in Eastern Europe and the Soviet Union. And then there is 5 May, the anniversary of the Prague uprising against the Germans in 1945, a modest event now glorified into an act of heroic resistance. Official calendars

inelegantly refer to 5 May as a Significant Day of the Czechoslovak Socialist Republic. Three days off in nine days clearly
strikes the Czech authorities as an excessive display of thankful-
ness, so 5 May is marked only by the solemn guard posted on
numerous official buildings by young Pioneers, in their smart blue
shirts and red cravats. The final movement of this trio of
festivities is performed on 9 May, the anniversary of the liberation
of Prague by the Red Army in 1945.

I knew by late April that these treats were in store because the
slogans told me so. 'ZDRAVIME SLAVNE MAJOVE DNY.' I
translate: 'WE GREET THE GLORIOUS MAY DAYS.' Can't be
clearer than that. By the morning of 1 May itself, a bright and
sunny day, the flags were all out. I was deeply disturbed by my
landlady's failure to decorate my window with flags, but my
anxiety was short-lived, for when I returned from the parade later
that morning, she had done her duty. There were other gaps,
though, occasional unadorned windows on high-rise apartment
blocks. The flying of flags is no longer compulsory during the May
Days, though the pressure to display them remains strong. Here
and there, no doubt, are old people or other happy-go-lucky folk
who are probably immune from the petty vindictiveness of the
state. I was particularly charmed, on visiting acquaintances a few
days later at their suburban villa, to see only the Czech flag flying
from the stout pole over the porch. 'Yes,' beamed my host, 'it
irritates them even more to see the Czech flag alone than to see no
flag at all. But what can they do?'

At eight o'clock on May Day morning, I joined thousands of
other jubilant citizens and took the metro to Hradčanská, from
which it was a short stroll to the Letná parade ground. A sports
stadium flanks the northern side of the huge open space, and
backing up against it was a lengthy stand, brightly draped in red.
Behind the stadium gates were parked dozens of black Tatras, the
sleek high-roofed cars reserved for the use of Party officials. Mere
mortals used public transportation or walked. On the grassy
expanses of Letná, people of all ages clustered around the banners
that represented their organizations. Later they would march past
the official stands and greet their leaders, who would return their
greetings. But for now the atmosphere was comparable to that of
any factory or school outing. Children gnawed at sausages or
slurped up zmrzlina, while their elders smoked and laughed and
wandered about. Some groups were uniformed, such as the police
and the airline pilots from CSA. There were more amorphous

gatherings around the banners of various state enterprises such as Energotechnika, Strojimport, and many others with names that only remain in my mind in distorted versions, such as Inter-smegma and Slobexport and Bossprojekt. Some of the banners were home-made, hurried last minute jobs, while the children were equipped with sticks resembling jester's tops to which paper streamers in the Czech colours (red, white, blue) were attached, or with circular paper representations in blue and white of doves. MIR (peace) was a useful slogan, short and meaningless, and it made its appearance in four languages. 'Peace' in the context of Czech propaganda, Václav Havel – the country's best known playwright and best known dissident – has written, is 'nothing more than an unreserved concurrency with the policy of the Soviet bloc and a uniformly negative attitude towards the West'.

I turned my attention to the official stand, which from end to end must have measured 500 yards. Army officers and Party officials and their spouses, together with honoured guests and factory managers, filled the distant extremities of the scarlet stand, while its grandest stretch was reserved for the Politburo and other senior dignitaries. This holy of holies was marked with a particularly lengthy red sheet hanging from the rail and adorned with a red star. Above the stand were four immense blow-ups: of Karl Marx, Friedrich Engels, V.I. Lenin, and – wait a minute. No, it's not Gustáv Husák, the long-reigning president. Those features do resemble – no, it can't be – he's a man of the left, to be sure, but hardly a hero of the Czechoslovak Socialist Republic. Still, to me it looks like Ray Buxton, leader of ASLEF, one of the more obdurate British trade unions. However, the history books assure me that Buxton's double is none other than the late Klement Gottwald, who ruled Czechoslovakia from 1948 to 1953. It is not a pretty face, for Gottwald exudes a thuggishness alien to the good Mr Buxton. Gottwald's somewhat bloated features were addition-ally distended by his fondness for strong liquor, an attachment said to have speeded his death, though some loyal citizens attribute his demise to grief at the death of Stalin, whose passing away preceded his own by a matter of weeks.

Shortly before nine o'clock the national anthem was played – or relayed across the loudspeakers. The crowd stood to attention, but as soon as the music ended, the chatter resumed. On the stroke of nine, the president of Czechoslovakia, Gustáv Husák, began to speak to his people. They did not listen. Children continued rolling on the grass and lapping ice cream, while their elders turned their backs on the rostrum – not, I'm sure, out of disrespect, but simply because it was more important to discuss the new extension to the country cottage than to listen to what Husák had to say. After all, they'd heard it all before. For almost twenty years the same platitudes have rolled forth from that thin mouth. Two or three rows of people pressed up against the fence to secure a good view of the parade that would shortly be passing by, and these few hundred spectators did appear to be paying some attention to their leader's words. But for the overwhelming majority of the people assembled at Letná that morning, 1 May was a day out with the kids and colleagues more than a political rally. The buzz of chatter subsided slightly when the loudspeakers crackled out the Internationale and some joined in the singing of the sturdy melody. Military officers and uniformed Pioneers gravely saluted.

Then the parade began. While the loudspeakers relayed the contents of a ten-minute tape of marching music over and over again, waves of cheerful factory workers, schoolchildren, uniformed pilots and officers strode past the stands. The Politburo went in for some heavy waving, their hands flapping epileptically as the official march-past marched past. As each group of striding citizens neared the stands they gave a great cheer, to which Husák, who was contorting his features into his annual smile, responded with even more energetic waving, as did his cohorts. Given the casualness of the assembly ten minutes earlier, such coordinated enthusiasm seemed odd to me, and I moved nearer to investigate. Beneath and about fifty yards before the Politburo stand, a small glass booth had been built just above ground level. Within stood a bespectacled man declaiming from a piece of paper, bawling out slogans at the top of his voice. At the end of his batch – it took twenty seconds or so to work his way down the list – he would yell: '*Hoo*rah!', and the marching crowds would take their cue, shout '*Hoo*rah!' in turn, and wave their streamers and Russian flags and peace posters. This was timed by the cheerleader in the booth so that the joyful shout would rise to the welcoming ears of the Politburo just as the main wave of each section of marchers was strolling by. It must have looked great on television.

I went to a great deal of trouble to scribble down the slogans picked for 1987. Friends kindly translated them, and now you are going to have to read them. Do not complain, for you only have to read them once, whereas the Czechs have to stare at these mindless words draped over thousands of buildings for weeks at a time. I can offer you:

'SOVIET UNION: GUARANTEE OF THE HAPPY AND PEACEFUL FUTURE OF MANKIND.'

'LENIN'S WAY TO THE FURTHER DEVELOPMENT OF OUR SOCIALIST FATHERLAND.'

'FOR LIFE IN PEACE AGAINST DANGER OF WAR.'

'FOR FURTHER DEVELOPMENT OF OUR SOCIALIST SOCIETY.'

'REVOLUTIONARY PRAGUE WELCOMED WITH GRATITUDE AND LOVE HER LIBERATORS.'

'HOLIDAY OF THE WORKING PEOPLE OF THE WHOLE WORLD.'

And finally, a great favourite with irreverent Czechs:

'THE AIM OF THE COMMUNIST PARTY: THE HAPPINESS OF MAN.'

Yes, they ask, but which man?

Slogans, like lettuce, rapidly become tired. The Party apparatus is busily engaged through the early spring of each year in devising new ones and, more importantly, dropping old ones. There used to be a spate of them on the theme of the USSR as the model for Czech society. These have now been jettisoned, and will presumably remain on the scrapheap until Mr Gorbachev stops rocking the boat.

'We couldn't help noticing,' said a former priest who was dismissed by the regime, 'that in recent years the slogans have been getting longer. We suspect it's because the factories that turn out the banners get paid by the letter. This year two of my colleagues in the cultural centre boiler room where I work were told to help out with draping the banners across the facades of our building. They spent hours on it, leaning out of windows, climbing up ladders, straightening out crooked strips of cloth, making sure everybody could see the words from the street. At the end of the day they came back to the boiler room cursing and groaning – as we always do when we have to do some work – and told me how they'd spent the day. I then asked them what our building slogans were this year. They'd spent the whole day hanging them, but they couldn't remember a single word of any of them. That amused me, but it also reflects a psychological reality: we no longer take in these dreary mottoes. They have no meaning. They make no impression upon us.'

I had expected, on coming to Prague, that the hard-line regime would have instilled a high degree of orthodoxy in its citizenry. If the people of Budapest do not take the reigning Communist

229

ideology and slogans seriously, this is in large part because their leaders clearly don't believe them either. In Czechoslovakia there is equal disbelief. The name of the game here is not ideology so much as power. By subscribing to the Party line, the ambitious have access to both power and privilege. Having attained both, their principal motivation is to stay in place and to keep the system as intact as possible. 'Ideology,' one particularly embittered Chartist told me, 'is merely a formula for staying in the same position.' Any deviation from Marxist-Leninist orthodoxy is a threat not to ideological purity, for the reigning ideology is utterly hollow, but to one's grip on power.

The defrocked pastor told me: 'Ideology certainly exists but it's not dogmatic. Remember that when Brezhnev was alive, it was his dogmas we declaimed. Now that Gorbachev is in power, we're required to echo his views, his dogmas. Here's an example. The ruling ideology used to require firmness in front of the imperialist enemy. But for the last year or two Gorbachev and Reagan have talked about little else than arms reductions and zero options. So our line has to change. Now the dogma isn't firmness but – you guessed it – flexibility. Dogma, even in orthodox Eastern Bloc countries, doesn't exist outside a specific context. It's crucial to know who's saying something and why. Our orthodoxy is one that exists without dogma. At all our universities and colleges the students are given classes in Scientific Communism and they must pass exams in the subject. The students consider it as no more than a catechism, formulae they're required to repeat but that have no connection with reality, with the rest of their life. Ironically, dissidents' children do very well in these exams, since most of them come from homes where Marxist ideas have always been under discussion.'

Václav Havel insisted to me that no one believes the slogans. Among young people, he said, there are few if any ardent communists. Even Party functionaries are not believers in the ideology so much as opportunists, prepared to go along with any mumbo-jumbo if it guarantees their access to power. 'The structure survives because power is self-perpetuating. The system doesn't require people to believe in it so much as people who are loyal to it.'

27

Is There a Foot That Fits This Shoe?

The Hungarians' reputation for deviousness is legendary, as the old definition proudly testifies: a Hungarian is someone who steps into a revolving door last and steps out first. The Czechs, however, have grown skilled at a form of deviousness that surpasses even the Italian gift for it – cheating foreigners. On only one occasion had I been cheated or short-changed in Hungary, but in Prague not a day passed by without a waiter or shop assistant attempting to relieve me of more money than I had contracted to part with.

I spent my first few evenings in Prague trying to get into some of its better restaurants. This was a fruitless exercise; a path had been beaten to their doors long before by countless *Gruppen*. Every table had been booked days in advance. Friends told me that a packet of classy British or American cigarettes slipped to the *maitre d'* would usually lead to the discovery of an available table tucked in a dim corner, but I have no talent for falling to my knees and begging to be allowed to spend a not inconsiderable sum in a restaurant. On my first evening in Prague, I went instead to the wine bar U Šuterů, famous, I was told, for its Moravian wines. A table was available, but there was no menu. After I placed my order – the waiter had given me a recitation of the dishes of the day – I did notice that other customers appeared to be reading what looked like a menu, but I thought nothing of it. Until the bill arrived. The glass of dry white wine turned out – surprise, surprise – to be the most expensive on the list, what the Czechs call an Archiv wine, what the rest of the world calls a vintage wine. For a second glass, containing a lesser and sweeter white wine, I was charged the same as for the Archiv wine.

I did the only thing one can do under the circumstances. I made as much noise as possible. This embarrassed me, but it also embarrassed the waiter into altering the bill downwards to make up for his 'mistake'. And so I learnt on my first evening that it is imperative to ask to see the menu. Such a request is always met by the usually untrue response 'But sir, the menu is in Czech.' To which one must always reply, 'Nevertheless . . .' even though such insistence is usually greeted with a scowl. Indeed, at the esteemed restaurant U Malířů, my request was treated with such surliness that I decided it was a bad omen for the meal to come, so I walked out.

Sometimes the waiter asserts the lie direct. At a wine tavern on Betlémské náměsti (square) I ordered two glasses of wine. 'Don't bring me Archiv wine,' I added, having learnt a thing or two by then. 'But', said the waiter,' we are such a fine wine tavern that we *only* serve Archiv wine.' I gave in. Later I checked a well-concealed menu. The waiter had indeed lied. If this irritation at being cheated became an excessive preoccupation, it was not merely parsimony on my part. Those two glasses of rather ordinary well-made wine set me back over £1.50 each, and such prices, which exceed those of even the fanciest London wine bar, are more or less standard in Prague wine taverns. The only excuse I can find for being cheated so regularly is that it was assumed that I must be German, and Germans, to most Czechs, are fair game.

Nor is cheating restricted to pulling the wool over one's eyes and miscounting the change or, as at the swish Hotel Alcron, in adding charges to the bill ('for the band') which do not appear on the menu. (At the Alcron I at least had the pleasure of sitting in an unspoilt 1930s room, complete with a life-size pewter statue of a nude enjoying a good stretch on emerging from the shower. The admirable service swiftly became supercilious once I queried the bill.) Czech restaurants adopt the admirable practice of listing not only the dishes on the menu, but the size of the portions. You will be offered 100 or 150 grams of steak, say with 150 grams of potato salad or 50 grams of cabbage salad. But if the waiter spots a tourist, the poor sucker is likely to end up with a severely reduced portion. After my souring experiences at U Šuterů and similar establishments, I took to eating every night at a small neighbourhood restaurant called Demínka on Anglická behind the National Museum. It was a place of faded grandeur, a suite of high-ceilinged rooms with chandeliers. The food was edible, the beer excellent, the prices reasonable, the clientele unpredictable. My usual waiter had the suavity of a merchant banker; he acted with such perfect politeness and attentiveness that I was sure he considered himself wasted at the job. Perhaps he had been a university professor or diplomat before Husák cracked the whip in 1968 or 1977. One day he brought me a miserable slice of pork that fell far short of the 150 grams stated on the menu. I complained. Without a word, he slid off and returned moments later with another plate, on which a second slice of remarkably fatty pork was swimming in its gravy. I thanked him, and that was that. From then on, the waiter and I enjoyed a very fine relationship, distant but respectful.

Some days later I was enjoying a glass of good wine with a plate of spicy salami at the excellent Three Graces wine bar close to the weir across the Vltava. (The bill here too was wrong, but the waitress had clearly made a mistake and happily adjusted it.) Opposite me – for sharing tables is routine – sat a very sophisticated Czech of about forty-five wearing a leather jacket, a broad pinstriped shirt, and what Americans mysteriously call 'aviator' glasses. We spoke in German, until he was joined by an equally dapper friend of his, who spoke flawless English. In the course of a fairly bland conversation, for my attempts to ask them how they felt about Gorbachev were met with skilful evasions, I mentioned that while I was revelling in the sheer beauty of the city, I was heartily sick of being cheated at every turn.

The English speaker shrugged. 'Oh well. You must realize that in Czechoslovakia, cheating is a way of life.'

And so it is. It is not only the tourist who is dunned. Czechs routinely double-cross each other. When I asked Helena which were the most lucrative occupations in the country, I was surprised when she replied: 'Apart from Party officials, greengrocers and butchers.' Others agreed. Indeed, anyone who has frequent contact with the general public is well positioned to make a great deal of money. Sharp practice in the greengrocers' trade includes injecting fruit, especially oranges, with water in order to increase their weight, and relabelling Grade II produce as Grade I, which obviously carries a higher price tag. As in Hungary, shortages, which are endemic, create opportunities for the entrepreneurial spirit. If you want some size nine nails, for example, your local building supplies outlet will sadly inform you that they are not currently available, nor are they likely to be back on the shelves in the foreseeable future. However . . . I know somebody who might be able to lay his hands on a box or two by the end of next week, so I may be able to help you then. Of course I'll have to pay over the odds for them myself, and I'm afraid I'm going to have to ask you for three times the usual price . . .

The regime is well aware that a substantial proportion of the Czech population is on the take, but does little about it. Special departments do investigate economic crimes, but their inefficiency is legendary, and it is possible that such units are as corrupt as the professions they supposedly investigate. Because official salaries are relatively low, some prosperous tradesmen have difficulty explaining how they earned their fortunes. One way in which they get round this problem is to keep their ears open when the results of the lottery are announced. A butcher laden with excess earnings will contact someone who has a winning ticket, for, say, 50,000 crowns. He will then offer to buy the ticket off the winner for, say, 55,000. Then, if and when the authorities question his vast income, he can say: 'Ah well, you see I won the lottery two months ago. Here's the stub to prove it.' It's worth paying a few thousand crowns to have so firm a financial alibi.

It is not only individual traders who manipulate the system for personal gain. Entire industries sink into a morass of double-dealing that, while not overtly corrupt, has the similar effect of undermining any legality established by the regime. One evening I went to visit Ivan, who, like the majority of Prague's intellectuals, passes his working hours tending a few boilers. His boiler room, which heats a complex of workshops on the outskirts of the city, is reached through a formidable series of 'No Entry' signs which he instructed me to ignore. I asked him whether he could earn enough as a stoker to feed and clothe his growing family.

'As a manual worker I am reasonably well paid. But only because the managers of this yard connive at it. Ministry regulations stipulate that workers at my level should be paid about 2500 crowns per month. Now the managers realize that no one will work for such wages here, so they've agreed to pay us more. That means they must find our extra wages from other sources. In other words they have to juggle the figures, fix the books, falsify the quotas to explain away the excess payments. This makes our bosses, technically, economic criminals, and they could be sent to jail for many years. This rarely happens, even though the ministry knows this kind of thing goes on all over the country. What I am telling you is common knowledge.'

The very fact that the government rarely takes punitive action against managers who doctor the figures – whether to feather their own nests or, as in this case, to retain their work force – gives the regime tremendous leverage. It keeps the managers in line. The same is true of the legion of greengrocers and taxi drivers on the take. Because the government knows that only a small proportion of their incomes has been earned legally, they can lean on such people when it suits them, often requiring them to act as informers.

'Most of those who commit economic crimes,' Ivan continued, 'are not criminals in any real sense. The regime puts people in a position where they have little choice but to act illegally. Laws here are made by bureaucracies and have little to do with real circumstances. The result is a system that disillusions and disgusts not just those of us who openly oppose the regime, but ordinary men and women who must bear silent witness to the degrading consequences of the government's indifference to the realities of daily existence.'

A similar point was made in a different way by a law professor who signed Charter 77 and lost his job as a consequence. 'People have come to believe they have the right to rip off the state. As we say in Czechoslovakia: "Anyone who doesn't steal from the state is stealing from his family."'

Czechoslovakia may be corrupt, but it is also prosperous. Among Eastern Bloc countries it enjoys the probably unique position of having no foreign debt. Its economy is well integrated with those of other Bloc countries, and although its industrial base is considerable for a country of its size, Czech agricultural production is also expanding. As in Hungary, there are no shortages of basic consumer goods and foodstuffs in the shops, even though their quality leaves much to be desired. The complete absence of even tokens of private enterprise means that the smooth running of shops and enterprises is solely dependent on the efficiency of the state. And since the state, with its insistence on Party loyalty rather than managerial performance, is not particularly efficient, the outcome is bad news for consumers. Although Czech incomes are considerably higher than Hungarian ones, the quality of life seems lower. Czechs may well buy more meat and more clothing than their Hungarian neighbours, but they have to queue for them and the choice is less ample. On the other hand, while the Hungarians may have more goods in their shops, they also have less money with which to buy them.

The relative prosperity of Czechoslovakia is not new. Indeed, it can be viewed not as indicative of the regime's success, but as one of many instances of its failure; for before the Second World War Czechoslovakia rivalled Germany in terms of its economic performance. This is clearly no longer the case. After the war Czechoslovakia's industrial capacity increased mightily, and it turned out large quantities of machinery, textiles, glassware, and electronic goods. After 1958 the regime switched to one-year plans, in the hope of providing greater flexibility than the five-year plans that had dictated economic planning from 1948. Other economic reforms were instituted, until the Russian invasion of 1968 and the installation of the Husák regime put an end to them. There would be no more talk, as there had been in April 1968, of introducing 'small private enterprise' into the economy. In 1970 five-year plans were revived. The industrial base continued to expand and new industries, such as chemical production, were started up, but this proved a mistake. It was pointless to maintain and expand manufacturing capacity at a time when markets could obtain such goods more cheaply from other parts of the world. By the late 1970s the regime switched gears once again, and instead of expanding the industrial base began to restructure those industries that seemed most viable.

Although some years ago the government found it necessary to borrow $7 billion from foreign banks, it also managed to repay the loan and has not found it necessary to take out new loans. Indeed, Czechoslovakia enjoys a hard currency reserve, which will supposedly be used to invest in new plant and equipment for industries that have grown outdated. The emphasis remains on traditional industries – looms, knitting machines, turbines – and Czechoslovakia performs more sluggishly in such fields as electronics and microchips. Despite the rigidity of the regime, some reforms have been introduced, but, as in the Soviet Union, they have met with resistance, though for different reasons. In the late 1960s managers were urged to adopt reforms, and many of them paid a harsh price for their compliance. It is hardly surprising, then, that present-day middle management is reluctant to take risks, to lead the way in diversification or imaginative marketing.

Although no one sees any possibility of Czechoslovakia adopting the reforms that have become commonplace in Hungary – if only because a highly industrialized economy is less amenable to a loosening of the reins – it seems likely that factories will be encouraged to operate more independently. Middle managers stubbornly prefer to operate five-year plans that stipulate production targets, since this absolves them of responsibility for the outcome; all they are required to do is turn out the required quantity of goods, and leave others to decide how to market them.

Such attitudes are being discouraged, and state enterprises are being urged to investigate the market for their products. In the future the ministries will not be satisfied with quantifiable production alone; factories will also have to make a profit, and that means they must devote greater attention to producing goods that people want to buy.

One woman told me how she had been unable to find shoes that would fit her daughter's feet. The particular size had been unobtainable for a year. Such lacunae are the direct result of excessively rigid economic planning. Under a five-year plan a factory would have been told how many shoes it had to produce, but it was less likely to be told to ensure that its output corresponded to the needs of the population. From the factory manager's point of view, all that mattered was to turn out a zillion shoes per year. That they happened to be in only two colours, three designs, and six sizes was of no importance – except, of course, to the harassed housewives unable to find shoes that would actually fit their children's feet.

The pacesetter among the more market-conscious enterprises is the agricultural cooperative of Slušovice in Moravia. It functions, to all intents and purposes, as a capitalist organization. Managers with poor performance records are likely to be demoted – not a word you hear very often in other sectors of the Czech economy or bureaucracy. Nor is Party membership a prerequisite for managerial jobs. In addition to agricultural produce, Slušovice also manufactures computers, thus showing an entrepreneurial spirit rare indeed in Czechoslovakia. As far as I was concerned, the cooperative's most important product is ice cream. Most Czech ice cream is grainy and of the soft variety composed principally of putty and molten vinyl, but the Slušovice confection is delicious. I joined a queue at its small retail outlet behind the (Swedish-built) Kotva department store in the Old Town, and was rewarded with two scoops of bilberry ice cream that actually contained flecks of the fruit after which it had been named.

The thrusting enterprise of Slušovice is atypical; shortages and bad management are still endemic in Czechoslovakia. Yet the standard of living, if not the quality of life, continues to rise. Every third family in Prague runs a car, and one family in four owns a weekend cottage. Wages are comparatively high, but because there are so few goods available that are worth spending money on, vast sums are kept in savings accounts rather than returned to the economy. People complain not about earnings, but about shortages. It is depressing to walk around Dům Módy, a five-storey department store on Wenceslas Square devoted to 'fashion', and filled with largely inaccessible racks of clothes made from tacky fabrics in drab colours to atrocious designs and offered at high prices. If this is the best that Prague can offer its women, one might deduce that the country is going through hard times. Yet this is not so, and only a few yards away you can buy – with crowns, not hard currency – the latest Japanese cameras, bottles of Scotch and Cognac, and foods imported from Germany and France. Cedok offers exotic holidays in China and Japan and, despite astronomical prices, such tours are sold out within hours or days of being announced. Czechoslovakia is the only Eastern Bloc country where new cars are instantly available. No five-year waiting lists here. All you need to buy a Skoda is 67,000 crowns, quite a markup when you consider that the production costs are just over 20,000. Soon, the economists say, even foreign cars will be available for crowns. It struck me as a topsy-turvy approach, offering luxury goods at inflated prices rather than ensuring a steady supply of basic necessities at affordable prices.

The second economy is less of a feature of the Czech system than the Hungarian one, but families must work hard if they are to afford their cars and cottages.

'It's impossible to afford these little luxuries on a single salary,' said Helena. 'So the women have to go to work too. Many of them don't want to, as Czech men are still very macho. In most families where the wife goes out to work, she also has to get up at dawn to take the children to nursery school, then she has to shop, and that can mean standing in queues for an hour or more. Then, after she gets back from work, she has to collect the children from school and cook for her family. Meanwhile her husband's sitting in the pub with his mates.'

Despite pious talk about equality, the reality is quite different. According to official figures, average monthly wages in 1984 were 3469 crowns for men, but for women only 2287. Czechoslovakia has probably the smallest differential between highest and lowest salaries, the range being approximately from 1800 to 7000 crowns per month, with military and police officers, Party officials, and approved artists at the top of the scale. Workers in occupations lauded by communist ideology – miners, farmers, construction workers, metalworkers – also earn good money, while more intellectual and technical professions, such as medicine, are poorly rewarded. The base income of a doctor could be as low as

2000 crowns per month, but such statistics do not reflect the true earnings of the profession, which can be as high as 6000 per month. Factory workers, on the other hand, are badly paid and their working conditions are widely recognized as appalling: work-safety standards are often abysmal and innumerable factories lack proper ventilation. Many of those who labour in such industries work for long hours at low salaries, and rely on overtime, second jobs, and theft in order to supplement their incomes.

As in Hungary, many Czechs live way beyond their means and go deeply into debt in order to acquire an apartment or car. On the other hand, loans are easy to come by – either from state banks or trade unions – and rates of interest are blissfully low, rarely exceeding 4 per cent. Workers in organized industries also benefit from canteen lunches and union-sponsored camp holidays at nominal prices. Rent control keeps prices low for those who enjoy such accommodation. Food prices are also controlled, and for some years the price of milk and butter has remained stable.

Czech economists speak of labour shortages throughout the country, but the claim is perplexing. At a government building in Budapest I once watched six women, their heads wrapped in kerchiefs, as they washed an equal number of steps. It is no different in Czechoslovakia. Since a sizable proportion of dissidents are employed as stokers, the profession of boiler maintenance is one with which I soon became intimately acquainted. One afternoon, my friend the parishless pastor took a couple of hours off from his tour of duty in the boiler room of a cultural centre and explained his profession to me.

'I've been a stoker for about twelve years now. Do you have stokers in England?'

'I'm not sure that we do. I don't think I've encountered one since my schooldays, though I suppose somebody must keep an eye on the heating systems.'

'Well, here we need four. We also have an electrician who sits in another part of the building watching a panel of instruments. If anything looks fishy to him, he rings down to the boiler room, where there are usually two of us on duty at any time. But this building is relatively understaffed. Not far from here is a newly built clinic, quite a nice place, only forty beds. There they have nine stokers.'

'What do you do all day? Apart from having coffee with foreign writers.'

'Of course we do keep an eye on the boilers. The system has to be kept running around the clock.'

'Why? Only part of the building needs to be heated in the evenings, surely, and only during the colder months.'

'Ah, but we also have to provide hot water for the restaurant. Otherwise they couldn't wash the dishes.'

'Surely they could instal a small heating unit in the kitchens to provide hot water without keeping all the boilers going.'

'Yes, they could. But they don't. Anyway, we have to keep the boilers going nonstop so as to use enough oil.'

'?'

'If last year I used, say, 100,000 litres of oil, and this year I economized and used only 70,000, that means that in following years we'll receive only 70,000, whatever the needs of the building. Can't let that happen, can we?'

'Is it arduous work, being a stoker?'

'Indeed it is. Walking from my room to the actual boiler room and checking the gauges, that must take me all of – let me see – oh, forty minutes. In winter perhaps an hour. And if there's a real emergency, I might have to work as much as two hours a day!'

I spent many hours in the boiler rooms of Prague, and on only one occasion do I recall a stoker rising to his feet and saying, 'Excuse me for a second, I have to check the boilers.' A former law professor, now a clerk in a government office, spent two hours with me one morning at a coffeehouse. 'I sit in a large office with nothing to do. Every morning I shuffle a few papers, but after an hour or so my work is over.'

'Surely you can read, or write your articles, during all that spare time?'

'It is difficult. I am surrounded by colleagues and while nobody minds if I am doing nothing, there is uneasiness if I pursue my other activities at the office. It is most depressing.'

For those out of favour with the regime, especially, there is little possibility of relief from the tedium of menial employment. The small private enterprises dotted around Hungary have no place in Czechoslovakia, where the state remains the sole employer. There are self-employed workers and artisans who sell their own handicrafts, but their activities must be officially approved and they are forbidden to employ additional labour. Although many workers have second jobs, these too are within the state sector. A would-be part-time car mechanic may not set up in business without an official permit. Such permits are often granted, especially to craftsmen and artisans, as there is a demand for bricklayers and other such workers that the state cannot meet. Even though the regime prefers to make such services available through organized enterprises under its own control, it has had to permit a degree of self-employment in order to counter the growing black market in these professions.

This black market still thrives. An architect told me how dependent he was on the unofficial second economy. 'I often need to hire an electrician, say, at short notice. There are plenty around. It's a good line of business, since they not only do these additional jobs during official work hours, but they often make use of stolen materials which they then charge you for. Of course under such a system they have no incentive to do a good job. It's all the same to them. If I complain about their workmanship, they'll just shrug and take on other jobs elsewhere. It's like that throughout the economy. Managers, who are often paid less than the workers they supervise, have no means of inducing their employees to perform more efficiently or productively. Not surprisingly, most managers are incompetent. How the system keeps going is a mystery to us all. It must be some kind of natural momentum.

'For someone like me, dependent on the work of numerous professions if I'm to complete a project, life is a continuous struggle against unavailable parts and materials. Whenever I need a component, there's a "shortage". Of course my plumbers and masons just happen to be able to provide the unavailable items – as a "special favour" to me – but they'll also charge between three and five times the official prices. "Shortages" are commonplace within the bureaucracies too. If you need something in a hurry – a flat or a permit to travel or urgent medical treatment – the only way to get it is to bribe someone.'

One evening, sitting in a boiler room with a philosopher, as was my wont, there was a pounding on the door and two men burst in. I tensed and concealed my notebook, for surely this could only be a visit from the police. The two men ignored me completely and strode up to where the philosopher was sitting and harangued him at length. He nodded and smiled and argued back. After five minutes of noisy discussion, they went into a huddle over his desk and started scribbling on a sheet of paper. Eventually they appeared to reach some kind of agreement and the two men, with a polite nod in my direction as they headed for the door, left as boisterously as they had arrived.

The philosopher raised his arms in a dramatic gesture and declaimed: 'You have just witnessed Czech private enterprise in action. There is no central heating in my flat. Working through official channels it would take two years to have it installed. But these two gentlemen will have the job done in a month. It will cost me more, but at least my children will not freeze this winter. They came to see me because we need three different sizes of piping, and they can only find two. So we are making minor adjustments to the heating system. It will sort itself out.'

28

'Terror Aids Rulers'

In Vienna the aura of the Habsburgs had been impossible to avoid. The double eagle soared over dozens of buildings, the hearts and intestines of the ruling house were distributed among the city's churches, the great institutions founded by Franz Josef along the Ring remain virtually unaltered. In Budapest, too, there were echoes of the Habsburgs, not only in the eclectic architectural styles that mirrored those of Vienna, but in the coffeehouses and boulevards and the broad bulk of Maria Theresa's palace high above the Danube.

In Prague, however, the echoes of the imperial past were faint indeed. Delving through the palimpsest presented by the city, the Habsburg era seemed just one of many historical periods through which the city passed. Whereas Budapest is an overwhelmingly nineteenth-century city still redolent of the bourgeois prosperity that swelled under the Habsburgs, Prague is, in its visual and atmospheric impact, medieval and baroque. Although Prague has its share of nineteenth-century museums and theatres and apartment houses, they dominate the city far less than their counterparts in Pest and Vienna. The coffeehouse, another institution inseparable from Habsburg culture, survives only in a debased form in Prague. In Budapest I would make daily visits to Ruszwurm and the coffeehouses along Népköztársaság útja. In Prague the only coffeehouses I found remotely congenial were the stylish Europa on Wenceslas Square, with its charming chandeliers and lanterns, and the vast Obecni Dům, admirable less for its coffee than for the Art Deco palace of which it forms a part. As for the Slavia, opposite the National Theatre, and the Malostranská, I never set foot in these dingy establishments more than once. It often seemed to me that the most enduring vestige of the Habsburgs was *Protektion*, that cosy system of corruption initially perfected by the Viennese.

The house of Habsburg had little time for the Bohemians, who were as fractious and raucous in their nationalism as the Magyars. Franz Ferdinand, however, had stronger links with Bohemia than most of the ruling house, for he married a Czech countess. The poor woman had to suffer numberless indignities from Emperor Franz Josef on account of her lowly perch in the aristocratic aviary, and it is not surprising that the heir apparent and his wife spent a good deal of time away from Austria, at their castle at Konopiště, southeast of Prague. In one of its original guises Konopiště must have been an impressive building, for it was founded in the early fourteenth century and reconstructed three times in succeeding centuries. Franz Ferdinand, however, initiated in 1889 a final reconstruction marked by that extreme vulgarity that was second nature to the Habsburgs. Konopiště must be the only castle in Europe with a pebble-dash exterior. In its present form the castle adopts a vaguely Renaissance mantle with some neo-Gothic trappings in the form of towers.

The moment I stepped into the castle I was met by that trademark of the Habsburgs – dead animals. Snipe and other game birds are suspended from spikes, together with deer's feet and foxes' heads. Trophies are everywhere: chamois horns, mounted tail feathers of nameless birds, antlers, even stuffed bears, stilled in mid-attack by the Archduke's bullet. The hacked souvenirs begin at shoulder level and rise to a height of twenty feet. The few corridors free of heads and feet are lined with sporting prints, most of which, I was pleased to note, were fittingly foxed. A glass cabinet contains tray upon tray of deer teeth, all dated. In a display cabinet in the hall is Franz Ferdinand's 'Schuss Liste' which records, in painstaking detail, exactly when and where the sporting Archduke killed 171,537 birds and animals between 1880 and 1906. For once I felt some sympathy with the propaganda exhibition with which the visitor to Czech monuments is routinely confronted. Of course the point of such displays, with their photographs and banners, is not to shed light on history but to argue for the inevitable triumph of Marxist-Leninism. (I noted a typical example of the genre at the castle of Karlštejn: 'Riches and corruption of the priests and all the clerics shows most conspicuously the parasitism of the non-working class . . .') Nevertheless, after gazing at countless photographs of the strutting conceited Archduke and his entourage, it did come as a breath of fresh air to encounter the sharp intelligent features of V.I. Lenin as the culminating image, however misplaced, of the exhibition.

Naturally, as the most powerful Habsburg after the Emperor, Franz Ferdinand couldn't help acquiring, if only by inheritance, a few items of interest which are on display at Konopiště: some tapestries and pietra dura tables, Gothic altars and statuary of fine quality, chandeliers of Bohemian crystal, and a superb collection of weaponry and armour inherited from the Este branch of the family. Here too the Czech authorities had stepped in, like kindly old pedagogues, to instruct us on the true significance of all this exquisitely engraved Renaissance artillery and armour. The Este collection was supplemented with a handful of images, each married to a pithy slogan from literature. Most startling of all was the photograph of a lynching, for beneath it was the following quotation from John Webster: 'Terror Aids Rulers'. Not Czech rulers, surely!

While the Habsburg rulers were undoubtedly an unappetizing bunch of people, they did at least allow their subjects a measure of freedom. Freedom of the press was granted in 1867, a tradition maintained by the republic until 1938. Franz Josef's tottering steps in the direction of democracy were of course painfully slow, and his principal motive for making concessions to the liberal elements in his Empire was not some theoretic enthusiasm for the idea of democracy but to maintain the unity of his wellnigh ungovernable domains. Viennese *Schlamperei* and the inevitable confusions of trying to persuade dozens of nationalities – nationalities that felt no love for one another and even less for the Austrians who ruled over them – to pull together for the greater glory of the House of Habsburg left little opportunity for sustained repression. And certainly the ideological uniformities and the denial of individual rights that became entrenched in Czechoslovakia since 1948 had very little place in the Monarchy's conception of its rule.

Between the fumblings of the autocratic Habsburgs in decline and the murderous excesses of the Stalinists in the 1950s, Czechoslovakia did manage to enjoy a brief era of true democracy. The provinces of Bohemia, Slovakia, and Moravia were welded together under the leadership of Tomás Masaryk. The idea of the new country was formed by Masaryk and Eduard Beneš during World War I, and the notion accorded with the principles of self-determination which were the basis for the postwar reconstitution of Europe. Under Masaryk's social democratic regime, the new nation prospered; an advanced social security system was introduced and many of the industries on which Czechoslovakia still depends were developed. Although there were, and still are, tensions between the three principal tribal groups within the country, it was the German population living within its borders that provided the pretext for the destruction of the republic in 1939. Prague, and Bohemia in general, had always sustained a large German presence, and the culture was as much German as Czech. The sophisticated urban culture that flourished under the republic was, of course, not merely German but in large part German-Jewish, and this strain of German influence in the country had little connection with the *Sudetendeutsch* to whom Hitler so successfully appealed. The ground was laid by the Sudetendeutsche Partei under the leadership of a nasty piece of work named Konrad Henlein. With Hitler's ultimatum of 1938 and invasion the following year, the republic was dismembered. Bohemia and Moravia became German protectorates, while Slovakia was granted a greater degree of independence.

After the war Beneš, who had succeeded Masaryk as president in 1935, returned to Czechoslovakia to head a new government, an uneasy four-party coalition of Social Democrats and Communists. In the postwar elections the Communists had polled 40 per cent of the vote, and were thus in a powerful position. Moreover, the Russians had been the only major power to support the Czechs in 1938, and many grateful Czechs regarded them as saviours. The Communists, while operating within the democratic restraints of the bourgeois democracy under which the country was still governed, also mobilized the active support of the armed workers' militias that repeatedly demonstrated in the streets. The non-Communists in the government retreated further and further, while the influence of Klement Gottwald, who had led the Czech Communists since 1929, and his supporters grew. The coalition regime tottered on until 4 June 1948, when Beneš resigned and Gottwald replaced him as president and rapidly transformed Czechoslovakia into a faithful reflection of its Stalinist model in the Soviet Union. Since his death, a few days after Stalin's in March 1953, it is Gottwald and not Masaryk who is seen, according to official propaganda, as the father of the nation.

It seems astonishing that so revered a figure as Masaryk, whose reputation extended far beyond the borders of his small country, should have been relegated to a footnote in the nation's history books. At Charles University library, his books have the same status as pornography in the British Library: you need special permission before you are allowed to read them. Indeed, the very democracy over which he and Beneš presided is dismissed as no more than the temporary triumph of the despised and reactionary bourgeoisie. Hard-line politicians, such as Vasil Bilak, have remarked that for the Czech working classes the interwar republic was by no means a bed of roses; for his family it was a time of deprivation and harsh strikes, and only a communist revolution offered genuine hope for the future. To men such as Bilak, a roof over one's head and bread on the table are more important than the frills of parliamentary democracy and freedom of expression that can be exploited by forces hostile to the will of the people.

To experience the official line at its most stately I made a visit to the Klement Gottwald Museum in the Old Town. I had the place to myself. It's a grand building, with a monumental staircase leading up to a landing on which are placed bronze statues and busts of the nation's heroes. The only full-length statue is that of Lenin, caught in a typically dynamic pose, while opposite him is placed a half-length Ray Buxton, one hand outstretched and a book in the other. The Leader as Teacher. The cult of the personality is not altogether dead in Czechoslovakia, and glass cases contain relics of the great man, such as his overcoat and many pipes. If Masaryk has been expunged from the history books, Stalin has not, it seems, for there is an abundance of photographs showing Gottwald and Stalin beaming at each other and shaking hands. The museum, which traces the history of Communism in Czechoslovakia as well as the glorious achievements of the frequently inebriated Gottwald, makes only minimal references to the events of 1968. A photograph of some youths throwing stones at a Soviet tank is captioned as an example of an anti-socialist act – it's as simple as that. After 1968 Gustáv Husák moves to centre stage. A large portrait of this dour man glowers down on the visitor, and elsewhere there are many life-size colour photographs of Husák shaking hands with other Communist leaders, for Husák too was not averse to a touch of the cult. The next rooms are devoted to graphs of economic production and photographs of heroic workers at their toil, smilingly. There is ample documentary evidence to support the view that Eastern Bloc politicians spend a large part of each day applauding each other.

Prague boasts its own version of Lenin's Mausoleum. The Czech adaptation is almost as grandiose, a bulky box of a building placed on top of a steep hill in the Žižkov district. Surprisingly, it was built between the wars as a monument to the newly independent nation, and it is no compliment to the style of the building that it could so easily be adapted to its new purpose. I grunted my way up the paths one hot afternoon only to find the structure barely visible behind scaffolding and, consequently, closed. When it is open to the gaze of bands of Pioneers and African students showing their gratitude for their scholarships – for who else would climb the hill merely to stare at a row of mostly empty sarcophagi? – it must be a curious sight, more a mausoleum-in-waiting than a true necropolis of the heroes of the nation. I asked a number of acquaintances in Prague what the place was like, but nobody had ever been there. Descending the hill, I passed the military museum. Tanks, fighter planes, and Russian-made missiles were parked in the forecourt and stood in odd juxtaposition to the bedraggled MIR posters still taped to a few windows in apartment blocks.

To make up for my disappointment, I visited instead the SNB (Police) Museum next to the Karlov church. There are graphic displays relating to the fight against Fascism – Gestapo guillotines and clubs, and no fewer than 444 pistols confiscated from 'spies and agents' (though whose were not clear to me) in the Soviet Union. It was hard not to be stirred by the visual displays testifying to Czech expertise at traffic control and handling sniffer dogs. I was impressed too by the vigilance of the border guards, who frequently bring to light caches of contraband inside the boots of cars crossing the border from the decadent West. Vivid photographic displays showed us a zillion watches in the back of a Mercedes, and a complete run of Playmate calendars seized from smugglers before too many Czech libidos could be aroused. (I was advised before entering the country that a few copies of *Penthouse* or *Hustler* hidden between my shirts might prove welcome gifts. However, my primness got the better of me and instead I took in copies of subversive books by the likes of Samuel Beckett and Joseph Heller.)

The museum had little to say about the continuing struggle against counterrevolutionary tendencies, though a brief allusion was made to 1968. Twenty years later the state security officers display undiminished zeal. Václav Havel has published a letter he wrote to the Czech General Public Prosecutor describing, just as a ten-year-old is usually obliged to do at the beginning of term, how he spent his holidays. Realizing that taking a spin through the countryside for a week might be a deeply suspicious act in the eyes of the regime, Havel had the courtesy to notify the authorities in advance of his travel plans. Nevertheless he was tailed constantly, the country homes of friends he was visiting for the night were raided, and he was arrested for two days, as is his wont. What interested me was his calculation that this vigilance on the part of the police had required the participation of no fewer than 300 men.

Such bursts of energy from the forces of law and order are, however, less common than they used to be. Individual Chartists – the most conspicuous of Czech dissidents, having signed the Charter 77 declaration urging compliance with the terms of the Helsinki Agreement – agreed that months, even years, could go by without any harassment from the police. Some argued that the police had little need for overt persecution, since the fuzziness of the law was always to their advantage. Since it is very hard for dissidents to know which of their deeds would land them in trouble with the authorities, and which were more likely to be overlooked, a constant atmosphere of uncertainty prevails. There are always exceptions to any rule; the police often appear to act at random, and this too creates a climate of unease. Everybody has a story to offer of how a chance word can result in a spell in jail. I heard tell of a youth in a village who had too much to drink in the pub one night and in a spat with a neighbour called him a communist swine. The lad was arrested and sentenced to eight months in prison for 'denigration of the nation'. There were stories about typists and copyists of underground publications who had been arrested, and I heard of a police search of a dissident's flat that unearthed an abusive letter to Gustáv Husák – though no one in his right mind, whatever his or her opinion of the president, would be so foolish as to scribble such a diatribe and leave it lying around until the police walk in and find it. The alleged author of this letter spent a year in jail. No one could say how many political prisoners there are in Czechoslovakia, because no one knows which offences are political. A political charge can easily take cover behind some technical infringement of the law. The leaders of the Jazz Section, for instance, were prosecuted not for subversion but for 'illegal trading', because the Section had published numerous articles that the regime viewed with disfavour. Political repression is thus able to skulk behind what appear to be merely economic infringements.

Why the regime should keep so tight a rein on the dissemination of information is something of a mystery. Even on my small portable transistor I could listen each day to English-language broadcasts from Austria, Sweden, and the Vatican, and many dissidents show you with pride their powerful and very expensive short-wave radios, with which they can pick up British and American news reports in Czech as well as English.

The writer and expert on propaganda Petr Fidelius welcomed me to his boiler room on a couple of afternoons. Unlike most dissidents, who were dismissed from their jobs either after the Russian invasion or after they signed Charter, Fidelius made a decision on leaving university to opt out of the system. He has exchanged the possibility of a university lectureship in philology for a room in the basement of a nineteenth-century building where, from time to time, he inspects the boilers. His room is a delight, cheaply but extravagantly furnished. (I must omit the description I originally wrote, as I am reliably informed that the Czech police would be keenly interested in any details that would help them identify Fidelius.) In these dingy surroundings Petr Fidelius wrote his excellent book *L'esprit post-totalitaire*, a detailed and wry analysis of the distortions and misappropriations of language practised by regimes such as the one from which he remains concealed. For Petr Fidelius is a pseudonym, and I had some explaining to do when, uninvited, I appeared on the doorstep of his hideaway.

'The fact is,' says Fidelius, 'that the regime no longer monopolizes information. Nevertheless it still likes to behave as though it did. We are treated like children. Take Chernobyl. Six months went by before we were offered any solid information. The Czech government was the slowest of any government, even in the Eastern Bloc, to acknowledge the extent of the calamity. This did a great deal of damage, because Chernobyl was, after all, not primarily a political matter. It shook the faith of a lot of people to know that the government had concealed from them matters affecting, for example, their children's health. Of course anyone who wanted to know what had really happened tuned in to a Western radio station. The government hardly ever bothers to jam foreign radio stations. There's no point. There must be a dozen or more German radio stations anyone can pick up from Prague. You can't jam them all.'

Moreover, although Western newspapers are less easily available than in Budapest, I did on occasion spot the *Herald Tribune* and the *Financial Times* tucked behind the porter's desk at the Hotel Jalta. The Czech press, I was told by those who occasionally cast a weary eye over its drab columns, does not usually indulge in outright lies. Instead it omits any stories that don't fit in with its view of how the world is constituted. Vast areas of knowledge and debate are simply not acknowledged to exist. My experience of the Czech radio's English-language broadcast was worse than that. Although Radio Moscow would not be my first choice as a source of information, there were times during the evening when my little radio couldn't pick up any other station broadcasting in English. The news was, of course, slanted, but gently so. This was not the case with the Czech broadcasts, which were peppered with snide footnotes and heavy-handed editorials, in the midst of what were supposed to be news headlines, stressing, for example, Israel's responsibility for the civil strife in Lebanon and the West's disdain for peace moves initiated by the Russians.

One morning I saw a long queue stretching outside a shop on Jungmannova that is the sole outlet in Prague for foreign press publications. Of course the range of publications was strictly limited to nonpolitical journals, but even so the queue stretched down the street on mornings when a new shipment arrived. I peered through the window to see what the Czechs were so eager to buy. The two most popular, apart from children's comics, were *Hobby*, a French DIY magazine, and a pair of women's magazines from Germany that sold for the relatively high prices of 30 and 40 crowns. Czech women are prepared to pay these high prices because the magazines contain clothes patterns far superior to anything comparable available in Czech magazines.

Perhaps the men and women reading those foreign magazines were also relieved to find publications devoid of propaganda. When I visited the eloquent dissident Pavel Bratinka, he tossed in my direction a philately magazine in which, he explained, an entire article was devoted to explaining how and why the history of Czech stamp design since 1948 had learnt to reflect 'socialist values'. Even the most trivial pursuits are bent to the service of the regime, and it is this all-pervasiveness of the totalitarian stifling, rather than any degree of effectiveness or brutality, that is so utterly oppressive.

29

Dalibore

La Bohème was not in the repertoire of the Czech National Opera that season, so I could attend performances without dread. Before the war, when there had been a German culture thriving alongside the Czech, two principal opera houses had served the city. The elegant German opera house has been renamed the Smetana Theatre and is now Prague's principal auditorium for opera. The most famous of the opera houses had been the Tyl Theatre, built in the heart of the Staré Město (Old Town) in the 1780s. In 1787 Mozart's *Don Giovanni* had received its premiere here, and once restoration of the tall neo-classical theatre is completed, it will once again be used for the performance of Mozart's operas.

But while I was in Prague the only way to see any opera was to join the queue outside the Smetana Theatre. The system for obtaining tickets is still not clear to me, since most seats are only made available about a week before the performance. Each Monday the seats for the week ahead go on sale, and I took my place in the queue, which was composed of Czechs and foreigners in equal numbers. I also wanted to pick up a ticket for *Don Giovanni*, which was being performed that evening, but was discouraged when two Italians ahead of me were told that the performance was sold out. After waiting an hour I bought some tickets for future performances. I thought I might as well ask about *Don Giovanni* that evening and received a different reply from that given the Italians. Yes, there were a few seats left, and so I bought a ticket.

As in Budapest, the interior of the opera house is more enchanting than the majority of performances to be heard within its walls. About the same size as the Budapest Opera, the Smetana Theatre employed an inexhaustible repertoire of white and gold rococo motifs, with fake windows opening onto pallid and indecipherable ceiling frescoes. All this rococo frivolity was pastiche, but at least it was more lively than the music-making. Battalions of statuary frame the four tiers of boxes and the balconies, which are also embellished with white, gilt and blue-gold paintwork. As for *Don Giovanni*, it was dire. Since the Czechs perform the 'original' version of the piece, as performed at the Tyl, audiences must put up with a *Don* shorn of some of its finest arias, such as '*Dalla sua pace*' and '*Mi tradì*'. Despite its profundity, *Don Giovanni* has many comic elements, a point lost on both producer and audience. Leporello attempted some comic business – ineptly, it must be said – but there was not even a titter from the audience, who betrayed no signs of enjoyment.

The performance was a disgrace. In Ulan Bator I could have made allowances, but not in Prague. The producer had given the complexities of the opera no thought at all, and the same was true of its simplicities. When, in the graveyard scene, the statue of the Commendatore nods his stone head and accepts the Don's invitation to dinner, it is reasonable to expect the Don and Leporello to express some surprise at discovering that a funerary statue is capable of conversation. But not in this production, where it was treated as the most natural thing in the world. Nor did the production convey who was giving the ball that ends Act 1. Both finales were ruined by silly ballets, and the terrifying scene when the statue comes to dinner was wrecked by using a silhouette to convey the statue's presence. At the climactic moments when the Don in an act of bravado grasps the statue's hand and is alarmed by its icy and tenacious grip, the dramatic point went for nothing, since silhouettes don't have hands. The Don was feeble and wooden, without menace, seductiveness, intelligence. Donna Elvira was sung as a soubrette – in other words, hopelessly miscast. Only the Donna Anna was up to the part, and she turned out to be a Hungarian guest singer. For the Czech singers, all words, all melodies, all phrases were given equal weight. As for the conducting . . .

Fortunately, the Czech Opera did rather better with native composers. I enjoyed Dvořák's *Jakobín* and Smetana's *Two Widows*; never having heard either opera before, I may have been less sensitive to the inadequacies of the performance, but I'll give them the benefit of the doubt. I had bought cheap standing tickets at the back of the balcony for these operas, as there had been a possibility that I might have to skip them in order to meet some

Czech acquaintances. Not that I mind standing, a form of opera-going that in some houses includes lying on the floor and taking quiet strolls during dull stretches.

As the lights were dimming before the curtain rose on *Two Widows*, an usherette pushed me into a free-standing chair and said: 'I'll find you a proper seat at the interval if you give me something.' No sooner had the tepid applause begun at the end of the first act than she was by my side again. I slipped five crowns into her open hand. Without even looking at the coin, she whispered loudly, '*Fünf Kronen ist nichts*' – and returned the coin to me. She expected, she told me, at least ten. 'But if,' I reasoned with her, 'I was prepared to pay an additional ten crowns on top of the five I've already paid for the standing ticket, I could have bought a seat in the first place. By giving you five, we both come out slightly ahead. If I give you ten, I gain nothing at all.' She didn't attempt to deny the logic, but her shrug of the shoulders made it very clear to me that she still wasn't going to lead me to an empty seat for less than ten. No deal. I spent the second act sitting in the chair I'd occupied throughout the first, and was perfectly content.

At *Jakobín* the same usherette approached me with her usual offer, which I declined, foolishly adding that I was quite happy to stand. When the lights went down after the interval I made a beeline for the unoccupied chair behind the seats. The usherette, spotting me from across the auditorium, approached at high speed and told me, 'If you've got a standing ticket, then you have to stand.' Her sharp-sightedness was unexpected, since when buying a programme before the opera began she had failed to give me change for my five-crown piece, excusing herself, when challenged by me, on the grounds that her eyesight was poor and it was hard for her to distinguish a small two-crown coin from a large five-crown coin. So by requiring me to stand, she took her revenge. She, however, lost the war, since after she had berated me I waited until she left the auditorium and then resumed my seat.

The Czech National Opera reached its nadir not at the Smetana Theatre, but on a visit the previous season to the Staatsoper in Vienna. They had brought with them Smetana's *Dalibor*. It was all part of some Czech culture festival, cementing the enduring friendship between the Austrian and Czech peoples and so forth; so I was expecting that the company would put its best foot forward. Have I ever seen a worse production of any opera? I can't recall one. I'd seen the English National Opera's production of

Dalibor about fifteen years ago and enjoyed it. In its native version it was unrecognizable. The production would have disgraced Vincent Crummles. At one point some peasants entered and clumped lumpishly through a dance; later in the scene they regrouped and performed the identical dance in identical positions. During the prison scene, performed in almost total darkness while the gaoler stumbled about carrying a badly needed lantern, enter the heroine accompanied by three knights, who proceeded to sit on their haunches, unpack a picnic hamper, and clink their mugs. They wandered off eventually, then reappeared and repeated the whole sequence without variation. The heroine herself, disguised as a man, wore a mini-skirt and labia-hugging black boots – very sexy, but she is supposed to be a brave woman on the lines of Beethoven's Leonora, not a Pigalle whore. A chatty Polish doctor standing next to me abandoned the opera after Act 1, but I stayed on. Act 2 contains some orchestral interludes, which were played while the audience stared at a blank wall for a full ten minutes. After Act 2 I too gave up.

When, some months later, I was in Prague, I had the pleasure of encountering a music critic whose sharp observations require him to publish in underground journals. 'I'm not an opera fanatic,' he told me, 'but an opera masochist. I've had to see some of these productions over six times.' Caruso, for that is his sly pseudonym, asked me what I thought of the Czech National Opera. I told him, adding that nothing I'd seen in Prague had been as dreadful as the flagship production of *Dalibor* they'd taken to impress the Viennese.

'You were there?' he asked, his bright eyes gleaming.

'I was there for most of it. No one with a modicum of taste or who was not a guest of the Czech or Austrian governments could conceivably have lasted longer than two acts.'

'I am so pleased to hear your views. I have collected all the reviews of that production from the Austrian press. I couldn't go myself, as I haven't had a passport since 1968. Naturally our newspapers only tell us what a triumph our opera company enjoys abroad. So I am printing the foreign press reviews to let people know that we don't have the brilliant international reputation that our authorities would wish us to believe we do. Did you see their production of *The Bartered Bride* which they also took to Vienna?'

'No.'

'A pity. The consensus was that it was even worse.'

Caruso was not gloating over the dismal standards of Czech opera, but he felt, quite rightly, that no improvement would ever be possible as long as everyone back home was duped into believing that the company was of an international standard.

The reasons for the awfulness of Czech opera are complex. It cannot be a lack of singers. Edita Gruberová and Eva Randová are great singers, but their appearances in Czechoslovakia are rare indeed. And who can blame them for wishing to free themselves from the constraints imposed on them by the Czech opera managements? Czech opera can never rise above a provincial level for as long as its producers and performers are deprived of opportunities to make comparisons and swop notes with their counterparts in other opera houses. Musicians, as well as music, have always been peripatetic, enriching all Europe in the process, but Czech musicians have little opportunity to acquaint themselves with music-making elsewhere in Europe, let alone in the United States. Opera house directors do usually have some affection for music, and can be held to account by governing bodies if the standard of performance noticeably falls. But those who direct the official theatre and opera in Czechoslovakia are civil servants, apparatchiks with scant interest in such marginal issues as artistic quality.

The same problem afflicts Czech theatre, though here there are at least possibilities for working outside the large, well-funded state institutions. Cost alone would make impossible the setting up of 'underground' opera companies. But there are numerous tiny theatre and mime companies that produce their work on the margins of official approval. Many are based either in theatre clubs, or in small theatres away from the city centre and often away from the capital itself. A favourite venue for some of the more avant-garde companies is the Braník Theatre, in a southern suburb. The more inaccessible the venue, the more likely that avant-garde productions can be mounted there. While I was in Prague I was asked to write about Edward Bond for a Czech publication. The answer had to be no, but the request indicated strong interest in contemporary drama from other countries.

Czech theatre has always been famous for mime, and I did manage to see the famous Fialka troupe, which was mounting a brief season at the Na zábradlí Theatre in a small square near the Charles Bridge. Mime, being neither ballet nor theatre but occupying the sag between the two, has never much appealed to me. Nor did I much enjoy this troupe. The gesturing seemed clichéd, the necessary exaggerations of the medium unnecessarily exaggerated. Ladislav Fialka himself, who founded the troupe almost thirty years ago, had a powerful stage presence, a natural authority that less experienced members of the company understandably lacked, yet the whole evening, comprising three one-acters accompanied by Czech classical music, seemed tired and lacklustre. Since the need to gain official approval for all new productions is a disincentive to artistic initiative, it is less of a headache to keep an old production on the boards than to mount a new one.

One morning I heard the voice of Kenny Rogers coming loud and clear from my radio which happened to be tuned to a local station. And I was surprised, soon after arriving in Prague, to see posters advertising a Rockfest to be held in the Palace of Culture. This proved to be a curious occasion, with up to six rock groups at a time performing in auditoria and conference halls. My credentials as a rock music critic date from the heyday of the Kinks, so I couldn't really assess the quality or style of music being played, though to judge from the degree of distortion coming over the loudspeakers there seemed to be a tendency in favour of Heavy Metal. The halls and foyers of the many-storeyed Palace of Culture were filled with fringe activities, including art exhibitions and fashion shows. The art shows had been hastily assembled, for permission to mount them had only been granted at the last minute. The majority of the paintings and sculptures on display were clearly from the margins of officially tolerated artistic expression, and bore little resemblance to the tame and decorous new work to be seen in Prague's downtown galleries. Little of it was especially good or even noteworthy, but I was pleasantly surprised to see such avant-gardisme at all.

The continuous fashion show wouldn't strike terror into the hearts of Parisian couturiers. The girls in mauve suits and long T-shirts doubling as dresses were pretty enough, but their shy smiles and extreme self-consciousness indicated that modelling was far from second nature. Both clothes and models were amateurish, and the show was upstaged by a small party of punks who weaved their way through the crowded halls. They were, to my amazement, the genuine article, metal studs and spiked fluorescent hair and all, though I later learnt that most of them had come from Poland. In another salon I watched a session of performance art, in which a young man sprawled on the floor, slowly coating his body in white plaster.

The Rockfest, which ran for three days, opened its doors at five each afternoon and closed them at eleven. 5000 kids paid 30 crowns each to gain admission and the festival was a sell-out. The Rockfest was no Woodstock, but on its own terms it seemed successful enough. It was, of course, an official concession to popular tastes. In the early 1980s the authorities launched a campaign against rock music, a foolish measure which predictably upset Czech youth, which has few enough enjoyable means of self-expression at its disposal. The authorities eventually relented, but kept the music scene under their control by selecting officially approved bands. Rock groups must be sponsored by institutions such as factories or offices; such sponsorship also functions as a form of control, since it complicates the existence of the bands, who can only act through intermediaries.

'Anything culturally worthwhile in Czechoslovakia,' Václav Havel told me, 'only functions on the periphery.' The Rockfest had taken place in the Palace of Culture, which would have been impossible without official sanction, and seemed a rare exception to this rule. The festival also provided an outlet for artistic enterprises that are just beyond what is officially sanctioned. The authorized Union of Artists consists of about 200 full members, who are rewarded for their loyalty and predictability with well-paid commissions and regular exhibitions in galleries, and 5000 registered freelance artists, some of whom have good reputations. Artists not associated with the Union find it almost impossible to exhibit their work in the main galleries of Prague and must try their luck in the provinces, where they may find a showcase in the foyers of state institutions. The film studios are also rigidly controlled, and no film can be made until the scenario has been approved by the authorities. It was cause for comment when, after a scenario had been rejected by the Czech film authorities, the scriptwriters went ahead and made the film independently and then persuaded the authorities to buy the distribution rights from them.

Words hold more terror for the authorities than pictures, whether still or moving, as a visit to Ivan Klíma, one of the country's finest writers of fiction, was to demonstrate.

30

Franz Who?

Whenever I had to climb a hill – to visit the ancient fortress of Vyšehrad in southern Prague, or to have tea with Ivan Klíma in the suburb of Braník just beyond – the sun would blaze from the sky and leave me drenched in sweat. I was bedraggled and ill-tempered by the time I'd hauled myself along the quiet street lined with undistinguished villas until I came to the one occupied, in part, by Klíma. He refreshed me with cool drinks until I stopped panting and regained my powers of speech. Although in his mid-fifties, the novelist looks younger and his intense, somewhat scrunched features repose beneath a pudding bowl thatch of hair that remains almost black. His shelves included books in a number of languages, and his own had been translated into English, Swedish, German, and other languages. There are, of course, no official Czech editions of his work.

As deputy editor of a literary journal that reflected the kinds of views that led to the Prague Spring in 1968, he was predictably unpopular with the neo-Stalinists who came to power after the Russian intervention. Indeed, in 1967 he and Ludvík Vaculík had been expelled from the Party, though they continued to enjoy the support of the Writers' Union. In 1969 he went to Ann Arbor to spend a year as a visiting professor at the University of Michigan, and although he was offered a chair in Slavic literature at the University of Indiana, he declined and returned to Czechoslovakia, despite the lack of cultural hospitality the new rulers were certain to offer him. Like hundreds of other writers who had taken advantage of the more liberal climate in the late 1960s, he was forbidden to publish by the new regime. There was a slight relaxation in 1970, when banned writers were offered the possibility of having their work published once again if only they would undertake self-criticism and thus lend their retrospective

259

support to the Soviet invasion and the Husák regime. Only four writers took up the offer; others emigrated. Of the writers left in Czechoslovakia, Klíma estimates that about a hundred are still banned.

Klíma is more fortunate than most. He, along with Havel and Vaculík, are probably the only writers in the country who are able to earn a living from foreign royalties. Emigré publishing houses in London and Toronto bring out his books in the Czech original, and they are widely translated elsewhere in Europe. I asked Klíma whether he'd seen a favourable review in a recent issue of the *Times Literary Supplement* of the English translation of his short stories *My First Loves*. Yes, he'd seen the review, only he'd never seen his book. Copies sent to him on two occasions by his publisher had been confiscated at the border.

Despite the official ban, Klíma remains highly respected in his own country. Samizdat thrives in Czechoslovakia just as it does in Hungary, though suppression, when exercised, tends to be more draconian. It is, of course, forbidden for individuals to publish anything, even chess problems, without official approval. The publications of specialist organizations occupy a middle ground between the official and the underground. The club of, say, Czech speleologists is entitled to publish a journal for its members, and while the majority of the articles must contain references to caves, it is sometimes possible for articles of more general interest to appear in such unlikely places. This is how the Jazz Section of the Musicians' Union ran into trouble. Its publications contained articles on a variety of cultural issues, and this catholicity drew down on its organizers the wrath of the authorities and a buckshot of prison sentences. Slipping articles of general interest into club publications can be risky, for all organizations are well stocked with informers.

Literary and cultural journals are not directly censored. However, you are unlikely to be offered the editorship of an officially approved magazine unless your political credentials are sound. Once appointed, editors are directly responsible for what they publish. Every now and again, an editor makes a 'mistake'. Everybody knows which writers must never sully the pages of literary journals. Any editor insane enough to print an article by Havel would soon be out of a job, even if, as would surely happen, informers ensured that the offending article were removed while still in proof. Still, editors do err: a short story that seems innocuous to one reader may strike another as subtly subversive. I heard about a writer of children's books who submitted a manuscript which was accepted for publication. However, a hard-line colleague detected an anti-Soviet subtext buried in this tale for eight-year-olds, and the book was not published. That was not the worst of it, for once it is known that a writer's work has been rejected on the grounds of political deviance, it is then extremely unlikely that any other editor will want to consider his work. This particular writer, whom I was asked not to name, has been cleared of wrongdoing, but the clearance may not manage to salvage his career.

So for most writers of ability, and for all writers of independent minds and original ideas, the only possible outlet for their work is through samizdat. The traditional method is for the author to bang out about fifteen copies of a book on the typewriter; these are then distributed to friends and admirers. Copies are then lent to other readers, some of whom will make additional copies for further distribution, especially in the provinces. No one, least of all the author, is concerned about copyright. Each copy will have about ten readers. This laborious method of distribution is likely to be improved now that there is greater access to roneo machines. A new theatre review in samizdat is published in an edition of 100 copies run off on a photocopying machine. It has been harder for Czechs than for Hungarians to avail themselves of more sophisticated print technology. It is not only novelists and poets who publish through samizdat. There are underground publications devoted to philosophy, popular music, translations, and even scientific research. Indeed, so tedious and outdated are most official academic journals that many apolitical academics feel obliged to read samizdat publications in order to keep up with the latest research. For playwrights such as Havel, distribution of his work presents no problem at all. A new play is simply recorded on tape, from which other copies are easily made.

The authorities are well aware of what is going on. Writers cannot be prosecuted for typing their own work, but distribution of unauthorized material is an offence, and hired typists have received short prison sentences. Nor is it an offence in Czechoslovakia to own Western books; only their dissemination is against the law. I was told of a man who lived in a village in northern Bohemia. For his own edification he translated some essays by George Orwell and handed a copy to his wife and another to his sister. For this act of dissemination he was prosecuted. Whether this story is true or not, I cannot be sure, but it is clear that the state has limitless powers, whether or not it chooses to exercise them. Laws concerning state subversion are so generally formulated that they can be wielded whenever there is considered to be a political need to knock a few heads together.

Samizdat is now so well established in Czechoslovakia that it is possible to talk not merely of underground publications, but of samizdat publishing houses. The leading underground journals include *Petlice* (Padlock), which was founded by Klíma and Vaculík, and *Expedice*, founded by Havel. Their publications are properly bound and have all the solidity of the hardcover book, and little of the provisional nature of the underground broadside. Although it is galling to know that you are unlikely ever to see your own work sold openly in your own country, there are compensations for samizdat publications.

'Being banned,' says Klíma, 'I have no access to the "general reader". But that also means that the readers I do have here form a devoted audience. Samizdat gives creative writers a kind of freedom. We are no longer dependent on the whim of the editor or censor, and we are also free from the pressures of the market. Of course we all suffer from the oppression under which we produce our work, but if that oppression is not life-threatening, then being banned needn't have an adverse affect on your writing. In a free society you are dependent on the whims of the marketplace, and we can all think of fine writers who end up making compromises, often for commercial reasons, that lead to a loss of their own integrity. Material success is a great danger for writers. They can lose their contact with everyday life. Here, where many writers have menial jobs such as window cleaning, they at least retain that vital contact with ordinary people. In Czechoslovakia there is no marketplace in which to lose our way, and, even if we're persecuted and harassed, which most of us are from time to time, we can still keep our inner freedom.'

Others take a less serene view. A former law professor told me: 'Whenever a new samizdat publication appears, it has to be read quickly. Because of the limited number of copies available, few of us can hang on to them. They have to be returned or passed on, just like a library book. This leads to a nervous, jittery form of reading. There are few possibilities for sustained critique – you can't refer back.'

The ex-professor sees other dangers in samizdat. When I spoke to him of Klíma's welcome of the freedom of expression that samizdat offered him, he said: 'Yes, underground culture here, as

I'm sure others have told you, is not unlike a ghetto. Our sense of solidarity gives us all a warm feeling, but we sometimes forget the terrible price we pay, that of isolation, isolation from our society as well as from the world outside. There are those who consider this ghetto-like situation positive, but there's a danger that we can become too inward-looking, too content to stay within that tiny circle.'

He was also concerned that the numbers of readers of samizdat were declining. Although the danger of detection if you have samizdat publications in your possession is slight, the climate of fear is still sufficiently strong, he maintained, to deter the faint-hearted from participating in the underground culture. Havel takes a more optimistic view, especially since it has become so much easier to make copies now that writers are not solely dependent on the typewriter. Nor does he detect any slackening of interest, among young or old, in samizdat; the numbers of readers have, in his estimation, definitely increased during the last decade. Demand, he insists, still exceeds supply.

For Havel, his prominence as Czechoslovakia's best-known dissident is a mixed blessing. As a writer who has maintained and increased his international reputation despite years of persecution and spells in jail, as a man of unflinching courage who refuses to mend his ways despite unceasing harassment, and as a leading impresario of samizdat culture, Václav Havel is to many of his admirers a national hero, a torch-bearer. 'I receive quite a few phone calls to thank me for this and that. They're anonymous calls, mostly students and ordinary people who are afraid to put their jobs on the line but just want us to know that they support what we do even if circumstances make it impossible for them to participate actively in the underground culture. Of course this is most gratifying. But I also find it unsettling, because it places on my shoulders an extra-literary power I do not seek.'

It is a burden he wears lightly. Havel lives in a spacious flat on the top floor of a building along the embankment facing Malá Strana. As I walked into the lobby on my way to see him, I was puzzled by a prominent plaque erected to commemorate one Vácslav Havel. Was, I asked the other Havel upstairs, the namesake any relation? Indeed, he was, and Václav Havel and his brother Ivan have the curious pleasure in living now in a building designed by their grandfather. The playwright was slighter than I had expected and his face more lined; his hair was unruly in what seemed a permanent way, as though unresponsive to the grooming

263

of a comb. His deep voice and somewhat grave manner suggested to me a quiet power, rather like some further advance into miniaturization which permits ever smaller objects to perform ever more remarkable feats. Havel would break from time to time into a winning smile that crinkles across his lively face. If he was weary of being visited by every Western journalist who comes to Prague, he was too polite to let it show.

The alternative to participation in the underground culture is depressing. A visit to the Museum of Literature in Prague gives one a quick introduction to the official line. The captions and explanations are printed in Czech only, so I may have missed the references to Franz Kafka and Jaroslav Hašek (who wrote *The Good Soldier Švejk*), though I doubt it. Karel Čapek is admitted into the canon, and one would have expected a small country to be proud of its Nobel-prizewinning poet Jaroslav Seifert, but I could only find two of his books in the display cases, one of them a children's book.

That Kafka, who died in 1924, is still regarded as a threat to the values endorsed by the Czech state is a tribute to the power of his writing, though a tribute most writers would rather do without. Even on the centenary of his birth, there was no official recognition of the occasion in the literary press. One guidebook to Prague makes no reference at all to Kafka, though when I asked a Cedok official where I could find the writer's birthplace, she did direct me to the house adjoining St Nicholas's Church at the top of U Radnice, where a portrait plaque is attached to the wall to commemorate the writer. This deliberate neglect of Kafka is not wholly explained by his depiction of the individual pitted against a bureaucratic and totalitarian state that has grown too complex to be understood even by those who control it. For Kafka wrote in German and was a leading figure in the Czech-German culture that prevailed between the wars. Czech nationalism is wary of that whole layer of its former culture, and the authorities would rather promote and perpetuate the work of those who wrote in Czech than those who, although Czech by birth and upbringing, belonged to the German-speaking community.

In the early nineteenth century Czech was little more than a peasant dialect. German was the language of administration, of the bourgeoisie; German culture was esteemed as the most cultivated in Europe. Later that century, as peasants moved into urban centres that were overwhelmingly German-speaking,

Czech nationalism grew as the only popular form of opposition to Habsburg domination, and the Czech language itself was conscripted into the cause. In 1882 a Czech university was founded, and the language increasingly became the vehicle for the intellectual life of the country. After the experiences of Nazi occupation it is hardly surprising that hostility to the German language was revived, even though this entailed blotting out many of the positive contributions German-Bohemian culture had made over the preceding century. It was yet one more round in the war between Slavs and Germans that had been waged since the Middle Ages in Bohemia and Moravia.

With such attitudes prevailing towards some of their greatest dead writers, it is not surprising that the living also get a raw deal. Buying books in Prague is not easy. On Thursday mornings, when new books are published, long queues, hundreds long, form outside the principal bookshops of the city. Forthcoming publications are announced in the newspapers, and everyone knows that if anything worthwhile is about to be published – perhaps a translation of a famous American novel – all copies will be snapped up in days, if not hours. Demand always exceeds supply. I only found one or two bookshops in Prague where one could browse. In the rest of them, you walk up to the counter, behind which a small number of books may be on display, and ask for what you want. At first I thought this was an absurdity, until I realized that any book that is readily available is probably not worth buying. The Czech publishing industry appears to be run along the same lines as the shoe industry: as long as quotas are filled, it doesn't matter what they are filled with. During my stay in Prague I was never able to find a Czech/English pocket dictionary, nor was any English-language guidebook to the city on sale.

Prague has half a dozen secondhand bookshops, some of which are well stocked. They are always full of browsers, since secondhand shops offer the only chance of finding certain coveted volumes. One Sunday I was gazing into the window of the large Antikvariát at Můstek when I spotted a used copy of the French edition of the standard guidebook to Prague. Since the only English guidebook I had to the city was a somewhat inadequate photographic guide I'd been lucky enough to pick up in Budapest, I decided I had to have this French version. The shop was due to open at nine on Monday morning, so I turned up at eight-thirty and joined the queue of about forty people. When the doors opened, a salesgirl emerged and handed out numbered cards to those in the queue. A multilingual inquiry to those ahead of me in the queue gave me the information that these cards were for those who wished to buy books displayed in the window. I was one of them, and was given the number 27. We then huddled round the display case while the salesgirl unlocked it, extracted the books desired by those with the lowest numbers, locked up again, and took the books into the shop to the till. She then returned and repeated the procedure for the next in line. She called out the numbers but I couldn't follow what she was saying, as became apparent to some of my fellow queuers, who kindly pushed me forward at the appropriate moment, thus ensuring that by 9.20, I got the book I wanted. As I walked back down Wenceslas Square, I found myself clutching the book hard, as though it were an ingot of gold. Extreme scarcity enhances value, and I could hardly believe my good fortune in having secured the *only* copy for sale in all of Prague of the only adequate guidebook to the city.

The English language sections of the secondhand bookshops give a curious idea of the average Czech's notion of the glories of our literature. Works by contemporary authors are hardly ever to be seen, but there is no shortage of books by Ernest Raymond, Charles Morgan, Quiller Couch, and Rose Franken – hardly *la crème de la crème*. It's not that Czech publishing houses fail to translate more modern, and more innovative, writers, but rather that the editions are so rapidly exhausted. It is also easy for translated authors to fall out of favour. Saul Bellow, John Updike, and William Styron have all been translated into Czech, but no sooner had they signed a petition in support of the persecuted Jazz Section than their works vanished not only from bookshops but from libraries too. Print runs seem random. Beryl Bainbridge's *The Bottle Factory Outing* was honoured with a printing of 20,000 copies, but Beckett's *Waiting for Godot* was printed in an edition of only 8000, which in terms of the East European appetite for good literature is negligible. When Joyce's *Ulysses* was published in Czech, only 7000 copies were printed. Within days the black market price had risen to 500 crowns, over ten times the publication price. Apart from secondhand bookshops, the most likely sources for out-of-print books are flea markets, which are less random and far more expensive than their Western counterparts, and advertisements placed by those with a supply of such books. Purchasing, and indeed selling, by mail order is risky, since it lays one open to the charge of speculation, which carries penalties that include a jail sentence.

It didn't surprise me that the books chosen for translation into Czech seemed an almost random selection, with Iris Murdoch rubbing shoulders with P.G. Wodehouse, and Kingsley Amis snug on the shelf next to Dorothy Sayers and Arnold Wesker. Far more serious is the refusal of the authorities to offer their own writers a platform. To deny publication to the many writers whose talent and vigour have gained them a high reputation worldwide is a perverse exercise in self-strangulation. A culture is no mere appendage; it is the core of a nation, its defining statement to the rest of the world, and for the living, erratic, unsettling and brilliant expressions of Czech writing which are available only outside the borders of the country, the authorities have substituted an ersatz literary culture that is a hollow mockery.

31

When I'm Cleaning Windows

While my fascination with underground Prague was growing, I was still making my way to some of the city's lesser known architectural marvels, especially now that I was properly equipped with a decent guide book. One day I walked south from the National Museum through busy unpromising streets and came to the Karlov church, a lovely building packed with baroque surprises. The drama of the Visitation is depicted in statuary above the interior of one of the doors, and three steep flights of steps swoop majestically up to side altars, while in the crypt the stone walls are painted in pastel colours to suggest gardens and views glimpsed through neoclassical ruins – a touch of Claude Lorraine in baroque Prague. Or by toiling up Úvoz, a glorious lane consisting of seventeenth- and eighteenth-century houses on one side and the Strahov Gardens on the other, I would eventually come to the Strahov monastery, with its magnificent rococo churches and two great libraries: the grand, balconied and frescoed Philosophy Hall, and the far more delicate though equally lavish Theology Hall which dates from the century before. In the anterooms to these two libraries cabinets contain eccentric collections of pinned butterflies, shells, lobsters, turtles, and dried fish and sea monsters with skins like rawhide.

On rainy days there were the museums and galleries to visit. The Applied Arts Museum proved a disappointment. Most of the furniture in the collection had come originally from Italy and Germany, and the Czechs' principal native contribution to the applied arts seems to have taken the form of huge glass and pewter beer tankards, cheerfully decorated with painted scenes. The National Museum, despite the exhaustiveness of some of its collections, was also a disappointment, though it was hard not to be awed by so many display cases exclusively devoted to the cockroach. Up near the castle the Šternberg Palace houses a fine collection of European art, from Italian primitives to the early decades of this century, with good Picassos and a few post-impressionists. The Šternberg also hangs a painting on its walls that it attributes to Piero della Francesca. Oh yeh? The gallery is on stronger ground with its German collection, which includes superb Holbein cartoons and many fine Cranachs. At the St Agnes Convent the authorities have mounted a large and highly un-memorable exhibition of nineteenth-century Czech painting, typified by sprawling nakeds daubed by one M. Pirner; while the exhibitions at the Riding School near the castle offer the visitor a cross-section of twentieth-century Czech art, of which the highly eclectic paintings of Jan Zrzavý proved the most arresting. More exhibitions are housed in the beautiful sixteenth-century Royal Summer Palace of Ferdinand I, which, with its long shady arcades, is the loveliest Italianate building in Prague.

Unquestionably the finest gallery in the city is to be found within the castle precincts at the St George's Convent, which is devoted to Czech Gothic art. Before Czech artists turned to the urgent business of decorating beer mugs during the Renaissance, they had produced a most ravishing sequence of fourteenth-century Madonnas, both painted and carved. This was work of such refinement, such delicacy and sophistication and purity of feeling, that it stopped me in my tracks over and over again. What I had intended as a half-hour stroll through the gallery lengthened into a stay of two hours. Before the sweetness of these Madonnas has a chance to become cloying, the gallery confronts visitors with a group of taut lean Crucifixions and the squat and powerful stone carvings depicting the enthroned Charles IV that were produced at Peter Parler's workshop. The fifteenth-century repre-sentations, whether of saints or the Madonna, were more plump and more coarse in feeling, though some of the carvings retained the exquisite refinement of the earlier work. I sped through the final galleries devoted to acres of drab mannerist and baroque canvases, as well as past the more arresting baroque sculptures of Brokoff and Matthias Braun, which certainly deserved a less hurried inspection.

It was a wrench to emerge from the convent into the squares and lanes of the castle, through which fifty-strong groups of tourists, Czech as well as foreign, were trooping, *zmrzlina* dripping down their chins. But I soon discovered that tourists groups in Prague, especially the majority under the constant care of Cedok guides, tread only the most well worn of paths. There were few tourists at the Karlov church. At night they seemed to confine themselves entirely to the beer halls and restaurants of Malá Strana and the promenades of Wenceslas Square and the Charles Bridge. One evening after dinner I took a long walk from the Old Town across the Charles Bridge into Malá Strana. I walked up Vlašská and down Nerudova and Valdštejnská, passing the beautiful but silent palaces on all sides.

Despite the gentle warmth of the evening and an entrancing lack of evidence that I was living in the later twentieth century rather than the early eighteenth, the lovely streets seemed strangely devoid of mystery and atmosphere. Venice, which has a similar architectural cohesiveness, is suffused with a nocturnal melancholy I never experienced in Prague. At night, when the tourists were off the side streets and hard at their pleasures, the lanes of Malá Strana seemed more beautiful than ever, yet devoid of life. There was no sense of continuity here. The palaces of the city have been institutionalized; the loveliest of them are now tightly guarded embassies, and the grandest of them government offices. They are still in use, and despite the omnipresence of scaffolding that sometimes looks as ancient as the structures it screens, there is little appearance of neglect or dilapidation. Yet the palaces have lost their sense of connection with the city which they so gorgeously adorn. They appear merely monumental, for all their sumptuousness.

When each morning I emerged from my lodgings and walked down Wenceslas Square, I would pass the tourists' cars parked outside the luxury hotels – the Mercedes and Saabs from Germany, Switzerland, Austria – and the video-equipped coaches from Germany and Italy crammed with teenagers, and as the day wore on I would pass the tourists following their guides through the streets and squares and churches of the city; and though I, indisputably, was one of them, my sense of distance from them increased day by day. The feeling grew on me that the city I was probing bore little resemblance to the city, designed by earlier centuries with colour slides in mind, that they were feasting on. Their Prague was a series of facades as elegant and exquisite as could be found in Europe, whereas my Prague was increasingly an underground city, with its true life beating not in the Europa coffeehouse or U supa beer hall but in dingy flats and claustrophobic boiler rooms where men and women strove against the odds to keep their voices heard, while all the power of the state was directed towards keeping them silent. I grew, quite unfairly, to resent the well-heeled tourists, crowing at the fistfuls of crowns handed them in exchange for their marks or francs. To them Prague was little more than a picturesque playground, a confection, a diversion. It offered a culture that could be patronized, and all the while you could congratulate yourself that you were doing the inhabitants a favour by spending your money and giving them a modicum of contact with rich and kindly Westerners. All tourists, myself included, participate in exploitation even while we hand over our money, yet the breadth of the gap between visitor and visited seemed wider here than in any place I'd been before in Europe. I wanted to grab passing tourists by the lapels and hiss: 'Do you really know what goes on in this city? There is a dream city here, like a laser show mounted for your benefit, but it is no longer related to the life that's lived here.' Mine was, I knew, a fruitless anger, tainted by self-righteousness. But there it was, and on this evening, as on so many others, I would seek to contact those aspects of the city that palpitated beneath the beautiful hard veneer of its facades, like the ripple beneath the cool sheen of snakeskin.

From the high points within the old city, it is easy to spot ranged along the horizon a series of tall off-white buildings as regular as the spikes on a rail. These are the postwar housing estates, hardly different from the concrete wastelands of Óbuda or, for that matter, certain corners of the East End of London. From the distance the ranged blocks have a certain grandeur, but as one draws near the bleakness becomes more apparent. At Kosmonautů, to the south of the city, the differing designs of the great slabs suggests the blocks have been built over an extended period, and some indeed remain incomplete. Like all such estates, these are characterized by the poor finish of the buildings, an apparent lack of amenities, and a bureaucratic fondness for planting lawns in inaccessible spots.

The blocks where Josef and his family lived were of better design and more varied layout. An example of cooperative housing, they had been built by the families who now occupied them. I did not know precisely where I would find Josef, as the address I had been given was incomplete. By inspecting all the names against the bells on four of the blocks I eventually found his, and pressed. A large somewhat shambling figure emerged and stood in the dimly lit hall examining me with a guarded watchfulness. I explained who I was and how it was that I had called, and he ushered me into his flat.

'I would have phoned first,' I apologized, 'but I didn't have your number.'

'That's all right,' replied Josef in excellent English. 'You're not the first foreign visitor to come out here.'

Josef's story is typical of those who are out of favour with the regime. A computer programmer by training, he was associated with the Chartists and, by returning to the Jewish faith of his forebears, was additionally tainted, in the eyes of the authorities, with the stigma of 'Zionism'. For the last six years he has worked as a window cleaner. His wife, however, has a good job and there were no signs of financial hardship. The authorities consider Josef tiresome enough to haul him into the police station for occasional bouts of interrogation, but attempts have also been made to persuade him to return to the fold.

'I have been offered jobs,' he told me as he brewed the black grainy stew that passes in Prague for coffee, 'but I couldn't accept them. For one post I would have had to stand as a Party candidate, which of course I couldn't do, and for another, a more academic job, I'd have been obliged, as most officials are, to report all contacts with foreigners. I couldn't agree to that either. If I'd taken that job, I'd have to give my superiors a detailed account of our conversation. So I'm a window cleaner, but at least I am free. Not entirely free, of course. I don't have a passport and I don't have a career, but to me the freedom to meet whom I please and say what I please is more important.

'Window cleaning has its rewards too. Not the kind Milan Kundera writes about in *The Unbearable Lightness of Being*. We work in cadres, so opportunities to slip into bed with beautiful women while on the job just don't arise.' Josef made a few more remarks, far from charitable, about Kundera, who is berated by many Czech dissidents for writing so eloquently about a situation in his native country with which he no longer has direct contact. 'But you learn about a few other things as a window cleaner. In April we had to prepare the streets around Letná for the May Day parade. We spent hours cleaning the windows facing the street, but were told not to bother with those along the back and sides. You've seen the new theatre alongside the National Theatre? A nice building, but they forgot to work out how the windows were to be cleaned. Usually we work from trucks with extension turrets, but we couldn't drive them onto the plaza around the theatre, because there's an underground car park beneath it, and the surface wouldn't carry the weight. Eventually, they had to import special lightweight scaffolding from the West. Now you know where your hard currency ends up.'

Josef's wife Ludmilla was away for a few days with the children, so he was quite content to have my company for a few hours. 'We have an allotment garden, and I have to go and water it. Come along, if you like. It's about two tram rides from here.'

We appeared to be skirting round the edge of the city, and a tram deposited us close to a long ridge entirely planted with small regular allotment gardens. On each plot stood a cabin that seemed large enough to live in.

'Most of the families who own these lots come here for weekends,' said Josef, unlocking the gate that led into the allotments. 'It's a great social occasion. Some people describe it as a form of internal emigration. Flats in town are small and cramped and lack privacy. At weekends the city empties. A third of all Prague families leave each weekend. People either drive out to their cottages in the country or, if they can't afford that, they take the tram to their gardens and spend the night in their cabins. People can meet their friends here, or drink beer all evening under the shade of a plum tree. The regime doesn't object to this form of property ownership, probably because it helps to relieve the shortages of fruit and vegetables.'

'There's no cottage on your plot,' I observed, as we approached what looked like a bomb crater bordered by a noble and upright row of tulips.

'We don't want one. But we're going to have to build one. It's part of the regulations. It's very annoying. We're going to have to spend 16,000 crowns we can't really afford just to build a weekend hut we don't want. My neighbours out here don't like me. They think I'm antisocial. You see, it's like a holiday community. People visit each other, take turns to cook, throw parties. I don't like that kind of thing, so they're angry with me.'

'What's that great hole in the ground you're watering?'

'That's where our fruit trees will go. I think we've left it all too late. By the time the trees are grown, the children will have grown up and moved away and there'll be nobody to eat the fruit. That other big hole is where the foundations of the cottage are going to be built. Oh yes, they all have to have proper foundations.'

'What's that large shed on the crest of the ridge?'

'That's the communal house. They've just finished building it.'

'What's it for, since you all have your own little houses out here?'

'Well, the committee has to have somewhere to hold its meetings, doesn't it? You can't have allotments without a committee, and you can't have a committee without committee rooms. That's where our real talent lies, in creating bureaucracies. They give people a feeling of importance.'

Once the muddy slope Josef laughably referred to as his 'garden' was thoroughly drenched, we made our way back down the hill to the tram stop.

'Once my wife is back from the country you must come to dinner with us. She will be most angry that she missed your visit, so you must return. Are you busy tomorrow evening?'

'I don't think so.'

'Perhaps you would like to come to the synagogue with me. I always go to the Altneu on Friday nights. It's very beautiful. It might interest you.'

We arranged to meet at the synagogue at eight the following evening. Josefov, the old Jewish quarter of the city, is one of its most famous features, not only because the Altneu is the oldest synagogue in continuous use in Europe, but because of the solemn beauty of the cluttered little cemetery nearby. The cemetery was used until 1768 and the oldest identifiable tombstone dates from 1439. There are said to be some 20,000 gravestones crammed into an area that can't occupy much more than an acre. More problematic is how 20,000 bodies managed to be deposited in so cramped an area. The expanse of leaning stones, resembling a petrified field of wheat, is now overlooked by turn-of-the-century apartment houses, while the old stones themselves are resting places for ladybirds whose scarlet shells gleam from the cracks and crevices. Heraldic devices as well as line after line of Hebrew script cover most stones from top to bottom. The Altneu synagogue predates the old cemetery by two centuries. Rebuilt towards the end of the fourteenth century, the small gabled building, which seems to repose at a level some feet below the street level, has an interior that could easily be mistaken for a Gothic chapel. It is lit by tall lancets and vaulted with strong ribs and bosses. Seats and prayer desks are ranged around the walls and alongside the raised central podium from which services are conducted. Beautiful knotty medieval ironwork screens this area from the congregation. When I visited the synagogue during the day, there were two Hasidim in black gaberdine coats fussing about, inspecting the inscriptions. They were, of course, from the United States.

274

The Altneu is not the only ancient synagogue in Josefov. There are four or five others, though only one other, dating from the sixteenth century, was open to visitors. The Jewish Museum, which snuggles into a corner of the Old Cemetery, has explanatory notices in five languages, which suggests to me that it is run by the Jewish community rather than by the state. It contained moving displays of children's drawings made at the closed ghetto of Terezín, established by the Nazis in 1942, as well as other mementoes of the camp where many elderly Jews from Prague and from many other cities were to die.

A noticeable proportion of those gathered at the Altneu on that Friday evening were foreigners. A French family were there in force, and an American sat in the pew opposite mine. The women, of course, sat in the back, leaving the menfolk to get on with the serious business of prayer. The majority of the regulars were old, but there were a few younger men, such as Josef. Many of these were, he told me, converts. As a child he had been baptized, and had made a conscious decision as an adult to reapply, as it were, to the religion his father had abandoned. Since the Czech/Hebrew prayer books had been destroyed during the war, the prayer books in use here had been facsimiled in New York from a 1930s edition and donated to the synagogue by American benefactors. Even including the visitors, there could not have been more than thirty in the congregation, and Josef mentioned that on some evenings it was difficult to get together the *minyan*, the minimum number of ten worshippers required before a service could be held. As in Budapest, many Czech Jews have lapsed both from religious observance and from cultural identification with the Jewish community, and though there are officially said to be 15,000 Jews in the country, there are probably 40,000 of fairly direct Jewish descent.

When the service was over Josef said he would take a walk. I joined him.

'Have you seen the Bartolomějská police station?'

'No, but I've read about it. They're always taking Havel off there for interrogations.'

'And not only Havel.'

As we walked down the long street towards the river, I recognized it as one of the few thoroughfares in the Old Town that was lifeless during the day. Josef showed me why. Much of one side of the street is filled with a long grim block, attached to a white-tiled building of singular unattractiveness. These are the police headquarters. The cells, however, are in another building which houses the criminal division and is reached through two courtyards not visible from the street.

'I've been brought here five times,' said Josef as we walked slowly past, taking pains not to show too close an interest in the building. 'Usually for the maximum forty-eight hours.'

'Are you allowed to let your family know where you are?'

'No.'

'So Ludmilla just has to sit at home with the children for two days and hope you haven't met with an accident?'

'That's it. Still, I haven't had any problems with the police recently. It's not always as direct as being detained for interrogation. A few years ago three women, all of whom I knew slightly, were approached by the police and asked to seduce me in order to compromise me. Two refused, but one agreed. She later told me she had been told she would never be promoted if she didn't go along with the plan.'

'Did she succeed?'

'No. In fact she ended up by confessing the whole thing to me.'

We walked back towards the centre of town, and found ourselves on the major pedestrian shopping street of Na příkopě.

'Ah, this brings back some memories,' said Josef as we walked past the Moskva restaurant, with its large lettered sign tacked onto the front of the building. 'In 1968, I watched people climb up to that sign. They took out the middle letters and replaced them with RA, so that the sign then read Morava, which is at least Czech.'

We then walked down the gentle slope of Wenceslas Square. Jerking his thumb in the direction of the broad dark facade of the National Museum, Josef said: 'In 1968, the museum was shelled by the Russians under their commander Marshal Grechko. The authorities filled in the holes but for a long time you could still see where the shells had hit. We were very intrigued by our new-look National Museum, and a saying made the rounds that it was a recent work by El Grechko.'

'Is it true that Jan Palach immolated himself just here?'

'Yes, close to the statue. There was talk of giving him a hero's funeral at Vyšehrad, but instead he was buried in a prominent spot near the entrance to the principal cemetery. But he didn't stay there for long. A couple of years later they dug him up and put in his grave a young woman called Marie Jedličková. That's when we all understood that he wasn't a national hero at all, but, as the authorities had told us, a helpless victim of imperialism.'

Before returning to my room, there was something I wanted to ask Josef, namely, why he persisted in refusing to make any compromises with the regime when his education and abilities would probably ensure him a long and fruitful career, not to mention a passport.

'It's a question of integrity, I suppose. If I make compromises I lose my independence. As I said to you before, it would be almost impossible for us to be having this talk, and for you to come to my home for dinner, if I held an important job. If I act in a particularly flagrant way, I could be arrested and given two or three years in jail. It's unlikely but it could happen. I'll take that risk if it means I can keep my freedom. Sometimes even the smallest gestures we make can have an impact. The other day three people were arrested for holding up Charter 77 banners during a May Day parade in the provinces. It may seem a futile gesture to you, but the news will get out and not only the world but the Czech people will hear of it and be heartened by that small act of resistance.' (He was right. Three days later the incident was reported on Austrian radio broadcasts, to which many Czechs listen.)

'But you're a married man with children. Of course I respect your stand, but doesn't it worry you that your children's prospects might be damaged by it?'

'Of course we've thought about that. I know many people who fully supported the ideals of Charter 77 but wouldn't sign Charter for that very reason. Yes, my children may have some difficulties in school or getting into university as a consequence of my position – though there's not much evidence that the children of Chartists are being singled out in this way. But I remember when I was growing up and we asked our parents how the horrors of the 1950s could have been allowed to happen, and why so few spoke up against the Stalinists. I'm not trying to say that things are as bad as they were in the 1950s – of course they're not – but I never want my children to be able to ask me why I didn't speak up for the values I believe in. I may be doing some short-term damage to my kids' future, but I'll take that risk because the long-term goals for which we are all striving are so vital.'

32

What a Swell Party This Is

It took me a couple of weeks to master the intricacies of Tuzex, the chain of shops where goods may be purchased only with hard currency or with vouchers purchased with hard currency. In exchange for handing over your hard currency to the Czechs, goods are made available at bargain prices. Out on Leninova, the boulevard that leads to the western suburbs and the airport, is the Tuzex emporium that specializes in food and drink. All manner of goods I'd never seen in downtown groceries were on the shelves: Italian olive oil, German chocolates, Cognac. Pilsner beer was priced at 2.50 crowns per bottle, instead of the 6 charged in ordinary shops. Czech wines – which are perfectly drinkable – that normally sell for 25 crowns or more were available here for 5. A bottle of Slivovitz priced, according to its label, at 100 crowns was on sale here for 18.

However, all is not what it seems. When I shopped in Wenceslas Square, I was using crowns purchased at the tourist rate, approximately 15 to the pound. At Tuzex the official exchange rate is used, about 9 crowns to the pound. Thus if I wished to compare wine prices at Tuzex with those I'd have to pay in the shops, I needed to multiply the Tuzex prices by 75 per cent. Even so, many goods were far cheaper there than in the shops. Not all the customers were foreigners or diplomats, and some fortunate Czechs shop here with Tuzex vouchers sent to them by relatives abroad.

It was rapidly becoming clear that there was no such thing as an exchange rate. Or, to put it another way, there were so many as to rob the concept of content. There was the base rate (also known as Tuzex crowns), the tourist rate (75 per cent higher), and a bonus rate (an additional 36 per cent higher) that rewards tourists who book a Cedok tour that includes accommodation and pay for the

278

lot in advance. And finally there is the black-market rate, which is approximately five times the base rate of any Western currency. It is, of course, the black-market rate which is the true rate of exchange, since it reflects the actual demand for the currency, while the three official rates are no more than a series of rip-offs of varying degrees of rapacity. Despite warnings to tourists that the death penalty is mandatory for any visitors caught changing money illegally, the black market clearly operates with a measure of official approval. Perhaps not approval, exactly, but certainly control. A friend who used to work at a Tuzex shop mentioned that from time to time the police would swoop down on the moneychangers always lurking near the entrances and get rid of some of them, while allowing others to linger. This, she thought, was a fairly clear indication that some moneychangers operated with police approval, and the reason why the other moneychangers were shooed off was that the police received their percentage only from the touts they protected. No doubt this is a terrible calumny against the probity of the Czech police, but it sounded convincing to me.

My shopping completed at Tuzex, I continued to walk another few hundred yards along Leninova to one of four shabby apartment blocks and rang the bell marked Slánský. It was a curious sensation, some moments later, to be shaking hands with a man in his early fifties by the name of Rudolf Slánský. In November 1951 his father, who bore the same name and happened to be secretary general of the Czech Communist Party, was arrested and denounced, with others, as a 'Trotskyist-Titoist bourgeois-nationalist traitor', which covered most of the possibilities. Slánský and ten other 'enemies of the Republic' (all Jews, it so happened) were found guilty of the bogus charges and hanged on 3 December 1952. His place on the praesidium was taken by Antonín Novotný, who emerged as first secretary of the party after the death, a year later, of Klement Gottwald. The purging of Slánský was particularly brutal since its sole purpose, despite the trumped-up charges, was to eliminate him from the leadership. There is no question of rehabilitating Slánský, and not even the most bitter opponents of the Communist regime think of the hanged politician as a hero along the lines of László Rajk. In 1963 Slánský's sentence was quashed by the Supreme Court but he was not readmitted posthumously to the Party. Novotný's generosity didn't extend that far. 'If Gottwald wanted to stay in power and retain Stalin's approval, he had to get rid of Slánský. It was as simple as that,' a

Prague architect put it to me. (There had been, I later learnt, a moment when László Rajk, on a visit to Prague, had shaken hands with Rudolf Slánský. This meeting of the sons of executed fathers must surely have been, in an obscure way, rather moving.)

The Rudolf Slánský who was pouring me coffee must be a remarkably resilient man. He was sixteen when his father was executed, and bearing the same name he found it extremely difficult to pursue his studies. He eventually trained in economics and engineering management, but was only offered the most modest of jobs. His association with the Prague Spring didn't do much for his career, and in 1970 he lost his passport. He compounded his errors by joining the Chartists.

'Signing Charter,' the mild-mannered Slánský told me, 'earns you a black mark that seems to stay with us forever. There were a few who retracted, but those that did so retracted very soon after signing. Hardly anybody else has changed their minds. Many of those who signed in the early days underestimated the pressure. To lose your job, your passport, your standard of living, that's all bearable as soon as it happens, but you and your family must live with the consequences indefinitely. About a third of the signatories emigrated. For ordinary citizens, emigration is impossible, but anyone who signed Charter was free to leave the country – as long as he or she never returned. Of the 1500 or so who signed Charter, perhaps a thousand are left. It's certainly possible that a few people signed Charter because they had emigration in mind.'

Slánský, a bachelor, lives in a tiny flat. What most people would choose as a bedroom he uses as a study, while a third room, only a few feet wide, serves as his bedroom. The total area of the flat is 38 square metres. Although the flat seemed very cramped to me, Slánský did not complain. For many others the situation is worse, since the official allocation of space in state-owned flats is 12 square metres per person, plus 8, though many flats are in fact considerably larger. There are three categories of housing in Czechoslovakia: state-owned property, cooperatives, and privately owned dwellings. State-owned property is especially attractive, since rents are very low. However, such flats are in short supply, indeed virtually unobtainable unless you are a Party member or a military officer. 'It's unfortunately true,' observed Slánský, 'that the highest earners tend to pay the lowest rents. Some state-owned apartments are made available to factories, which rent them to workers who have given long service. But that's a very small percentage of the accommodation.'

More and more people are joining cooperatives as the only way to secure a flat of their own before they reach retirement age. Helena had told me that it was almost impossible for single young people or childless couples to obtain their own flats, and many spend a decade or more living with parents or in-laws. When joining a cooperative, you must reckon that a three-room flat in Prague will cost you 200,000 crowns. For such a flat you must lay down a deposit of between 30,000 and 40,000 crowns – roughly a year's wages – and you may have to wait many years before it is ready for occupation. The state donates to the coop 1000 crowns for each square metre to be constructed. This might average out at 70,000 crowns for each 70-square-metre flat. The balance must be borrowed by the coop and paid off by the tenants over thirty years or more. Tenants also pay a maintenance charge. Monthly repayments, however, would be on average a bearable 500-600 crowns.

Despite the deposits and loans and repayments, the occupant of a cooperative flat is not its owner, and such flats cannot be sold on the open market. If you wish to move, you must return the flat in exchange for some kind of rebate from the cooperative. For those wishing to move, the most common method is to exchange flats; indeed, in practice there are few other options. For those moving from Prague to the provinces there is no problem, but those wishing to move from the provinces to the capital will find the exchange extremely difficult and costly. Flats can be inherited but they must be occupied by the recipient.

There are private properties for sale, especially small country cottages and suburban villas, which are usually far more spacious than all but the most sumptuous flats. A villa will, however, set you back at least a million crowns, which is a tidy sum, even if most of it is acquired through loans. For many senior Party members, acquiring such a property is one of the principal rewards for their slavish loyalty. One of the most powerful politicians in Czechoslovakia, Lubomír Štrougal, is reputed to have owned no fewer than thirty such villas. Not that he lived in them all. Instead, he rented them out, which must have provided a pleasant supplement to his already considerable income. For the benefit of those of you who wish to acquire a villa at a knock-down price, here's how you do it. When you hear that someone has emigrated, you rejoice, for this means that their property will be confiscated. There are two price scales for property: valuation price and market price. Market price is of course much higher, but valuation price is the useful figure, as tax assessments are based on it. Party people are allowed to buy up confiscated property at their valuation price, which by any reckoning is a steal. I said steal. However, there are tough times ahead for Mr Štrougal. Rumour has it that the zealous Mr Gorbachev does not take kindly to the thought that certain leaders within the Socialist bloc have their snouts so deeply in the trough, and Mr Štrougal has been requested to divest himself of a dozen or so villas.

It was when returning from Slánský's flat – a far cry from Mr Štrougal's bagful of villas – that I glimpsed from the tram buzzing along Leninova another symbol of Party opulence. I later asked Josef what that gleaming, low-slung, elegant concrete and glass showcase of modern architecture was on the slopes above Leninova, not far from the leafy villa district of Dejvice. A hospital, perhaps?

'It's the Hotel Praha.'

'A hotel? Really? It's not mentioned in the tourist kits. Is it expensive?'

'The prices are not disclosed. The Praha is reserved for the Party. I don't think you'll ever find yourself staying there, not unless you disguise yourself as a visiting Bulgarian minister or a Libyan with an important contract in his pocket. The public is not admitted. A friend of mine occasionally does the windows there, so he's told me a thing or two. Most Party leaders have a suite there. Each morning lavish dishes are prepared for lunch, even though on some days nobody turns up to eat them.'

Private suites at the Praha are just one of the perks enjoyed by prominent Party officials. This elite, which consists of perhaps 200 people, also has access to specially imported foods such as yogurt and milk – which may not sound like luxury items until you recall that Chernobyl is not a vast distance from the Czech border. Farms in Moravia supply Party bosses with all-natural products, free from any contamination. The elite also has access to special clinics, though not all the leaders are keen on them, for while there is no doubt at all that the doctors are keen-as-mustard Party men, there is more uncertainty about their expertise as medical practitioners. Certain department stores, such as Dům Módy on Wenceslas Square, are said to have special floors reserved for top Party officials and their wives, where goods not available to the toiling masses are miraculously on offer. The young lady who had worked for a while at Tuzex told me what happened when a minister decided he needed a new briefcase. Tuzex were instructed to contact the best luggage shop in Vienna, and a snazzy briefcase was duly purchased, thus mopping up about $300 worth of hard currency. For some reason, the minister either had a stroke or was moved sideways in a hurry, with the result that he never claimed his briefcase. Tuzex, stuck with the bill, had to sell the case off at a loss.

Such privilege is not merely the icing on the cake, the just reward for decades of undeviating, unquestioning service to the state, for the prospect of participating in a life of luxury is a principal incentive for joining the Party in the first place. Membership is restricted to about 10 per cent of the population, and most of the important jobs are only open to Party members. Since there is no evidence that anyone in Czechoslovakia believes in the ideology spouted by the leadership, it's safe to assume that the overwhelming majority of those who join the Party do so for opportunist, careerist reasons. Many Party members will, I am told, admit that in their heart of hearts they despise the Party and all it stands for, but ambition requires them to put aside all scruples and toe the line. Just as important as the promise of goodies available only to the Party elite is the sure knowledge that Party members are rarely demoted. As in Britain, where failed politicians can look forward to a peaceful old age in ermine in the House of Lords, so hopelessly incompetent bureaucrats can be certain of eventual promotion to a well-paid sinecure where they can do little harm. After the sinecure comes retirement and a generous pension.

'Since the only source of power in the country is the Party,' a writer told me, 'those who support the regime tend to be opportunists. Inevitably, those who rise to the top tend to be the worst people. This will almost certainly have to change in the next few years, at least in managerial positions if not in cultural policy. Because Party appointments are determined by loyalty rather than by competence, we are ruled by idiots. Worst of all, there seems to be nobody around who can initiate change from within.'

Ironically, those who serve the regime most devotedly are often denied one of the most coveted privileges of all: permission to travel abroad. Heaven knows it's difficult enough for ordinary citizens to leave the country even briefly, but for former military and police officers and their families, it is impossible. If you are a private citizen and wish to travel to the West, you must be invited – by relatives, academic institutions, whatever. Your family is unlikely to be granted permission to accompany you, even if you can afford the fares, since the regime is keen to ensure that you return. Once you have secured the invitation you must purchase hard currency with which to finance your trip; you must do so, of course, at the least favourable of the many rates of exchange. You are only entitled to purchase foreign currency once every three years, though in practice you must often wait far longer between trips. The only way to speed up the process is to bribe someone. Once you have bought your hard currency, you must apply for a police permit, without which you cannot leave the country. This may or may not be forthcoming. All this applies to private travel only, since it is always possible to sign up on a Cedok tour to Paris or China; even though such tours are extremely expensive, they are invariably oversubscribed.

The Czech authorities save some citizens from having to go through this rigmarole by relieving them of their passports. It is not surprising, perhaps, that in a repressive society a government should seek to prevent dissidents from travelling abroad, but their families frequently suffer the same restrictions. Josef's wife, who has a responsible job in a ministry and is clearly not perceived as a threat to state security, told me she applies every year for a passport: eight years in a row she has applied, and each time her application has been rejected. In recent years, however, there has been a modest slackening of the reins and some of those who lost their passports after the Russian invasion have had them restored.

Nor is it much easier to travel within Eastern Europe. Far from being a happy family, united by singing the Internationale and membership of Comecon and the watchful presence within their borders of Soviet troops, there is far more tension and distrust between the countries of the Eastern Bloc than there is between Western European nations. The popular view of the national characteristics of the Bloc is expressed in the following joke: Gorbachev was travelling back to the USSR by train. As he passed through East Germany he put his hand out of the train, and repeated the gesture in Czechoslovakia, Poland, and Russia. Each time he was able to identify which country they were travelling through. How was he able to do this? his aides inquired. 'Easy,' replied Gorbachev. 'I put my hand out of the window and it was raining, so we had to be in East Germany. I put my hand out again a few hours later and people kissed it, so I knew I was in Czechoslovakia. I stuck my hand out again and

284

someone spat on it, so we had to be in Poland. A while later I poked my hand out once again and someone nicked my watch, so I knew I was home.'

Another view of inter-Bloc relations was provided by the following anecdote, which its narrator assured me was true. Some Poles came to Czechoslovakia to buy shoes for a young daughter. It is forbidden for such visitors to make off with Czech surplus products, so the shoes were confiscated by Czech border guards. As the Polish family crossed the border back into their country, the border guards spotted the barefoot little girl (a doubtful detail, in my view) and were outraged by what had occurred. So they stopped the next Czech car returning home from Poland, which happened to be rolling along on four spanking new Polish tyres, which the border guards had the pleasure of confiscating on the spot.

Private travel to the land of the protector, the Soviet Union, is well nigh impossible; only under the auspices of Cedok is it possible to go there. It is as difficult to go to Poland as to the West; an invitation is essential. This has been the case only since the rise of Solidarity; the hard-line Czech regime is anxious less the contagion should spread. In 1980, according to official figures, there were 1·7 million visits to Poland by Czechs; two years later the figure had dropped to 104,000. Travel to Yugoslavia and Hungary can be hampered by the difficulty of obtaining currency.

A learned stoker told me of a trip to Germany made by one of his colleagues in the boiler room.

'His daughter got married to a German, you see.'

'East or West?'

'West, of course! What would be the point of marrying an East German? You might as well marry the first person you spot on the street. Anyway, my colleague, who I should mention is a good Party member, returned from Germany with one of those fat mail-order catalogues. He was astounded. He had calculated how long it would take a German worker to earn enough money to buy a refrigerator, and then he worked out how long it would take him to earn as much. The difference was vast – one week against two months, or some such figure. Naturally we all patted his hand and assured him that material possessions were not everything in life, that he enjoyed much better social security in Czechoslovakia, and so on. Our colleague, who is a good Party member, nodded – then opened the catalogue at another page, and said: "And have you seen *this*?" And he read out more tempting, unaffordable offers. Perhaps I should point out that one of the reasons I was sent to work in a boiler room is that there, the authorities told me, I would be in the company of true workers who would soon correct my deviant opinions.'

33

Pastors and Masters

Despite reports in the Western press that churchgoers in Prague are often harassed by the police, I noticed no obvious surveillance, let alone harassment, on the two Sundays I went to Mass. There is no doubt that churchgoing is officially discouraged, but at the same time there are dozens of churches in the city open for prayer and regular services. Nor was it possible to generalize about the congregations, which contained all kinds of people, young and old, smartly dressed and scruffy.

On leaving the baroque church of St Ignatius after Mass, it occurred to me that the celebrated beer hall U Fleků was only a few hundred yards away. I thought it probable that the usual invasions of *Gruppen* would ensure that I was turned away at the door, but I had nothing better to do, so I made my way through the empty streets to the tavern entrance. Just off Charles Square I spotted a Trabant, the world's tattiest car, with the proud sign TURBO attached to its rear. Perhaps it was this mordant touch that had provoked a policeman into stopping the driver, whose papers were being scrutinized as I passed by.

U Fleků was crowded, of course, but there was room to sit in the courtyard, a pretty spot shaded by trees and overlooked by half-timbered galleries. It was still early in the drinking day for German tourists, but not, it seemed, for Czech soldiers, some of whom were almost too drunk to stand unaided and were responding with puzzlement to the joshing and taunting of the Germans. The one sober soldier in the party persuaded his colleagues it was time to go, but once on the street a fresh thirst must have developed, for two minutes later the platoon was back and calling for more. They didn't have to wait long, for briskly efficient waiters bring an unending supply of half-litre mugs of the dark beer for which U Fleků is famous. In other beer houses, especially during hectic lunch hours, I had noticed that waiters will weave through the halls with trays of freshly filled mugs of beer. Catch his eye and he will slide one down the table towards you and mark another notch on your tab. Of course such a system works like a dream because in most Prague taverns there is no choice of beer.

No sooner had I sat down than I recognized a teacher from Britain who was working for a year in Prague. He joined me for a beer and a lunch of greasy pork, bracing sauerkraut, and squidgy dumplings, a meal less disgusting than it sounds. Rory and I spoke nostalgically of our native country, of promiscuous Cabinet ministers, the decline of lacrosse, the edibility of dogs, and other delightful topics. I did ask him for advice on one matter that had been puzzling me. A bus or Metro ticket costs one crown, a reasonable sum, and is valid for ninety minutes. It was not clear to me whether this entitled the bearer to make a single journey, or to interrupt a journey as long as it was continued and completed within that ninety-minute period. If the former, then I failed to see the point of stipulating a time limit, since no single journey in Prague could possibly take more than an hour or so from the time it began, which is recorded when the ticket is punched. Rory put my mind at rest: it was indeed permitted to break one's journey, and he had been doing so for months.

After a second mug of beer, we went our separate ways. I lazily took the Metro to Muzeum, returned to my lodgings to collect a few items, and then walked back to Muzeum and through the barrier into the subway. No sooner had I done so than a tall skinny man blocked my path and jabbered at me. He was gesticulating with his hand and in his open palm I spotted a red enamel badge. It was a public holiday, yet again, so I assumed he was a hawker trying to sell me one of those lapel badges with a portrait of Lenin or some other acceptable motif. Having no use for such trinkets, I waved him aside and continued on my way towards the escalator. Once again the tiresome fellow interposed himself and waved his badge. He seemed to be saying the same word over and over again: 'Control! Control!' I soon gathered that he wished to see my ticket, which I was happy to present to him, since only thirty minutes had elapsed since I'd purchased it. Since he spoke none of the five languages I offered him, he had to call over a colleague, who addressed me in German. He made quite a long speech, the upshot of which was they they expected me to hand over 100 crowns, the standard fine for evading the fare. How fortunate that I had only an hour before been discussing this very point with Rory. Since I was on firm ground, I replied with some heat that my ticket was valid and I had no intention of paying a fine. Unfortunately, the two officials were equally adamant that I should. It was not permitted to break one's journey using the same ticket; I had done so and thus broken the regulations and must now pay up.

I abhor injustice, especially if it's going to cost me the price of two dinners. I pointed out, accurately, that nowhere on the ticket was it stated that it was forbidden to break a journey, and, moreover, why impose a ninety-minute limit if only one journey may be made? The logic did not impress them, and their manner was growing increasingly truculent. Any minute now they would lay their hands on me. I thought of attempting a bribe, but decided to see this thing through. The linguist asked whether I was from East or West Germany. Neither, I replied, and told them with pride that I was British. He asked to see my passport. I don't normally hand my passport to unauthorized individuals, but it seemed to me that the longer I could prolong the negotiations, the better my chances. He jabbed with his finger at the date on my visa, some ten weeks old.

'You said you had only been in Prague for a few weeks. But it's clear from your passport that you've been here for almost three months.'

The man was an idiot, and I had to point out to him that he had mistaken the visa stamp for the stamp of admission from the immigration authorities, which I found and showed to him. Once he grasped this, he went into a huddle with the other plainclothesmen, whose number had risen to three. Rather to my surprise, he returned a moment later and, handing my passport back to me, murmured, 'You may go.' I suppose, in retrospect, that he had paid me the double-edged compliment of thinking I was a German, and thus fair game. Then, on discovering I was instead an Englishman, he had realized I could not possibly be guilty of a wilful evasion of the law. Hats off to the perspicacious Prague Metro Police!

I continued on my journey, though not before I had purchased a spanking new ticket and given a cheery wave to my new pals. I waited for the train to Malá Strana, marvelling as I did each day at the interior decoration of the wall facing the platform. This is lined with bands of what can only be described as individual poached-egg pans, some of which are inverted to provide visual variety. Apart from this error of taste, the Metro is efficient, clean, and pleasant to use. In sharp contrast to commuters in Budapest, hardly anybody reads newspapers on the Metro. The majority of those travellers who did have an open newspaper before them were invariably scanning the sports pages. Clearly there is nothing worth reading in Czech papers. Magazines dealing with cars were far more popular.

I was on my way to see Radim Palouš, another Chartist and a convinced Catholic who, I was hoping, could tell me more about the position of the churches in Czechoslovakia. An imposing man in his early sixties, he lives in a charming converted mill close to the Vltava in Malá Strana. He settled me into his study with a glass of Finnish vodka and began to talk.

'Signing Charter was only the most recent of many hard decisions I've had to make. In a way everything has been conditioned by what I saw here in 1938 when I was fifteen years old. I saw the anti-Hitler demonstration in Wenceslas Square, and from that moment on, though we didn't quite realize it at the time, Czechs have had to live in hope of better times. Ever since those days and the end of the Republic, we have lived provisionally, as it were. The worst times were the 1950s, of course. In 1951 I was asked to sign a petition demanding the death penalty for a woman in the publisher's office where I was employed. Her alleged offences were political and I couldn't bring myself to sign. My colleagues said to me: "Look, we understand. We all know she's probably innocent of the charges, but the fact is they're going to hang her anyway. If you refuse to sign, you won't save her from the gallows and you'll be dismissed from your job." But I wouldn't sign and I lost my job. I had a number of jobs from then on, working in a steel mill, teaching Russian, and continuing my studies in chemistry and educational philosophy, which have always fascinated me.

'By the late 1960s I was a professor at Charles University. After 1968 I lost my tenure but was allowed to remain at the university on a provisional basis. Ten years later I was asked to sign Charter. I was then fifty-two, and my career was at its peak. I had a long talk with my wife and family, and decided to sign. For those with young families the decision was more difficult, since important matters such as university admission depend not only on school grades, not only on the pupil's political orthodoxy, but on the political position of his parents. Two weeks later I was dismissed from the university. Of course I am one of the luckier ones, since my articles continue to be published in the West in a variety of journals, and I also write for samizdat publications here. I am not idle. As for my wife, she didn't lose her job, but all prospects of promotion have been blocked, and her salary remains very low. But, as you can see, we live in a nice apartment in a beautiful part of the city, and things could be much worse. Of course I have had no passport since 1969, so I have no choice but to stay here.

'But you have come to talk about religious tolerance in Czechoslovakia, not my personal history. I'm not surprised that you saw no harassment at the churches you've attended. Catholics don't have too bad a time of it in the cities, where we're protected by anonymity. But in the villages it's a different matter. In the countryside it's quite common for worshippers to be photographed as they leave their churches. Some may be questioned by the secret police. All churches belong to the state, which also pays the salaries of the clergy. This isn't a Communist ploy. It's been so ever since Habsburg times. An anticlerical tradition is something else that Czechs have inherited from the Habsburgs. In those days church and state were closely linked, and one way to oppose the Austrians was through anticlerical action. Of course the regime today controls the Church in a more rigorous way. Possession of religious books can be regarded as subversive and arrests do take place. And of course it is the state that decides where priests shall take up their duties. If a particular priest becomes too popular he can be transferred or even lose his position.'

It grew dark as he talked and I was having difficulty in scribbling my notes. I asked Palouš to be so kind as to turn on the light. He didn't understand me.

'*Mehr licht,*' I said. More light.

He rose. '*Das wollen wir auch.*' (We'd like that too.)

Some days later I took up the theme again with a priest who had in fact been dismissed. His name is Miloš Rejchrt. We met in the entrance hall of the building where he tends the boilers. I hadn't been told what he looked like, and didn't at first grasp that the blue-overalled man with animated features and thinning sandy hair was the former pastor. Instead I suspected he was the caretaker, and I was doing my best to look inconspicuous for fear that he would turf me off the premises before I'd made contact with Rejchrt. Eventually we put two and two together and went off to a coffeehouse.

Rejchrt had lost his pastoral position in 1972 when he was simply informed that he was no longer authorized to practise. When he asked for an explanation he was told vaguely that he hadn't fulfilled his conditions of employment. His parishioners, dissatisfied with so bland an explanation, demanded more information. It then transpired that it had been brought to the attention of the authorities that Rejchrt had been holding seminars on the work of the Russian philosopher Berdyaev, who died in 1948. Moreover, in the course of one of these seminars the achievements of Lenin had, it was alleged, been calumniated. No charges were brought against the youthful pastor, but he was instructed, like so many others, to seek enlightenment in the company of the proletariat. In short, he went to work as a stoker.

'And were you enlightened by your colleagues in the boiler room?'

'Most definitely. They are men of strong opinions.'

'Ardent Marxist-Leninists?' I ventured, suspecting I was feeding him a cue.

He grinned. 'You must be joking. Reaganites to a man. But' – and he raised a cautionary finger – 'some of them are now expressing some doubts about Reagan, on the grounds that he's getting soft on Moscow.'

Rejchrt felt it was going too far to say that the regime actively persecuted the Church. Clearly it was able to limit the activities of the Catholics in particular, but while it was able to weaken the tradition of churchgoing in Czechoslovakia, it was almost inconceivable that it could be eliminated entirely. The Protestant churches are somewhat less constrained, as they, unlike the Catholics, are in the position of being able to instruct young people in the tenets of Christianity without simultaneously teaching Marxist-Leninism. However, the state has other ways of making life difficult for Protestants, as he had discovered: pastors can simply be denied the right to preach and practise.

'Implicitly, you must remember, what isn't authorized is forbidden. Thus it's very easy for Catholics to find themselves breaking laws which land them in jail. It's wrong to think of priests as inherently rebellious. The vast majority just want to get on with their religious vocation. But the constraints are tremendous. Whenever I wanted to invite a neighbouring pastor to preach to my congregation, I had to seek special permission. All affairs concerning the churches are controlled by a Party secretary for religious affairs. In every region there is a branch of the secret police that deals exclusively with church affairs. They even pay us the compliment of coming to hear our sermons. Sometimes priests are asked for information about their colleagues. "Be frank, be open with me," is the line the police take, but this soft line can still turn into a nightmare. It's so easy for the authorities to step up the pressure. For instance, a priest may be invited to the West for a conference for the first time in ten years. It's a delicate moment, because he won't be able to travel without a police permit, and if there's no cooperation with the police, that permit may not be forthcoming. Who needs persecution when the regime has this kind of leverage over ordinary parish priests?

'In Czechoslovakia, I regret to say, most priests and pastors spend less time dealing with the Holy Trinity than with the police.'

34

Suspicious Minds

Despite my fondness for the Demínka, where I could enjoy a decent helping of pork and a half litre of beer for under 20 crowns, I did on occasion hanker for a change of diet. The Baltic Grill, the only fish restaurant in Prague, is tucked into an arcade off Wenceslas Square, and since it was close to the opera, I went there for a pre-opera meal one evening. It was a rather dingy place, but uncrowded, free of tourists, and reasonably priced. I ordered carp, which seemed a sensible thing to do in central Europe, and waited. And waited. Since I didn't want to miss the start of the opera, I expressed some impatience to the unperturbed waiters. Not so the other customers, who clearly expected to have to wait almost an hour for a simple plate of food in a half-empty restaurant. With very little time to spare before the opera began, the dish was finally brought to me after forty-five minutes. For my patience I was rewarded with Moravian carp, which revealed itself to be a portion of fish with a rather nasty cheese omelette on top of it. On another occasion I visited the Baltic Grill after the opera, and found myself the only diner, though a few teenagers were sipping Cokes at a corner table. This time a waiter, on taking my order, warned me that it would take forty minutes to grill the fish I'd ordered. When I asked why, no intelligible explanation was offered. At the Klášterni vinárna on Národní, I was kept waiting equally long for a small portion of pork, incorrectly garnished. When I pointed out the error, the dish was taken away. Two minutes later it returned correctly garnished but stone cold.

As the weeks went by, I longed to taste again the hearty, well-cooked, inexpensive meals I'd enjoyed daily in Budapest, and decided to try the establishment of that name in Prague, the only Hungarian restaurant in town. Prices were quite high, but I was past caring: the prospect of paprika and cream sauces and *galuska* and a glass of Szürkebarat was worth any price. Unfortunately, the cooking bore no resemblance to anything I'd eaten in Hungary. I was brought a very fatty pork chop garnished with decidedly Czech dumplings. Nor were any Hungarian wines available, although they can be found in every grocery shop.

At lunchtime my hunger could be satisfied more easily. There were cheap, cheerful, noisy restaurants patronized by office workers and students, such as U Mestske Knihovny on Valentinská, the huge yellow-walled U Medvidků near Národní, and a nameless little place on Betlémské náměsti, where substantial portions of schnitzel and potatoes were always available. Here the service was extremely rapid in the interests of turnover, and the custom of sharing tables raised the possibility, which rarely materialized, of having an interesting conversation or two. Once I managed to talk to an elderly office worker, who told me he had twice seen Gorbachev on his recent visit to Prague, but when I sought his views on the Soviet leader, he changed the subject to the war years and how the city centre had been spared serious bomb damage. As one of the very few tourists to make regular appearances in the Betlémské náměsti restaurant, I soon became known to the waiters, who endeared themselves to me by being the only waiters in Prague invariably to wish me, as I rose to leave, an enjoyable afternoon in the city.

Food may be cheap and plentiful in Czechoslovakia, but there is little of the splendid variety of foods readily available in Hungary. The excuse given is one of national preference, that the Czechs are as stolid in their culinary habits as in everything else, blissfully content with a steady diet of pork and dumplings and beer. There is some truth to this, and the scarcity of decent vegetables in Prague can be attributed to the Czechs' distaste for greenery as much as to any shortcomings of the agricultural wing of the economy. Nevertheless the main market in Prague, now located in a former abbatoir, is both feeble and poorly maintained. Much of the interior was run as a local supermarket and bore no resemblance at all to a true market. Tired bunches of radishes and grubby piles of potatoes on sale at some stalls looked scarcely edible. In the Old Town there's a small market along Havelská, but this is an even more miserable affair, with just a few stalls selling flowers and herbs in plastic yogurt tubs, and a few bunches of fresh herbs and carrots.

There are, however, some special groceries that stock imported goods. This is not simply to satisfy any Czech yearnings for French wine and cheese, but another government scheme to persuade the thrifty citizens to part with some of the crowns they keep stashed away in the savings bank. On Jindřišská, at the shop called Paris-Praha, you can buy a basic rosé wine from Provence for 72 crowns and a box of Coulommiers cheese for half as much. Gourmets will be puzzled to note that other imported French delicacies on offer include dried mushrooms, vanilla cream, vinegar, and ketchup. Despite this bizarre and limited range of goods, the queues at Paris-Praha were always long. My own favoured grocery was on Žitná, where the queues were shorter, and I supplemented my rations of pork with Czech imitations of Emmental and Edam cheese that were bland and flabby, but cheap and edible, which is more than can be said of their so-called Balkan cheese, a violently salty version of Feta.

I had to learn to kick the pastry habit I had acquired in Budapest, for there were few such confections in Prague coffee-houses to tempt me. Friends spoke highly of the cakes at the Pařiž Hotel, but I never managed to get a seat, let alone coffee and pastry, when I wandered into its café. I did venture into a *Cukrarna* – Czech for *Konditorei* – near náměsti Míru, and it was here that I saw the oddest pastry I have ever laid eyes on. It consisted of chocolate sponge with, above, an equally tall slab of yellowish jelly the colour of motor oil glinting in the sun, and within the whole were embedded slices of banana.

The stodginess of the diet has its effect on the collective beauty of the nation. Although there were dozens of pretty girls and slender youths gliding around the city, by early middle age those lithe figures seem to thicken out. Lean and dark good looks in men were gradually subsumed within an increasingly four-square body, over which receding hair is slicked back into a kind of widow's peak; despite the gradual advance of the forehead, like the toe of a glacier, into the hairline, many Czechs sport a fine head of greying hair. The young women, often blonde in their youth, develop with the passing years an alarming sallowness of complexion, as well as pendants of flab around the neck. Portraits in my room of my landlady as a young wench show her to have been a remarkably pretty woman, the flower of Slav womanhood, but despite a sweet smile that matched her generous disposition, her good looks had long deserted her. This is the price you must pay for habitually consuming three slices of cake with whipped cream for breakfast each morning. Despite a look of furrowed concern whenever she was required to think or make a decision, my landlady had lively features with all the plasticity of a fine actress. Deeply worried, she might stop me in the corridor to ask whether I liked that morning's flavour of yogurt, and the swift transition from mortal anxiety to radiant relief that took place when I reassured her that everything was blissikins was miraculous to see.

In this she was atypical, and most Czechs I encountered casually had impassive features I found bewildering, simply because I couldn't read them. The impassivity extended to more than physical appearance, and an experienced observer of central Europe told me he found it significant that in 1956 thousands of Hungarians had defended their revolution and fought the invading Russians with all the vigour and ingenuity at their command, while in 1968 the Czechs, though aghast at the ruthlessness with which 'socialism with a human face' was repressed, did not take up arms against the Russian tanks. No doubt this is as much a contrast between political realism and hopeless romanticism as a sign of impassive acquiescence, but it did seem that there was no urgent desire for change in Czechoslovakia. However much people grumbled about shortages and difficulties in finding housing, there was broad appreciation of the reasonable standard of living that had been attained, especially in rural areas. Many agricultural cooperatives function efficiently, even innovatively, and there are few farmers now who yearn to have their land back. Nor does there seem to be any great yearning on the part of former entrepreneurs to start up their own businesses again, since that would entail taking on responsibilities of which they are now free. For all the restrictions imposed by the state and the bureaucracy, goods still circulate with ease. In the Laterna arcades off Wenceslas Square are a dozen glass panels, behind which are pinned index cards advertising goods for sale, goods as diverse as cars, prams, model railways, bridal dresses (800 crowns), stereo systems, puppies, a 1977 Lada (33,000 crowns), a 1975 Volga (12,000 crowns), television sets.

The social security system does deliver the goods; the system was established during the days of the Republic and the model has proved sound. I heard complaints about medical services, about a shortage of nurses and a lack of medical supplies. Bureaucratic tangles certainly induce some patients in need of prompt convenient treatment to slip a doctor 100 crowns in order to get it. Life can be hard for pensioners, since their pensions are not index-linked but are calculated on the basis of the wages they last earned years or decades before. Free transportation for pensioners only

297

becomes available at the age of seventy, and rents are not reduced for the elderly. But in general – as long as you don't feel compelled to think original thoughts and desire to express them, and as long as you have no wanderlust – life is not bad.

Critics of the regime point out that Czechoslovakia's prosperity has been attained at a terrible cost to the environment. Natural resources, especially timber, have been plundered at a reckless rate, and strip mines and chemical industries have been expanded with scarcely a thought for the ecological consequences. Northern Bohemia is now so badly polluted by sulphur and other emissions from local factories that not only have entire forests and rivers been destroyed, but an alarmingly high incidence of infant mortality, deformity, and illness have been recorded among the population; indeed, doctors and other necessary professional people can only be induced to move to the region if offered exceptionally high salaries. Since many Prague residents have, or had, weekend cottages in the region – and in other parts of Bohemia that are almost as badly polluted – the people as a whole are well aware of the problem. Even if they are not politically alert, they know that when they hike through the woods to pick mushrooms – a favourite weekend occupation – they are finding fewer and fewer.

A few years ago Charter 77 made public a secret report from the Academy of Sciences concerning environmental damage. Since the cat was now out of the bag, the regime has found it easier at least to acknowledge the problem by printing occasional newspaper articles. Moreover, since the problem affects both the Germanies, there has been greater international cooperation in order to reduce sulphur emissions. The government remains enthusiastic about nuclear power, however, but in this respect hardly differs from many West European governments. Nor are Czechs unaware of the fierce controversy over the Danube dam. This is not due to any admissions on the part of the regime, but once again to Charter 77, which in September 1985 published the Danube Circle reports on the proposal, with a detailed analysis of the deleterious effects the construction of the dam would have on Slovak forests, the quality of drinking water, and the loss of farming land.

The publication of these reports aroused considerable anger against Austria. One Chartist said to me: 'We're extremely bitter about the cynicism of the Austrians. It's quite clear they're determined to go ahead with the project at all costs, even though we in this country will suffer the greatest environmental damage, while the Austrians will enjoy the greatest economic benefits. It just shows they don't give a damn about Czechoslovakia, for all their protestations of friendship. You can't drink toasts to friendship and cooperation one minute, and then wreck part of the environment of your neighbour the next.'

If the regime is gradually being forced into a greater public acknowledgment of concern for the environment, there are few other signs of willingness to tolerate a wider openness in the discussion of government policies. The regime's grip on education, where free and inquiring minds are, or should be, encouraged to develop, remains tightly clenched. At the primary school level, discipline is rigidly enforced. The patterns of learning would have found favour with Mr Gradgrind, and the emphasis is on memorization and regurgitation of texts. In secondary schools, as pupils reach the age when they become preoccupied with university entrance, the pressures to conform grow more intense. Students are well aware that political profiles of themselves and their parents will be taken into consideration by university admissions officers. Children are not so much indoctrinated as made aware of the need to dissemble, while within the classroom the extent to which freedom of discussion is tolerated very much depends on the attitudes of teachers and their degree of servility to the government.

'The danger,' says Petr Fidelius, 'is not that our children will succumb to the propaganda that is pushed at them every day, nor do most of us fear that they will adopt a false view of the world. No, the danger is that they will accept the need to conform. Many parents are well aware of the ridiculous distortions that our children are being fed with in class, but we all have to deal with it pragmatically. It's no use presenting children with dilemmas and choices before they are old enough to understand the consequences. If we encourage our children to take an independent line, that could damage their chances of receiving higher education. Not that higher education amounts to much these days, except as a stepping stone to a career.'

There is widespread agreement that most university departments in the Humanities are moribund. Heads of departments have to be Party members, and lecturers and other staff members who are reluctant to join the Party may be denied promotion. A few prominent non-Communists are employed in some faculties, largely as window-dressing, but even they must smile sweetly upon the regime, whatever their private opinions. Faculties such as philosophy and law, once hothouses of intellectual vitality, are, in that respect, dead; some of the science departments remain of high quality, if only because the regime has a continuing need for well-trained technicians.

'Very little is published that's of any interest in the field of philosophy,' Fidelius told me. 'Historical accounts of some value are published, but no original work. And the same is true in linguistic research, my own field. One of the problems is not only the iron hand of the Party, but the lack of information about developments in our disciplines in other parts of the world. Apart from Soviet textbooks, it's hard to find foreign publications in our university libraries – not only for ideological reasons, but because the libraries lack the hard currency which is needed to buy them.'

The students themselves, some lecturers told me, seem fairly dismissive of the need for political correctness, though their willingness to conform increases as they near the end of their five years of study and are faced with the need to find suitable employment. There are informers within most student bodies, so indiscretions tend to diminish as final exams draw nearer.

'Most students simply cultivate detachment,' says Radim Palouš. 'They steer clear of politics, since they know from their parents how much suffering earlier generations have endured as a result of political involvements. Of course they all know that the ideology they must endorse is a sham, and even the opportunists among them who will go on to enjoy splendid careers within the Party know it too. Most students go along with the requirements of the regime because they have little choice, but I always sense that they do so wearily. Few have the courage to adopt an independent line, because they know that to do so is to risk forfeiting not only their careers, but all the benefits that come from those careers – the car, the country cottage, and even the prospect of a good education for their own children in years to come.'

35

Untune That String

Mikhail Gorbachev had been and gone. Those who had hoped he would make a dramatic gesture – such as meeting Alexander Dubček or lecturing his hosts on the virtues of *glasnost* – were disappointed. Indeed, he said little in public that could have caused the regime much disquiet. So clearly did he seem to endorse the Husák regime that many Czechs, who may have felt a glimmer of hope on learning that Gorbachev was coming to Czechoslovakia, felt almost betrayed, though it was surely absurd to expect him to utter serious criticisms of a regime that has been unswervingly loyal to the Soviet Union from the day it took power in 1968. In Radim Palouš's view, 'The enthusiasm for Gorbachev springs from weariness and a need for hope. But nothing has changed, and people seem even more disillusioned now Gorbachev has gone. Surely we must keep in mind that Russia has no democratic tradition. Pluralism as a concept means nothing to the Russians, so it's foolish to expect much from them. It hasn't escaped our notice that the Russian word *perestroika*, of which we hear so much these days, is very close to the Czech word for "disguise".'

An architect told me: 'Before Gorbachev came to Prague, people were full of hope. They even started reading *Pravda*, which they never did before, hoping for more news or information about what was happening in the Soviet Union. And there's no doubt that the regime was very frightened before Gorbachev's arrival. It was most amusing to hear our leadership parrot Gorbachev by making open attacks on the Brezhnev era, when everybody knows that without Brezhnev's support in 1968 they wouldn't be in power today. Their discomfort was delightful. Knowing Gorbachev's views on the matter, many of the leaders may have been worried by their own unconcealed corruption. But although Mr Štrougal may have to get rid of a few of his villas, nothing of any importance is likely to change. Gorbachev's main interest is not to bring greater democracy to Czechoslovakia, but to ensure that our deliveries to the USSR are made on time.'

Nevertheless many were convinced that the regime would eventually bow to pressures for reform. 'Pressure from Gorbachev is bound to bring changes,' according to Rudolf Slánský, 'though they will happen slowly. What's new is that people are now talking about politics again, even at their place of work. Party and trade union meetings are still formalities but questions are being raised about reform at such meetings, which wouldn't have happened a few years ago, and the regime is very sensitive to these signals. The first changes will be economic, and that probably means some reforms on the Hungarian model, though Czechs certainly don't want to copy the Hungarians in everything. It's only been a year since Vasil Bilak declared that talk of reform was counterrevolutionary, but reform there will be. Quite apart from pressure from the Russians, the Czech leadership is old, and some change at the top is inevitable. Whether the next generation of Party leaders will be technocrats or apparatchiks it's too early to say. And once economic reforms are under way, cultural reform may follow. One encouraging sign is that the pressure on Chartists seems to be diminishing.'

Josef agreed with this. 'The leadership seems unsure of itself now, and police control is weakening. Even during the Jazz Section trial the police kept a low profile. I remember watching as they tried to lead away some protesters with banners, but we talked them out of it. A few years ago that couldn't have happened, you couldn't have argued with the police and won. The trouble is that any changes in the regime's attitudes, any softening towards us, could be reversed at any time without warning. These changes tend not to last.'

'In the 1950s,' says Ivan Klíma, 'the police were ideological, mostly uneducated and quite sadistic. Now it's different. They're bureaucrats, functionaries. Beatings are rare, though there are always a few people who deliberately provoke the police and are punished for it. Dissidents' homes are still searched and their papers confiscated, but the last time this happened to me most of my books and papers were later returned to me. My hunch is that if Gorbachev survives, the Czech government will have to bring in serious reforms within the next three years.'

An economist who was no dissident accepted the need for

reform but could see difficulties ahead. 'Managers know what needs to be done, but the bureaucratic procedures make actual changes slow and cumbersome. All ideas and proposals have to go to the Central Committee for decisions, and that can take ages. The Committee is very wary of any reforms that smack of a return to the ideas of 1968. Political constraints obscure any coherent conception of how to run the economy: the regime is afraid to move too fast, as happened in the 1960s. Ever since 1968, when the screws were tightened and the old models of economic planning revived, there has been no effective way to exert pressure from below. At Party meetings you can complain that your bus stop has no shelter, but more weighty matters are hardly ever raised. The only condition under which pressure will induce major reforms is when the health of the economy is clearly threatened.

'I went down to the pub a few times after Gorbachev's visit, and my drinking companions down there spoke about their desire for more travel, a freer press, and so forth. But these people aren't prepared to work harder and be more efficient – I'm talking about managers as much as workers – and that's the other side of the coin. Of course people were disappointed by Gorbachev's visit, but their expectations were naive. Our economy is integrated into the Russian economy. The Husák regime will go along with anything the Russians say as long as it can remain in power, so why should Gorbachev give them a hard time while he's here as their guest?

'I don't suppose much will happen before 1990, when the next major Party congress will be held. Perhaps Husák will choose the occasion to retire. The next generation of leaders will be more pragmatic, they'll be technocrats rather than ideologues. Still, I don't expect the changes to be very profound, if only because there's no obvious leader on the horizon who can spearhead such changes. The upper ranks of the Party are filled with time servers and opportunists, but, as Gorbachev has shown, all it takes to turn a country around is one man.'

As it happened, a few months later Husák stepped down. The alacrity with which the Soviet government greeted the change, and its remarkable failure to pay the usual cloying tribute to the freshly retired leader, suggests that Husák did not reach his decision unaided. He retained the largely ceremonial office of president, while his more important position of First Secretary was given to Miloš Jakeš. Jakeš was not the obvious choice, but while the more vocal and visible Štrougal and Bilak were jockeying for position the grey bureaucrat who happened to be in charge of the nation's economy played his cards correctly and came up trumps. There are few indications that Jakeš will initiate major reforms. He devoted the first half of the 1970s to arranging for the removal of almost half a million Party members who were tainted through association with the Dubček regime. Husák ordered the purges and it was Jakeš who implemented them. More recently, as the Party boss in charge of economic policy, he has opposed the mildly reformist Štrougal line, though some observers attribute this to personal distaste for his rival rather than to ideological differences. Moreover, the 65-year-old Jakeš, though nine years Husák's junior, represents less a new generation of leadership than the tail end of the old guard. In his first speech as Czechoslovakia's new leader, Jakeš stressed 'the principle that more democracy means more socialism' (whatever that means) and assured the nation that the reins would be grasped as tightly as before: 'Everything that is alien to socialism must be criticized.'

The arrival of Mr Jakeš on the scene will clearly make no difference in the short term. Whether, like Kádár, he will eventually perform a volte-face and come to abandon his hard-line instincts, no one can say, but there is no reason to be hopeful. Nevertheless, Fidelius was one of a number of observers who agreed that the next generation of leaders is likely to be more pragmatic and technocratic that Husák ever was. 'But that doesn't mean they'll be more amenable to change. Reforms could certainly take place in the next few years, but within a monolithic regime such as ours there can be very swift reverses and any reforms could prove short-lived. You must remember that our leaders have been talking about reform for fifteen years, and nothing has happened. The present regime has no political will for change. When you're old and your pension's around the corner, why rock the boat?'

There are many whose predictions are more gloomy and embittered. The former law lecturer who is now a lowly clerk in the parks department told me: 'How can you have reforms under the old leadership? The regime talks of reform, but nobody believes it. Only a dramatic event – a scandal or ecological disaster – can bring about change. I'm not one of those who looks ahead eagerly to when the old leadership, Husák's generation, is replaced by a younger team. In my view, the next generation is even worse. The heirs apparent achieved their rise to power and prominence after 1968. These are people with no scruples at all. They're cynics, only interested in power and privilege. Why should they allow us any more freedoms than the present Politburo? And as for the ordinary people, well, they're cautious, and it's not hard to see why. Change means uncertainty, it means risk. Most of us are old enough to remember very clearly what happened last time there was pressure for radical reform. After the experiences of 1968, many people who favoured reform have grown more cautious. Why, they argue, should I be the first to put my head over the parapet by demanding reforms? There are a few people, reform communists, who talk of a return to the 1960s, to socialism with a human face, but they're all outside the power structure. Nobody on the inside would dare to reintroduce such ideas.'

Václav Havel shared many of these reservations. 'Tourists, casual visitors to our country, can't appreciate the tragedy of this society. People have come to accept the restrictions in exchange for a degree of prosperity. I find this acquiescence dangerous rather than harmonious. There is a glimmer of hope, I suppose. Because of the prevailing orthodoxy, no politician dares to express his real opinions publicly. If there is a Gorbachev-style reformer within the power structure, it would be almost impossible to know about it. It's possible that changing conditions may create reformers within the Party. That's what happened in 1968. Dubček was no reformer in 1967.'

'Reform? Forget it,' says Miloš Rejchrt. 'We're talking about a regime that still locks people up for dissent, denigration of the regime, subversion, and all the other catch-all offences. Not long ago, just after Gorbachev's visit, Husák made a speech to a trade union conference, and rebuked the delegates quite sternly for failing to be sufficiently critical of Party policies. Ah, you may think, reform might be on the way if criticism is being encouraged from the top. But the delegates remained silent. And for good reason. Everybody in Czechoslovakia knows about Husák's background, and to think of him as a new convert to the cause of reform is absurd. To reproach people for lacking the courage to criticize the regime is rich coming from a man who has betrayed his colleagues and locked up his opponents.'

The most complex prognostications came from a dissident I've called Ivan, whose views have been heavily influenced by the New Right in Western Europe. It was with some dismay that I learnt that Roger Scruton's *Salisbury Review* is regularly translated in digest form and published in samizdat in Czechoslovakia. Ivan was a fervent admirer. In the late 1960s he had been working outside Czechoslovakia but made a conscious decision to return.

'I had good prospects in the West, but life back here seemed vastly more interesting. By the time I returned many thousands of people had been purged, indeed anyone associated with 1968. It wasn't just academics and writers who were sweeping the streets and cleaning windows. It was ministers and ambassadors too. I had a clean record, since I'd been out of the country. I was doing research at the university after my return. But I refused to join the students' union, which was regarded as highly suspicious. I was told: "It's a small thing, a token, so why not do it?" To which I replied: "If it's so small, then why are you making all this fuss about it?" Anyhow, my research contract wasn't renewed, which comes to the same thing as being fired. The state had spent thousands on training me as a scientist, and then, because I wouldn't join the union, they threw it all away.

'I found another job, good pay, not much to do. I was sent along one day to a trade union meeting where we had to discuss, or should I say pass, a resolution condemning Charter 77. I abstained, on the grounds that I hadn't been mandated either way. The vote was eighty-four to my one. Since my abstention was technically correct, they couldn't throw me out of my job, but my travel permit was taken from me, and in 1981, when there was a fresh round of repressive activity, I was dismissed for "endangering the security of the state". Since 1982 I've been a stoker and a sweeper in this delightful works yard.

'Do you like the view? All my windows, you'll be pleased to learn, face west. That reminds me of a joke. Do you know how the Communists discovered the world was round? It's because they shit to the West and it comes right back at them from the East. I'm very comfortable here. I have a bed for when I'm on the night shift. It's quiet here, I can work, nobody bothers me.

'But on the outside life is less simple. Keeping conscience and reason intact in this society involves continuous pain. If you accept the lie we live under, you'll feel constantly sick. Of course everybody has to make some kind of accommodation, and after all these years we refuse to get excited about the things that humiliate us. The result is that there's a smouldering hatred in the air, and one day it could explode because of the endless humiliations which we accept in exchange for a peaceful life. There's a constant tension between your beliefs and the way of life that's forced upon you. Naturally the system has its collaborators, but there's no one left who is prepared actually to *defend* the system. We Czechs are reasonably prosperous, I admit, but even so we must constantly rub up against the system in the form of bureaucracy, queues, shortages, bribes, delays, all of which keep us needled into an awareness of the nature of the system.

'All institutions are discredited now. No economic plans are fulfilled, and the regime is simply unable to rule. Their power and authority are not derived from society. The regime despoils the countryside, and instead of repairing our houses they chop down our forests to obtain lumber to sell for hard currency. Only power counts in this country, and because of this no judgments on performance are permitted. Incompetence, corruption, evil – none of these has any meaning or value, as long as power is served. All standards are subverted. That's why I believe that Western values are the only hope. If the Eastern Bloc reforms, it's solely for the sake of efficiency, to sustain its Manichaean ideology and its fight against what it perceives as reaction. It needs that fight, because without it its ideology would be defunct.

'The regime is so unbending because there are no rival sources of power in Czechoslovakia. In Poland the regimes before 1982 always had to worry about the army and the police. Not here. Our government here can do as it pleases because it knows the people will never rebel. Thus the regime, which has never needed to woo the population for support, acknowledges no limit to its power. Any weakening, any concessions, would be taken as a sign, not of responsiveness to the wishes of the people – which have never troubled it in the past – but as a sign that the regime is crumbling. The leadership can't give any ground without undermining its own existence.

'That's why in my view it's only a matter of time before the system collapses. The Russians have changed the tune and the regime doesn't know how to play it. There are already signs of internal dissension. We have Strougal attacking Bilak in public, and for the first time since 1968 members of the Politburo are giving diverging views in public – that's an extraordinary change. When the regime collapses – I give it six months [been and gone] – then the 5 per cent of the population who are politically concerned may act, and when that happens there will be no one to defend it. That's why the passivity of the people doesn't really matter. People acquiesce for as long as the government has the power to oppress them, but when the crunch comes, they will not lift a finger to save the regime.'

Ivan's apocalyptic view was not shared by others I spoke to. His forecast, however unlikely, seemed at least hopeful. The prevailing view of most dissidents was far more gloomy. They recognized that the system was now so entrenched that not only did the leadership lack the political will to initiate reform, but that too large a proportion of the population now had a vested interest in the system, however much they might despise it. They have learnt how to manipulate the system, invent shortages, bribe officials. From the chaos of daily life they can extract high profts. Reform, even a modest tidying up of the system and a crackdown on corruption, is sure to mean hard times ahead. The Czech regime can depend to some extent on its willingness to overlook and thus encourage the greed and corruption of the populace, which it has allowed to flourish in the absence of a well-ordered and responsive political and economic system. As Miloš Rejchrt suggested to me, the opportunism of the system is such that even the genuine idealism of socialism has become discredited and denigrated. Those ideals were still alive when people made sacrifices in 1968, and look where it got them. No wonder few are willing to gamble again on behalf of an as yet unscripted programme of reform.

There was one point on which all were agreed. It was idle to expect serious reform from a leadership that had devoted almost twenty years to suppressing not only reform itself but any talk of reform. This widespread scepticism is most succinctly expressed in the form of a very typical Czech joke: 'New winds don't blow from old arseholes.'

36

Can the Centre Hold?

When this book was conceived I imagined that the three cities I would be visiting would all, as former Habsburg strongholds, reflect different aspects of the same culture, that all three would, in very different ways, be labouring or prospering under the weight of a magnificent heritage. Of course, it didn't work out that way. The three countries are part of no commonwealth of nations. The cords that once tied them to the Habsburgs have long been broken, often brutally. In Vienna Habsburg influence remains powerful, not in any political sense, but culturally, architecturally, and in some respects in terms of the mentality of the inhabitants, their attitudes towards officialdom, their self-importance. On the other hand, the Viennese do not seem to resent their diminished role; few of them hanker for the past.

Budapest and Prague, however, have been defined in their modern phase by their resistance to the Habsburgs. Budapest certainly attained its prosperity under the Monarchy, but Prague was a great medieval city while the Habsburgs were still minor princelings. The delectable baroque and rococo architecture of the city is a legacy from Habsburg days, but that plain fact seems little more than an accident of history. Prague owes its beauty not only to the nobles who built their palaces in Malá Strana but to the good fortune of the city in having escaped the bombardments that destroyed large parts of so many other European cities which during the last century displayed an architectural heritage every bit as glorious as that of Prague.

The more I journeyed, the more the Habsburgs receded into the background. In Vienna the double eagle was everywhere. The Habsburg rulers had strewn their bodies as well as their architectural commissions and warrants of trade around the city. In Budapest Maria Theresa's castle and the Austrian-built citadel on a neighbouring hill loom over the Danube and the bustling streets of Pest, but their presence no longer intimidates. The Budapesters seem as oblivious of these reminders of past Austrian rule as they are contemptuous of present-day Russian influence. In Prague the manipulative totalitarian state has done its best to remove from the national consciousness any notion of the nation's past as anything other than a catalyst for revolutionary change. If Masaryk can be written out of the books as easily as a weary actress can be written out of a Hollywood soap opera, there is no reason to dwell on the intricacies of Bohemia's Habsburg past. Indeed, in Prague the Habsburg heritage seemed the least interesting aspect of the city.

Vienna proved in many respects as rich and sustaining as its pastries and cuisine. A cultural life of great splendour, a wealth of museums, an excess of palaces, and a growing prosperity that was allowing more and more Viennese to measure up once again to the opulence of their city – all this proved a great pleasure for this visitor. I was cushioned by the city, though wary of the Viennese, whose devotion to *petit bourgeois* values could be at times quite suffocating. The Budapesters proved more unbuttoned, managing to find time in their hectic lives for immense enjoyment. The sense of ferment in the air was invigorating, even though the debates and discussions take place within clearly circumscribed limits. It was quite apparent that with every year that passes, those boundaries gradually recede. The momentum of Hungarian society drifts away from Soviet models and towards a Western-style market economy, all the while protesting that it is doing nothing of the kind. Where the Viennese are stolid, predictable, cautious, the Budapesters are ingenious, alert, imaginative.

What the people of Prague are like I have no idea. While the Budapesters ignore their official constraints, and revel in their capacity for indiscretion, the citizens of Prague have to be more careful. Only those who have openly rejected the system are entirely free to speak. Inevitably my impressions became one-sided. By signing Charter and thus insisting that the government uphold its own laws (freedom of speech being guaranteed by the Czech constitution), the dissidents have laid down their challenge to the great sham of the system. For this act of intellectual honesty, they have all paid a great price, but they have gained the freedom they desire by the simple yet courageous act of grasping it. Václav Havel has used the phrase 'living in truth' to convey in its essence the challenge the dissidents are making. Until I went to

Prague the phrase seemed high-flown. But I soon realized that it had real content, that the system is so compounded of lies and deceptions that it does indeed require bravery of a high order for a Czech to state what is soon obvious to the observant visitor.

In his fine essay 'The Power of the Powerless', Havel writes of the all-encompassing nature of what he calls the 'post-totalitarian' system. In Prague there are few armed police in the streets, mutilated bodies are not found in the gutters at dawn, men and women no longer disappear without a trace. The system attains its total control simply by penetrating every aspect of daily life from cradle to grave. It exercises this control in the name of an ideology that no one believes in. Havel writes: 'That is why life in the system is so thoroughly permeated with hypocrisy and lies: government by bureaucracy is called popular government; the working class is enslaved in the name of the working class; the complete degradation of the individual is presented as his or her ultimate liberation; depriving people of information is called making it available . . . ; banning independent thought becomes the most scientific of world views; military occupation becomes fraternal assistance. Because the regime is captive to its own lies, it must falsify everything. It falsifies the past. It falsifies the present, and it falsifies the future.'

Individuals need not and mostly do not believe in these perversities, but they must act as though they do. 'They must *live within a lie*. They need not accept the lie. It is enough for them to have accepted their life with it and in it.' It is only when one has grasped at first hand the cynicism of such a system that Havel's phrase 'living in truth' takes on its full heroic force.

Because the system permeates everything, the Czechs no longer believe in the possibility of change except as a response to dire circumstances, such as an economic crisis or intense pressure from the Soviet Union (which is unlikely to be forthcoming). There will be no revolt against the system. With very few exceptions almost the entire population is implicated within it. The machinery of government and its handmaiden repression has become self-perpetuating. Even though the power of the state is absolute, no one, as Havel has pointed out in 'Politics and Conscience', 'actually possesses such power, since it is the power itself which possesses everyone; it is a monstrosity which is not guided by humans but which, on the contrary, drags all persons along with its "objective" self-momentum – objective in the sense of being cut off from all human standards, including human reason and hence entirely irrational – to a terrifying unknown future.'

For the Hungarians, utterly dependent on expanding foreign trade, change was unavoidable, and the system, while remaining firmly in control, could be loosened sufficiently to permit at least a semblance of freedom in a few carefully demarcated zones. For the Czechs there are no chinks of light opening up in the wall of absolutism that surrounds them. It is significant that the only names in this book that I have disguised are those of some Czech dissidents. My journey ended as a probing of an intractable situation. I left Prague filled with admiration for those who, whether noisily or quietly, have spoken out against the system, but also with a feeling of sadness that so many people have chosen to give up and accept the sop of material prosperity granted as the price of their acquiescence. I went to three cities, and found not only three urban personalities, but, unexpectedly, three ways of living in the uncertain centre of Europe.

CODA: THE DEAD

Coda

The gates were locked, so I climbed the wall. I was in the small town of Gänserndorf, about twenty miles east of Vienna and midway between the capital and the Czech border. It's a nondescript place set among flat and featureless farmland. I had walked out of town along the main road in the direction of Vienna, past a straggle of houses, garages, and uneventful fields. The fields were interrupted by a small pine grove, and in the midst of the grove, down a short broad drive, was a walled enclosure. Over the main gate I could still see the outline of a Star of David, though the metal star had clearly been removed some time ago. I rattled the gate, but it was firmly closed, and so I climbed the wall.

After ten minutes I found what I was looking for. Among some thickly growing shrubs was the unkempt grave of Lizzi Eisinger, marked by a stone slab that had settled into the earth and was now slightly askew. Born in Gänserndorf in March 1923, Lizzi had died a few days before her eleventh birthday. On her tombstone was inscribed '*Unersetzlich – Unvergesslich*' (Irreplaceable, Unforgettable). The grief-laden words had proved, as the decades rolled by, ever less true, and Lizzi Eisinger is now almost entirely forgotten. I have her photograph before me now, taken when she was a round-faced child, perhaps two years old. Dressed in a frilly lace tunic, her round eyes staring directly at the lens, she is seated on a shaggy rug that has been placed on top of a small stepladder so as to bring her face to the same height as that of the camera. Standing next to Lizzi is a pretty little girl, five or six years old. Clutching a doll, she is wearing a sailor suit and sensible shoes and white ankle socks and on her head a most extraordinary kind of turban secured with an enormous bow; a small earring glints beneath her left ear. Solemn and slightly shy, her mouth set firm, my mother poses before the camera patiently if not altogether

315

happily. She too is dead now, though she outlived her little sister, who died of tuberculosis, by thirty-five years.

In Budapest, in the large Kozma utca cemetery not far from Ferihegy airport, I found the spot I was looking for, but it was blanketed with snow. Scraping away at the mound with my hands, I uncovered a low slab that had almost sunk into the ground. I had to use sticks to chip away at the ice obscuring the inscription until I read the words: Siegfried Eisinger – Wien – 1890–1939. In 1938 my mother and grandmother had left Austria for good. My grandfather, whose health was poor, had not gone with them but had moved to Budapest, where he died a year later in October 1939. My grandmother, who lived into her eighties, never visited her husband's grave. My mother did so a few years before she died. I made the same visit twenty years later because no one else ever will.

In Prague the large Jewish cemetery, two miles west of the city centre, is still in use. As I walked through its alleys I watched a sandy-haired man in a yarmulke as he chanted the Kaddish over a fresh grave. Some tourists come here too, for Franz Kafka is buried near the entrance. On the northern side of the cemetery, some distance from the main entrance, is a black marble slab mounted on a pedestal over the grave of Filip Brod. Its height had preserved it better than the stone over Siegfried Eisinger, but I had to snip away at ivy and other creepers in order to read the inscription. Filip died in December 1935 at the age of fifty. The stone also memorializes his wife Meta and her mother Jette Rosengarten. The inscription gives their date of birth, but not their date of death. Instead I read the following two words: *Beide Deportiert* – wrongly spelt. Meta was deported to Lodz in Poland on transport E–152 on 3 November 1941, and nothing more is known of her. It seems likely that she shared the fate of many others who were deported to Lodz from Western Europe. From 4 May to 15 May 1942, ten thousand of these mostly German and Czech Jews were relieved of even the lightest baggage and dispatched to Chelmno and gassed. I have to assume that Meta Brod, if she'd survived until then, was among them. Her mother died closer to home, in the ghetto the Nazis established at Theresienstadt north of Prague. Meta's two sons were more fortunate: they left Prague in 1938. Meta had also left in February 1939 and joined her sons, but after only a couple of weeks in London she returned to Prague to extract her own mother. A few days later the Germans invaded Czechoslovakia. Although my father and uncle arranged exit

316

visas so the two women could leave for Tangier, once France fell all escape routes from Czechoslovakia were closed. The women lived on in Prague until their eventual deportation and death.

Compared to many other Jewish families from Central Europe, mine were lucky. My mother and grandmother and great-grand-mother, and my father and uncle and aunt, all escaped to England; my two grandfathers and my uncle died of natural causes, and only Meta and Jette perished as a direct consequence of the Holocaust. Even had the war never taken place, I could have made the same melancholy pilgrimage through the cemeteries. For me, the invitation to write a book about these three cities was also, unknown to my publishers, an invitation to visit the three cities from which my forebears stemmed. Their history was a perfect illustration of the fluidity and cosmopolitanism of central European Jewry.

Filip was born in Vienna, but after the First World War, in which he had fought in the Austrian army, he opted for citizen-ship of the new-born Czech Republic, for his parents had come from Boskovice, near Brno. Two of his sisters were living in Germany; Filip joined them and tried to establish himself as a photographer, without success. He married young, but his wife died a year later, childless. Next he married Meta, who came from Westphalia, and went to live in Fürth, Bavaria, where my father was born. When Hitler came to power, Filip had the good sense to leave Germany; taking advantage of his Czech citizenship, he brought his family to Prague in 1933. My father, then fourteen years old, spoke no Czech and had to take classes in the language. Meta never learnt to speak Czech. It wasn't really necessary. Czech was useful when shopping, but the Brods' social life was conducted in German. The two cultures existed side by side. Filip established himself as a wine merchant, representing various German producers in the Rheinpfalz. Two years later he died of a stroke. His elder son had a good job as a European agent for Scottish textile manufacturers, but he was the sole breadwinner and times were hard. My father, still at school, supplemented the family income by giving German lessons. In 1938 the two young men emigrated to England.

Siegfried Eisinger was born in the Austrian town of Hohenau, close to the Czech border, in 1890. In 1919 he married Jolanka Reich from Budapest and they moved to Gänserndorf, where their two daughters were born in 1920 and 1923. Siegfried was a cattle dealer, and prospered sufficiently to be able to afford a town flat in

Vienna's Leopoldstadt. Photographs show a burly man, double-chinned and with a small moustache, well dressed and self-confident. He was no peasant, and neither was Jolanka, who brought to her new home a trousseau of magnificent linen and silver, embroidered and engraved with her new initials. Jolanka grew up in the heart of Budapest, close to the main Jewish quarter. Her father, Ignácz Reich, had been born in Nyitro in what is now Czechoslovakia; he was a wine and spirit merchant. In 1894 he had married Teréz Grünwald, also from Nyitro. A photograph which must have been taken just before the First World War shows Ignácz, a stocky little man with close-cropped hair and a bushy moustache, standing on the steps of his large shop; the exterior is plastered with paintings of bottles of Cognac and rum. Jolanka stands beside him, her hand resting on his shoulder, and eighteen other people – babes in arms, dour women in kerchiefs, lads in overalls, shop assistants in wing collar and tie – pose for the camera in front of the shop. When Ignácz died I do not know. Teréz remarried in 1926. What happened to her husband, Mr Farkas, is also unknown, but Teréz survived the war long enough to be my babysitter. I remember her dimly, a severe old lady dressed in remorseless black, with white hair neatly parted. We communicated somehow, she in Hungarian, I in English.

The Jews of Budapest were luckier than most. By the late nineteenth century they comprised an even larger percentage of the population than Jews did of Vienna. By 1910 one quarter of the population was Jewish. The old Jewish quarter is in the 7th district, very close to the commercial centre of Pest. The main synagogue, on Dohány utca, is a vast neo-Byzantine structure with extensions and courtyards and a memorial garden adjoining it. It is hardly ever used as a place of worship, though there is still a large and active Jewish community in Budapest. Other vestiges of Jewish life in the quarter are less easy to find. Walking down Vasvári Pál utca I peered into a courtyard at random and spotted twin round-headed windows at the rear of the yard. As I suspected, the windows did indeed belong to a small synagogue, now unmarked. A darkened flat adjoined the synagogue at right angles, and old prayer books were piled against a window. The district is now dilapidated, as are most older streets of apartment buildings in Budapest, though in Klauzál tér some of the houses have been most elegantly facelifted, their whitewashed walls in startling contrast to the dark green trim of windows and doors and the gleaming black paint on stair rails and balustrades.

Along Dob utca stands the Orthodox synagogue. I stared through broken windows into the large space within. Although this large synagogue is also unused, its furnishings remain intact: immense bell-shaped chandeliers hang from the ceiling, massive neo-Byzantine columns flank the Ark, and row upon row of carved pews stretch the length of the interior. The Jewish community has raised $100,000 from the United States, matching local contributions, in order to restore this synagogue, but much more is needed.

I knew that my grandmother had lived as a child on Nemet utca, but the street was renamed long ago and I had no idea where it was. I visited the Jewish community centre on Sip utca to gain more information and also to locate my grandfather's grave. I was assisted by plump old ladies with dyed hair, who dragged from the shelves immense old ledgers and card indexes so worn that they were as furrowed as corrugated board. Exactly why Siegfried failed to travel with his family to London I do not know. The explanation usually given was that he was too ill to travel to England, but separation from his wife and daughter could hardly have been much of a boost to his health. However, in coming to Budapest he made a wise choice. Had his health not failed, he might well have survived the war, in the company of the majority of Budapest Jews. Nemet utca, I discovered, is now Bacsó Béla utca, and the building where my grandmother grew up is an ugly four-storeyed yellow-brown apartment block on the corner of Rákóczi tér. The crudely neoclassical building is very run down, and in the courtyard the sagging balconies are supported on rough timber frames that double as posts from which washing lines are strung. My grandmother was prudish in the extreme, and it gave me malicious pleasure to observe that the building now overlooks the main cruising ground of the whores of Budapest.

My grandmother despised her fellow Hungarians as antisemites and never returned to Budapest after the war. She undoubtedly had a point; there were many antisemitic Hungarians, but the record suggests they were rather less virulent in their hatred of the Jews than large sections of the Austrian, Polish, and Ukrainian populations. The regime of the Hungarian dictator, Admiral Horthy, had been responsible for much anti-Jewish legislation, but nonetheless the vast majority of Hungarian Jews were untouched until 1944. Hungarian Jews were among the most assimilated in Europe, and some were as fiercely nationalist as any Magyar hussar. Even after the Germans occupied Hungary in

319

1944, Horthy blocked the deportation of Jews from Budapest, though the Germans transported most rural communities in Hungary to extermination camps. Consequently the Jewish intelligentsia in Hungary survived the war more or less intact, and they remain influential. Whereas only a few thousand Jews still live in Austria, there are almost 100,000 Jews in Hungary. Countless Budapest families must have more than a trace of Jewish blood in their veins. Budapest is the home of the only rabbinical seminary left in Eastern Europe. Jews, now as then, are prominent in the middle-class professions. One doctor told me: 'Any Jews among the factory workers are likely to be sociologists doing field work.'

Few Jewish Budapesters complained to me about antisemitism. Some recalled incidents of name-calling and possible job discrimination, but none sought to maintain that overt antisemitism is a feature of modern Hungarian life. In one way this is remarkable, for many of the most unsavoury politicians in the 1950s were of Jewish origin. Rákosi himself, police chief Mihály Farkas, AVO Chief Gábor Péter, prime minister Ernő Gerő – all were Jews, and all had a lot to answer for by 1956. A large number of Hungarian Jews became Stalinists because it seemed the only feasible way to oppose Fascism in the 1930s, though this historical explanation for the high proportion of Jewish Communists in Hungary does not excuse the appalling reign of terror which they directed. When these despicable men were ousted in 1956, no outbreak of antisemitism followed. Rákosi and his henchmen were despised as evil men, not as Jews. Moreover, many of those who fought most bravely for the revolution in 1956 were themselves Jews. All this merely confirms the extent to which Hungarian Jews are assimilated. And while most East European regimes maintain a firm anti-Zionist and anti-Israeli line that easily lapses into antisemitic pronouncements, the Hungarian government has in recent years gone out of its way to admit that antisemitism does still exist in the country and that Jews have the right to assert their cultural and religious identity within the society as a whole.

In Prague I found the various houses where my father's family had lived in the 1930s: the block, now rebuilt, where Meta had lived until her deportation; the block on Soukenická, still standing, begrimed but handsome, from which her mother was sent to Theresienstadt; and the Art Deco house where the family lived before the war in Vršovické náměsti, an asymmetrical baroque square about a mile east of Charles Square. I also followed the path of the last journey my great-grandmother made, to Theresienstadt, known in Czech as Terezín. Built as a fortress town by Emperor Joseph II in the 1780s, the neat little town, its orderly streets still lined with barracks, is much visited by tourists. On the edge of town is the so-called Little Fortress, which has been converted into a museum – unlike the rest of the fortifications, which are still used by the Czech army. The Little Fortress was for decades a camp for political prisoners, and Gavrilo Princip, who murdered Franz Ferdinand, was imprisoned here. In June 1940 the Gestapo used the fortress as a police jail to accommodate about 3000 prisoners. Conditions were harsh and about 250 prisoners were executed; others were tortured.

The Little Fortress was, no doubt, a thoroughly unpleasant place, but it was fairly idyllic compared to what was going on just down the road within Terezín itself. Towards the end of 1941 the 3000 Czech residents of Terezín were evacuated and the entire town sealed off and converted into a ghetto. Terezín was not an extermination camp, but a transit camp; 140,000 Jews, half of them from Czechoslovakia and the remainder from all over Europe, were brought here. 87,000 inmates were later dispatched to Auschwitz, Treblinka, and the other death camps. Conditions at Terezín must have been appalling, for 34,000 people, almost a quarter of the intake, died here, either from hunger or from epidemics. Among the prisoners were many old people and thousands of children, who left some of the most poignant records of the Holocaust in the form of drawings now displayed at the Jewish Museum in Prague.

The crematorium at Terezín, built to dispose of the corpses from the ghetto, is still standing, but no serious effort is made at the Little Fortress to apprise visitors of the fact. The Czech regime, with its usual heavy-handedness, stresses at every turn how those who died at Terezín included many Communists who resisted Nazism. All honour to them, but the downplaying of the ghetto and crematorium is a disgrace. The only reference to the ghetto at the museum in the Little Fortress is a case containing two yellow stars and some of the special ghetto currency, and a drawing by Leo Haas of a crowded Jewish cell. The rest of the exhibits depict the history of Nazism, Communist resistance, and the liberation of Terezín by the Russians. The main task of the museum, states the guidebook, is 'on the basis of scientifically verified facts and in dialectic continuities with this recent and cruel past, by means of

321

all specific forms accessible to our institution, to arouse conscience and thinking of our contemporaries, especially that of our
youth, so that fascism, which has not disappeared from the world
yet may never more have a chance to set world war fire'. The
museum, in pursuit of its illiterate but educational aims, illus-
trates the persistence of neo-Fascism with photographs of German
neo-Nazis, British skinheads, and Israeli actions towards
Palestinians. While I wouldn't wish to deny for a moment that
Israeli treatment of the Palestinians has often been indefensible,
the equation of Israeli actions with neo-Fascism, just hundreds of
yards from where tens of thousands of Jews died for no other
reason than that they happened to be Jews, made my blood boil.

So did the downplaying of the Jewish suffering at Terezín. The
brief guide to the Little Fortress ignores the crematorium entirely,
though it is described in the souvenir booklet. If one asks for the
whereabouts of the crematorium one is directed to a map posted
near the main entrance, but you have to know about it in order to
ask for it. It's on the far side of town. Walking there, I skirted the
main square, where a military band was practising for the May
Day parade and where schoolchildren were running races and
where teenagers were lounging on the grass in the warm sunshine.
The windows of the mustard-coloured barracks were plastered
with propaganda slogans saluting the glorious May Days. Passing
some outer fortifications, I followed a lane for a few hundred yards
until I came to the large anonymous structure that houses the
crematorium. In the car park a coach was loading up with Dutch
tourists; by the time I arrived the site was deserted. Around the
crematorium are the symbolic graves of Jews from all over Europe
who died in the ghetto. Inside the building is the 'laboratory'
where corpses were relieved of gold teeth and rings and hair, and
of course the ovens themselves. Here, almost certainly, my great-
grandmother was reduced to ashes on 3 October, 1942.

Returning to Prague on a crowded bus, I talked to the only other
foreigner on board, a German girl whom I recalled seeing at the
Little Fortress. She told me she'd been very impressed by what she
had seen. She had tagged along with some parties of German
students as they toured the prison. And had she been to the
crematorium? I asked her. To which she replied: 'What crematorium?' The Czech propagandists have done their job well, for here
was an intelligent and adventurous seventeen-year-old schoolgirl
who had journeyed out to Terezín on her own while her
classmates from Munich lingered in the taverns of the capital, and

322

she was now leaving Terezín only vaguely aware of the true history of the dapper little town. The Czech presentation of the story of Terezín is an insult to the memory of all but 250 of those who died there.

By the turn of the last century about one-tenth of the population of Vienna were Jews. Their legal emancipation in 1867 stimulated a movement of population from the provinces to the imperial capital. Although barred from the most prestigious professions, such as the army and the civil service, Jews experienced fewer obstacles to a career in law or medicine or the arts and sciences. Jews, the beneficiaries of a religious upbringing that stressed literacy and disputation and memorization, were swift to lap up a secular education too; by the turn of the century their impact on Austrian culture was already colossal. But it would not be appropriate to see this Jewish influence on the culture as primarily a religious or ethnic one. As in Hungary, most Austrian Jews were highly assimilated. Many of the great men who are remembered as Jews, such as Gustav Mahler and Karl Kraus, were for at least part of their lives active Catholic converts, while the pioneer of Austrian socialism Viktor Adler converted to Protestantism.

With the Jews of Vienna so visible, so prominent, and so successful, it was not surprising that demagogues such as Karl Lueger should have built their political careers by exploiting popular resentment felt towards them. Not all the Jews of Vienna were intellectuals or artists, of course. Enormous numbers of rural Jews from the furthest flung corners of the Habsburg Empire arrived in the city and plied their trades as tailors or cobblers or merchants, thus bringing them into direct competition with the working-class Viennese, who often responded with alarm and envy. The more settled Viennese Jews also looked askance at this invasion from the provinces, and there was disdain for the new arrivals, fresh from Poland in their gaberdine coats and traditional costumes, from some of the Jewish bourgeoisie.

When the rise of Nazism encouraged Austrian antisemites to abandon any restraint they may have shown up to that time, Viennese Jews found themselves in a situation of exquisite if deadly irony. The Jews, as much as any other sector of the population, revered German culture. They had escaped from persecution and pogrom in Slav lands and chosen to come to civilized Vienna. The educated Jews, the intellectuals and artists and doctors and financiers and journalists, were part and parcel of

German culture. For some of them, it was hard to fathom that people were turning so murderously against them in the name of Germanic values. My father recalls how he and his brother were returning from a business trip to Italy in March 1938. Driving through Austria, he was surprised to see Austrian border guards wearing swastika armbands, although the Anschluss had not yet taken place. The brothers were driving a car with German plates and were harassed by Austrians for failing to display swastikas. At 11.55 p.m. they crossed the border into Czechoslovakia. Five minutes later the border was sealed and the Anschluss began. In 1938 there were close to 200,000 Jews in Vienna. In the following eighteen months half of them fled. My mother would recall how eagerly the Viennese, rather than the invading German soldiers, humiliated the Jews around them. It was another horrific irony that many of the persecuted Jews were far more Viennese in their roots and culture than many of the Slav Viennese who were attacking them. The Eisingers, with their house and cattle pens in Gänserndorf, and their town flat in Heinestrasse overlooking the pleasure grounds of the Prater, with their bourgeois comforts and trunkloads of linen and clothes and household goods, did not linger. By late summer they had made their escape, and a short time later, safe in England, my imperious, not to say snobbish, grandmother and her eighteen-year-old daughter entered domestic service.

By the end of the war Viennese Jewry no longer existed. 100,000 Viennese Jews had been murdered in extermination camps. Of those who'd escaped, very few returned to the city, preferring to remain in their newly adopted countries. I asked the part-Jewish painter Georg Eisler why he had returned to Vienna in 1946. Austria was his country, he replied with some defiance, and nobody was going to dispossess him. 'My family has lived in this part of the world for three centuries, and I can trace some of my ancestors back to the Middle Ages. This is my home. I love England, I went to school in England, but my home is Vienna.' The 7000 Jews who now live in Austria now find themselves the unwelcome focus of attention once again. As mentioned earlier, many Viennese Jews, while despising Waldheim, share the widespread resentment within Austria at what is perceived as outside interference. Austrian antisemitism, which has always simmered below the surface, became almost respectable during and after the election campaigns, as electors raged against those who would interfere with their democratic right to choose the odious Waldheim as their president.

The Austrians have never gone out of their way to make amends for what happened after the *Anschluss*. The convenient fiction, to which the Allies subscribed, that Austria was a victim of Nazism absolved them of legal responsibilities. Whereas postwar German governments have compensated German-Jewish refugees with fairly generous pensions for the loss of their property and livelihood, successive Austrian governments have felt no such obligation. Hardly any monies have been paid to Austrian Jews as compensation for their losses, and the government has always maintained that whereas the German government is the legal successor to the Third Reich, no such claim can be made for the Austrian government. 'It's nothing to do with us' has been the general line, and legally it may be justified. Morally, it seems niggardly. In the late summer of 1987 the Austrian Council of Ministers, no doubt anxious to improve the country's faltering international image, proposed a package of measures, including the renovation of the main synagogue and one-off payments to needy Jewish refugees from Austria. Better than nothing, I suppose, but such reparations are conveniently cheap, since half a century has been allowed to lapse between offence and penance.

There are still many Viennese who feel no responsibility whatever for what happened to the Jewish population. In the view of Frau Mayr, who must have been a teenager at the time of the *Anschluss*, social conditions were to blame. 'In the 1930s conditions were far worse in Austria than in England. Educated people as well as labourers were out of work. People slept under bridges. We had rulers like Dollfuss and Schuschnigg, and the Catholics ran this country. After them, Hitler didn't look so bad. He offered hope to Austria. There was no way we could tell what was going to happen to the Jews! We didn't even know which of our neighbours were Jewish. The record isn't all bad. There were even some Jews that were redefined as Aryan and survived the war right here in Vienna.'

Her argument is not a pretty one. It reminded me of some lines from *Der Herr Karl*: '*Alles, was man darüber spricht heute, is ja falsch . . . es war eine herrliche, schöne [Zeit] . . . Naja, Österreich war immer unpolitisch . . .*' ('All those things that people say today, none of it's true . . . they were wonderful, beautiful times . . . Anyway, Austrians have never been interested in politics . . .') Frau Mayr may well not have known who was Jewish or not Jewish among her acquaintance, but thousands of others certainly did. It was the Viennese, not the Germans, who laughed and kicked as Jews were brought literally to their knees and forced to scrub the streets. George Clare, whose family fled to Germany to escape Viennese persecution, spent a year of relative calm in the heart of the Third Reich. Both Hitler and Eichmann were Austrians. I don't suppose Frau Mayr is an anti-semite, but her eagerness to shrug off the whole matter as none of her concern is clearly widely shared by many Austrians. The danger that lies in the growing popularity of men like Jörg Haider is not that they will persecute Jews once again, but that they will reawaken, legitimize, and exploit attitudes that all civilized Austrians had hoped were at long last dying out.

When I visited the Central Cemetery on All Saints' Day, I turned off one of the main avenues and strolled down a side alley. I noticed a sudden change. These graves were untended; autumn leaves, unswept, were strewn everywhere; most gravestones were entirely obscured by ivy and weeds. Here and there ornamental urns had been knocked over, and one or two heavy tombs had, I can't imagine how, been turned on their side. Almost all the graves dated from before 1930, though I did spot one or two new additions to family plots. I was of course in the Jewish section. I walked for half an hour without retracing my steps, for it covers acre after acre of burial ground. A hare ran across the path in front of me. In all that time I saw three other people, while a few hundred yards away thousands of Austrians were laying wreaths on the graves of their relatives and heroes. The only wreaths in the Jewish section were at the small rotunda within which are inscribed the names of Austrian Jews, many of them officers, a few of them noblemen, who fought and died in the First World War. A dishevelled old man appeared while I was standing there. 'They fought for their country,' he muttered to me, 'and much thanks they got for it! I'm a Christian, mind you.' He then launched into a tedious denunciation of capitalism, and I left.

It is not the fault of the municipal authorities that the Jewish section of the Central Cemetery is now reverting to wilderness. The authorities are responsible for maintaining the paths through the cemetery, but not for the upkeep of individual graves, which is the responsibility of those who own the plots, usually the descendants of the dead. There are no descendants of most of these dead. A handful of Viennese Jews descended from old families who are buried here, and an equally small handful of descendants now living abroad, do maintain a very few graves, but the rest are left untended. The Jewish community in Vienna, the Kultus gemeinde, understandably spends its limited resources on the living rather than the dead.

The explanation is a rational one. No one is responsible. Yet the sight of these abandoned graves in their thousands shocked me more than anything else I saw in these three cities, more even than the mass graves and crematorium at Terezín. Here are the graves of an entire community, rich merchants and housewives, ennobled bankers and masons, bakers and surgeons, cellists and swindlers, some in simple graves simply marked, others in grandiose tombs with heraldic flourishes. The vast majority of them were as Viennese as the Christians buried half a mile away within the same cemetery. Those buried here are the lucky ones. Their descendants were the ones who were driven out or murdered. The Jewish cemeteries in Budapest and Prague are poorly tended too, and for the same reasons, but not nearly to the same extent. My first enraged reaction was to wonder why somebody – who I didn't know – didn't come along and tidy the place up, out of respect for the dead. But I began to feel differently before long. Let this place be left as it is, for as the years go by and the desolation becomes ever more complete, it will become an increasingly expressive memorial not only to the deaths of individuals but to the extermination of a culture that endowed Vienna with a vitality it has subsequently lost.

I had made two journeys simultaneously, one for the purposes of this book, and one to flesh out the stories I had been told of my ancestry. The two journeys, public and private, could not be separated as easily as I at first thought, for the story of my family differs only in its details from thousands of others that could be told. Relatives who died before I was born can touch me only sentimentally, but what happened to an entire culture in count- less communities across the face of central Europe is more than a private matter. Few of those now walking the streets in the three cities I visited have any direct responsibility for what happened, though 7 per cent of Austrians still admit to holding antisemitic views. The Viennese tabloid, the *Neue Kronen Zeitung*, still writes of Austrian Jews as 'foreigners'. The world has moved on. Nothing is gained by worrying unduly about a Jewish community that scarcely exists. Jews now thrive elsewhere, and enrich to the best of their ability the cultures of other nations, other cities. But one should not forget the extraordinary, possibly unparalleled contribution the Jews of Vienna made, and one should equally not forget that their absence from modern Vienna is no accident of history. When I next visit Vienna, I shall visit my friends, and stand happily through the longest operas, and stroll in the Belvedere Gardens, and look for Waluliso in the Stephansplatz. And I shall also return to the Central Cemetery and walk for an hour through its alleys and groves, and remember, just for an hour, what used to be.

INDEX